The Fragility of Law

The Fragility of Law examines the ways in which, during the Second World War, the Belgian government and judicial structure became implicated in the identification, exclusion and killing of its Jewish residents, and in the theft – through Aryanization – of Jewish property.

David Fraser demonstrates how a series of political and legal compromises meant that the infrastructure for antisemitic persecutions and ultimately the deaths of thousands of Belgian Jews was Belgian.

Based on extensive archival research in Belgium, France, the United States and Israel, *The Fragility of Law* offers the first detailed exploration in English of this intriguing and virtually unexplored episode of Holocaust history. Belgian legal officials did not hesitate to invoke the provisions of international law found in the Hague Convention and those guarantees of individual freedom found in the national Constitution to oppose the demands of the German occupying authority. However, they remained largely silent when anti-Jewish persecution was at stake. Indeed, despite the 2007 official report of expert historians on Belgian state collaboration in the persecution of the country's Jewish population, the mythology of 'passive collaboration' which has dominated Belgian historiography and accounts of the Holocaust in that country, must be radically rethought.

David Fraser is Professor of Law and Social Theory at the University of Nottingham. His primary research interest is in legal and jurisprudential aspects of the Shoah and National Socialism.

The Fragility of Law

Constitutional Patriotism and the Jews of Belgium, 1940–1945

David Fraser

Routledge·Cavendish
Taylor & Francis Group
a GlassHouse book

First published 2009
by Routledge
2 Park Square, Milton Park, Abingdon, Oxon OX14 4RN

Simultaneously published in the USA and Canada
by Routledge
270 Madison Ave, New York, NY 10016

A GlassHouse book

Routledge is an imprint of the Taylor & Francis Group, an informa business

© 2009 David Fraser

Typeset in Times by
HWA Text and Data Management, London
Printed and bound in Great Britain by
CPI Antony Rowe, Chippenham, Wiltshire

British Library Cataloguing in Publication Data
A catalogue record for this book is available from the British
Library

Library of Congress Cataloging-in-Publication Data
A catalog record for this book has been requested

ISBN10: 0–415–47761–1 (hbk)
ISBN10: 0–203–88500–7 (ebk)

ISBN13: 978–0–415–47761–1 (hbk)
ISBN13: 978–0–203–88500–0 (ebk)

Contents

Acknowledgements

This book is the product of several years spent in archives and research libraries in Belgium, France, Israel and the United States. These archives provided facilities with varying degrees of salubrity and with differing states of technological advance. Wherever I went, however, I was always welcomed and given assistance far beyond what a researcher familiar only with the formal, sometimes legally rigid, rules of archival access might believe was possible. To all those archivists and librarians who met my requests with efficiency and kindness, I am most thankful.

The research for this book received the generous support of several organizations and individuals, to whom I am particularly thankful. Original work on the project was begun several years ago under the then Large Research Grant scheme of the Australia Research Council. Subsequent financial assistance was provided by the Arts and Humanities Research Council of the UK under Research Award (APN 16324). I would like to thank the AHRC for its long-term funding of this project on legality, resistance and collaboration in occupied Belgium.

Much of the archival work on the millions of pages of documents concerning the occupation of Belgium was undertaken while I was a Charles H. Revson Foundation Fellow at the Center for Advanced Holocaust Studies, United States Holocaust Memorial Museum, Washington DC. My thanks go to the Foundation and the Center and to the staff of the Archives and Library there, without whose help and support this work would not have been completed. Holocaust researchers are indeed fortunate to have the support and the resources of the Center and the USHMM available to them.

The final stages of writing up were made possible by the Leverhulme Trust by means of a Research Fellowship. The Fellowship allowed me the necessary time away from student demands to finish the manuscript. I am grateful to the Trust for this support.

The staff of many archives and libraries generously gave their time and effort to assist me: CEGESOMA and the Archives Générales du Royaume, in Brussels, the Archives de la Ville de Bruxelles, the Jewish Museum of Belgium, the Archives de l'État in Liège and in Anderlecht, the CDJC in Paris, Yad Vashem in Jerusalem, the Library of Congress in Washington and the Hoover Institution at Stanford University all provided invaluable resources and assistance. In Belgium, the Honorable Freddy Thielemans, the Mayor of Brussels, kindly granted me access to the files from the Mayor's Office (Cabinet du Bourgmestre) for the years of German occupation. Madame Rolande Depoortere of the Archives de l'État at Anderlecht helped in obtaining the files of the Conseil de Prud'hommes of Brussels. Special acknowledgement must go to two individuals in particular: Madame Christine Renardy of the Archives de la Ville de Liège and Madame Laurence Schram of the Joods Museum van Deportatie en Verzet in Mechelen, for extraordinary kindness and support throughout. Historian Maxime Steinberg generously offered his time at the early stages of my research. Thierry Rozenblum also facilitated access to files relating to the history of Liège's Jewish population.

Parts of Chapter 3 originally appeared in volume 14 of *Law and Critique* (2003), 253–75, and the work appears here with the kind permission of Springer Science and Business Media. Sections of Chapters 6 and 7 were first published in the *Brooklyn Journal of International Law*, 30 (2005), 365–420, and appear by the kind permission of the editors of the *Brooklyn Journal of International Law*.

As usual friends and colleagues offered valuable insights and criticism and to them I am also grateful. Early versions of parts of this project were presented at the Center for Advanced Holocaust Studies, the Universities of Reading and Warwick, and the joint seminar series in history and law at the European University Institute. The insights and comments of the participants in these seminars have contributed to this final version of the project. Dr Frank Caestecker, formerly of CEGESOMA and now of the Department of History at the University of Ghent, and Professor Herman Van Goethem of the Department of History at the University of Antwerp have given excellent advice and assistance. Professor Christian Joerges of the European University Institute in Fiesole has always been incredibly supportive of my work and this project was no exception. Diane Afoumado of the CDJC has also been ready to render assistance when called upon and to offer necessary encouragement in the darker days of archival dust and chaos. Bernard Suchecky, formerly of the Jewish Museum of Belgium, has also provided assistance, encouragement and conversation when they were most needed.

Above all, I am grateful to Kathryn, who has suffered, for longer than I could expect, a house filled with boxes of archival documents and dusty books on the history of this period in Belgian history. She also tolerated innumerable trips back and forth to airports. For all her support, and for being there, I am grateful beyond words.

More than ever, the usual caveat applies. I alone am responsible for the content of this book.

Abbreviations

AGR	Archives Générales du Royaume
AVB	Archives de la Ville de Bruxelles
AEA	Archives de l'État à Anderlecht
AELg	Archives de l'État à Liège
AJB	Association des Juifs en Belgique
AVLg	Archives de la Ville de Liège
BEF	Belgian francs
BTG	Brüsseler Treuhandgesellschaft
CDJC	Centre de Documentation Juive Contemporaine
CEGESOMA	Centre d'Études et de Documentation Guerre et Sociétés contemporaines/Studie- en Documentatiecentrum Oorlog en Hedendaagse Maatschappij
JCB	*Jurisprudence Commerciale de Bruxelles*
JMDV	Joods Museum van Deportatie en Verzet
SG	Secrétaire-Général-Secrétaires-Généraux
SVG	Service des Victimes de la Guerre
USHMM	United States Holocaust Memorial Museum
VOBIB	Verordnungsblatt des Militärbefehlshabers in Belgien und Nordfrankreich für die besetzten Gebiete

Chapter 1

The taxonomies of an anti-Jewish legal order

This book deals with an understudied and often misunderstood aspect of the Shoah. The role played by local governmental and legal authorities in implementing anti-Jewish Decrees in Belgium has been shrouded for too long in national myth. This work seeks to explore, through archival sources and other documents, the nature and extent of local Belgian involvement in the persecution of that country's Jewish population between 1940 and 1944. There was no directly or overtly fascist domestic, or puppet, regime in Belgium during the occupation. While the influence of collaborationist elements increased as the occupation continued, the period for implementing anti-Jewish legal measures occurred before this influence was truly significant. Local officials who assisted in implementing the anti-Jewish Decrees of the occupiers were not, for the most part, adherents of a vision of a New European Order. Most considered themselves to be Belgian patriots, serving as a buffer between the civilian population and the German occupying authority. The Jewish population of the country, however, was by and large excluded from this protection, however slight, offered by Belgian government and legal officials. The following chapters seek to explore the complex questions which surround this phenomenon characterized by officials whose self-belief was one of patriotism but whose understanding of the norms of that patriotism, of that loyalty to the Belgian nation and the Constitution, excluded any idea that anti-Jewish persecution violated any of those norms in a significant way.

Much of the literature concerning occupied Europe under the Nazis is situated along a taxonomical axis two key components of which are the categories of "resistance" and "collaboration". Works which focus more specifically on the events known as the Holocaust might also add the difficult concept of "rescue" to treat the exceptional cases of non-Jews who attempted to save their fellow citizens identified as Jews by the Nazi conquerors and their domestic collaborators. What is striking about many of these histories of German-occupied Europe is that there is not a categorical correlation in fact or in any satisfactory intellectual sense between the idea of "resistance" on the one hand and the events of the destruction of European Jewry on the other. "Resistance" in histories of the period of occupation during the Second World War is resistance to the foreign invader. It is national and/or nationalistic, or it is ideologically based, or it develops from some complex combination of all such factors. But what it is not is the story of "rescue", which remains taxonomically distinct. Nor is resistance ever a more simple tale of the rejection of anti-Jewish persecution and ultimately of extermination.

Of course, there was resistance throughout the continent by Jews themselves.[1] But non-Jewish resistance to the occupier was never, as a matter of daily and existential political or tactical reality, focused on the fate of a country's Jewish population. It is by now a commonplace to refer to the fact that the French *cheminots*, the railway workers, sabotaged trains and tracks and did their best to disrupt German military rail traffic in their country, without ever attempting to stop, delay or disrupt the trains which left France filled with Jews destined for the death factories of the east. This is but one of a myriad of examples which could be used to underline the fact that resistance to the German occupier and the fate of Europe's Jews do not fall within the same taxonomies of historical analyses. This does not mean that resistance was unimportant, nor does it mean that it is an area undeserving of further study, nor does it mean that some of those who resisted did not also rescue Jews. But it does mean that we must always be aware of this absence of a necessary connection between any idea of resistance and rescue when we deal with the historical fate of the Jewish populations of Europe.

In this book, I focus on a country of occupied Western Europe, Belgium, where in fact, there was an attack on a train carrying Jewish deportees, where for one brief moment at least there was an intersection between resistance and rescue, when the fate of a country's Jewish population seemed to become central to an understanding of what it meant to resist.[2] But, as is often the case, this overlapping of resistance and rescue in the case of the twentieth convoy, has been overstated. The Venn diagram of the incident which might show the area in which resistance and rescue came together would present an incomplete and therefore inaccurate picture of the Belgian case. The attack on the twentieth train carrying Belgian Jews to their fate in the east was carried out not by members of the broader Belgian resistance, but by an armed "Jewish resistance" group. This raises at least two issues which are central to the framework which informs and underpins this book. The first underlines the now broadly accepted historical and historiographical idea that there is no necessary correlation between the taxonomical category "resistance" and those events we know as the Shoah. What is true for Holocaust history more generally applies equally in the Belgian context.

The point of the disconnection between "resistance" and the Holocaust is one which is based on a study of the record of the Second World War, which I cannot repeat here. In equal part, some of this disjunction is grounded in the factual and theoretical complexity of the category "resistance" itself. Anyone who has attended a conference on the Shoah will recognize the fundamental and ongoing debates which arise around the components of the taxonomy: perpetrators, victim, bystander, resistance, rescue, etc.

Considering the actors with whom this book is concerned, high-ranking governmental officials and members of the legal professional elite, judges and lawyers, the taxonomical difficulty, the question of resistances and collaboration become complex. What exactly counts as resistance among members of this social stratum? Membership in a clandestine resistance group which provides intelligence information, for example, clearly fits most understandings of "resistance", as does publishing underground newspapers.[3] But what about "professional" resistance? How does a member of the Bar resist? Does an advocate refuse to participate in any proceeding before a German field court or other military tribunal on the grounds that s/he is a Belgian lawyer, whose duty is to represent clients only before duly constituted and constitutionally recognized domestic jurisdictions? Or does one understand one's duty as requiring professional expertise in the protection of the interests of Belgian citizens, perhaps especially when they stand accused before the military judicial apparatus of the occupying power? Neither position appears at first blush to be unacceptable from a professional ethical or moral deontological understanding of a lawyer's role or professional self-image. Either can be justified by reference to an understanding of Belgian legal patriotism, and indeed might be grounded in a conception of legal positivism. Each is based in a normative position relating to a kind of constitutional *grundnorm*, that the Constitution of Belgium continues to exist and Belgian sovereignty is unbroken. This idea that the Nation and the Constitution continued to exist even under military occupation was in fact the principled position adopted by the members of the legal professions and the judiciary from the beginning of the occupation of the country and maintained throughout.

The position becomes more complicated when the question is one of how best to deal with a set of anti-Jewish legal norms established by the occupier. In such cases, the nexus "resistance/Jewish question", if it exists, must be starkly confronted. Does a lawyer, realizing that potential serious consequences will befall the client if they are found to be legally classified as a "Jew", undertake steps to convince, with documentary evidence of ancestry in support, the German authorities that their client is not, under the operative German legal definition, a "Jew"? Or does the legal profession, the Bar, notaries, solicitors and the judiciary, mount a united front by refusing any participation in such a process because it violates both the fundamental principles of freedom and equality guaranteed in the Belgian Constitution and the normative system of the international law of armed occupation as enunciated in the Hague Convention? Are "refusal" and "resistance" synonymous in these circumstances? The converse of this problematic also arises. If resistance as a category for comprehending the Shoah is complex, then collaboration, its mirror image, "is simultaneously contested and multifaceted".[4] Does simply complying with existing legal norms constitute collaboration when those norms are inherently antisemitic?

These questions will arise throughout the rest of this book. It is not my intention to offer definitive answers to the taxonomical complexities which inform the literature underpinning this research, nor to propose a deontological solution to the questions of law and legality under crisis, it is my goal to bring these issues to the light of day by a careful examination of one specific historical circumstance, the application of anti-Jewish legal norms in occupied Belgium.

The second issue of major and central importance to this project is the distinction between "Belgians" and "Jews". If constitutional patriotism of some sort, however complex or nuanced, did inform the actions of the legal and governmental elites of Belgium in this period, a key question of citizenship, narrowly or broadly construed, would also inform all acts by these social leaders. While there are important discussions to be had about the role of political ideologies in the structures of the Belgian underground and armed resistance, the major focus in what follows is on the national aspect of resistance and the fate of the Jews of Belgium between 1940 and 1945. The core idea of resistance in Belgium was informed by a construction of national identity, of Belgium as yet again the victim, a mere twenty-two years after the horrors and depredations of the brutal occupation of the country by the Germans during the First World War. In 1940, the same foreign invader, once more attacked and undermined all the institutions and values of the Belgian nation. While adherence to national constitutional values was at the heart of the resistance in Belgium, it also carried with it the seeds of the destruction of the country's Jewish population. The nation as the site of resistance was constituted, literally and figuratively, by "Belgians" and its concomitant and necessary constitutive element, that "Jews" were the constitutional Other. This idea of foreign Jews and of Jews as foreign to Belgium, its constitution and the nation itself, informed much of the reaction by the Belgian leadership, from the royal family,[5] to the top government officials, to members of the legal professional elite, from the introduction and subsequent implementation of German anti-Jewish measures.

Files maintained by the royal household include documents which carry the handwritten inscription, "Foreign Hebrews for whom nothing was done. No follow up. Receipt was not acknowledged."[6] Jews appealed to the head of state, the King, to come to their assistance against the persecutions of the German occupier. That head of state, or his minions, classified such requests based on one criterion, citizenship, Belgian nationality. The history of the application of anti-Jewish measures reveals the tragic consequences of this predominant attitude expressed in the royal family files and found throughout the ruling elite of the country. Belgian officials felt able to resist attempts to incorporate anti-Jewish laws into the domestic juridical order by insisting that such measures were clearly contrary to the constitutional guarantees of religious liberty and equality. At the same time, they coupled this "resistance" with a pragmatic application of these very measures as part of the daily practice of Belgian state and administrative structures. They also appear to have done so without experiencing any form of constitutional, cognitive dissonance. The Belgian constitutional order at one and the same time was invoked to refuse to pass anti-Jewish Decrees as part of Belgian domestic law and to justify the unquestioning application of measures identifying "Jews" and "Jewish" property, excluding individuals from civil society and finally expropriating their property as they were sent to the east, all as part of the ordinary business of the Belgian state and legal apparatus.

This second informing framework, the key role of "Belgian" versus "Jew", plays a clear and central role in the existing scholarly research on the Holocaust in Belgium. Maxime Steinberg, the leading historian of the Belgian Shoah, has identified and studied in detail the problem of "xenophobia" and the role it played.[7] Of the nearly 56,000 Jews in Belgium at the outbreak of the war, fewer than 3,700, or less than 7 per cent of the total, were Belgian citizens. The vast majority were recent immigrants from the Soviet Union, Romania and Poland or refugees from Germany, Austria and Czechoslovakia who sought safety in Belgium from the Nazi onslaught. This statistical reality of the Jewish population of Belgium also served as a basis for a more generalized idea that there were at least two vital distinctions abroad at a constitutional and constitutive level in Belgium. There was a difference between "Jews", who were foreigners, and Belgians, who were therefore not Jews. Likewise there was a distinction, best articulated in the French-language terminology of the period, between those Belgians who happened to be Jewish, Hebrews (*Israélites*), on the one hand, and on the other side of the legal equation, "Jews" (*Juifs*) who were and would remain foreigners, aliens, the constitutive and constituted Other.

The history of the application of German anti-Jewish Decrees, which framed the gradual process of identification, registration, exclusion, expropriation and then deportation and death, was characterized by a ludic deployment of this distinction by the occupying power. The Germans played on the distinction between Belgian and non-Belgian Jews, between Hebrews and Jews, in order to gain the cooperation and collaboration of Belgian officials and of the apparatus of the Belgian state in the practical and efficient application of the antisemitic legal order of the occupation. Belgian Jews were exempted from the harshest application of many anti-Jewish Orders in the early period of anti-Jewish Decrees. This "protection" was extended to include Jews who found themselves in so-called "mixed marriages", i.e. whose spouses were non-Jewish Belgians.[8] Belgian authorities from the royal family, to the heads of various Belgian government departments and agencies, to the legal elite, to the representatives of the Jewish community itself, the leaders of the Association des Juifs en Belgique, the AJB, the "official" organ established by the Germans in late 1941,[9] all participated in this discursive process under which clear, important, constitutive and deadly distinctions between "Hebrews" and "Jews" were constructed and put into practice. In the end, of course, such distinctions proved meaningless as far as the German vision of a Europe which would be *Judenrein* was concerned and Belgian Jews joined the transports to the east.

Concern with foreigners or aliens was already firmly situated within the structures of the Belgian state, as it was in other European states. The refugee crisis of the mid to late 1930s, which followed Hitler's rise to power, German expansionism and persecution of Jews, greatly exacerbated the situation in many countries.[10] The outbreak of war and the hysteria which surrounded it meant that "foreigners" now became enemies and German Jews, for example, became Germans. In 1940, Belgium, like other European nations, had a well-established pre-existing legal framework as well as a police and bureaucratic machinery to deal with foreigners present on the country's soil.[11] Policing of foreigners was directed from Brussels at the national level, but each municipality had an Aliens' Office. When the anti-Jewish legal order was established late in 1940, because of the statistical reality of the make-up of the Jewish population in Belgium, these pre-existing Belgian bureaucratic services would be intimately involved in the implementation and application of the German Decrees.

One example from the occupation period illustrates the Belgian state's involvement not merely in implementing anti-Jewish Decrees, but in implementing them within the normal structures and jurisdictional division and competencies of domestic governmental structures. It serves as an introduction to a principal theme of this book, that the Shoah in Belgium was necessarily dependent on Belgian state and legal cooperation. When the Eleventh Decree under the Reich Citizenship Law was introduced in November 1941, all German Jews residing outside of German territory lost their citizenship. All their property was then forfeited to the German state.[12] This created several issues and matters of concern under Belgian law for Belgian state and legal officials. Jurisdictional disputes and questions soon arose. The Decree (§ 8) required the active involvement of the German Security Services (*Sicherheitsdienst*) in verifying the change in citizenship status. Yet as far as the Belgians were concerned, the application of the Decree to the status of "former" German citizens recorded in Belgian bureaucratic files was a matter of Belgian law. The right to deliver a passport or to issue a marriage certificate for example, to a newly stateless person was purely a matter of domestic law and no German interference could be tolerated.[13] Belgian central authorities made it perfectly clear that no Belgian institution was inherently competent to determine whether the Decree applied to a particular individual. As far as the question of who was or was not a German citizen, this was a matter solely for the German authorities. But once such a determination was made, Belgian files had to be modified. Since all former German Jews no longer possessed German citizenship, they were, legally speaking, stateless. This change in their status therefore had to be entered on their files in every Aliens' Office file in the country. An elaborate procedure under which each individual had to be notified and informed to bring all official documents indicating German citizenship to the appropriate agency of the Belgian state to have those documents officially modified was put in place for each municipality in the country.

Not only did the idea of an important legal difference between Belgians and foreigners fit into this pre-existing legal bureaucratic machinery within the Belgian state apparatus, but the more fundamental distinction, one which lived in the minds of the Belgian elite, came to the fore. This attitude drew a bright-line distinction between Belgians who were Jewish, the Hebrews, and all the other foreign Jews.

When the First Decree concerning Jews was introduced in late October 1940, the legal definition of the new legal subject "Jew" drew no distinction based on nationality. It was, quite naturally and unsurprisingly, one grounded in Nazi racial ideology. Among the few formal protests from Belgian officials which followed the introduction of the Decree, was one signed by the King's aide-de-camp, General

Six. He wrote to von Falkenhausen, the German Military Commander,[14] and intervened as the representative of a number of Belgian veterans' organizations.[15] The substance of the letter involves a plea for the exemption of veterans of the 1914–18 war and for those who had fought under the Belgian flag in 1940. The veterans and the royal aide-de-camp wrote as follows: "We cannot believe that the occupying power wished to include under such measures these categories of individuals against whom no reproach in relation to the highest form of patriotism can be made."[16]

This plea encapsulates the problematic nature of the Belgian elite's understanding of the issues at play in relation to the introduction and implementation of the new German antisemitic legal system. Six's letter contains more than just a heartfelt intervention in favor of those who had demonstrated their patriotism and loyalty to the Belgian nation on the field of battle. It is at the same time an implicit condemnation of those who did not fall into the war veteran category. More pointedly, by strong implication, it is an argument that all those foreign Jews are in fact demonstrably "unpatriotic". A reproach could and was being made against the vast majority of Jewish residents of Belgium and General Six appears to accept it. That reproach in effect is that Jews are Jews and not loyal patriotic Belgians. The ideal of the nation, as evidenced by this early intervention from a highly placed royal official, is one from which the vast majority of the Jews in Belgium are automatically excluded.

The two problematic taxonomies relating to "resistance" and to "Jews" which inform these brief examples would come to operate in a synergistic relationship which would have almost entirely negative consequences. "Jews" were largely excluded from understandings and practices of resistance more broadly construed and, at the same time, when acts of professional resistance to anti-Jewish measures did in fact occur, they were almost inevitably infected with the distinction which favored a narrow idea of citizenship, patriotism and nationality. They created a small and special category of "Jews" deserving of protection because they were "Hebrews", Belgians who happened secondarily to be Jewish. This meant that by constitutional definition, in the minds of those charged with the onerous task of protecting and maintaining Belgian national sovereignty in the trying and difficult circumstances of German military occupation, the vast majority of "Jews" on Belgian soil were constitutively excluded as Other. Xenophobia was not just an important factor in the Holocaust in Belgium, but in many ways, in so far as the role of the Belgian governmental and legal professional elite upon whom this book focuses is concerned, it was literally the constitutive factor in an active collaboration with the new German anti-Jewish legal order.

Resistance and collaboration among the legal elite

When Belgium fell to the might of the German military forces in May of 1940, the legal regime under which the country would operate was reasonably well-known, in principle at least, to the main actors. While following chapters examine the situation in more detail, several factors relating to the extant legal system in occupied Belgium need to be highlighted in order to provide some context for those acts of "resistance" which would come to characterize the broadly accepted professional self-understanding of the legal professions from the immediate post-war period to the present day.

Belgium had suffered a bitter and harsh period of German occupation in the First World War. Many of the leading political and legal officials who filled key roles in 1940 had lived through that period and it was embedded in their existential and professional being. During the First War, Belgian institutions had effectively ceased to function. The courts had refused to operate under the Germans, policing was carried out by the German military and daily government was in the hands of the occupiers.[17] Belgian officials in 1940 were dedicated to avoiding a repeat of this history for the country and its citizens. They stayed behind and, as they saw it, did their best to maintain Belgian institutional integrity and national sovereignty.[18]

In this task, they relied upon a continuing legal framework which they did not hesitate to invoke, often with apparent success, against actions by the German occupier. On the domestic legal front, they relied upon the institutional arrangements for emergency government found in Belgian legislation, and on the general principles of the country's Constitution. This document guaranteed *inter alia* the equality of all Belgians (Article 6); rights of access to Belgian courts and the application of basic rule of law principles (Articles 8, 9 and 10); protection of private property (Articles 11, 12); freedom of religion (Articles 14, 15, 16). International norms, in the form of the Hague Convention, guaranteed that, under the law of armed occupation, Belgian sovereignty would be maintained and German legal power strictly limited (Article 43).

The historical record is replete with instances in which both governmental officials and leading members of the legal professions proffered formal protests to the German authorities based on the argument for the application of domestic and international legal norms.[19] Informed by the tragic experiences of forced labor during the First World War, Belgium's leading lawyers and judges were quick to protest in late 1942 when the Germans began a similar process. On 16 October 1942, the *Bâtonnier* (President of the Bar) of the Court of Cassation, the Chief Justice of the Court, the Attorney-General, the Chief Justice of the Brussels Court of Appeal, the *Bâtonnier* of the Bar of the Brussels Court of Appeal and the Attorney-General before that same Court, wrote a letter of protest against the deportations of Belgian civilians for forced labor in Germany and relied specifically on the relevant provisions of the Hague Convention.[20]

Likewise, the German practice of taking of civilian hostages and using them as human shields on military transport trains and especially the use of members of the judiciary and the legal professions as hostages, also gave rise to frequent and vociferous protests from the legal elite of the country.[21] When the Germans arrested members of the judiciary and of the Bar because they perceived their legal arguments as being too directly "anti-German", professional solidarity and the task of upholding the ideals of Belgian constitutionalism again and again resulted in the filing of strongly worded protests. More often than not, these protests resulted in the eventual freeing of incarcerated members of the Bar and the judicial branch.[22] Throughout the occupation, the Bench and Bar of Belgium, together with many of the leading governmental legal officers protested against German violations of domestic and international law. There was protest and there was, if the two are synonymous, resistance.

In 1945, after the liberation of the country, a leading member of the Brussels Bar, Charles Van Reepinghen, took over as editor of the profession's most important periodical, the *Journal des Tribunaux*. The 13–20 May issue paid tribute to the fallen of the profession and the heroic struggle undertaken by colleagues during the occupation. Most importantly, it celebrated the "victory of law".[23] Later in the year, on 5 November, the journal celebrated the traditional beginning of the judicial year and the 11 November national holiday with a call to its readers to remember the traditional values to which the publication and the profession had always been dedicated. The editor insisted that the members of the profession must now rededicate themselves after the travails of the last few years under German rule.

> When the freedoms of the homeland were torn asunder, when weakness and sometimes even cowardice came to the support of those who usurped power, when attacks insulted justice, when judges and lawyers were paid for their resistance by harassment or constraint, they dreamed of the proud principles that they and their predecessors had defended since Edmond Picard, one December evening in 1881, founded this journal to serve law and truth.[24]

Van Reepinghen justly celebrated a history of resistance and of support for the basic norms of the international and domestic legal orders. At the same time, he forgot or elided the historical truth about the founder of the *Journal des Tribunaux*, whose name figures prominently not just in this editorial invocation of the principles of truth and law, law and truth, but at the head of the journal's title-page, Edmond Picard. Picard was a notorious antisemite. Picard's writings were republished by the anti-Jewish press, in France and Belgium, during the occupation.[25] This unquestioning invocation of Picard as the embodiment of the finest traditions of the Belgian Bar, dedicated to law and to truth in the immediate aftermath of the German occupation and the deportation of tens of thousands of Belgian Jews, brings into stark relief the informing matrix of this book.

The question which arises is whether the history of the glorious resistance of the Belgian legal profession includes a record of protest and resistance in so far as "the Jewish question" was concerned. Jews were arrested and deported, first as slave laborers in the Atlantic Wall camps of the Organization Todt in the north of France and subsequently to be killed in the east. There was little or no protest at these events, either from the governmental, political leadership of Belgium or from the Bench and Bar. They protested formally only when their colleagues were subjected to unlawful arrest and when "Belgians", including judges and lawyers, were used as hostages, as retaliation for acts of sabotage or attacks on German troops, or as human shields to protect German transports from Allied bombing. Mass arrests of Jews, their incarceration in the camp at Malines and their deportation, did not give rise to any agitation at the Bar of the Court of Cassation.

Subsequent chapters will show the picture of Belgian legal and governmental resistance to anti-Jewish legal measures is not unambiguously negative. There was protest based in constitutional and international legal principle. There were clear attempts to subvert German attempts to use the Belgian legal system as a tool in the process of eliminating Jews from Belgian civil society and the economy. But the ambiguity of "resistance" by the legal and democratic elite to anti-Jewish Decrees was itself filled with further ambiguity. The story which unfolds in this book can be told in terms of black and white, right and wrong, good and bad, resistance and collaboration. It is also often one which can only be recounted in shades of gray, of doubt, of uncertainty. In this, it is perhaps a distinctly legal story, in which black can be made white, and everything can be made into some shade of gray, because lawyers and judges live in a world in which practice turns certainty into uncertainty, in which the clear language of the Constitution or the Civil Code or a statute, is rendered ambiguous through the technical legal skill of the lawyer or the art of judicial interpretation. Lawyers, notaries and judges in occupied Belgium did many good things in relation to the application of anti-Jewish Decrees. But like their political colleagues, they also did many bad things. What is crucial to the stories which unfold in the following chapters is that all of these things, good and bad, took place within a political and existential professional life world in which law and constitutionalism continued to be the overarching and operating framework for all involved.

The stories which are recited, almost without exception, deal with legal professionals and government officials who saw themselves as Belgian patriots. The bad guys, the collaborators, the fascists who welcomed the New Order and a Belgium free of Jews, do not figure prominently here. The anti-Jewish Decrees introduced progressively by the occupier called starkly into question exactly what self-understanding these legal actors and patriots had of "Belgianness".

The governance of antisemitism in occupied Belgium: the framework of constitutional suicide

While the morally correct choice appears simple and straightforward in retrospect, the existential reality involved a complex set of circumstances and considerations which makes the study of such an historical question so fascinating. This does not mean that the taxonomical line between a morally acceptable decision and one which evidences a failure of ethical behavior is not a clear one. It does mean, however, that the paths which lead to such a decision can be and are complex and in many instances are inherently contradictory.

In her important work on the role and rule of law in the demise of French republican democracy under Pétain's Vichy regime, Vivian Curran highlights the pedagogical function embodied in the Vichy model:

> even nations like our own, constituted as democracies, can be undermined from within, by and through the very democratic processes designed to ensure self-perpetuation, for the most important of all constitutions, the one written in the citizen's minds is ever renewable and ever destructible, recreated continuously, invested with inevitably transitory meanings that fluctuate with time and history, through the perpetual vagaries of individual and collective perception and sentiment.[26]

There is an increasingly developed and sophisticated body of work on the nature and role of French law, judges and lawyers in democracy's suicide, and resistance thereto, under Vichy. A key factor appears to separate the French and Belgian examples. In France, Vichy continued to exist. Vichy law, that is French law, imposed discriminatory measures on the Jews of France. In Belgium, at the formal and constitutional level, the Orders or Decrees identifying, excluding and targeting Jews were measures of the German military administration.

This idea of an anti-Jewish legal regime imposed on a reluctant, resisting Belgian administration and institutional structure by the German occupying force, long dominant in most Belgian Holocaust historiography, tends to obscure and often to ignore or deny, the real and active role played by Belgian state and related bodies in the removal of Jews from the Belgian state and from civil society. The Belgian case of democratic suicide, this complex history of state and institutional involvement in the implementation of measures against the country's Jewish population, exemplifies the embodiment of the voluntary destruction of the principles of democratic citizenship by and through law so carefully articulated by Curran. The destruction of Belgian values of equality and democratic citizenship did not occur as the result of German anti-Jewish Decrees. It is more centrally attributable to the voluntary actions of Belgian officials in implementing those anti-Jewish measures, at a level and to a degree beyond that which the Germans demanded.

In occupied Belgium, national government officials were faced with the task of creating and maintaining a functioning relationship with the occupying German military forces. While the Belgian government-in-exile sat in London, the Belgian King remained in the country. The day-to-day administration of the country was left in the hands of the senior government officials, the Secretaries-General (SG). Faced with the second German invasion and occupation of the country in just over twenty years, the SG sought to carve out a form of governance of the country which they themselves characterized as the policy of the lesser of two evils. This idea of *le moindre mal* operated throughout the occupation.

At this introductory stage, it is sufficient to note that following the advice of the country's leading jurists, sitting as the Conseil de Législation, the government of Belgium found a way to accommodate itself to this Nazi process of the legal identification, exclusion, spoliation, arrest and killing of that country's Jewish population. They convinced themselves that the role they played was consistent with their duty to obey the Belgian Constitution and to uphold its immutable foundational norms of individual liberty and the free exercise of religion.

Leading lawyers advising the governmental officials attempted to draw a fine, some might argue a Jesuitical, distinction between active "collaboration", which was forbidden by Belgian law and was contrary to the Hague Convention, the international legal regime governing armed conquest and military occupation, and a "passive collaboration" in the implementation of German measures, which was violative of neither Belgian domestic legal rules nor of the relevant international norms.[27] How Belgian lawyers and leading governmental officials construed their involvement in the persecution and exclusion of the country's Jews as part of a broader construction of patriotism and loyalty to constitutional principle unfolds in the stories which follow.

Chapter 2

The Secretaries-General
Passive collaboration, Belgian law and the Jews, 1940–1945

A set of congruent historical myths has dominated Belgian collective memory and discourse on the subject of the Shoah in that country. According to this narrative, anti-Jewish measures were imposed on a reluctant and resisting Belgian public and officialdom by the Germans or the "Nazis". Compliance was minimal. Measures were implemented largely at the behest of the victims. In the loop of traditional Holocaust taxonomical structures, perpetrator/victim/bystander, the first two categories are filled easily by the Germans (Nazis) and the Jews. The Belgians were, in their own collective narration of the period, either passive observers or active resisters. At worst their activities could be classified as falling into the category of "passive collaboration".[1] It is this incongruous historical category, passive collaboration, which characterizes the myths about local participation in the persecution of Jews. This passivity and its construction are the direct results of the creation of the limits of permissible, lawful, constitutional, conduct by the highest legal and governmental instances, which in turn led to the narration of the national mythology of the Jewish question in occupied Belgium.

Legal discourse served to limit, if not the actions, then at least the ways those actions were understood by some of the actors, when the local and central administrations throughout Belgium began to implement German anti-Jewish Decrees.[2] It is also important to underline that, as in all such discussions, competing counter-narratives might be available. While dominant myths support the story of resistance and reluctant, begrudging, minimalist compliance by Belgian officials in implementing anti-Jewish Orders, Dan Michman has accurately noted: "the implementation of the anti-Jewish measures – both the legal and the economic – could be carried out (even if only partially) by the Belgian bureaucracy".[3]

Beginning in October 1940, "passive collaboration" has been invoked, almost without interruption, to create and re-enforce the constitutive mythologies of resistance and the problematic question of Jewish compliance. These complex historical and legal phenomena might be understood in light of the simple historical fact underlined by Michman, i.e. that the implementation of the first phase of what became the Final Solution in Belgium was carried out not by the Germans, but by Belgian officials, acting in accordance with their interpretation of Belgian constitutional law and of the binding norms of the international law of war and armed occupation embodied in the Hague Convention. These Belgians were not proponents of the New Order. They were the highest-ranking civil servants, the SG, left in the country after the elected government fled following the German invasion in May 1940. They perceived themselves to be patriotic Belgians and constructed their actions in terms of acting as a shield between the demands of the Occupying Authority and the population at large. How did loyal, patriotic Belgians, aware of that country's constitutional guarantees of equality and religious freedom, proceed to register, identify and participate in the economic and physical exclusion of those defined as "Jews"? Why was there no constitutionalized cognitive dissonance or resistance?

Part of the explanation lies in the notion of "citizenship" and in the statistical and historical reality of the Belgian Jewish population in 1940.[4] Of the 55,671 Jews registered in Belgium under the anti-Jewish Decrees, 3,680 were Belgian citizens; the rest were Jews who had come to the country from Eastern Europe, fleeing pogroms and poverty, in waves of immigration to feed the demands of Belgian industry, and more recently from Germany itself. Most of the Jews in Belgium at the time the German measures against them were introduced were not Belgian citizens. They were more recently arrived, and therefore less integrated, immigrants. They were not, in fact or in law, "Belgians". One key factor of local compliance can be found in this limited understanding of constitutional citizenship operating in the minds of the Belgian officials of the time.[5] Indeed, the Constitution itself differentiated between citizen and foreigner. Article 128 provided that "Any foreigner who is on Belgian territory enjoys the protection accorded to person and property, other than exceptions provided by law."[6]

In an environment of military occupation, German Decrees and a generalized "state of exception", it is hardly beyond comprehension that Belgian authorities could have adopted an attitude and a jurisprudential position according to which, psychologically if not legally, "Jews" became synonymous with "foreigners". In this constitutional, constituted worldview, all legal measures affecting Jews occurred in a normative context, permitted under the Constitution, in which aliens could be treated differently. The entire history of the implementation and consequences of anti-Jewish measures in Belgium demonstrates clearly that the Germans understood this. They consistently adopted a position whereby assurances were given to Belgian authorities that "Belgian" Jews would not be subjected to the strict legal regimes applied in practice to foreign Jews. The synergies between and among the demographic realities of the Jewish population in Belgium, understandings of Belgian citizenship and national identity, a well-established bureaucratic and legal system of policing aliens as part of normal governmental practice, and the existence of a constitutional framework which allowed lawful discriminations against foreigners more generally must all have been at play as Belgian authorities established the legal and constitutional mechanisms which began the juridification of anti-Jewish measures in Belgium.

The Belgian experience of anti-Jewish measures under German occupation highlights the role played by the legitimating function of law and legality in permitting domestic compliance with these decrees. National and local officials throughout the country did not hesitate to obstruct many German demands, from the collection of non-ferrous metals to the use of local police to assist German forces, through refusal and often by way of legal argument. They invoked the provisions of international law, of the Hague Convention, in order to place legal and constitutional sticks in the wheels of German actions. The one area in which they failed to act in such a way was in the implementation of anti-Jewish laws.

This book proposes, if not an answer, at least a framework, a legal historical reading of the situation in Belgium, which might go some way towards allowing us to explore this radical discrepancy. The failure of Belgian officials to invoke the Constitution in defense of their fellows defined and identified as "Jews" can be understood, albeit not exhaustively, by way of a careful study of the legal background of the phenomenon of the "passive collaboration" which at a minimum defines and frames this still understudied part of Belgian history. In effect, constitutional guarantees of equality and religious freedom, like the Hague Convention, were rendered irrelevant to the implementation of anti-Jewish measures in Belgium by the interpretation and operation of Belgian law itself. The "participation" of local officials in putting into practical effect Nazi antisemitism in its legal form was made lawful by the operation and interpretation of Belgian constitutional and international legal norms.[7] In other words, the officials in question did not invoke the constitutional guarantees of religious freedom and equality, or those found in Article 46 of the Hague Convention,[8] protecting property rights and religious freedom, because those guarantees ceased for them to exist as a matter of law. Domestically, "Jews" were read out of the Constitution as un-Belgian, as non-Belgian, as non-citizens and therefore as legal subjects excluded from the operative and constitutive norms of the nation. When that Constitution was further limited by a series of legally binding interpretations of its force and effect under German occupation, Belgium's Jews became extra-legal subjects ripe for administrative identification.[9] "Passive collaboration" was lawful by the operation of the normative and legitimating structures of the Belgian state and juridical apparatus under occupation. Local and national officials did not raise the Constitution as a shield to offer legal protection to the Jews because they had to all intents and purposes already been removed from its protective cover by the operation of Belgian law itself.

Creating the framework of legalized antisemitism: the Belgian role

While local officials worked under the arduous and dangerous conditions of wartime occupation, they also operated under a well-understood and functioning legal system. This does not mean that there were not constitutional and other legal ambiguities which arose during the period of occupation. Instead, it is clear that a system of Belgian government and law continued to function at all relevant times. Indeed, the German occupation of Belgium from 1940 to 1944 was to a large extent both premised and dependent upon this legitimate continuation of Belgian governmental and legal structures.

After the defeat of the Belgian armed forces in the *Blitzkrieg* of May 1940, the elected government of Prime Minister Pierlot fled first to France and then to London where a government-in-exile was established. The King, the head of state, remained in Belgium, and the nature of his role and attitude during the Occupation continues to be a matter of historical, political and constitutional controversy.[10] Issues soon arose out of the nature of constitutional government in Belgium and from subsidiary questions about the actual text of the Constitution itself.[11] Article 26 vested legislative powers in the King, the Representative Chamber (Chambre des Représentants) and the Senate while Articles 32–59 enumerated the powers of each chamber. Articles 60–85 dealt with the authority of the King and Articles 86–91 with ministers. Circumstances were such that the bodies empowered under the Constitution were dispersed geographically, and/or no longer functioning. Article 82 of the Constitution dealt with the case where the King could no longer rule. Then ministers were entitled to call together the two chambers of Parliament who, acting in concert, were empowered to appoint a regent. While the King could no longer effectively rule in an occupied Belgium, the two chambers no longer existed. The generally accepted constitutional position was that Pierlot and the other ministers-in-exile in London were in the circumstances of occupation the only legitimate seat of Belgian governmental and state authority. Unlike France, with a continuing and functioning state apparatus in Vichy and a counter-claimant to legitimacy in the form of De Gaulle's Free French in England,[12] the government, in the accepted political and constitutional sense, of Belgium was the government-in-exile in London.

More importantly from the perspective of the day-to-day operation of Belgium and the Belgian state throughout the period of German occupation, and for the evolution of the system of anti-Jewish legal measures, a core of the prewar judicial and civil service structures remained on Belgian soil. The highest-ranking public servants in all the main departments of government, the *Secrétaires-Généraux* stayed behind and the day-to-day practical (and constitutional) running of the country was in their hands.[13] The role and activities of the SG during the occupation has also been and continues to be a matter of controversy.[14] Because they had the quotidian carriage of the business of the Belgian state apparatus between 1940 and 1944, the SG had ongoing contact with the occupier.[15]

There can be little doubt about the real difficulties faced by those remaining behind to see to the daily government of Belgium. The country had suffered serious physical and psychological damage as a result of the defeat. Many officials at all levels of the government structure had fled the country and would not return. Staff shortages were endemic throughout the governmental and legal bureaucracies. The infrastructure of the country was in disarray and the legal framework necessary to get Belgium back on its feet and functioning in as normal a way as possible had to be rethought. Food shortages imposed enormous hardships on citizens. The demands of the military occupier had to be juggled, fitted into other priorities and eventually complied with. Informing all of this were relatively fresh memories of the harshness and brutality of the previous German occupation during the First World War.[16] During the previous war, Belgian institutions, the police, the judiciary and the civil service had essentially ceased to function and their roles had been filled by the German occupier. The SG in May 1940, like the Court of Cassation, the highest judicial body, and other members of the ruling elites who had stayed behind, wanted at all costs to avoid the repetition of those events. Belgian police would patrol the streets of the country to insure law and order, not the German *Feldgendarmerie*. Belgian courts would render ordinary justice to Belgian citizens, not occupation military tribunals. The Belgian state would subsist. The SG would govern to maintain Belgian sovereignty under German occupation.

The situation as a matter of Belgian law of the SG is essential to understanding the dynamics of the juridical framework in which the Belgian officials would put into effect measures against those identified and defined as Jews. Without the actions of the SG, the constitutive body of day-to-day Belgian government, the embodiment of constitutional continuity and competence, the role of local administrations and officials who were charged with the practical implementation of anti-Jewish measures, would have become much more legally, if not ethically and morally, ambiguous.

On 10 May 1940, at the end of the period of the "phony war", the Belgian Parliament passed a Law Relating to the Delegation of Powers during Wartime, a measure intended to avoid any constitutional uncertainty and to allow for the continuity of Belgian sovereignty under the by then inevitable German invasion and occupation.[17] Article 5 provided that:

> When, as a consequence of military operations, a judge or a civil servant, or a body of judges or of civil servants ... is unable to communicate with the appropriate superior authority, or if this authority has ceased its functions, he possesses, in cases of emergency and within the limits of his professional activity, all the powers of that authority.[18]

Under these provisions of Article 5, the SG subsequently found themselves with the effective power to govern Belgium until the return of the Pierlot government. After the fall of Belgium, the Germans installed an occupying military authority but they never imposed their own system of civilian rule. There would be no *Gauleiter* in Belgium. In the early days of this new occupation arrangement, the SG themselves were however still unsure of their authority. Could they "legislate" or merely "govern"? They wished, to the most extensive degree possible, to maintain and ensure the continuing functioning of Belgian institutions of law and government. Since the Germans also wanted to have a fully functioning, efficient Belgian government administration to which to delegate, or more accurately upon which to impose, certain functions and tasks, the legal question of the nature and extent of the delegation envisaged under Article 5 became one of central importance. Both parties, each for their own purposes, wanted to ensure that a Belgian structure of governmental authority would remain in place. All that remained in doubt were the precise legal rules of the game.

The German Military Commander immediately after the fall of the country issued a "Proclamation to the Population of Belgium" in which he urged everyone to "stay at work and look after their own affairs. By doing this, everyone will do his duty to the country, to his people and at the same time act in his own self-interest."[19] The question of the constitutive framework for government was debated in the days and weeks which followed.

On 5 June 1940, following the first formal meeting between the Occupying Authority's representative and the SG, the *Militärverwaltungschef* Reeder announced that the German authorities would leave the Belgian government with a great degree of autonomy and that the occupiers would not introduce measures which the Belgian officials would find offensive (*des mesures qui pourraient blesser ses sentiments*).[20] The SG responded by praising the German decision not to ask them to do anything which would be incompatible with their duty to the nation.[21] In order to ensure the proper framework for a government structure in which the Germans would act as the military authority occupying Belgium and the SG would maintain and represent Belgian sovereignty, a set of legalized criteria relating to jurisdiction and other aspects of the dual system of governance had to be established.

The SG sought an opinion from two leading Belgian jurists, J. Pholien and P. Tschoffen, on several interrelated questions concerning the nature and extent of their powers under the 10 May statute. Two principal questions which informed the legal opinion are central to the subsequent history of anti-Jewish measures. The SG inquired as to whether they possessed, under the terms of the delegation contained in Article 5, legislative powers. If they did not possess such powers, could they be conferred on them by the Germans?[22]

The legal opinion from Pholien and Tschoffen set out the general juridical context within which the Belgian government, on Belgian soil, would operate for the next four years. First, it was established that the delegation of authority to the SG took place only in the framework of "the limits of (the) professional activities" of the SG. Since they exercised power, whatever it might be, by virtue only of their functions within the different ministries, the sole authority which could be delegated legally was ministerial, not legislative, power. While they could not legislate, they could emit ministerial decrees (*des arrêtés ministériels*).[23] On the second question, the delegation of legislative powers by the German military authority, the two eminent Belgian jurists affirmed that under Article 43 of the Hague Convention, the occupying power was vested with legislative authority to maintain peace and order over the conquered territory and that such a power could not be delegated.

The SG had a theoretically limited, but practically quite extensive, power to enact measures having legal force in Belgium by way of ministerial orders or decrees (*arrêtés*). They could not be granted more extensive authority by the

Germans who had, by reason of the international law of armed conquest and occupation, legislative jurisdiction to enact measures which would have the same effect as Belgian law.[24] After this legal opinion clarified the position of the SG under Belgian law, an agreement was signed between the German Military Commander and the SG formalizing a joint understanding on the operative legal framework for occupation.[25] The SG recognized the limits imposed under Article 5 of the statute and also that all occupation decrees passed in accordance with the Hague Convention would be treated and enforced as if they were Belgian law (paras 2 and 1). There was at this stage no explicit definition or understanding of the limits of the relevant provisions of the Hague Convention, especially Articles 43 and 46, which might have been invoked in relation to anti-Jewish measures.

The SG asserted, and the Germans agreed, that any measure which was "purely political" (*purement politique*) would be introduced and enforced by the occupying authority. The legal and constitutional stage was now set for the debate over the jurisprudence of anti-Jewish laws in Belgium.

In early October 1940, the German military administration in Belgium decided that the time had come to introduce measures regulating the legal status and rights of Jews.[26] They entered into contact with the SG with the intention of having them introduce prohibitions and discriminations against Jews as part of Belgian law. On 10 October 1940, a meeting was held between the SG for the Interior, Jean Vossen, and General von Craushaar, deputy head of the military administration, to discuss the practical implementation of the German decision to introduce anti-Jewish legal measures. Von Craushaar informed his interlocutor that the Germans wanted the Belgian authorities to impose an order-in-council or decree excluding Jews from public employment, registering Jews and their property, imposing compulsory signage indicating that a business was "Jewish" and banishing all Jews who had fled the country in the mass exodus of Belgians during the invasion and the ensuing chaos and forbidding them from returning.[27] If the local authorities refused to take these steps as part of Belgian law, the Germans would introduce the measures themselves and would impose upon Vossen as SG for the Interior the obligation to enforce the decree. In the case of a refusal by the Belgians, the Germans would reluctantly take steps themselves to enforce the measures against the Jews.[28]

The SG met the next day and "after a brief exchange of views", they asked Vossen to convey the unanimous results of their discussions to the Germans.[29] On 11 October 1940, Jean Vossen wrote to von Craushaar, outlining the legal position of the Belgian government. At this early point, the SG staked out what would appear to have been an eminently sensible, ethically supportable and legally sound position of refusal. Vossen said "the Committee of Secretaries-General is of the opinion, after an in-depth examination, that it cannot, for constitutional reasons, take on the responsibility for the measures envisioned concerning the Jews".[30] This statement is followed by a rather detailed exposé of the provisions of the Belgian Constitution guaranteeing equality and an outline of Article 43 of the Hague Convention which permitted the occupying power to legislate itself, for the maintenance of public order. This letter from the SG has been read as constituting the beginning of a history of administrative and governmental refusal, rejection and resistance to anti-Jewish measures, based in overriding Belgian constitutional discourses of equality and the rule of law. But of course, the story is not yet complete.

A more nuanced interpretive practice might begin by underlining that Vossen (and the SG as a body), use the term "juifs" and not "israélites". The use of the latter term might have underlined their commitment to some more profound understanding of and commitment to an idea of Belgian citizenship and equality broadly understood and applied. More importantly, the proper characterization of this letter might be more accurately put as one of partial "refusal" than as one of "protest". What Vossen and his colleagues actually say is that they cannot, for constitutional reasons, assume the "responsibility" for anti-Jewish measures. Such legal prohibitions cannot be made part of domestic Belgian law. At the same time, they argue that such a matter could be and is the responsibility of the occupying power. More damagingly for the mythology of Belgian protest, reluctance and resistance, they assert, by direct implication, that it is within the jurisdiction of the Germans, as a matter of valid and existing norms of international law, to enact measures against the Jews. In other words, the SG clearly adopt the legal position that measures against the Jews of Belgian can be imposed by the Germans pursuant to their powers under Article 43 of the Hague Convention, which limits the occupier to measures necessary for maintaining public order and safety. This moment of constitutionalized and principled protest might then be seen as the moment at which Belgian officials entered upon the slippery slope of involvement in the implementation of anti-Jewish laws. They could have asserted that neither domestic Belgian law nor applicable international law norms as found in the Hague Convention permitted the occupying power to enact such discriminatory measures. They had already apparently imposed a limit on German authority by asserting that that power existed only within the framework of the Hague Convention.

> The authority of the legitimate power having actually passed into the hands of the occupant, the latter shall take all steps in his power to re-establish and insure, as far as possible, public order and safety, while respecting, unless absolutely prevented, the laws in force in the country.

These anti-Jewish measures clearly violated Belgian law. The SG's refusal to introduce such measures offers irrefutable and incontrovertible evidence that they understood this. The only legal justification available to legitimate and legalize measures against "Jews" therefore was if such measures were necessary "to re-establish and ensure public order and safety". While the presence of Jews may have been *per se* contrary to public order in Nazi ideology and legal practice, this was not a valid basis for the introduction of such provisions in international law. The SG did not avail themselves of any such argument or position of principle.

Instead, they accepted, implicitly but unequivocally, that such antisemitic decrees were within the jurisdictional remit of the German occupier. They based their "refusal" on purely domestic legal grounds and yielded without protest to a German claim of jurisdiction to identify, record, exclude and expropriate individuals and businesses classified as "Jewish".

What is contested, in fact and in law, in the letter from the SG, is limited to a discrete legal question as to exactly which body has the right and power to persecute Jews. The SG do not assert, as they might have, that there is no legal basis, as matter of international law or Belgian constitutional law, for the persecution of those identified as Jews. Instead of taking this absolutist position, they present a relative rejection of the German request. They could have asserted that the Hague Convention did not permit the legalized persecution of Jews under international law. The legal authority of the occupying power is limited strictly to matters of public safety and the persecution of Jews, because they are Jews, is not a matter of public safety or national security.[31]

Instead, the SG adopt a more nuanced, domestic and self-serving juridical position, which would haunt and inform the entire history of Belgian collaboration in implementing anti-Jewish measures. They do not object to anti-Jewish measures *per se*. They object to explicitly "Belgian" anti-Jewish measures. By arguing that the matter was one within the legislative power of the occupier under the Hague Convention, they began a process, albeit one with its own ambiguities, of "passive collaboration" under law in the persecution of Jews in Belgium. Under the terms of the constitutional understanding abroad in Belgium and pursuant to the agreement between the occupying power and the SG which established the legal framework for the occupation, such measures under the Hague Convention would have precisely the same effect as Belgian law. This is the basis not just for all that would follow in the sad story of Belgian complicity of anti-Jewish persecutions, but also for the legal gray area which informed this "passive collaboration". The Belgian Constitution prohibited discriminations based on race or religion. Belgian criminal law also prohibited and penalized all active collaboration in such practices. Yet at the same time, under the SG's interpretation of the Hague Convention, anti-Jewish legal measures would have the full force and effect of Belgian law and all Belgian government officials and agencies would be bound thereby. Belgian law at one and the same time appeared to prohibit and permit anti-Jewish persecution under the Catch-22 legality operating following the June accord and the SG's mealy mouthed position concerning the Hague Convention.[32]

The SG again discussed the German intention to establish a legally binding framework for the identification, registration and separation of Jews from the body politic of Belgium. On 25 October 1940, Vossen informed his colleagues that the Germans would introduce anti-Jewish laws themselves and that, crucially for what would ensue, they would "charge the Department concerned with the application of the Decree".[33] The President of the Committee of SG then stated that "under these conditions, the Belgian administration could not avoid complying with the enforcement of such a Decree".[34]

The recorded discussions of the officials themselves contain a complete refutation of the politics of rejection and resistance, so central to mythologies and understandings of occupation history. Faced with the German threat that Belgian government departments, bound by the Constitution, would be given the task of applying discriminatory laws against the Jews, the Committee of the SG clarified the issue of "responsibility" for anti-Jewish law which they invoked in their "letter of protest". They could not accept legislative responsibility by way of a Belgian *arrêté* but they could not avoid administrative responsibility for enforcing a German decree against the Jews. Yet this was precisely a possibility considered by Von Craushaar and reported by Vossen in his account of the 10 October meeting detailing the options for implementation. The Germans clearly foresaw a possible Belgian refusal and considered implementing the measures themselves. This cave-in, based in a limited and incorrect interpretation of the Hague Convention,[35] meant that the SG placed the entire apparatus of the Belgian state at the disposal of the occupiers for the process of identifying Jews. The stage was set for the next series of legal positions and dispositions which would seal the fate of Belgian Jews and establish the lawful framework for a Belgian "passive collaboration" in enforcing anti-Jewish measures.

"The dirty work":[36] the constitutional legitimation of anti-Jewish law in Belgium

At the end of October, after their first constitutional and legal skirmishes with the SG had set in motion the informing juridical dynamic of the earliest stages of "passive collaboration", the Germans introduced the first set of specifically anti-Jewish Decrees.[37] The so-called first Jewish Decree[38] (*Judenverordnung*) offered a legal definition of the new legal subject, "Jew" (§ 1); it banned Jews who had left Belgium from returning (§ 2) and imposed both the obligation for the creation of a Jewish Register covering all individuals, setting out the process of registration (§ 3), and required the identification and declaration of all businesses defined as "Jewish" (§ 5–12).[39]

The second Decree ordered the removal of public employees identified as "Jews" and forbade "Jews" from the judiciary, from practicing as lawyers, teaching in public education and from holding management positions in newspapers or radio (§ 1).[40] Jews were to be removed from their functions by 31 December (§ 2). Jewish schools and religious education were exempted from the operation of the Decree at this time (§ 3).

The central procedural elements of the two Decrees which would frame the legal process of Belgian officialdom's "passive collaboration" in the identification, registration, exclusion, spoliation and finally killing of the Jews can be identified. The so-called Jewish Decree provided in § 3 (1) that the Register of Jews of all male individuals over the age of 15 and identified as "Jews" would be created and held by the appropriate municipal officials, depending on the size of the city, town or village in question. It also set out what information the Jewish Register would contain: name, place and date of birth, address, profession, nationality and religion, as well as the names, place and date of birth and religion of the wife, parents and grandparents. The files of foreign Jews would also carry a special indication of how long they had lived in Belgium and of their previous home. In the case of a change of residence by a Jew § 3 (3) provided that the competent municipal authority would forward the file to the appropriate local officials in the new place of abode. Finally, § 3 (4) indicated that all identity cards of registered Jews would carry a notation that the individual was listed in the Register of Jews.

The Second Order relating to the removal of Jews from public employment by the end of the year imposed the obligation for compliance on the appropriate Ministerial Department with a special duty on the Interior Ministry to ensure that the required instructions for the application of the anti-Jewish provisions were given to all concerned (§ 4).

The stage was set for the final debates and clarifications concerning the lawful nature and framework for the first specifically anti-Jewish Decrees. The SG had refused to accept legislative responsibility for these measures by invoking the various guarantees of the Belgian Constitution. At the same time, they had recognized, in a way which left little room for backtracking or resistance, that the operative system of governance in Belgium, to which they had given their consent in June 1940, allowed the Germans, as the occupying power pursuant to Article 43 of the Hague Convention, to introduce valid and binding laws targeting Jews. The Germans had at this stage chosen the second of the three options put forward by von Craushaar in early October: i.e. they would enact anti-Jewish laws and put the enforcement and application of those measures largely in the hands of the Belgian officials.

From the earliest stages of the "Jewish question" in Belgium the first pillars in subsequent constructions of Belgian legal and historical amnesia are in evidence. The measures against the Jews are "German". The Belgians are forced, by law, to cede to the will of the occupier. Of course, they are forced to submit to the will of the occupier in large part because they refused from the beginning to assert what Richard Weisberg has called the "jugular" argument.[41] They did not assert as a matter of unequivocal principle that anti-Jewish laws were antithetical to their understanding of their position as upholders of the Belgian Constitution and as the representatives of the Belgian "nation". They offered the beginnings of such an argument, but it was fundamentally and fatally flawed because it was followed by their acceptance that the Hague Convention gave the Germans a lawfully binding way to achieve their aims in relation to "the Jews". Any principled, ethical, constitutional, argument, grounded in ideals of equality and liberty, as embodied in Belgian law and in the limits on an occupying power found in the Hague Convention, was reduced to empty and self-justificatory rhetoric. The laws against "Jews" were German laws, as fact and mythology will agree, but that did not make them un-Belgian as popular myth long asserted.

At their meeting of 8 November 1940, just after the Decrees had been published, the SG discussed in some detail the question of what status, in terms of the law governing civil service pensions, should be afforded to government employees who would lose their jobs because they were "Jews". They also debated what was for them a more basic question: how would they know if a public servant were a "Jew"?[42]

The answer came from Vossen who stated that "interested parties must make the declaration to the municipal administration. If they do not make this declaration, they will be liable for very severe penalties. As a result, all the administrations must, within the limit of their jurisdiction, consider what steps to take."[43] The parameter of the dominant historical paradigm in Belgium runs from resistance to "passive collaboration", avoiding by definition any idea of complicity, responsibility or "collaboration" in the legal sense. The rhetorical and semiotic strategies deployed by Vossen and his colleagues in positioning (or not) themselves as Jew hunters are vital. They invoke the trope of the passive voice and/or the use of the French reflexive verb construction. Jews must make the declaration, they must present themselves, and they must request their registration. Jews, apparently of their own volition, make the declaration. This has the effect, rhetorically and psychologically, as well as legally, of turning the SG issuing the circular setting out the modalities for registration of Jews, and the municipal employee who fills in the card (*fiche*) as each Jew presents himself, into a transcriber of the will of the Jews themselves. These Belgian officials become mere scriveners, recording passively the information provided. The constant use and historical repetition of the French verbs *s'exécuter* and *s'inscrire* executes its own legal semiotics of responsibility in Belgian Holocaust history. The language of official legal documents inscribes its own mythology of just who was "passive" and who was actively involved in the registration process. The Jews in law and in the mythology of Belgian "passive collaboration" inscribe themselves in the Register of Jews. This is a Jewish and German process, not a Belgian one.

The second point of importance, as a matter of legal and historical precedent, comes at the next stage of the official construction of the juridical framework of Belgian complicity in the Shoah. At the 8 November meeting, the SG put into force the provisions of the two Decrees. They discuss what to do with employees who will lose their jobs because they are "Jews". They do not discuss whether Jewish civil servants should or will be dismissed, that question had been decided when they declined to engage in any overt refusal. Instead the highest representatives of Belgian political sovereignty focus on the practical issues of pension payments when the civil servants are finally dismissed at the end of the year. They worry about how they should go about identifying Jewish civil servants and find the answer in the fact that the Jews will be obliged to present themselves for registration or face severe punishment. There is no "should" (*devraient*), only a compulsion, a "must" (*doivent*). The die is cast for the highest Belgian officials, sworn to uphold the principles of the Constitution. There is no protest, no jugular argument. The Constitution has been rendered null and void by their simple, unquestioning acceptance of one of several possible interpretations of the Hague Convention. They signed away their responsibilities to their Jewish fellows at the moment they reached an agreement with the military authority which did not include any clear understanding that the Hague Convention did in fact impose substantive limits on the Germans' legislative powers in "political" matters. The SG abandoned any sense of moral, ethical or legal duty to their fellow Belgians under the guise of an overriding lawful obligation imposed on them by international law.

Similar discussions on the implementation of the anti-Jewish Orders broke out at the meeting of 19 November. The President of the Committee of Secretaries-General, Ernst de Bunswyck, who would soon be compelled to leave his post by the Germans, reported to his colleagues that the Germans had written demanding that Vossen, who did not attend this meeting, as SG for the Interior, take all necessary steps to ensure that Jews were properly registered by the local and municipal authorities. German General Reeder wanted Vossen to create a model for the registers as well as for each card to be completed during the registration process.

De Bunswyck informed his colleagues that he had already himself drafted a circular for the Ministry of Justice informing local prosecutors and others of the procedure to be followed for removing Jewish employees. He reiterated the line of thought and legal argument which would become so important in the days and years to follow.

> He replied that Jewish persons must declare themselves to the local Administration, under penalty of finding themselves subjected to very severe sanctions.
> There is no need therefore for local authorities to take steps for this registration.[44]

The themes repeat and reinforce themselves. The Jews "must" declare themselves. The obligation is theirs and theirs alone. Failure to comply will result in them "seeing themselves having sanctions imposed on them" (*se voir appliquer des sanctions*). The deployment of the reflexive verb structure is not accidental. It creates and deepens the self-image of the SG, and subaltern Belgian representatives, as ethically, practically and legally divorced from the process of identification and separation of those classified as "Jews". De Bunswyck's draft memorandum for the dismissal of Jews employed by, or responsible to, the Ministry of Justice does not implicate him personally in any legal liability for the racial/religious discriminatory practice. Only those employees who have identified themselves as "Jews" will be dismissed. In reality and in law, they are responsible for their own fate.

Four days later, the SG again met to discuss various matters arising out of the anti-Jewish Decrees. The question of pension benefits for full and part-time employees dismissed as "Jews" was again mooted. M. Adam agreed to send a copy to all his colleagues of his circular to the various municipal authorities concerning the registration process. This time de Bunswyck read his memorandum to his colleagues as an example to be followed by all Ministries. The goal of the memorandum was, according to the minutes of the meeting "to invite the Jewish employees concerned (by the measures) to request their retirement".[45]

Once again, "passive collaboration" required that Jewish public servants be "invited" to "request" their "retirement". The position of the SG shifts none too subtly over the few days from the end of October to late November 1940. Active steps to put into effect German measures against Jews are being taken by the heads of each Ministry, even as such activities continue to be couched in terms of passivity and Jewish agency. More importantly, Adam has begun to draw up a series of instructions to municipalities throughout the country for the implementation of the registration process. Gone is Baron de Bunswyck's assertion that the Jews had full responsibility for registering themselves. His claim that no steps need be taken by the local government authorities gave way to practical and legal bureaucratic necessity. This becomes the key jurisprudential point of reference in relation to the process by which Jews were identified and entered into the Register of Jews. The municipalities did not "take steps", they merely complied. The Jewish Register was created at the request of Jews who demanded their registration pursuant to a German Decree. This limited technical legal distinction between active agency and compliance with superior binding orders is the point at which "passive collaboration" begins and ends in Belgian law and history. Predominant mythologies have replicated this strict jurisprudential position that Belgian state and legal officials merely complied and did not in any moral or juridical sense actively collaborate in the persecution of that country's Jewish population.

The Permanent Council of Legislation: legitimating and legalizing antisemitism

These developments are essential to our understanding of the ways in which, in reality, Belgian compliance with German anti-Jewish measures was early and active. They also serve to displace, or perhaps to re-emphasize in a somewhat more nuanced fashion, the next step in the construction of the jurisprudential bulwark permitting the legalized persecution of Belgium's Jewish population. Maxime Steinberg has rightly pointed to the importance played by the Permanent Council of Legislation (Conseil Permanent de Législation) in the processes which legitimated Belgian official compliance in executing German anti-Jewish Decrees.[46] Although the SG do seem to have accepted in no uncertain terms the jurisprudential inevitability which informed the fate of their Jewish fellows, they did turn to the body of jurists and eminent figures whose task was to offer advisory opinions on the constitutional validity of Belgian legal measures before reaching any final positions on the modalities of implementation. The legal advice given by the Permanent Council would come to embody and legally inscribe and circumscribe the subsequent history of "passive collaboration" as justified by a respect for the rule of law in occupied Belgium.

The legal, historical and rhetorical legitimating role in permitting local and national officials to put into effect anti-Jewish laws of the Permanent Council's opinion cannot be overestimated. Nor can its importance in the construction of the discourses and mythologies of resistance and awkward, limited compliance which have informed many understandings to this day be ignored. But these mythologies have an earlier and equally powerful origin, in the discursive practices and legal interpretations of the SG as evidenced in their own records. "Passive collaboration" began and was legally justified from the moment in early October when the SG indicated in their letter to von Craushaar their clear understanding that, under the Hague Convention, the Germans could validly introduce anti-Jewish measures pursuant to Article 43 and that those measures would be obeyed as having the same effect as Belgian law under the accepted juridical norms of war. The Permanent Council did nothing more than provide a more explicit legal basis for the position already adopted by the government and embodied and inscribed in their writings, their discussions and their practical steps to implement the anti-Jewish Decrees well before the Council delivered its advice on 21 November.[47] The advice of the Council must be read not just on its own textual terms but in the context of the practices and discourses of the SG and others who were already a good way down the path of full-blown "passive collaboration" before the formal legal framework had been established.

The first legal principle from which the Council proceeds in its letter of advice is the supremacy of the Belgian Constitution. The provisions of Articles 6 and 14 which guarantee equality and religious freedom and Article 100 enshrining judicial independence are for the Council the textual embodiment and the very foundation of the Belgian state structure. These provisions "are the fundamental principles of our public law, situated as the very basis for our administrative and judicial organizations".[48]

The racial and religious exclusions found in the anti-Jewish Orders are clearly violative of these founding, constitutive principles of the Belgian nation. As a matter of constitutional principle and criminal law "*participation* in these Decrees clearly exceeds the legal power of the Secretaries-General and of all public servants, since it would constitute a breach of their oath of loyalty to the Constitution".[49] This is a legal opinion from the most powerful and eminent group of jurists in the country, informing the SG that all *participation* in the execution of the anti-Jewish Decrees would violate their sworn allegiance to the constitutional principles of the Belgian nation and the Belgian state. This text, had it stopped here, could have served as the basis for another (sadly hypothetical) jugular constitutionally based refusal by the highest authorities in the land to enforce the various measures, such as the registration of Belgium's Jewish population, or the dismissal of governmental employees or judges identified as "Jews", set out in the Decrees.[50] By this time the SG were already intimately engaged in a process of legalized compliance and obedience. What would they do when faced with this legal opinion that any *participation* in the anti-Jewish measures was a violation of their sacred oath and of their self-perception as the institutional embodiment of the continuity of the Belgian state and nation?

Fortunately and not surprisingly, they were saved by the next part of the Council's letter of advice. It is here that the legal textual basis on which the legal practice of "passive collaboration" which was put into place in Belgium can be located. This is the moment at which Belgian law betrayed itself and its Jewish subjects. The Constitution must be situated and understood in light of the law of armed occupation. This opinion serves as the embodiment of the legality of measures taken by Belgian officials against the Jewish population. In part at least, the answer to the legal historical question as to why Belgian legal and governmental officials did not consistently (or ever) invoke Belgium's constitutional guarantees of equality and religious freedom when faced with these Decrees can be traced to this legal opinion. The strict and narrow legal framework as set out in the Permanent Council's opinion defining the limits of acceptable state involvement is not the sole explanatory factor at work in the history of "passive collaboration" by Belgian officials in implementing anti-Jewish measures. The social imaginary's construction of Jews as foreigners, as non-citizens, serves as an equally strong explanatory factor for their absence from constitutional discourse. The Constitution was not invoked because the constitutional authorities, the Permanent Council and the SG, removed the Constitution from the parameter of acceptable, applicable, legal discourse. In combination with a constitutional imagination in which "Jews" became foreigners and a constitutional text in which protections could lawfully be removed from foreigners, the fragility of Belgian constitutional legality and patriotism became the operative factors in permitting state collaboration in antisemitic persecution.

Thus, the Permanent Council, after denouncing *participation* as contrary to the foundational principles of Belgian constitutional government, went on to define *participation*. Hayoit de Termicourt, the Solicitor-General (*Avocat-Général*) at the Court of Cassation wrote for the Council:

> Without a doubt, every enforcement of the obligations contained in these Decrees is not a "participation" therein.
> The person in relation to whom, or against whom a measure is taken by the Occupying Power and who, under the compulsion on which the Authority bases its power, completes the material act imposed by the law, submits to the provision, he does not participate therein.[51]

As matter of law, submission to the legal compulsion which accompanies and characterizes these Decrees imposed by the Germans, is not "participation" in those Decrees and therefore, is not a violation of the oath of loyalty to the Constitution and to the Belgian nation. The thematic repetition is striking. The measures taken against the Jews are German Decrees and at most the Belgian officials who put them into effect submit themselves under a threat of compulsion and military force. As Maxime Steinberg so powerfully argues, this juridical argument posits the Belgian government as the first and primary victim of Nazi antisemitism.

The Permanent Council expanded and clarified its understanding of the position in which compliant Belgian officials would find themselves, as a matter of constitutional and criminal law.

> Thus, in the opinion of the Permanent Committee, the following are not acts of illegal participation: the submission of persons defined in § 1 of the 1st Decree to the prohibitions and obligations imposed on them by §§ 2 and 3, paragraph 2, (§ 14 of the 1st Decree and § 1 of the 2nd Decree); submission to § 9 of the 1st Decree; keeping a Register of Jews by municipal or local administrations as a result of the spontaneous declarations of interested parties (§ 3 of the 1st Decree); the posting of signs by municipal authorities requested from them by interested parties pursuant to § 14 of this Decree.[52]

"Passive collaboration", lawful within the limits of the Belgian constitutional state, allowed government departments to dismiss civil servants identified as "Jews", exempted municipalities from penalty for registering "Jews" who spontaneously presented themselves for registration, or printing "Jewish Undertaking" signs to be posted on Jewish businesses. But even here there were limits. "Passive" submission under legal constraint of the occupying power was permissible and permitted but "active" participation, the key legal and taxonomical defining concept in all that would follow, was still clearly in violation of the basic norms and fundamental principles of the Belgian constitutional state. Therefore

> On the other hand, any initiative, all investigations or complementary steps, with the aim of ensuring the full efficacy of any of the provisions of the Decrees by Belgian public servants is forbidden. The taking of such an initiative or such steps would mean no longer being compelled to submit to the enforcement of the Decrees, but would be their promotion, and as a consequence would mean participating in the transformation of our public law.[53]

The constitutional law, if not the nuances and complexities of its practical application, is clear. Submission to the Decrees is permitted; active enforcement is not. The Permanent Council takes up the theme not just of "passive collaboration" but additionally underlines the idea that "Jews" must take the initiative themselves. The Register of Jews may be held by local authorities but such a Register is constructed, has a legal existence, only as a result of two active steps. First, the Germans compel Belgian officials to keep such a Register and the Belgians passively submit to the compulsion. At the same time, the Permanent Council makes it clear that the other actors in the drama of anti-Jewish Decrees are the objects of the law themselves, "Jews". The Jewish Register is compiled only on the basis of declarations of "interested parties" (*les intéressés*) and in each Belgian local area, the signage for Jewish businesses is "requested of them by the interested parties" (*requis d'elles par les intéressés*). Even in its carefully constructed grammatical language, the jurisprudential semiotics of the Permanent Council makes it clear that "Jews" ask to be registered; they request the proper signs for their businesses.

Always in the history of Belgium's official "passive collaboration", the participation which is not *participation* takes place in a jurisprudentially sanctioned world in which Belgian actions are not "actions" because they are always passive, mere compliance under threat of force and lawful occupying power authority. They authorize themselves to act as everything but the authors of the identification, exclusion and elimination of their Jewish fellows. Belgian officials are protected by Belgian law and by its inherent authority. Passive collaboration is not, for the SG, the Permanent Council or the postwar legal construction of the question of local compliance and resistance in applying anti-Jewish laws, unconstitutional or un-Belgian. It is precisely the contrary, faithful from its grammatical construction through its rhetorical deployment, to its practical implementation, to the highest norms of public service and the constitutional rule of law.

The taxonomical question which underlies all of the issues of the fragility of law in occupied Belgium is presented in its starkest, most lawful form. The categories "collaboration" and "resistance" are central to our understanding of this part of Holocaust history. The black and white divisions between active believers in the New Order and those who took up arms against the German invaders pose few difficulties beyond the merely historiographical account books. The idea of "passive collaboration" which characterizes the role and self-understanding of the bureaucrats and elected officials in Belgium in implementing anti-Jewish laws raises fundamental issues not just for the taxonomy of Holocaust history, but for our understandings of the nature and role of legal legitimacy in the construction of the category of "collaboration" itself. As Zygmunt Bauman puts it, "In that grey area bystanders confront the risk of becoming accessories to the devil and turning into perpetrators."[54]

We confront the essential importance of the micro-level study of the role of local officials in the implementation of those anti-Jewish Decrees which served to identify, classify, exclude, expropriate, incarcerate, deport and kill the Jews of Belgium. The self-understanding of Belgian officials, the legal framework constructed to legitimate their passive collaboration which was not *participation*, all serve to mask and obscure the taxonomical complexity and ethical importance of this aspect of Belgian Holocaust history. The ideological and jurisprudential basis for the creation of occupation history has been the legality of passive collaboration and the adherence to constitutional principle by Belgian officials during the occupation. And yet there is an affinity between "doing evil" and "non-resistance to evil" – much closer and more intimate than the scholars engrossed in the exploration of one but neglecting the other would notice and admit.[55]

This gray area of obedience, compliance and of self-described passivity which characterized the self-understanding of Belgian officialdom after the constitutional opinion of the Conseil de Législation embodies in a concrete case study the very dilemma of the role of law and legality in the Holocaust.[56] The actual construction and interpretation of the legal situation by the Permanent Council must be critically analyzed.[57] The actions of the various official Belgian participants in anti-Jewish persecutions need to be looked at in light of legal limits on their actions set out by the Permanent Council in order to determine the extent to which these actions were on their own self-defined terms legal. A critique of the history of Belgian official participation in anti-Jewish persecution will need to be constructed based on an analysis which combines the first two elements. Was the collaboration which took place limited to passive collaboration and to the self-created legality of Belgian officials? If so, how can we now understand resistance, collaboration and legality as interacting concepts in the history of the Shoah? If not, the same question takes on a different substantive complexion but must still be addressed.

Postwar repressive measures against collaboration in Belgium clearly focused on those who actively participated in the creation of the New Order.[58] The construction of that process of repression reflected the complex understandings of and conflicts over Belgian identity and citizenship. French-speaking Belgians understood the necessity of punishing anti-Belgian Flemish collaborators and bemoaned the arguably artificial process of reconciliation and amnesty which followed. Flemish understandings of the idea of collaboration itself differed sharply from those of their Walloon fellow citizens, who seemed blind to their own history of collaboration.[59] What all parties shared throughout the process of repression and reconciliation, no matter how flawed either may have been, was the foundational notion of the illegality of "collaboration". While exactly which actors, or what types of acts, fit into the definitional confines of the category itself remained open for political and legal contestation, all participants in postwar debates in Belgium shared this common starting and finishing point.[60]

Law served as the mechanism and as the taxonomical definer of "collaboration" as a Belgian phenomenon. Collaborators acted illegally and law would serve to punish these deviations from the constitutional and legal normative structures of Belgian national identity. The concept of passive collaboration which is deployed from the beginning in the process of Belgian self-understanding and justification therefore involves, at some epistemological level, an apparent dissonance. The very passivity of the collaboration made those acts and those actors who performed them as mere executors of German will and power, non-collaborators as a matter of law. They collaborated passively under law and therefore, by definition, not unlawfully. From the very earliest moments of the constitutionally grounded refusal and subsequent negotiations by the SG about the role to be played by the Belgian state apparatus in enforcing and applying anti-Jewish measures, and then of the Conseil de Législation's opinion which constructed the legal framework grounded in the fine, but apparently essential, distinction between collaboration and execution, between *participation* and submission, Belgian state and administrative collaboration was never considered by participants to be collaboration in the legal sense. The collaboration which features in the chapters of this book was not perceived or understood to be "collaboration" in the legal sense precisely because it *was* collaboration in the legal sense, i.e. collaboration which could not be collaboration because it was consistent with the Hague Convention and the Belgian Constitution, or at least with an operative and operating shared understanding of those legal texts. What precisely did this passive collaboration entail at the practical level?

The Secretaries-General and the Jewish question 1940–1945: the constitutional practice of antisemitism

With the framework set for the introduction and implementation of the first anti-Jewish Orders, the SG met again on 3 December 1940.[61] What emerges from the minutes of this meeting is that the exact permissible limits on Belgian "participation" in the process were still unclear. M. Adam, the Inspector-General of the Ministry of the Interior, reported that he had met with the German authorities and presented a draft of a circular to be sent to all local and regional authorities regarding the practical aspects of the creation of the Jewish Register. The Germans approved the wording of the text but insisted that the document itself must carry the imprimatur of the Belgian Ministry of the Interior. The circular was sent two or three days later. When the Ministry of the Interior circulated its letter of instructions about the duty to comply with the anti-Jewish Orders to local officials on 6 December 1940, it did so against a background of legal and practical compliance with German anti-Jewish Decrees. The circular under Adam's signature to the mayors and other government authorities throughout the country simply confirmed what had become the juridical reality of passive collaboration. Continuing the common theme of passivity, of non-*participation,* Adam made it clear once again that the registration process was at the demand of the victims. Local authorities were advised that

> It is also ordered that municipalities shall urgently publish a notice indicating that Jews are required to have themselves entered in the Register of Jews and that those in charge of Jewish establishments must request that the local administration proceed with the signs set out in the Decree.[62]

The dominant position of the SG, which would become the shared understanding of a core Belgian mythology, was already well-established. "Jews" would present themselves. Local authorities would simply comply with their request to be registered as "Jews" under the permissible rules of passive collaboration. At this historical juncture, the finer points and details of the actual limits of permissible Belgian involvement were still being negotiated both with the German authorities and among the Belgian authorities themselves. The SG recognized there were still things which Belgian state officials could not lawfully do. The rules of the game were still being clarified for Belgian non-participating participants in the Jew hunt.

At the 3 December SG meeting, it was noted that the Germans had insisted that local mayors and other municipal authorities should report the names of those "Jews" who had not registered to the military authority. Adam informed his colleagues that the Germans had, after discussion, withdrawn this demand. While the details of the discussions are not recorded, it is not difficult to imagine that Adam would have informed his German interlocutors that such a request could not be complied with. First, any such report would have had the effect of completing and/or perfecting the German anti-Jewish Order, thereby exceeding the constitutionally permissible limits of Belgian passive collaboration as set out by the Conseil de Législation. Second, Adam most probably would (should?) have indicated to the Germans that Belgian mayors had no way of identifying "Jews" who had not registered since the country's Constitution guaranteed religious liberty. No such category existed in Belgian law. There was no way, legally speaking, for Belgian officials to know who was or was not an unregistered Jew, since they could not know who was a "Jew".

The issue of implementing the provisions of the Second Jewish Order, compelling the removal of all Jewish civil servants, was also discussed at this early December meeting. After some hesitation, the SG decided that they should proceed through the already existing mechanisms of Belgian employment law.[63] Under their plan, Jews in public employment would be "laid off" (*mis en disponibilité*), thereby retaining the right to some form of salary substitution payment. No mention was made of the fact that the Secretary-General for Finance, Oscar Plisnier, had already sent out a circular (*ordre de service*) advising all heads of department to inform civil servants subject to the Jewish Order that they were to leave their posts by 31 December, and that notice of their "wish" to take advantage of being laid off had to be received by 10 December.[64] Once again, "Jews" take the initiative, they benefit from certain advantages if they leave their jobs, and all the Belgian state does is make their life less onerous.[65]

Plisnier followed up on his earlier circular with a letter dated 16 December 1940 in which he informed the heads of relevant departments that the mechanism of a compulsory laying off of "Jewish" employees had been decided upon by the SG and that the relevant legal provisions under Belgian law would be followed in all cases. He attached to his letter a template of the administrative order (*arrêté*) which would be completed in relation to each Jewish civil servant subject to the German Decree. The internal administrative document itself states clearly that the employee in question had been removed because he could no longer fulfill his role as a result of the German Decree of 28 October 1940.[66] The textual embodiment of Belgian passive collaboration at this early stage can be read as a combination of unquestioning obedience to the new German legal order concerning "Jews" and an attempt at some level to mitigate the consequences of that new juridical arrangement. Collaboration and resistance coexist. Employees maintain a significant portion of their salary, at least in the first year of their unemployment, through the application of the standard rules of Belgian civil service employment law. At the same time, ambiguities and apparent contradictions emerge.

Plisnier's letter of 16 December indicates that the Belgian state and its representatives had simply adapted to and adapted the language of the German occupier. He writes without hesitation of "Jewish civil servants and agents" (*fonctionnaires et agents Juifs*). There are no longer any government employees who might be Hebrews (*Israélites*). At the same time, the actual Belgian legal instrument which he attaches as a template makes no reference at all either to Jews or Hebrews. Instead there is a simple reference to the German Decree of 28 October. The documentary record of the early days of implementing the anti-Jewish Orders perhaps indicates that at some level, both juridical and psychological, the SG were attempting to tread carefully through the administrative and legal minefield of passive collaboration.

Nonetheless, cooperation with the process of eliminating Jewish civil servants went ahead. On 11 January 1941, Plisnier issued another letter to heads of department asking them to report to him the number of employees subject to the German Decree, together with information including their names and positions.[67] After this first wave of activity involving the creation of the Jewish Registers throughout the country and the removal of Jews from all designated public employment, there was a lull in the involvement of the SG in the "Jewish question", just as there was a short respite in German anti-Jewish legislative activity generally.

In November 1941, however, the SG had to deal with the practical and legal consequences of their actions of the previous year. The regular provisions of Belgian law came face to face, as they would in a number of other circumstances throughout the occupation, with the practical consequences of German anti-Jewish provisions. Belgian law, subordinate in matters relating to "Jews", had to be applied in a concrete context created by or resulting from the German measures. This double legal system, hierarchically constructed, would characterize Belgian juridical involvement in the active enforcement of German persecutory practices against the country's Jewish population.

Decisions had to be taken about the operation of Belgian labor law provisions governing the status of laid off government employees. As Plisnier explained in his letter, after the first year of unemployment, the normal payment regime changed.[68] While they received full salaries in the first year, former employees' rights to remuneration or its equivalent were reduced by a complex formula directly related to their years of government service. According to the examples given by Plisnier, the potential reduction in the second year, if normal rules of Belgian employment law were followed, was radical. An employee with twenty years service at the time of being laid off would see the entitlement reduced from 30,000 BEF to 10,000 BEF. A 21-year-old employee with two years of service would fall in the second year of his "lay off" from 12,600 BEF to 420 BEF. Because such an employee would have only worked for two years, after that same period of inactivity, they would be barred from receiving further payments. After the second year of unemployment, all payments would cease.

The problem which arose therefore was that many former civil servants would soon find themselves reduced to a state of penury if the provisions of Belgian law were to be followed, since their period of entitlement under which their rights to payment were determined would be rather short. Furthermore, as Plisnier points out to his fellow SG, there was a technical legal conflict between the actual wording of the German Decree and the practice adopted by the Belgian government. The Second Jewish Order § 2 (1) sets out that Jewish civil servants should be "retired" with effect from 31 December 1940 (*mis en retraite*). However Belgian law provided that civil servants could retire only at the age of 65 and after thirty years of employment. It would therefore have been unlawful for the SG to have forced Jewish civil servants to retire before they fulfilled the dual criteria of age and years of work. Plisnier explains that the solution of laying off the state employees was the only legal means available to the SG in November and December 1940 because they had to comply with the German Decree and Belgian law. The dual legal system of executing German anti-Jewish Orders and at the same time complying with ordinary rules of Belgian employment law resurfaced as the first year of Jewish "lay offs" came to an end. For Plisnier, the equity of the case was clear. It was not possible or permissible to leave to suffer those civil servants who would find themselves in dire financial straits if the strict provisions of Belgian law were to be adhered to.

Plisnier sought a solution to this real and legal dilemma in the world of the new dual legal system. Since the Germans had left the actual practical (but legally passive) application of the removal of Belgian Jewish civil servants to the appropriate domestic governmental authorities, compulsory "retirement" as found in the Decree, which would be contrary to Belgian law, should be ignored and a new solution found. The SG for Finance therefore suggested to his colleagues that another Belgian solution was available. He argued that the application of another article of the operative domestic *arrêté* relating to civil service employment permitted them to adopt a formula under which a 20 per cent reduction in payments would occur after the second year as long as the monies received never fell below a threshold established according to another formula based on years of service. This would also be combined with another equitable solution which would apply the same calculations to any employee whose years of service were not sufficient to cover the lay-off period.

Plisnier's solution which sought to alleviate the suffering of Jewish former civil servants did not convince his colleagues. At the meeting of the SG which took place on 5 December 1941, G. Claeys, SG for Communications, objected that the proposal would have the effect of privileging dismissed Jewish civil servants over those government employees who had lost their jobs for other reasons, for example, following German Decrees relating to the removal of undesirable individuals from public office.[69] The SG collectively decided that in these circumstances they could not adopt Plisnier's advice since that would in fact be a case of special treatment for Jews. Instead they decided that any civil servant who had lost their post for whatever reason could come to them for individual assistance if they had been unable to find another job. One year after Adam's circular establishing a special Register of Jews throughout the villages, towns and cities of Belgium and a year after all Jewish public employees were removed from their posts, the SG categorically refused to accept that there was in fact or in law any specifically identifiable issue concerning these "Jews". All former civil servants now simply fell into a single category to be dealt with on a case-by-case basis of individual equity.

Other departments of the central government began to ask what was to be done about their former Jewish civil servants. The Department of Public Education wrote to Plisnier on 8 December asking about the situation of their colleagues dismissed one year before pursuant to the German Order concerning "Hebrews" (*Israélites*).[70] On 12 December, Plisnier issued general instructions reiterating the collegial decision.[71] He added that, if the application of the provisions of Belgian law in the matter caused particular hardship, one should seek redress from the German authorities.[72] Plisnier changes semiotic strategies from his previous correspondence when he refers specifically to "Jewish civil servants" (*fonctionnaires juifs*), just as he changes jurisdictional strategies. While he had previously sought to convince his colleagues of some existing duty under Belgian law to help impoverished former government employees, following their rejection of his proposal, he informed department heads that any hardship cases needed to be referred to the Germans, who as a matter of law were responsible for the Jewish question. Whether he actually thought that the German military administration would obviate Jewish suffering at this point is unclear. What is evident is that the Belgian SG continued to adopt a position which placed responsibility for Jewish civil servants dismissed from their posts squarely in the hands of the Germans.[73]

In June and July 1942, when German deportations of Jews for "compulsory labor" were under way, the SG intervened with the German authorities. On 12 June 1942, the SG discussed a report to the effect that, while some deportation measures had already taken place against foreign Jews, it now appeared that Belgian Jews were being subjected to the same measures.[74] At their meeting of 27 June, Claeys inquired if Secretary-General Vervaeck, of the Ministry of Labor, had written a letter of protest to the Germans. Vervaeck promised to present the letter at the next meeting.[75] The subject of their disapproval was the deportation of Jews to forced labor in the north of France under the auspices of the Organization Todt. More specifically, the intervention signaled by Claeys and Vervaeck concerns only the planned deportation of Jews who are Belgian citizens (*Juifs de nationalité belge*). The pernicious distinction between Belgian Jews, who are apparently worthy of protection, and the tens of thousands of foreign Jews subjected to deportation measures is invoked by the SG in what appears to be their first official protest against the mistreatment of Jews.

The next time "the Jewish question" was addressed at the collective level by the SG was at their meeting of 8 September 1942. Again, the subject was the arrest of Belgian Jews by the Germans.[76] The meeting reported that nine Jews arrested in Antwerp and sent to the camp at Malines had died in transit as a result of the inhumane conditions to which they were subjected. The intervention by the SG was in vain, since German military officials simply claimed that orders to arrest all Jews and to seize all Jewish property came directly from Berlin and they could do nothing about it.

The recorded internal discussions of the highest Belgian government authorities demonstrate the desperate state of affairs. While they recognize that something must be done, they are realistic enough to recognize that the only person with enough authority to intervene is General von Falkenhausen, the Supreme Military Commander in Belgium.[77] Gaston Schuind, SG for Justice, reminded his colleagues that these harsh new measures would affect 5,000 Belgians. The emphasis once more is not on "Jews" or measures against "Jews", but on Belgian citizens who are Jews. Schuind made special pleadings to Von Falkenhausen that Belgian Jews should enjoy the benefits of the exemptions afforded to Romanian, Italian, Portuguese and even American and English Jews. He received assurances from the Germans that Belgian Jews would not be deported to the east; that pleadings in favor of veterans could be made to exempt them from "work" in the north of France and that some Belgian Jews might be given permission to not wear the Yellow Star.[78]

Major actions against Belgian Jews would take place in 1943, when the Germans sought to end the "Jewish question" in Belgium.[79] By this time, the vast majority of the 25,124 Jews deported from Belgium, mostly foreigners, had already been sent to the east.[80] Maxime Steinberg records a total of 55,671 Jews living in Belgium with 3,680 Belgian citizens among them. Of the deported, 23,921 or 95 per cent were foreigners. Only 5 per cent or 1,203 "Belgian" Jews were deported.[81]

Schuind was able to report again a little over one year later that the Germans had agreed to halt arrests, temporarily at least, of Belgian Jews.[82] He insisted however that the SG must continue their efforts to arrange a meeting with Von Falkenhausen.[83] A meeting with high-ranking German military officials took place that day and the SG reconvened that afternoon to learn of the results of the discussion.[84] Von Falkenhausen, according to his representatives, would not meet with Secretary Schuind whose recalcitrant attitude in general, and specifically to German complaints about the failures of the Belgian police and judiciary to adequately deal with rising terrorist activities, was unacceptable.[85]

At this point in time, two facts were clear. The arrest, imprisonment, spoliation and deportation of Jews from Belgium had already occurred to a highly significant degree. All of these persecutions of Jews had taken place in Belgium without significant protest or intervention by the SG. Their collective interventions, after the first anniversary of the "laying off" of Jewish civil servants, were virtually unknown. When they did act, they acted almost exclusively to protect the interests of Belgian Jews. The joint impact of the general policy of passive collaboration in the Jewish question and a deeper constitutional, constitutive understanding of Belgian citizenship and identity had resulted in the active identification and registration of tens of thousands of Jewish individuals and property defined as

"Jewish" and the removal of foreign Jews from the country without a word of protest from the representatives of the Belgian nation.

Secondly, the interventions on behalf of Belgian Jews were not only too little too late, but also can only be properly situated in the context of the evolving political situation, domestically and internationally. By late 1943, German victory and a thousand-year New Order in Europe were no longer inevitable or even likely. In Belgium itself, resistance activity was on the increase. Some Belgian organisms were displaying disconcerting signs of less than complete compliance and obedience. The courts were increasingly reluctant to allow the SG to proceed by decree without judicial review. Belgian police appeared more and more to have "lost" their weapons or to have been "forced" to surrender them to Resistance fighters. Most significantly, at this historical juncture, compulsory labor service for Belgians had begun. Young Belgian men were being drafted to work in Germany. This provoked bitter memories of compulsory deportations of Belgian workers in the First World War and raised the ire of ordinary Belgians. Protests about this compulsory labor service came from all walks of Belgian officialdom and, as in France, many young men joined the resistance as a direct result of having received their notice to report for deportation and work in Germany. The protest of the SG in September 1943 and the German reaction must be seen and can be understood and interpreted only in this broader historical context.

At their meeting of 1 October 1943, for example, the Belgian officials first discussed the labor issue generally and then turned to the specific case of civil servants subjected to this regime of compulsion. Then they addressed the issue of the continuing arrest of Jews.[86] They emphasized the fact that, despite their protests and certain German assurances, many Belgian Jews remained incarcerated and others had already been deported to Germany. They noted that the Germans also continued to confiscate Jewish property.

Plisnier, who presided, stated that this confiscation of property was clearly contrary to the provisions of the Hague Convention (*est en opposition formelle avec la Convention de la Haye*). Finally, in October 1943, the SG appear to have realized that Article 46 of the Hague Convention might have some significance. One can only speculate as to the effect the invocation of these provisions might have had when the Germans decided to involve the entire Belgian state apparatus in the process of identifying and registering Jews, and of declaring all Jewish property. One might also ask why the provisions relating to private property under the Hague Convention were never invoked when all Jewish commercial activity had to cease operations and all businesses surrender their licenses in March 1942, or why the Aryanization of Jewish property belonging to foreigners was not contrary to these same provisions in the eyes of the SG? Article 46 of the Hague Convention enters the legal and constitutional consciences of the SG far too late and in a far too limited fashion to make for a convincing argument for placing their actions in a taxonomical structure of resistance without further contextualization and counter-analysis.

Nonetheless, the SG did decide to draft a letter of protest to the Germans concerning the measures taken against Belgian Jews. A letter concerning the arrest and internment of Belgian Jews was drafted and sent to Von Falkenhausen, without concrete results.[87]

In December 1943, three years after the introduction of the first anti-Jewish Decrees, the highest governmental officials in Belgium continued to intervene in favour of Jewish citizens. At this time, they were apparently reduced to arguing with the Germans that Jews who were currently under arrest should be spared from deportation. To this end, the SG for Justice, De Foy, who had replaced Schuind when the latter was dismissed by the Germans, convinced his colleagues that they should argue for the establishment of an internment camp in Belgium in which these Jews could be held without being deported.[88] Passive collaboration had now come to this stage. Belgian government officials had abandoned all reference to the Hague Convention, which had in any event come far too late, and were reduced to asking for the creation of a Belgian concentration camp, in Belgium, for Belgian Jews. At the same time, they sought to adopt a strategy, in part at the behest of the AJB, for a further subdivision of those Belgian Jews on behalf of whom they might intervene with the German military authority.[89] The Committee of Secretaries-General therefore discussed making special pleadings to the Germans concerning combat veterans, those holding national honors, civil servants and teachers.[90] All of this led to naught. The Germans had already managed to deport those Jews they could still find.

In the letter of 5 June 1940, the SG expressed their happiness that they would never be asked to do anything which would bring them into conflict with their duty of loyalty to the nation. What is clear from the historical record is that the establishment of a legal framework of passive collaboration under which Belgian officials could implement but not perfect anti-Jewish Orders was both conceptually ambiguous, if not vacuous, and practically impossible to adhere to in practice. Combined with a self-understanding of the nation and of Belgian citizenship which constructed Jews as foreigners and foreigners as a group from whom rights could be lawfully withdrawn, the fate of Belgium's Jews was written in the context of the SG's limited constitutional hermeneutic. There is nothing in the records to indicate that they ever took a strong position about the German anti-Jewish measures until it was far too late and then only in so far as Belgian subjects were concerned. Their understanding of their duty of loyalty and fidelity to the nation was a narrow, technical and basically flawed one. They understood only that guarantees of equality and religious freedom, as well as judicial independence, might prevent them from placing the provisions of the first anti-Jewish Decrees within Belgian law. They did not understand that a passive collaboration, as conceived and practiced from the very first days of the occupation, would lead to the exclusion and persecution of the Jews of Belgium as an inevitable result of their lack of constitutional imagination and of the inherent fragility of their vision of the nation to which they had to be faithful.

Chapter 3

The fragility of law

Anti-Jewish Decrees and Belgian legal elites

Vivian Curran, in her brilliant study of the effects of legalized antisemitism on the constitutional order and legal tradition under Pétain's Vichy régime, describes the "internal or voluntary road to destruction" followed in France.

> Vichy France illustrates that the insidious potential for autodestruction and for the legalization of racism is embedded within the very structures and institutions of constitutional democracy. This potential came to fruition in Vichy without a violent usurpation of authority, for the Vichy régime did not result from a military coup d'état, nor was it imposed by Nazi Germany. Indeed, France was the only western democracy subject to Nazi occupation in the wake of military defeat that had an official, indigenous government dedicated to collaborating with the occupier.[1]

Like France, Belgium fell to the Nazi onslaught in the spring of 1940. The German conquest placed all Jews on Belgian soil in peril. Unlike France, however, the apparatus of the Belgian state did not directly introduce anti-Jewish legislation. All measures taken against Jews in Belgium were pursued under Decrees issued by the German Military Command, but implemented by local officials. Subsequent sections of this book will fill in the most important details of the daily legalization of antisemitism in Belgium and its state apparatus and the normalized process of eliminating "the Jew" from civil society.

Those who have studied in some detail the tragic story of the law's implication, indeed centrality, in the process of exclusion, expropriation and killing of French Jewry, point to the failure of legal actors in that country to combat official legislative antisemitism. They underline the absence of any invocation of the great and overriding, and still existing, constitutional principles of *liberté, égalité et fraternité*, as a legal bulwark against anti-Jewish laws. This failure is to some extent exacerbated for Francophiles by the fact that Belgian judges and lawyers, the "county cousins", did precisely what their French counterparts failed to do. In Brussels, lawyers and judges protested against the German Decree which sought to remove Jewish legal professionals by claiming that such actions violated the norms and provisions of the Belgian Constitution. They invoked Article 100 of the Constitution.[2] They asserted that its provisions, guaranteeing life tenure for judges and strictly limiting the grounds of removal of members of the judiciary, were the only legal norms to which they were subject. No restriction based on race or religion was part of the Belgian constitutional order. In later periods of the German occupation, judges and government lawyers in Brussels refused to process the paperwork for the adoption of Jewish children when the German authorities requested the files from such cases.[3] Notaries throughout Belgium eventually refused to authenticate (legally certify) any transactions relating to the Aryanization of Jewish property on the grounds that such procedures violated Belgian law.[4] Belgian courts rejected any action instituted by the German nominated administrator (*Verwalter*) of Jewish property or businesses because their appointment was contrary to the Belgian legal order.[5]

In other words, the Belgian legal profession and judiciary appeared to place legal and constitutional roadblocks in the way of German anti-Jewish measures. They protested, they used their legal skills and they ensured that the legal system of Belgium was not implicated in the enforcement of legalized antisemitism. German measures targeted at the "Jew" remained German measures. Belgian law and the Belgian Constitution were, according to the dominant and current mythologies of professional history, untainted and unimplicated in the Holocaust as a juridical event. Belgian lawyers and judges remained loyal to their professional oaths to uphold the laws and Constitution while French judges took the oath of loyalty to Pétain and the New Order of Vichy.[6] Richard Weisberg in his insightful study of Vichy law and the Holocaust bemoans the French professions' failure to invoke the higher normative standards of the Constitution and contrasts it with the example of Belgian objection. Indeed he characterizes the Belgian position as "admirably pro-Semitic".[7] Noted French jurist Robert Badinter also underlines Belgian protest and adds that no leader of the French Bar raised a voice of protest at the exclusion of their Jewish colleagues. "As far as French Bar Associations were concerned, no voice of a current or former Bâtonnier (President) was raised to publicly denounce those racist measures which were contrary to principles the Bar had always elevated as its own."[8]

I shall examine what appears to be the most dominant myth of Belgian legal resistance to German anti-Jewish Decrees, the refusal to comply with the German Order banning judges and lawyers identified and defined as "Jews". German legal historians interrogate the Nazi legal regime with an eye to establishing norms of civic education for a vigilant, democratic profession and citizenry, French lawyers like Badinter look upon the Vichy record with a sense of shame. Badinter and Weisberg praise the unequivocally positive response of Belgian lawyers to institutionalized antisemitism. The Belgian case, in which the legal profession and judiciary invoked the Constitution to protest against the legalized racism which informed attempts to ban members of the judiciary and legal profession, is for them a beacon. It can serve to highlight many of the complex and still troubling issues surrounding state practices which enshrine racism as part of the juridical order and which threaten the very existence of the democratic polity

... for the most important of all constitutions, the one written in the citizens' minds, is ever renewable and ever destructible, recreated continuously, invested with inevitably transitory meanings that fluctuate with time and history, through the perpetual vagaries of individual and collective perception and sentiment.[9]

In looking more closely at part of the mythical and foundational story of Belgian legal resistance, I want to highlight, interrogate and add nuance to this historical representation of Belgian juridical opposition to Nazi antisemitism. Ideas and understandings of citizenship, equality and constitutional principles no doubt informed some Belgian legal responses to Nazi anti-Jewish Decrees. Yet the protest was, in part at least, more equivocal and much less "pro-Semitic" than mythology and incomplete historiography would have us believe. Ideas of the nation, of "Belgique" and/or "België", were not universal or universalized. The Bar in Brussels invoked the principles of constitutional patriotism only in defense of a small number of colleagues who shared social, historical, professional, class and ideological backgrounds. While subsequent attempts to subvert the application of various German anti-Jewish measures underline the significant level of legalized opposition by the Belgian professions, other contrary examples which highlight the daily implication of Belgian officials and lawyers in the regular application of anti-Jewish legal norms must also be examined in order to draw a more nuanced, complex and complete picture of Belgian legality in this time of crisis. The lessons we might learn, or the questions we might begin to ask, from and about the legal history of the Nazi period, inform the broader project of this book. What exactly might we mean by invoking legal normativity as a basis for "resistance?" What role, if any, do the rhetoric and practices of the rule of law play in fighting racial and religious oppression in times of crisis? What, if anything, can the story of the Belgian legal system under Nazi occupation teach us about our ideas of citizenship and constitutionalism, of law and justice, of legality and ethically and morally correct behavior? Is this history of resistance and collaboration a useful introduction to broader discussions about ideals of legal constitutional patriotism or even about the professional self-understanding of the rule of law?

The first question which faced the Belgian legal and constitutional order was where lawful authority was seated. The King and some of the structures of government remained on Belgian soil. Memories of the brutality of German rule during the First World War served to inform the decision in favor of maintaining a Belgian authority to deal with the Germans.

As part of the policy of the lesser of two evils (*le moindre mal*) it was necessary for the Belgian court and legal system to continue to function. Again, bitter memories of the punishments meted out by German Military Courts in the First World War, scenes of German police patrolling the streets of Belgium and the judicial "strike", generally convinced lawyers and judges that a Belgian legal bulwark against the Germans was absolutely required if the nation were to be saved. Again, it is not my purpose to detail the twisted and tragic path of the policy of the lesser of two evils generally or in relation to the legal system in particular. Others have done this.[10] Instead, it is necessary to underline for any study of the history of German anti-Jewish Decrees in Belgium that the legal profession and judiciary made a clear decision to remain in place under the occupation. They did so in order to preserve, as much as possible, Belgian institutional sovereignty and the Belgian constitutional order. The very existence of that sovereign order was challenged in October 1940 when the German Military Command decided to introduce the first two in a series of anti-Jewish Decrees.

The Second Decree concerning the Jews banned those defined as "Jews" under the First Decree from government and public service positions. They were also eliminated from the legal profession and the judiciary. Again, all "Jews" were to be removed from their posts or positions by 31 December 1940 (§ 2). This was the moment at which Nazi anti-Jewish measures struck at the heart of the Belgian constitutional, legal order. Jewish civil servants, judges and lawyers were to be removed from their posts. The Decree (§ 4) charged the departments and governmental authorities themselves with the implementation of the exclusion order, under the supervision of the Ministry of the Interior.

While much of this book focuses on the pernicious ways in which "passive collaboration", permissible within the positivistic construction of the Constitution and the Hague Convention adopted by the Permanent Council, quickly transmogrified into collaboration in persecution, there are counter-narratives and evidence which tend to undermine the categorical condemnation of the Belgian officials when faced with the anti-Jewish Decrees of October 1940. There was in fact delay, obfuscation and subversion by local administrations and by some of the higher ranking officials in implementing the Decrees aimed at the Jews of Belgium. The highest instances of the legal profession and judiciary drew a constitutional and moral line in the sand from the earliest days of the German anti-Jewish legal system.

Resistance behind the scenes at the Brussels Bar

Paul Struye, who was present as secretary at all the important meetings of the Bar of the Cour de Cassation in Brussels during the occupation, and who would become a postwar Minister of Justice, was a keen observer of, and participant in, the actions of the Bar in relation to the first set of measures aimed at Belgium's Jewish population. Struye had been named as a legal adviser to the government of the province of Brabant, which included the Brussels region, from the earliest days of the occupation. He was specifically tasked with briefing the provincial authorities on the legal regime under which the occupation would operate.[11] On 27 May, he went, along with a colleague, to the deserted law library of the Université Libre de Bruxelles and "requisitioned" the international law collection to familiarize himself with the legal principles of armed occupation.[12]

His diary entry for 6 November 1940 describes the divisions which manifested themselves among the members of the profession when news first emerged of the anti-Jewish Decrees.[13] What comes out of Struye's first-hand account is a picture far different from that postwar image of the Bar, united and in solidarity with their Jewish *confrères*, vociferously asserting the fundamental and foundational provisions and principles of the national Constitution against the pernicious and immoral German regime. Instead, Struye characterizes a faction among the members of the Bar as more than willing to adapt to the principles of the New Order (*les adaptés*), who accepted the measures as a good idea.[14] Others, the "timorous" (*les timorés*), thought there was no choice but to bow to the wishes of the Germans. Finally the third and eventually most influential group emerged, the "exalted" (*les exaltés*), who felt that there was no choice but to vigorously protest and possibly to strike.[15] The formal minutes of the first meeting of the members of the Bar of the Cour de Cassation to deal with the question of the appropriate response to the Decrees on 8 November 1940 give little evidence of the controversy which had swirled around the question in legal circles. They indicate simply that the *Bâtonnier* Veldekens underlined the strong emotions provoked by the Decrees, particularly in so far as the exclusion of Jewish lawyers was concerned.[16] Struye vigorously argued that the Bar should both file a protest with the occupying authority and decide, as a matter of principle, that in the eventuality of the exclusion of their Jewish members, any lawyer taking over a client's file in those circumstances would be acting purely as the agent of the excluded lawyer and not in their own name.[17] The decision on this latter question of principle was put off until a subsequent meeting and Struye was given the job of drafting a letter of protest which would be discussed at the next meeting of the Bar Council.

The rather dry minutes of the meeting hide what from Struye's contemporaneous private diary account was a very heated encounter. According to this narration of events surrounding the debate on 8 November, *Bâtonnier* Veldekens argued long and hard to prevent any protest against the Decrees.[18] Instead he wanted only to make special pleadings for exemptions in favor of lawyers who were war veterans or otherwise prominent citizens. In other words, the leader of the lawyers in Brussels who practiced and pleaded before the Cour de Cassation was in favor of adopting the "hermeneutic of acceptance". The exclusion of Belgian lawyers and judges was acceptable or at least inevitable as long as some accommodation and special pleadings were permitted. Veldekens was willing to passively comply with a system the effect of which was to institute a *numerus clausus de facto*, similar in effect to that which would be part of the French legislative framework. The idea that in principle Jewish judges and lawyers could be excluded did not appear to raise issues of fundamental constitutional norms and national ideals, at least not to a level which would warrant principled rejection or protest. For whatever reason, he chose to ignore the clear provisions of Article 100 of the Belgian Constitution and to countenance the exclusion of members of the judiciary simply because they were "Jews". The head of the leading section of the Bar in Brussels wanted to adopt a limited Constitution, one whose protections and freedoms would apply only to "meritorious" Jews, eminent Jews, Jews who had fought for Belgium and demonstrated, because unlike all other "Belgians" they had to, their loyalty to the nation. All other Jews, apparently, could be abandoned by their colleagues and excluded from the judiciary and the professions without causing any injury or slight to the Constitution or to the profession's normative deontological principles.

Struye's accounts of what was happening behind closed doors and in the robing rooms and corridors of the Palais de Justice in Brussels reveal a heated political contest over the meaning of the lawyers' oath of allegiance to the Constitution, the outcome of which was at this point far from certain. While these lawyers had decided that their presence in a German-occupied Belgium was necessary to maintain the sovereignty of the country and the continuity of its institutions, the place of the proposed anti-Jewish legal order in that scheme was still highly problematic. For a distinct minority, the New Order was welcome and the purge of "Jews" would return Belgium and the legal profession to their proper place. For others, the facts of life and the harsh reality of occupation required a passive acceptance of the unconstitutional exclusion of some of their colleagues. For some, the exclusion of Jews was not worthy of principled protest but could and should give rise to individualized pleadings in favor of some colleagues identified as meritorious Jews. Finally, those who at some level carried the day insisted that still operative normative legal and constitutional principles and their own professional framework left them no choice but to protest and to protest vigorously. Loyalty to the Constitution demanded it. The foundational norms of the profession itself were unequivocal. "Lawyers shall freely exercise their calling for the defense of justice and truth ..."[19]

Struye's draft argument asserts forcefully that the exclusion of Jews is contrary to the international rule of law and to the basic provisions of the Belgian Constitution. He wrote in part:

> The lawyers of the Court of Cassation of Belgium were profoundly moved upon reading the Decrees of 28 October 1940 relating to measures against the Jews.
>
> These Decrees do not apply to any of our number; but we can nonetheless not remain indifferent to them, first because our members might be called upon to cooperate in the application of these measures and secondly, because of the irreconcilable conflict between these Decrees and Belgian legislation, which remains in force, and to which we have sworn an oath of obedience.[20]

This draft contains a clear enunciation of the principle of obedience to Belgian legal norms which informed the official and public position of the all sections of the Bar in Brussels throughout the occupation. Struye then went on:

> We must also add that because of the very nature of our professional activities, it is not possible to demand that lawyers collaborate in any actions of which the consequences will be to exclude from society and to finally reduce to

a state of misery, men who, with no responsibility for their origins, have justly laid claim through the dignity of their lives and often by their unfailing devotion to public life, to the right to be Belgian citizens and to enjoy all of the privileges attached to this status.[21]

The draft protest letter appears in some instances to limit itself to cases involving the exclusion of lawyers, although the language elsewhere is somewhat more ambiguous. But what is not ambiguous is the idea again that Belgian law and the rights of Belgian citizenship (*la qualité de Belge*) are what are at stake in relation to the measures seeking to exclude Jews from the legal profession and judiciary. The annex to Struye's draft protest contains a lengthy discussion of the constitutional and legal principles and relevant texts. Among other sources, he reiterates the oath which lawyers take requiring "obedience to the Constitution" and the demands of fraternal solidarity with one's fellow lawyers. He adds part of the text of the Imperial Decree of 10 December 1810, the "organic base" of the legal profession, which makes part of the lawyer's professional duty "the love of truth and justice, and an enlightened zeal for the weak and oppressed".[22] Removing the rights and privileges of those who have earned this status and these rights is simply not something which can be countenanced by those who have sworn their allegiance and loyalty to Belgium's legal and constitutional order. But even for the "exalted" of the Brussels Bar, their concern was in large part limited to their colleagues, Belgian citizens, and not, it would appear, for all "the weak and oppressed". This is hardly surprising if one takes into account the heated and at the time relatively recent debates which had circulated around the question as to whether non-Belgians could become lawyers. In other words, there was a broadly accepted professional self-understanding and view that there was a citizenship requirement for membership among "the exalted". Particularly in the bitter aftermath of the First World War, in which the ideal of Belgian citizenship and loyalty to the constitutional order confronted the reality of the traitorous actions of a few under German occupation, the vast majority of members of the Bar insisted that the oath of loyalty required of members was radically incompatible with foreign nationality.[23]

Less than a week after Struye was asked to draft a possible protest, at their meeting of 14 November 1940, the lawyers of the Cour de Cassation urged the *Bâtonnier* to join with another planned protest to the Germans. They reserved their decision on what steps to take next.

The Constitution and the nation as legal resistance

On 26 November 1940, the *Bâtonnier* of the Bar of the Court of Appeal,[24] Louis Braffort, the *Président* (Presiding Judge) of the Cour de Cassation, Jamar, and the *Procureur Général* (Director of Public Prosecutions or Attorney-General) of the Cour de Cassation, Gesché, wrote to the German Military Commander for

Belgium and the North of France, General von Falkenhausen. They requested an interview with him in order to explain in detail the constitutional and legal questions raised by the two anti-Jewish Decrees of 28 October.[25] They wrote:

Excellency

The Decrees of 28 October 1940 concerning the status of Jews in Belgium have profoundly moved the legal world.

The undersigned scrupulously avoid any discussion of the basic principles of the institutions of the Reich.

But the Decrees in question apply in Belgium measures which are opposed to the principles of our Constitution and of our laws.

Belgium continues to exist as a Nation. Foreign occupation has in fact the effect, under the terms of the Hague Convention of 18 October 1907, of substituting the power of the occupier for that of the lawfully constituted authority, but only within the limit of measures which are required for maintaining order and public life.

It is not apparent that in the administration of justice, the presence of Hebrews has been such as to trouble order or public life.

The number of judges of the Jewish race is minimal; the number of lawyers is very low.

Any deviation by them in the observation of the rules of honor or delicacy would be immediately punished by our disciplinary procedures.

The Decree, in excluding Jewish judges from the judiciary, is contrary to Articles 6, 8, 14 of the Constitution, as well as to Article 100 thereof, pursuant to which a judge, appointed for life, may only be removed by way of a judgment. As far as lawyers are concerned, they can only be struck off following disciplinary proceedings.

The undersigned wish to bring to Your Excellency's attention the irreconcilable nature of the Order with these principles, in the hope that you would take this into consideration before proceeding to put these measures into effect.

As you have been able to recognize in carrying out your extremely important functions, the Belgian justice system has so far acquitted itself in its difficult and delicate task, for the greater good of the country, without any conflicts with the Occupying Power, and its heartfelt wish is to continue to smooth out any difficulties by way of conciliation. The undersigned request the honor of a meeting with your Excellency in order to clarify more completely for you the full thrust of the Belgian Constitution and our laws and the important questions raised by these Orders,

Signed

Braffort (*Bâtonnier*)
Jamar (*Premier Président*)
Gesché (*Procureur Général*)

The position of these leaders of the legal community is, on the surface, quite clear. They invoke the Belgian Constitution with its principles of religious freedom and the equality of all citizens against the racist vision of Nazi legality. They argue that there can be no justification under international legal norms for the German measures. "Belgium continues to exist as a Nation" and Belgian law must be the rule, Nazi law the exception. The Hague Convention clearly establishes that German law can be justified only in cases where it is required to ensure order and public life (*l'ordre et la vie publique*) and no such justification exists in the circumstances. The leaders of the Brussels legal profession and judiciary engage in what might be called the "hermeneutics of rejection".[26] The normative content of the German Decrees violates basic principles of Belgian constitutional law and practice. Discrimination on the basis of race or religion is a clear violation of Belgian norms of equality and freedom. In addition, the German attempt to interfere with the rights of Jews to hold public office or to be members of the legal profession not only strikes at the heart of the ideals of Belgian citizenship enshrined in the Constitution but also directly and illegally interferes in the sovereign independence of Belgian institutions under occupation. Belgian government employment is a matter for the Belgian government. Belgian law and Belgian institutions provide the mechanisms for removing judges and lawyers for misconduct. German interference with Belgian sovereignty brings into question the very nature of the occupation and the occupying authority's compliance with international law.

At the same time, of course, the text is ambiguous and like all texts subject to interpretation. This ambiguity may well have been intentional. Belgium was recently defeated and occupied. The history of German atrocities in the First World War was still part of collective and individual experience and fresh in the memory of all concerned. The desire to maintain Belgian judicial and legal institutions as a buttress against the Germans and to serve as a symbolic embodiment of the nation was strong. *Bâtonnier* Braffort himself, a leading criminal lawyer and professor of criminal law and criminology at the Université Catholique de Louvain, had been one of a small number of Belgian lawyers, fluent in German, who had defended Belgian citizens before German military tribunals during the First War.[27] For lawyers like Braffort, the essential role to be played by the Bar and the national courts in maintaining and protecting Belgian independence and the sovereignty of its constitutional order was grounded in recent bitter experience as well as principle.

General public opinion was largely indifferent, for a variety of reasons, to the anti-Jewish measures imposed by the Germans.[28] The three representatives of the Belgian legal profession and the judiciary had to proceed with caution while still expressing their moral and constitutional outrage.

There is at a basic level no equivocation or ambiguity about the Constitution or the Belgian legal system. Sovereignty and equality are the clearly enunciated norms of the 26 November letter. "Belgium continues to exist as a Nation". The use of the term "Nation", in upper case letters is in the context something more than a simple declaration that a nation state, subject to the Hague Convention, known as Belgium, exists. Instead it is an invocation of the idea of "Belgium", a nation of citizens guaranteed constitutional equality and freedom and the exercise of those rights despite foreign occupation. The Belgian nation, the Belgian Constitution, these define and embody for the legal elite who wrote this letter, an ideal and a reality which they must defend when they are attacked. They write that they will explicitly refrain from any discussion of the underlying principles of the institutions of the Reich, which are, of course, by this very abstention, discussed, invoked and compared. There is Belgium with its Constitution and its founding principles and then there is the Reich with its "principles".[29] The letter's signatories argue about the small number of Jewish lawyers and judges, not as an excuse to allow the application of anti-Jewish laws, but instead, to support and underline their legal position that the Hague Convention does not permit German action aimed at excluding Jews from the profession or from the judiciary. If there are very few Jewish judges (in fact only one) and a small number of lawyers (possibly forty), such low numbers could not in fact or in law justify an assertion, implicit in the first two Decrees, that "Jews" in the legal profession or the judiciary posed a threat to public order or life. There is no indication that the presence of Hebrews in the administration of justice has caused any problems. Indeed, any act or activity by them which might have such an effect could be adequately addressed under existing disciplinary and legal procedures.[30] Public order would not be troubled since adequate Belgian measures to deal with Belgian problems are already in place. The Belgian nation continues to exist.

This is, of course, a potentially dangerous hermeneutic practice. The letter moves between the rejection of the German legal regime *per se* and the invocation of a more accepting position which addresses the proposed anti-Jewish system more on its own terms. There is an implication of the idea that the presence of Jews/ Hebrews might, in theory, if their numbers were more significant, be a possible source of trouble. While this is a response to the German Decrees, it might also be read as being perilously close to legitimating the legal premises of the Decrees, but rejecting their practical application based on the extant circumstances. Similarly, the specific mention of an abstention from discussing the informing principles of the Reich can be read as an implicit recognition of their legality and of their acceptability, when a stronger and unambiguous condemnation of legal antisemitic norms was perhaps called for.[31]

Other ambiguities can be found. The letter, while referring to the "presence of Hebrews" also mentions in the next sentence "judges of the Jewish race". In liberal, free and constitutional Belgium, "judges of the Jewish race" should have been a completely foreign and legally dissonant idea. "Jews" and "Hebrews" are not the same. "Judges of the Jewish race" are not, semiotically and constitutionally, Hebrew judges. The former are the subjects of German Decrees, the latter are Belgian citizens, dedicated, as are all other Belgians, to the principles of freedom, equality and loyalty to the Constitution. This use of the phrases "judges of the Jewish race" and "Jewish judges" is troublingly ambiguous and potentially dangerous in the context of a letter which seeks to uphold and defend Belgian constitutionalism in the face of Nazi anti-Jewish legal Decrees.

Whatever the potential semiotic, hermeneutic or historically determined and contingent difficulties which might flow from the letter of protest, the fundamentally significant point remains. There was a protest in Belgium and for this Belgian lawyers must be recognized and their example studied. Perhaps the ambiguities and limits found in the text of the 26 November letter can be explained by the historical context. There was a strong sentiment that the continuation of Belgian legal structures was essential to the country's and the nation's survival. This was relatively early in the occupation and there could have been no certainty about the duration of the war or the New Order. The lawyers and judges could not have foreseen the horrors of the destruction of Belgian Jewry. But they could have, and they did, see that these anti-Jewish Decrees were in essence fundamentally "illegal" and un-Belgian. They may also have felt somehow compelled to refer to "Jews" in order to make themselves understood semiotically by the intended readers of the letter of protest, the German authorities for whom only *Juden* appeared to exist.

This letter is not a protest against anti-Jewish measures in general but instead it is a limited one aimed primarily at the exclusion of Jews from the legal and judicial professions. While this is clearly the direct and immediate institutional concern of the three authors, their duties and ethical obligations arguably should not be seen to end there. They are high-ranking national and moral authorities who have sworn an oath to uphold the Constitution and who have opted to remain in their positions in order to act as a legal bulwark against the German occupiers. As lawyers they must remain dedicated to truth and justice, as the foundational norms of their profession demand. A letter of protest which deals primarily with the fate of one judge and forty lawyers, out of a total Jewish population of around 56,000 souls, raises important questions. What exactly is the relationship in these circumstances between the authors' understandings of the principles of constitutional government, freedom and equality and the limited nature of their appeal?

The guarantees of the Constitution applied as well to the rights of Jews not to be registered as Jews, or to have their businesses recorded and labeled as Jewish enterprises. Or did it? Is there some idea that the public life and order of occupied Belgium might somehow be threatened by the presence of a large number of Jews and Jewish businesses? Is the limited hermeneutic structure of their protest such that it might actually justify in some sense an understanding that, outside the strict limits of the Bar and the Bench, numbers of Jews are sufficient to trouble the public order? Why did the legal elite remain silent about the bigger question of citizenship and equality? Can their silence be understood in part at least as some veiled acceptance of a *de facto* or *de jure* position that general measures against Jews might somehow be justified, as the Permanent Council and the SG had accepted, as provisions falling under the operative public order provision of Article 42 of the Hague Convention?

All Jewish lawyers in Brussels ceased their practice at the end of December. There was no strike. But *Bâtonnier* Braffort did write a further letter of protest after the German authorities made it perfectly clear that they did not need to meet with the Belgian legal hierarchy and that they intended to proceed with the implementation of the anti-Jewish Decrees.[32] This letter contains none of the textual ambiguities found in the earlier joint protest. Braffort writes of "Hebrew lawyers", "lawyers of Hebrew origin" and "Hebrews" of the Bar. He denies the existence of a "Jewish question" at the Brussels Bar, and employs quotation marks to semiotically ensure that the pernicious language of Judeophobia is not attributed to him. Again and again he refers to the Belgian Constitution and fundamental law of the "Belgian people". He invokes his oath of office and refuses to take any steps to exclude Jewish lawyers from the Bar. Indeed, faced with constant German demands to provide a list of the names of Jewish lawyers in Brussels, Braffort with the support of the Bar Council refused to publish any membership list at all for the rest of the occupation.

The Brussels Bar refused to institute proceedings to exclude its members who fell within the German legal definition of "Jew". Under Braffort's unbending leadership, they argued that any such proceedings would violate the constitutional guarantees of liberty and equality and the norms of Belgian law and professional practice which provided for the striking off (*radiation*) of lawyers only in specific circumstances and according to prescribed rules of procedure. That individual lawyers, identified as "Jews" under the First Decree, had ceased to practice law pursuant to the Second Order concerning Jews, was a matter for them. As far as the Bar was concerned, they had not been formally excluded or banned from the Bar itself. They suffered no Belgian disqualification or impediment. The Bar in Brussels did not provide lists of Jewish lawyers to the Germans. Instead, they simply refused to provide any lists of lawyers at all, much to the frustration of the occupier. While Jewish lawyers could no longer practice law and had to absent themselves from the Palais de Justice, they did so out of fear of the Germans and not because their colleagues had turned against them and used an illegal legality to exclude them.

The Antwerp Bar and the unconstitutional and illegal exclusion of Jewish lawyers

If the actions of the leaders of the Brussels Bar evidence a circumscribed but uncompromising adherence to the principles of constitutional and legal equality, the response of their colleagues in Antwerp embodies the fragility of law in times of crisis. Antwerp is and was, unlike the officially bilingual Brussels, a Flemish-speaking city.[33] The Bar communicated with its members primarily if not exclusively in Flemish. The city itself also was and is the home of an internationally renowned diamond industry and of a significant, observable and observant Jewish community, as well as being the center of right-wing Flemish nationalism and collaboration. Antisemitism played a significant part in the rise of a fascist version of Flemish national identity. Antwerp would be the one place in Belgium in which the Jewish community witnessed a burning synagogue, set alight by their countrymen. Antwerp also saw Belgian police rounding up Jews for the Germans.[34] Members of the legal profession in turn played a significant role in anti-Jewish politics and agitation, both in the prewar period and during the German occupation. These nationalist lawyers had long struggled for the elimination of Jews and any "Jewish influence" from legal circles in Antwerp.[35] The events which would unfold at the Antwerp Bar were largely an internal Belgian affair, in which a different conception of the nation would inform the actions of the legal elite in that city.

Anti-Jewish agitation among legal professionals in Antwerp in the prewar period can be traced most importantly to the controversy surrounding the nomination to the Antwerp Bench of Henri Buch in 1936.[36] Buch was a foreigner, born in Paris, a naturalized citizen, and a communist, in addition to being Jewish. Moreover, he lived in Ixelles, a Brussels suburb. In other words, he simply was not, in the eyes of Flemish nationalists of Antwerp, sufficiently Belgian, or Flemish, to warrant such a judicial position.[37] A series of antisemitic protests came from various elements of the Catholic and nationalist Flemish right, including the Flemish Lawyers Association, the Vlaamsche Conferentie der Balie van Antwerpen.[38] This group, at the time an unofficial fraternal association without official professional responsibilities, passed a motion asserting that Buch was unfit for office because he was foreign-born, a non-native speaker of Flemish and therefore not sufficiently imbued with an appropriate judicial sensitivity to Flemish life.

From 1936 onwards, the Vlaamsche Conferentie der Balie van Antwerpen came increasingly under the influence of Nazi ideology, as key offices were taken over and held by fascist nationalist and Nazi sympathizers. In early 1939, the organization, still without any legal status to determine the right to practice law, decided to exclude Jews, although most had already resigned during the Buch affair.[39] The motion was not accepted by all members of the association, but nor was antisemitism in the Antwerp Bar limited to the Flemish-speaking members of the profession. At around the same time as the Vlaamsche Conferentie was making itself *Judenfrei*, the smaller Francophone Conférence du Jeune Barreau also experienced some antisemitic outbursts.[40] Well before the introduction of the Second Order in October 1940, there was nonetheless abroad among certain elements of the Antwerp Bar an understanding that membership in the profession was or should be directly linked with an idea and ideal of Flemish nationhood. This in turn was also increasingly understood by leading elements of the profession to be racially based. Jews were not and could never be Flemish.

The case of Régine Orfinger Karlin is the best known episode in the next phase of antisemitism at the Antwerp Bar and exemplifies the tale of constitutional compromise and the legal profession's slide into illegality in Belgium's second city.[41] Like their counterparts in Brussels, by the end of December 1940, the few Jewish lawyers remaining in Antwerp had stopped practicing law. At this stage, however, despite agitation from Flemish nationalists and adherents of the New

Order, they had not been formally excluded from the local Bar. One of these Jewish lawyers, Régine Orfinger Karlin, continued to go to her office and meet with colleagues since, as her senior partner explained to objectors at the time, she was on vacation and where she chose to spend her free time was entirely a matter of personal choice.[42] She was eventually denounced by a colleague for violating the Decree banning Jews from the practice of law. The Bar Council (Raad der Orde der Advocaten) began proceedings against her, as well as against other Jewish lawyers.[43] She was summoned to the meeting of the Council to take place on 28 April 1941, shortly after the Antwerp pogrom. According to the letter from the Bar Council, the purpose of the meeting was to determine whether, in compliance with the German Decree, she and the other Jewish lawyers should be struck from the Roll.

She replied by way of a lengthy written submission arguing that the Bar could exclude her only on grounds of misconduct and then only pursuant to the rules and practices regulating matters of professional discipline. Being a "Jew", as defined by a German Military Decree, she argued, was not recognized by Belgian law or by the rules of the Bar as grounds for being struck off. She replicated the arguments and legal positions adopted earlier by the Brussels Bar. She further asserted that the prohibition found in the German Decree referred specifically only to the "practice of law". Having gone to Brussels to seek advice and information, she had determined that the Roll there included individuals who had retired and who had not been seen in court or in an office in years but who continued to pay their annual dues.[44] Being a member of the Bar, counted and included on the Roll, she argued, was not by definition synonymous with practicing her profession, which she confirmed she had ceased on 31 December. Moreover, the Decree itself imposed the obligation for the enforcement of its provisions on the Ministries of Justice and of the Interior. It placed no obligation or power on the Bar Council to act as it proposed to do.

The Bar, she asserted forcefully, with authorities cited in support, had no power or jurisdiction to act except according to the rules and practices of Belgian law, and its own internal disciplinary mechanisms. None of these recognized the fact of being identified as a "Jew" by the German occupiers as grounds for automatic disqualification. Nor, she added, was being a "Jew" a moral failure which brought the profession into disrepute Again this reason could not inform an exclusion (*radiation*) from the Roll.

Her legal argument convinced her colleagues. At its meeting of 9 June 1941, the Council voted 11–4 to take no action to remove her or the other identified Jewish lawyers from their Roll. At this stage the Bar of Antwerp, like its counterpart in Brussels, accepted, if not unanimously, the argument that Belgian law and legal principles did not permit them to comply with the wishes of the Germans and their native collaborators to remove "Jews" from Belgian professional life, at least as far as having their names figure on the Bar Roll was concerned. Nonetheless, the same Bar Council decided that, since "Jews" were forbidden to practice law, they could no longer attend any official Bar function or vote in any professional election. They upheld Orfinger Karlin's principled argument on a central point, while at the same time illegally banning "Jews" from all but formal membership.

A weekly lawyers' bulletin, the *Juristenblad*, now controlled by the forces of fascist Flemish nationalism, denounced the Bar Council and demanded the immediate exclusion of all Jews from the profession. They labeled the members of the Council who voted to maintain Jews on the Roll as enemies of the "nation". The collaborationist newspaper, *Volk en Staat*, slammed the decision and published the names and voting record of each member of the Council in an obvious attempt to shame those who had supported the Jews in the eyes of right-thinking Flemish people. Less than one month later, on 2 July 1941, the Vlaamsche Conferentie passed a resolution condemning the continuing presence of Jews on the official Roll of the Bar of Antwerp. The next day, on 3 July 1941, the newly constituted Bar Council voted to strike off, allegedly at the request of the German commander, all "Jews", "members of the Jewish community" and all those "for whom some doubt remained as to their Jewish origin" (*Verordnung über das Ausscheiden von Juden*, §2(2)). As a result, Auguste Roost, Niko Gunzburg, Marcel Roost, Joseph Jacobsohn, Jacques Cypres, Henri Rueff, Marcel Laufer, Harry Torczyner, Van Hentenryck-Burstenbinder, Birnbaum-Blankstein, Orfinger Karlin, Michel Liverant, Jacques Herbach, Theodoor Lorie, Jaak Nutkewitz and trainee lawyers (*Advocaten Stagisten/stagiaires*), Robert Borisewitz and Alfred Soldinger, were removed from the Roll.[45]

This radical reversal indicates the ease with which compliance with legalized racism can be accomplished. Constitutional patriotism or at the very least adherence to the positive limits of domestic law and professional rules of self-regulation disappeared without a whimper. The case of the Antwerp Bar also demonstrates that lawyers can exceed what is legally required of them if the circumstances, or their personal ideology, demand it. Mere technical compliance, submission to overwhelming military authority and strict legal positivism do not, alone or together, explain the actions of the Bar Council. This is more than passive collaboration. They did not try to argue that the German demand was inconsistent with the German Decree which imposed the duty to take actions in compliance with the Order only on the Ministry of Justice. They did not argue that the Decree only required that Jews stop practicing law, not that they be removed from membership in their professional bodies. Orfinger Karlin made these arguments. The Bar Council, once the inevitable evolution of a new legal ideology had taken over, ignored them and struck off their Jewish colleagues.

The Bar Council reversed its original decision to maintain its Jewish members on the Roll after pressure from local fascist antisemites and the Germans. It struck off members of the profession, identified as Jews, in clear violation of the norms of Belgian law and of their professional oath of allegiance. Where their Brussels counterparts stood firm and refused to do anything which would have compromised their adherence to the principles of Belgian law and the Belgian constitutional order, the leaders of the profession in Antwerp abandoned their dedication to law and the Constitution in favor of extended and vigorous collaboration with the New Order, and a new ideal of the "nation" from which Jews were organically and legally excluded.

On 11 September 1944, following the Liberation, the Bar Council of Antwerp voted to readmit those it had excluded three years earlier. A letter dated 25 September was sent to Régine Orfinger Karlin informing her that she had been "reinscribed on the Roll between Me Hens and Me Van der Haegen". Antwerp's legal profession had returned to the constitutional fold and Jews were once more Belgians, although apparently it was felt that a formal vote on the question was still required. In his 1960 history of the Flemish Bar, leading Antwerp lawyer René Victor describes the German Decree excluding Jews from the profession as "stupefying and inhuman". Yet even at that relatively late date he insisted that the Bar could have done nothing to prevent the application of the German Decree and that the organization did all it could to resist.[46] He did not mention the important fact that he was one of the original four members of the Bar Council to vote from the beginning for the exclusion of Régine Orfinger Karlin and her Jewish colleagues.

What explains this historical, quasi-official amnesia about events in Antwerp? Where does the story of Régine Orfinger Karlin fit into the myth that "Belgian" lawyers resisted the Nazi legal regime while their French counterparts eagerly joined in the implementation of anti-Jewish legal norms? First, it is true that the leadership of the Brussels Bar did resist. They invoked the ideals of legally and constitutionally entrenched guarantees of equality and freedom. They refused to identify and exclude their "Jewish" colleagues. But the history of the wartime leaders of the Antwerp Bar is one of gradual and then open and vigorous collaboration with the New Order. Jewish lawyers were informed on by their colleagues and struck off by the Bar Council for no other reason than that they were Jews. The rest of the occupation period is characterized by a similar legal ambiguity.

The "Jewish" question and legal resistance

Leading legal officials especially in Brussels continued to resist German attempts to "Belgianize" the juridical persecution of the country's Jews throughout the occupation. In September 1942, the occupying authority wrote to the chief government legal representative, the Crown Attorney (*Procureur-Général*) demanding that all requests to adopt Jewish children be forwarded to German headquarters. The Attorney representing the Crown before the Court of Appeal issued a circular on 20 October 1942 requesting that all Crown Attorneys cease certifying adoption requests. He issued a further request to the courts on 18 March 1943 asking them to delay any decision in all adoption cases before them and for which final judgments were pending.[47] By not taking official action to certify adoptions and by simply suspending all decision-making in adoption cases, the court system in Belgium was able to keep the identities of Jewish children out of German hands and to allow many of them to find shelter safety in "Aryan" homes".[48]

Other Jews were given at least temporary protection through the process of marriage with non-Jewish Belgian citizens, sometimes through purely fictitious marriages. For a certain time during the German implementation of anti-Jewish persecution, arrest and deportation, Jews in such "mixed" marriages were placed outside the grasp of the occupier who persisted in playing the game with Belgian authorities by offering exemptions to "Belgian" Jews while the foreign majority was targeted. The local collaborationist press, as well as the Germans, complained vociferously that local Crown Attorneys were waiving publication periods normally required for banns and were ignoring other temporal requirements in order to allow as many "mixed" marriages as possible to take place.[49] The Germans summoned a representative from the Ministry of Justice to officially complain about the number of obviously fictitious marriages taking place between Jewish women and elderly Belgian men.[50] The government official met with the Attorney and requested a report on the matter.[51] "Mixed" marriages continued nonetheless to be celebrated for some time. Still other local Crown Attorneys continued to approve applications for naturalization from Jews in an attempt to offer whatever small protection such a change in legal status might offer.[52]

Other Belgian lawyers opted for individualized strategies which relied upon and invoked a "hermeneutic of acceptance". They acted in what they perceived to be their clients' best interests by seeking whatever room for maneuver could be found within the framework established by the anti-Jewish Decrees.[53] In the city of Liège, the case of brother and sister Joseph and Fanny Dietz demonstrates the extent to which Belgian lawyers became involved in these attempts to "save" Jewish clients. On 2 February 1942, the mayor of Liège wrote to Messrs Servais and Laurent-Neuprez, attorneys at the Court of Appeal to inform them that he had agreed to their request to remove their client Joseph Dietz from the city's Register of Jews.[54] A month later on 6 March, Servais wrote to the mayor requesting the removal of Joseph's sister Fanny's name from the Register as well. If her brother was not a "Jew", she could not be one either. The mayor passed on the request to the bureaucrats responsible for the Jewish Register in the city's Population Office. They informed him by return memo on 9 March that they had already removed Fanny from the Jewish Register on their own initiative.[55]

This case evidences not only the active involvement of Belgian lawyers in the legal process of deciding who was and who was not a "Jew", but local government officials seemingly willing to by-pass the occupying authority by deciding for themselves who fell under the operative definition of "Jew". On 26 August 1942 the Germans demanded an explanation.[56] On 1 September the Population Office set out its procedures and explanation for the mayor. Lawyers Servais and Laurent-Neuprez acting on behalf of their clients had approached the Bureau and requested that the Dietzes be struck off the Register of Jews. The lawyers submitted a detailed genealogical document outlining the Dietz family's non-Jewish origins, together with an official declaration from the Hebrew community of Liège stating that the Dietz family was unknown to them. Finally the file submitted by the two lawyers included a copy of a letter from a member of the Brussels Bar, Raymond

Ledoux, setting out what was apparently the standard practice in such cases in the capital. The letter stated:

> As I have previously told you, the German Office for Jewish Property LEAVES IT UP TO THE BELGIAN AUTHORITIES TO DEAL WITH STRIKING OFF individuals who have registered themselves in the local Register of Jews.
>
> I have been able to obtain this removal from the list in a Brussels suburb in behalf of an individual who had registered "in case" and who was later able to prove that he had 50% Jewish ancestry. This striking off, carried out by the local government was communicated to the German Authorities who raised no objection.[57]

This letter and the Dietz file more generally indicate an intimate level of involvement of Belgian lawyers in creating legal arguments about their clients' Jewish, or non-Jewish, or in Ledoux's case *Mischlinge* status, as a matter of course. It seems that they operated as if they had the burden of proof, especially since their clients had in fact registered as Jews and that they brought traditional forms of evidence recognized in Belgian law. In Liège, however, the local German authorities were not as apparently complacent as their Brussels colleagues.

Dr Busch of the *Oberfeldkommandantur* in subsequent correspondence made it clear to the mayor that Belgian procedures did not suffice. He underlined the key provisions of the anti-Jewish Order which gave sole jurisdiction in the matter of who was or was not a Jew to the Military Commandant of Belgium and which operated, in his view, a presumption of Jewishness for anyone whose name figured in the Register of Jews. Moreover, he reminded the mayor, standards of proof are particularly stringent. "A family tree which is not supported by official documents cannot be considered as proof, any more than a statement from a Jewish association."[58] Belgian lawyers, and Belgian law, were put in their place.

Jewish property, Belgian Law: legalized resistance and collaboration

A more detailed examination of important aspects of the processes of Aryanization is found in subsequent chapters. The present discussion is limited to an overview of the role of the Belgian legal professions in attempts to "resist" this legalized theft of Jewish property.[59] Jewish property was also protected, to an extent at least, by the actions of Belgian lawyers and judges. In addition to the various "straw man" transactions which formally transferred Jewish property into Aryan hands with the sole aim of sheltering it until the end of the war, more direct and formal action, grounded again in the basic principles of Belgian law, also took place.

The most celebrated example of such behavior is that of M. Victor Vander Perre. Vander Perre was the *Référendaire* of the Commerical Court (Tribunal de Commerce) in Brussels. The *Référendaire* acted as a legally trained permanent expert who gave advice on points of law to members of the Commercial Court. Vander Perre had practiced at the Brussels Bar for some time before taking up a full-time position at the court. In this role, he acted during the occupation to prevent the Aryanization of Jewish property, or at the very least to resist the implication of Belgian judicial bodies in a process which he saw as illegal and unconstitutional.[60] German administrators of Jewish companies attempted to appear before the Commercial Court in Brussels, representing or acting on behalf of Aryanized business entities. Vander Perre paid a visit to the offices of the Chief *Verwalter* on 24 March 1943. He informed the German official in no uncertain terms that administrators named by the Germans had no standing to appear before Belgian judicial bodies. Belgian courts could not and would not be bound to enforce German measures aimed at Jewish property which clearly exceeded the limits permitted under the Hague Convention.[61] In June of 1943, he refused to provide copies of the declarations found in the Commercial Registry concerning Jewish businesses. He informed the Brüsseler Treuhandgesellschaft (BTG), the organization established by the Germans to deal with the administration of Aryanized businesses, that he could not participate in such an endeavor because German anti-Jewish Orders were contrary to Belgian law and to Belgian ideals (*contraires au droit belge et aux conceptions belges*). Only because he could not prevent the consultation of otherwise public documents did he recognize that a German representative could himself consult the relevant files at the court clerk's office.[62] According to his colleagues, Vander Perre also refused to allow the officers at the Registry of the Commercial Court to participate in the removal (*radiation*) of Jewish business from that Registry pursuant to a German command.[63] In each instance, Vander Perre relied on his self-understanding as a legal professional who had sworn an oath of allegiance to his country's Constitution and obviously to his self-conception as a Belgian citizen. For his colleagues, "He did not submit to the laws of the Belgian people; he brandished them like a flag in the face of the enemy. And if the law was his standard, it was also his best weapon."[64]

Belgian constitutionalism and the Jewish question: the fragility of law

There can be little doubt that Belgium, like all other nation states, is constructed in part at least through a series of mythological self-imaginings.[65] One of the essential myths of a country like Belgium, founded on the basis of linguistic and religious (not to mention social and economic) difference, must be the ideal of "citizenship". If local identities as Walloon or Flemish are to be displaced or superseded by a "Belgian-ness", some form of transcendent ideal needs to be found and supported. There must be a relationship to the nation which avoids ideas of sectarian or linguistic identity. Loyalty and identity must be given to and derived from the nation embodied and enshrined in the Constitution and the institutions and national myth structures of shared public life. Clearly when the Brussels legal elite wrote to Von Falkenhausen and insisted that "Belgium continues to exist as a

Nation", this ideal/ideology informed their actions, as it must have been the basis of *Bâtonnier* Braffort's steadfast refusal to comply with the German demands for lists of "Jewish" lawyers. Vander Perre's persistent invocation of the foundational principles of Belgian law and ideals to resist Aryanization was always grounded in a national constitutional ideal. The nation was for them embodied in the Constitution and its values and clearly informed their professional self-image.

This is hardly surprising given the role of Francophone lawyers from Brussels in the very historical constitution of an independent Belgium. The construction of the Belgian Constitution which embodies its fundamental freedoms not in a separate Bill of Rights but in the founding text itself is the legalized creation of freedom and equality as essential, constitutive elements of the nation and of citizenship. The ideal of an independent Belgium as a rule of law state, and of the notion that the constitutive power comes from the nation, were the result of the complex politics of law among the French-speaking legal elite at the time of the founding of the Belgium state in the 1830s.[66]

The Brussels Bar, faced with military defeat and occupation, living with the memories of the previous brutal occupation by the Germans, held its solemn procession for the war dead in November 1940, despite the German insistence that 11 November would not be observed. They defied the Germans to honor their country, the memory of the fallen patriots and to inscribe the continuation of the nation in their public practice. The Bar was faced several days later with the German Decrees targeting Jews. Their self-understanding as Belgians and as lawyers was at risk. They had stayed in the country in order to preserve the legal order and that legal order as they grasped it was endangered. They had just defied the military authority in a public act of patriotism. Their protest should be read as an embodied plea to themselves as much as it is to the Germans about law and about Belgium as the nation which continued to exist.

The Antwerp Bar eventually took another stance, abandoning its constitutional duties to pressure from a vocal and violent powerful group of indigenous fascists whose ideas of the nation were in fact ideas of the *Volk*, a linguistically and culturally homogeneous, *Vlaamse* nation to which the "Jews" could not and did not belong. One could put down the Antwerp's Bar's ultimate concession to fear of violent reprisal and the lack of moral courage. The existence and power of indigenous fascism no doubt must go some way to explaining the different response in Antwerp to that of Brussels. But parts of the Bar in Antwerp had taken up Nazi antisemitism long before the First and Second Orders concerning Jews were introduced in October 1940. The Jew Buch could not in their eyes be a judge because he was not, and could never be, Flemish. The Vlaamse Conferentie became increasingly antisemitic before the fall of the country in May 1940. Jews were excluded from the brotherhood before the war as the necessary consequence of the construction of a particular Flemish ideal identity.

There is no doubt that the Antwerp Bar more broadly became increasingly subject to pressure from local collaborationist forces, their press and parts of general public opinion in the early months of 1941, leading up to elimination of their Jewish colleagues. Yet Louis Braffort, *Bâtonnier* of Brussels, was constantly targeted by collaborationist groups, Francophone and Flemish-speaking alike. He was threatened with death because of his and his profession's failure to concede the future of Belgium to the New Order. He never wavered in his insistence on the dignity of Belgium and the adherence to its foundational constitutional principles. He upheld the ideal that "Belgium continues to exist as a Nation" until he was kidnapped and murdered by Rexist thugs near the end of the war.[67] Physical danger and moral cowardice cannot, in these circumstances, be the only explanatory tool, nor can they exculpate the Antwerp Bar or mitigate the penalties of the judgment of history on the legal profession in that city and its collective betrayal of the Constitution. René Victor chose to rewrite history and his own role in that antisemitic story in 1960, but the record of his and other moral cowardice remains.

One of those Jewish lawyers excluded by the Antwerp Bar in 1941 was Nico Gunzburg. He was a world-renowned criminologist and Professor of Law at the University of Ghent. He was also lucky enough to have escaped Belgium at the beginning of the war and spent the occupation in exile. In addition to his international academic reputation, Gunzburg was known as a major proponent of Flemish identity and a leader in propagating and enshrining the place of Flemish language and culture. He was what Belgians call a *flamigant*. He played a central role in the transformation of the State University of Ghent into a Flemish-speaking institution.[68] For Gunzburg and for others, one could be a Belgian, Flemish, Jewish and a patriot. Yet for the majority of his professional colleagues, he was worthy only of derision, discrimination and exclusion because he was, and could only be, a "Jew".

Clearly, one could be Flemish and a Belgian patriot, just as one could be a French-speaking Belgian patriot. The overall history of resistance to the Nazis in Belgium underlines the fact that patriotism to the Nation did not know linguistic boundaries. In light of the emerging record of Antwerp's exceptionalism in the history of the Holocaust in Belgium, the possibility that, at some level at least, the understanding of "Belgium" and constitutional patriotism was different in elite legal circles in Brussels and Antwerp must nonetheless be an informing factor in historical analysis. There was, if the case of the Jewish lawyers is any indication, some fundamental jurisprudential distinction between a Francophone understanding of "Belgique" and a Flemish legal elite concept of "België". The long and intense history of anti-Jewish sentiment and activity among elements of the legal profession in Flemish-speaking Belgium did not have an institutionalized equivalent in prewar Brussels. We must at least be open to exploring the idea that the construction of professional self-understanding and duty to the nation was informed by different positionings of constitutional patriotism based in part on different linguistic groupings and historical experiences.[69] However, we must also avoid all hasty generalizations. Antwerp is not Flanders and Flanders is not Antwerp. The Bar in Antwerp was perhaps dominated by a Flemish fascist elite but other instances of patriotic resistance to anti-Jewish Orders can be found for example in Ghent where the courts and Flemish-speaking judges were firm in their refusal to incorporate Nazi antisemitic legal norms into Belgian law.[70]

The degree of ambiguity which remains in the legalized resistance by the Brussels Bench and Bar should also be remembered and subjected to ongoing and deepened analysis. The protest was limited. A week before the First and Second Orders concerning Jews were published, a Decree was introduced prohibiting ritual animal slaughter.[71] While the Order does not mention Jews specifically, it was clearly targeted at observant members of the Jewish communities of Belgium. The SG, the Bar and the judiciary all remained silent. The measure entered the legal landscape almost unnoticed. Can we detect here a latent antisemitism which found nothing objectionable in regulating the bizarre ritual practices of Jews? Can we detect a more subtle distinction between Belgian Jews and weird and strange foreign practices which because they are not "Belgian" were considered undeserving of protection and incorporation inside the norms of Belgian constitutional citizenship? Is this a window into the pernicious operation of a constitutional normativity which welcomes Hebrews but excludes Jews as un-Belgian?

The Germans consistently played the xenophobia card and offered differential treatment for the small "Belgian" Jewish community. Belgian government officials made special pleas and received promises and concessions for their own citizens, which they did not in reality seek for all "Jews". "Mixed marriages" provided shelter for some individuals but relied on a double distinction, between Jews and non-Jews and often between Belgians and non-Belgians. In the end of course, this special status for Belgian Jews did not prevent the deportation of Belgian Jews to the killing factories of the east. What we can detect not just generally in official Belgian responses to German measures against Jews, but more specifically in the action (or inaction) of the Bar in Brussels, might at this stage at least be identified as hints of a narrow and even potentially antisemitic understanding of Belgian citizenship.

"Jews" were foreigners. "Hebrews" were Belgians. "Jews" engaged in ritual slaughter, "Hebrews" were judges and lawyers, loyal to the Constitution like all good Belgians. The guarantees of equality and freedom which the Bar and *Bâtonnier* invoked so eloquently in defense of the existing Belgian nation and of their colleagues applied for the lawyers of Brussels only to "citizens", to "Belgians", since the loyalty demanded to the Constitution of members of the legal profession excluded foreigners in any event. *Bâtonnier* Louis Braffort proved himself to be less ambiguous as time went on. He acted purely to defend and uphold a vision of concretized Belgian national sovereignty and constitutional order. There was resistance. There was constitutional patriotism, however narrowly conceived.

Chapter 4

Aryanization, legalized theft and Belgian legality

The history of Aryanization in Belgium is well-documented, in official reports, historical accounts and more popular literature.[1] It is not my intention to examine German attempts to engage in the legalized theft of Jewish assets in Belgium in detail. Instead I will simply offer an account of several key aspects of the program of Aryanization in order to highlight some areas of the complex processes of the removal of Jewish property in which Belgian officials and citizens played an important role. In other words, I wish to highlight the Belgian part of the Aryanization program. In this chapter I will touch briefly on some important aspects of this involvement before turning to more detailed and contextualized accounts in subsequent parts of the book.

In addition to creating the definition of the new legal category "Jew", the First Order of 28 October 1940 officially framed the process for the identification and ultimate removal of the Jewish influence in the Belgian economy. The idea of a pernicious presence of Jews in the economic power structure of Europe was central to Nazi antisemitic ideology.[2] This remained true in Belgium despite the early German recognition that there was little if any factual basis for a belief that Jews played a predominant and/or disproportionate role in the economic structure of the country. Nonetheless, the process of removing Jews and Jewish property from the Belgian economy was a central part of German anti-Jewish policy and practice throughout the occupation.

Indeed, the legal framework for Aryanization began even before the introduction of the first specifically anti-Jewish Order in the autumn of 1940. From the earliest days of the occupation of Belgium, the German Military Command took control of key economic institutions and economically important facilities. An administrator (*Verwalter*) was appointed in most important parts of the economy in order to ensure that the Belgian economy was directly incorporated into the overall occupation system.[3] Some firms which would later be classified as "Jewish" fell almost immediately under the control of a German *Verwalter*.

Still more "Jewish" businesses came under more indirect German control as the occupier introduced a system of compulsory declarations for "enemy property".[4] The Second Order of 2 July 1940 imposed an obligation to declare all "enemy" property interests and extended the definition to include "Belgian" property the owners of which were now on "enemy" territory. This category included the thousands of Belgians, including Jewish individuals, who had fled, especially to France, in the hectic and confused early days of the invasion and occupation.[5]

The First Order concerning Jews extended the control of Jewish property by introducing a system of compulsory declaration (§ 5 et seq.). Any commercial operation which had a sufficient "Jewish" content, on or after 1 May 1940, had to complete and submit a declaration form by 10 December 1940 to the Office for the Declaration of Jewish Property in Brussels (§ 11), whether or not a prior declaration in relation to enemy property had been made (§ 7). Control over Jewish assets was to be centralized in a special section of the German occupation bureaucracy in Brussels.

In § 6 of the Order were set out those businesses or undertakings which were subject to the mandatory declaration process. Non-incorporated businesses had to be declared if the individual who ran the enterprise, directly or indirectly, was a Jew (§ 6 (1)). Incorporated entities had to make a declaration if 1) one of the legally responsible owners was a Jew; 2) a legally authorized representative of the company was a Jew; 3) a member of the board was Jewish; 4) Jews possessed a "decisive" participation in the business, i.e. by possessing one-fourth of the capital or one half of the voting shares or, in the case of a publicly held company, Jews possessed enough shares to influence the management of the company; or 5) Jews possessed a real or *de facto* predominant interest in the company (§ 6). Finally § 17, which also operated in relation to the Jewish Register for individuals, was applicable here. In any doubtful case, a company or business was obliged to make a declaration.

It is hardly surprising that the German authorities would be interested in obtaining information which was as complete as possible on the level of Jewish participation in the Belgian economy. What is intriguing from the point of view of the participation of non-Jewish Belgians in the process of informing the Germans by means of these declarations is their apparent willingness to exceed the strict legal limits of what was required. Certainly, the catch-all provision of § 17 requiring declarations in doubtful cases and the penalty of imprisonment and fines (§ 18) for failing to declare may have had an operative influence on these non-Jewish Belgians in the relatively early days of the occupation. Nonetheless, even a cursory examination of the archival record reveals, I believe, perhaps something more than mere compulsory compliance by these Belgian citizens. Indeed, the principal question which must have arisen in relation to the application of the Decree to many of the companies which lodged "Jewish declarations" was exactly how they would "know" if one or more of the eligible persons within the company fell under the operative definition of Jew pursuant to § 1 of the First Order. Would the legal representatives of a company or the board of a business operation be in a position to know if one of their fellows had three Jewish grandparents or two Jewish grandparents and was married to a Jew or practiced the religion as required by the Order? If not, on what basis would they act to complete a declaration in case of doubt according to the provisions of § 17? Would a "Jewish-sounding name" suffice?

It would seem that in some instances the answer to the last question was a resounding yes. The Liège porcelain manufacturer and publicly held company Teco filed a declaration under the First Order because on 1 May 1940 Mr P. Meyer, who had resigned from the board on 3 June, had been a director of the company. The company added in its statement that "we are unaware if Mr. P. Meyer is a Jew as defined in the Decree of 28 October 1940".[6] Likewise, the Société Belge de l'Azote filed a declaration because it had one director "believed to be" (*réputé*) a Jew. As with Teco, that director had already resigned his post. The company was also quick to underline in its declaration that not only had he resigned but that they had properly publicized that resignation in the Official Gazette (*Moniteur Belge*).[7] In a similar fashion, the Union des Centrales Electriques de Liège was at pains to point out that it did not know if its director M. Walter Liberman was Jewish or not, but because of the provisions of § 17, it was filing a declaration.[8]

In Brussels, a similar attitude obtained. The company Proma identified Mr Borys Rabinovicz as its only Jewish shareholder.[9] The First Decree (§ 6 (d)) imposed an obligation to declare Jewish shareholdings in a publicly held company only in those cases where that shareholding exercised a decisive control or power in the decision-making of the company. Proma stated that it did not know the actual level of Rabinovicz's participation in the company.[10] Another company, Simon Brothers, indicated that its two "Jewish" directors had resigned in March 1940 and that those resignations had been ratified by the shareholders in August 1940.[11] The Belgian subsidiary of the Delaware-incorporated Borvisk Belge SA filed a declaration on 17 December 1940 because of "doubt on the racial identity of a director of the business, Mr. Gaston Lehman".[12]

These few examples indicate quite clearly that Belgian businesses were anxious to comply with the first important German legal measures identifying and attacking the Jewish presence in the country's economy. For the most part, the seemingly zealous obedience might be seen as an attempt by the various businesses not just to comply with the provisions of the First Order concerning the Jews, but perhaps more importantly for them, to avoid being characterized as being really "Jewish" undertakings. Teco indicated that Meyer was no longer with the company, as did the Société Belge de l'Azote and Simon Brothers in Brussels in relation to their "Jews". The other declarations made clear for the most part that the company was lodging the required paperwork only because there was some doubt about the "origins" of an individual. Only Proma specifically identified its shareholder as Jewish. The doubt which persisted for them was as to the level of his shareholding and therefore as to whether Rabinovicz exercised a legally significant level of control over the company under the Order. What seems to emerge from the other instances is that the doubt about the individuals in question, for example Mr Lehman at Borvisk or Mr Liberman at the Union des Centrales Electriques, must to some extent at least have been based on the sound of their surnames. Lehman and Liberman did not appear to those in charge of the companies to be names which resonate as "Belgian". They did not sound native. They were, in other words, "Jewish-sounding names", or at least Jewish-enough-sounding names to raise a doubt which then caused the system of declaration to operate in the minds of the companies' directors.

These companies, like countless others found in the archival records, declared the apparent Jewish presence in their midst, on a basis which is at one with the entire operation of German anti-Jewish Orders within Belgian society as a whole. By seeking out and indicating in their declarations Jewish-sounding names, these Belgian corporations cooperated in a process of identification and exclusion with which, at some level, they were already existentially familiar. "Jews" were identifiable because, at the most basic level, they were not Belgian. This notion of Belgianness and of the concomitant establishment of Jews as not Belgian was central to the implementation of the first antisemitic legal measures by the various organs of the Belgian state. What we find in the system of declarations for Jewish businesses under the First Order in the last days of 1940 is perhaps the private version of the public, state-based distinction between Belgians and Jews.

The Notaries and Aryanization: the legal profession and Nazi law

The preceding chapter examined the reactions of the Belgian Bar to the introduction of the anti-Jewish Orders. These lawyers, joined by prominent members of the Bench in the case of Brussels, focused their protests and objections primarily on the provisions of the Second Order which compelled the expulsion of individuals identified as Jews from the profession. I now turn to the other branch of the legal profession in Belgium, the notaries and their involvement in the implementation of anti-Jewish legal measures.

As in the civil law world generally, notaries in Belgium form an important part of the legal professions. Unlike "notaries public" in common law jurisdictions, notaries are highly trained legal professionals. In Belgian law, notaries were and are considered public officials (*fonctionnaires*). Their role consists primarily of officially ratifying or authenticating all documents, contracts and other legal transactions which must according to law be legally recognized or to which the parties wish to attach an official and incontestable character.[13] In terms of professional self-definition and self-understanding, notaries act as the unbiased, disinterested legal advisers to all parties to a transaction, informing them of all legal consequences flowing from the transaction in question.[14] As public officials, they must also ensure the inherent validity and legality of the legal act, document or transaction before them. It quickly became apparent that the system of Aryanization introduced by the German military administration would pose specific deontological and practical legal problems for the country's notaries.

The First Order concerning the Jews (§ 13), as well as subsequent Aryanization provisions, would also prove to be of central importance in the subsequent application and practice of Aryanization in Belgium. It banned all transactions or other legal acts aimed at the sale or other lawful form of transfer of the business or assets of any undertaking or individual subject to the declaration provisions for Jewish property without the express consent of the German authorities. Since the SG had reached an accord with the German authorities pursuant to which the Belgian state adopted the position that German anti-Jewish measures would be applied as Belgian law in the country, there was strong authority for the idea that provisions such as § 13 now imposed new restrictions on the sale or other legal dealings with so-called Jewish property in Belgian law. How would such a provision be viewed by the notarial profession when giving advice to parties involved in an attempt to dispose of or to transfer such property? Would Belgian notaries now have to advise parties about the potential application not just of the various and normal rules of Belgian law but of the relevance of the new exceptional anti-Jewish Orders as well? The question of the reactions of Belgian notaries when faced with these anti-Jewish legal provisions has been detailed in the official reports of the Commission Buysse[15] and more recently in the official historians' study, *La Belgique docile*.[16] I can only summarize the history here and offer some brief practical examples of the ways in which the profession reacted.

At the beginning of the Aryanization process, with the provisions of § 13 of the First Order in particular, the leaders of the profession simply informed their colleagues of the content of the new rules relating to the transfer of Jewish property and urged them to comply therewith. The Order itself was reproduced in the leading professional journal.[17] Notaries, like their colleagues at the Bar, raised concerns about the actual meaning of the Order and its application, but not at this stage about its inherent validity. For notaries, practical issues relating to real property transactions came to the fore in their daily practice. Could mortgages on Jewish property be paid off and the proper entry made on the deed without German consent for example? The German authorities responsible for Jewish property questions responded that, since such transactions did not concern the transfer of Jewish property directly and therefore fell within the general domain of Belgian law, the application of ordinary domestic principles and practices should continue to apply.

While government officials in Belgium and the country's notaries under the authority of the German occupiers were seemingly content to proceed on a broad assumption that German Aryanization measures were both legal and operative, the government-in-exile in London warned them that this was not necessarily the case. The Ministerial Decree of 10 January 1941 clearly stated that all transfers of property, public or private, pursuant to any German measure definable as "confiscation, seizure, compulsory sale, or any other measure adversely affecting private property" were null and void.[18] Thus, Belgian notaries and other legal officials were faced at this early date, before the real process of Aryanization got fully under way, with the knowledge that the arguably legitimate seat of state authority to which they remained subject, considered any act relating to Aryanization to be outside Belgian law.

Nonetheless, the process of Aryanization and of transactions affecting the disposition of Jewish property continued to operate. Belgian notaries still functioned as if the anti-Jewish legal measures had full force and effect and seemingly ignored the edicts of the government-in-exile. During this period, other problematic legal cases began to arise as the sale of Jewish property to "Aryans" became central to German policy and practice. In addition, many creditors sought to realize their rights against their Jewish debtors in the ordinary course of business and legal affairs. Because many of the Jewish owners had fled the country before the arrival of the Germans, their regular and pre-existing debts were unpaid. The creditors sought relief through the normal mechanisms of Belgian law and eventually they sought the judicial sale of their debtors' assets to meet their legal obligations. Since most sales of Jewish property in this period were hardly "voluntary" on the part of the owner, the question for the notary who was meant to advise both parties to the sale was whether he needed to inform the purchaser of any possible taint on the title. As time went on and the Aryanization process picked up steam, Belgian notaries finally seem to have asked whether they could continue to authenticate such transactions in any circumstances.

An eventual response would come in the form of opinions from the Attorney-Generals in both Brussels and Antwerp who in late 1942 each informed the relevant leaders of the profession that any forced transfer of property instigated by the German legal order was contrary to the provisions of the Hague Convention. Notaries could therefore no longer participate in any fashion in such transactions.[19] In the end, faced with the refusal of Belgian notaries to authenticate any transactions relating to Aryanization, the German military authority was compelled to introduce a legal measure naming a German notary who was empowered to lawfully register all such transactions.[20]

The Commission Buysse concludes that the refusal and obstruction by Belgian legal officials, the Attorneys-General in Brussels and Antwerp and the notaries of the country, led to the ultimate failure of German attempts to Aryanize large swaths of Jewish property.[21] No Belgian legal professional would participate after 1942–3 in such transactions and no ordinary Belgian purchaser would be a party to a "sale" which would be authenticated and registered by a German military officer appointed as a notary by the occupying power. There is little doubt that this is true. The refusal by Belgian notaries had a profound effect on the extent of legalized theft of Belgian Jewish property, more specifically real property. Those legal officials who refused to permit the success of Aryanization through the invocation of and reliance upon the Hague Convention and the principles of international law can only be admired for their adherence to the highest aspirations of the professions and to an understanding that those principles remain imminently fragile in the absence of human intervention.

At the same time, the refusal and resistance did not occur until 1942 and 1943. This was more than a year after the Pierlot government in London had declared all such transactions null and void. The timing of the legal professions and their eventual refusal meant that some transactions Aryanizing Jewish property in Belgium did in fact take place and were authenticated by Belgian notaries. Transactions involving the compulsory sale of Jewish real property took place under the aegis of the Belgian legal system. Mortgage lenders were able to avail themselves of the general provisions of Belgian law when their Jewish debtors failed to keep up their payments. Judgments of mortgage defaults were part of the ordinary operation of Belgian law and resulted in a form of *de facto* and *de jure* Aryanization essentially without the involvement of German authorities.[22] Subsequent chapters detail other ways in which the Belgian legal system continued to operate, often to the detriment of Jewish individuals (although occasionally to their benefit as well), in a normal fashion or as a necessary adjunct to the German systems legally regulating enemy and Jewish property.

Meanwhile a small number of Belgian lawyers and notaries continued to collaborate directly with the Germans in the implementation of anti-Jewish Orders. Raymond Ledoux, whom we encountered as an expert in "Jewish" legal matters, in relation to the Dietz case in Liège, and as the author of a text on the contributions of National-Socialist legislation to corporate law, served as an administrator (*Verwalter*) for Aryanized Jewish property. Notary Léon Brunet formalized the incorporation documents, pursuant to Belgian law, for the Brüsseler Treuhandgesellschaft (BTG), the corporate body which directed much of the Aryanization process in Belgium.[23] While these legal adherents of National Socialism and the New Order remained a minority presence among the professional elite of Belgium, they did exist and they did, for a certain period, exercise professional, legal influence on the fate of the country's Jewish population.

The legal professions confront Aryanization

From the earliest days of the *Verwalter* system to the end of the occupation, Belgian legal professionals would be intimately involved in the juridical system regulating so-called Jewish property. In many cases, notaries authenticated and registered transactions relating to Jewish property. Some notaries would also act as trustees or legally empowered representatives of Jewish clients, reporting on their client's assets and making appropriate payments to the *Verwalter* charged with administering the Jewish property in question.[24]

Lawyers would also act as their clients', both Jewish and non-Jewish, legal representatives in any number of cases directly related to the application of anti-Jewish property measures and the interactions between the Belgian and Nazi legal systems. Some lawyers would act as temporary administrators appointed by the courts pursuant to Articles 112–14 of the Civil Code in instances in which the owner/debtor was absent. In such cases, Belgian law and the German occupation regime sometimes came into conflict. The sale of Jewish property could sometimes be delayed in instances where the Belgian court had appointed such a temporary administrator for an absent owner and the German request that the firm go into liquidation was not addressed to the administrator.[25] In these cases, the technical requirements of ordinary Belgian civil and commercial law served as a bulwark against the occupation Aryanization machine.

Still other legal professionals would make use of their legal skills in "ordinary" cases arising out of the application of the property provisions of the anti-Jewish

Orders. An example of this can be found in the case of Mme Nélis Kerkofs. Her furniture and other household property were seized by the Germans in late January 1944. Her lawyer, Me De Raditsky d'Ostrowick, consulted with his client and sent "all certificates establishing the Aryan origin of Madame Kerkhoffs [sic]"[26] to the appropriate German officials. Since only "Jewish" property was to be confiscated by the Germans, and because the definition of "Jewish" property was directly dependent upon the operation of the definition of "Jew" in the First Order (§ 1), the Belgian lawyer adopted a legal argument, supported by documentary evidence, that the seizure should be voided because his client was not a Jew and the property therefore could not be "Jewish". Years after the notarial profession had refused to participate in the validation of transactions affecting Jewish property, an eminent member of the Brussels Bar invoked a legal argument which depended in its entirety on the extant legal notion of a Jew. The hermeneutic of acceptance had a long and (un)healthy existence in Belgian legal discourse and practice.

There are of course several grounds which might be invoked to support the assertions of Me De Raditsky d'Ostrowick. First, his client's property had in fact been seized and she in all likelihood had a dire and pressing need for these basic belongings in the harsh winter of 1944. The Germans on such legal questions had always shown themselves to be willing adherents to a vision of strict positivist legality. The lawyer therefore may well have believed that this was the best if not the only way to get the occupier to agree to hand back the property. At the same time, of course, such a tactic is a far cry from the principled objection and jugular constitutional argument which characterized the Brussels Bar letter in 1940 or the refusal of the notaries of Belgium to play any further part in the Aryanization process. As we have seen in relation to attempts to deregister individuals classified as "Jews" and as we shall see in subsequent chapters, Me De Raditsky d'Ostrowick was certainly not alone in adopting this pragmatic practice in relation to the application of anti-Jewish Orders.

Winding-up Jewish undertakings: 12 Francs for the Belgian state

In June 1941, the German military administration tightened its grip on the Jewish presence in the Belgian economy by imposing further, more complete and more stringent reporting obligations and by extending and strengthening the *Verwalter* system through the introduction of the Third Order concerning Jews (Order relating to economic measures against the Jews).[27] This process reached its apogee in March 1942. In the first few days of this month, a circular in the three languages, German, Flemish and French, was sent to all registered Jewish businesses in Belgium.[28]

All such businesses were to cease operations no later than 31 March. In order to complete the process according to the appropriate legal framework, the Germans required that all businesses have their entry removed (*radié*) from the Commercial Register held at the local Commercial Court office. The registration could not be lawfully transferred. The process of eliminating Jews from commercial and economic life in Belgium took place in a lawfully ordered bureaucratic fashion. More importantly, the system and practice of Belgian legality were incorporated in the German Aryanization process. Being struck off the Commercial Register (*Registre de Commerce*) by means of *radiation* meant that the business was no longer in existence according to domestic law. Aryanization at this final stage became a Belgian process of giving formal domestic legal effect to the German removal of Jews from the economy, long after the government-in-exile's prohibition on Belgian involvement with expropriatory measures. A brief case study reveals how the Belgian judicial officials, in this instance the clerks (*greffiers*) of the Commercial Court (Tribunal de Commerce), attempted to deal with the reality imposed on them by the military administration with its *de facto* effect of removing Jewish businesses from Belgian legal existence while maintaining at some level a distance from direct, perhaps *de jure* involvement in the process.

An examination of the records of the Commercial Court for the district of Liège in March and April 1942 offers potentially intriguing and informative insights into the daily operation of this Belgian aspect of the German Aryanization program in Belgium.[29] Between 10 March and 4 April, approximately 155 Jewish businessmen went in person to the Clerk's Office of the Commercial Court in Liège to have their entries struck off the Commercial Register pursuant to the circular from the occupying authority. While 17 Jews had rapidly complied in the period up to 27 March, the vast majority waited until the deadline of the end of the month loomed. Between 28 and 31 March, 128 Jews came to the Court House (Palais de Justice) to officially close their businesses according to Belgian law but following German commands. On 31 March alone, the deadline, 83 Jewish businesses were struck off the Commercial Register in Liège. A few stragglers missed the official deadline, and 10 further businesses were removed from the Register between 1 and 4 April.

The Register documents indicate that while the formal removal of Jewish interests became increasingly important as part of the daily work in the Clerk's Office, particularly as the deadline approached, the business of the Commercial Court Office nonetheless continued as normal. Other transactions such as intra-family transfers of commercial interests and notifications of the death of a business owner were entered into the official Commercial Court records at the same time as the removal of Jewish businesses. It takes little imagination to picture the scenes at the Palais de Justice in Liège on 31 March 1942, as more than 80 Jews stood waiting for their turn to put a legal to end their livelihoods.

The records of the Clerk's Office also indicate that, on occasion during the last few days, so many Jewish businesses were "surrendered" that there was a delay, sometimes of two or three days, between the filing of the form by the owner with the Clerk and the official entry of the *radiation* in the court records. In addition, the archives show that, as the deadline of month's end approached, a number of businesses were wound up at the courthouse on the weekend. Thus, on 28 March 1942, a Saturday, 22 Jews legally terminated their economic activity. Four others did so the next day, Sunday 29 March 1942. Belgian legality knew no day of rest when it came to the end of Jewish business in Liège.

At the same time, however, it is clear from an examination of the documentary record that the Belgian court officers were at pains to indicate that they were unwilling participants in this stage of legalized Aryanization. Form E, the correct bureaucratic document for legally recording a declaration of Death, Winding-up or Winding-up by Transfer of a commercial enterprise, required a certain amount of identifying information relating to the business and the owner. There was, however, no place on the form to enter the reason for winding-up a business. Yet on the vast majority of the forms found in the Liège archives, a handwritten annotation which indicates that the business was terminated under German orders completes almost all of the documents. While the formulation varies, most of the forms contain the inscription, "By Order of the Occupying Authority" (*par ordre de l'autorité occupante*). Moreover, most of these entries made at the Clerk's Office are clearly written in the same hand, in writing different than that on the declaration completed by the Jews of Liège. In other words, in any number of cases involving the elimination of Jewish businesses, following the form and procedure imposed by Belgian law, local officials were clearly at pains to indicate "officially" that the real operating power was German.

While it is impossible to determine if the entry placing responsibility for the closing of the Jewish businesses on the occupying authority was made at the time the Jewish businessman signed and filed the paperwork, it would seem that this was the case. Within the archives of Form E found in Liège, there are several examples in which the individual owner himself entered similar information. Several examples exist, from the simple to the more complete: "Surrendered by order of the Occupying Authority" (*Remis par ordre de l'autorité occupante*); "I surrender my business pursuant to the Decree of the Military Commander for Belgium and the North of France of 31 May 1941 relating to economic measures taken concerning Jews" (*Je cesse mon commerce en vertu de l'ordonnance décrétée par le Commandant Militaire pour la Belgique et le nord de la France du 31 mai 1941 relatives* [sic] *aux mesures économiques prises à l'égard des Juifs*); and variations on these themes. What they share is the declaration that the German Occupying Authority is the source of the surrender of these Jewish businesses. Other declarations from other jurisdictions within Belgium contain similar statements placing the legal and practical burden for the application of these Aryanization measures clearly and unequivocally on the Germans.

Things were never really as simple and clear as they might appear however. Every form E filed in March and April 1942 pursuant to which Jews surrendered their business and took one more legal step in the process of exclusion, penury and suffering, contains one more piece of valuable information. The standard fee for the processing and registration of a *cessation* or *radiation* was 12 BEF. Every Jewish business surrendered "by order of the Occupying Authority" was charged this fee by the Belgian officials at the Commercial Court. While responsibility for the process might have been sheeted home to the Germans, the Belgian legal system, the Belgian state, compelled the Jewish victims of Aryanization to pay the legal cost of their exclusion. 12 BEF went directly to the Belgian state from each Jewish business.

Chapter 5

Belgian municipalities and the introduction of anti-Jewish Decrees

The role played by local, Belgian administrations and elected officials in implementing the first German measures against the Jews of Belgium has historically been underdeveloped in Belgium. While the implementation of the first two anti-Jewish Decrees was delegated by the Germans to the SG as a general matter, the real concrete work of identifying Jews and beginning the process of their legal exclusion was given to local government. The First Order concerning Jews created the general framework for the establishment of the Jewish Register throughout the country. Local governments in all towns and cities with a population of over 5,000 were vested with the responsibility for the registration process, while in smaller places the local police were to create and maintain the Register of Jews (§ 3). The Adam circular of 5 and 6 December 1940 outlined the process embodied in the Decree as well as a clear indication that the exclusion of Jewish civil servants was to be applied and enforced at the local, municipal level as well.[1] Municipal governments were at the very core of the implementation of anti-Jewish Orders.

This was hardly surprising given the nature of the structure of Belgian government. Towns and cities, mayors and councilors, were invested with significant legal authority, including an extensive law-making, quasi-legislative power.[2] At the local level, these officials in fact and in law represented the Belgian state and were the real embodiment, in the difficult period of German occupation, of Belgian sovereignty in the daily lives of most citizens.[3] The actual history of local administrations is central to the unfolding of the drama of the fate of the Jews of Belgium between 1940 and 1945. Until recently, the story has been largely untold. Most of the tales of local government under occupation dealt with the hardships encountered by officials as they attempted to find the finance necessary to carry out the various tasks of their daily responsibilities to their citizens. From the very beginning of the occupation until the days of Liberation, most mayors and councilors, as well as their civil servants, faced with the ever-increasing and more onerous demands of the Germans, were kept busy with the basic tasks of ensuring that the inhabitants of Belgium's villages, towns and cities had a roof over their heads, the means to heat their domiciles in the harsh winters and enough food to eat.[4] Other histories emphasize the hardships faced by local officials following the flight into exile of many of the most important elected officers and high-ranking employees in May 1940 and subsequent German edicts forbidding them from returning and banning many from their positions in government for any number of perceived political activities. In such official renderings of local government under the occupation, the fate of Belgium's Jews hardly figures at all.[5]

Whatever trials and tribulations these local administrations may have faced throughout the occupation, until they were replaced in the latter stages of the war by official collaborationist stooges of the occupying authority, mayors, councilors and civil servants continued to resist. As the embodiment of the Belgian state and the representatives of the values enshrined in the Constitution, they were beacons of solidarity and resistance.[6] At least this was the predominant historical narrative until a period of historical revision which emerged a few years ago. Belgian historians have begun to examine the role and activities of local government under German occupation with a more critical eye and with greater access to archival records. A primary focus of this new historical activity has been the question of the fate of the Jewish populations in various parts of Belgium. Historians have begun to pay close attention to, and to catch up with, the constitutional and governmental framework of occupied Belgium. If local officials were designated by the Germans and the SG to implement and oversee the day-to-day practicalities of the new anti-Jewish legal order, it only makes sense to focus research attention on the structures and officials of local government to gain a clearer insight into how the organs of the Belgian state reacted to this new role as the identifiers of "Jews".

Lieven Saerens has completed an intricately detailed study of the particular and peculiar situation which obtained in Antwerp.[7] Herman Van Goethem has more recently focused on the relationship between the decisions of the SG in relation to the constitutional issues surrounding the anti-Jewish Decrees and local implementation by legal officials in his important examination of Antwerp.[8] Thierry Delplancq has begun to publish his findings in relation to the officials of Brussels[9] and Ostend.[10]

For the most part, despite these more recent changes in emphasis on the specificity of the fate of local Jewish populations, Belgian historiography continued to focus on the wartime period and the occupation more generally. The question of Belgian participation in Nazi atrocities tended to be subsumed under the broader rubrics of collaboration and its mirror image resistance. When the focus has turned to the role of non-Jewish Belgians in the Shoah, historical study has primarily looked at various stories of rescue.[11] Other efforts have been aimed at the mechanisms of exclusion and death put in place by the German occupiers for the Final Solution. Attempts to examine in detail the precise role played by Belgians in that country's treatment of its Jewish population are only really beginning.[12] In this chapter, I want to begin to elucidate, however briefly, one key part of the most vexing and fascinating yet still understudied areas of Belgian Holocaust history: the role played by the Belgian state and legal apparatus in the exclusion of the Jews. I will look at the day-to-day practices and discourses of local administrative and elected officials generally, before subsequently turning to more detailed studies of the cities of Brussels and Liège, in order to cast light on the ways in which competing ideas about citizenship, "Belgianness", constitutional duty and obedience to law came into contact with what became for its practitioners the bureaucratic necessity to efficiently and effectively comply with obligations based in legal edicts from the German occupiers, to register, identify and segregate Jews. This examination is a useful way to begin to clarify our understandings not just of the historical reality but also of the institutional and political dynamics, of the broader question about modern governance, legality and the Holocaust.

For a variety of reasons this question of local participation in anti-Jewish persecution in Belgium has either been ignored, or else subsumed in debates about collaboration, and thence into mythological conflicts between French-speaking Wallonia and Flemish-speaking Flanders over each community's understanding of the nature of Belgian identity. It is perhaps deeply ironic, given the historical sense of superiority evidenced in Francophone Belgians' attitude to the active creation of a dominant mythology of Flemish perfidy and collaboration,[13] that the first real critical inquiry into local collaboration in the persecution of a city's Jewish population in occupied Belgium is Saerens's work on Antwerp.

As is the case in France with attempts to come to grips with its own domestic implication in the Final Solution, it has been easier, both morally and politically, to simply blame the Germans and a few local fanatics dedicated to the New European Order instead of engaging in a careful and nuanced, if traumatic, study of Belgian complicity. Part of the complex psycho-social, historical, political and legal, matrix of this forgetting in Belgium has been the creation, as in France, of a glorious tradition of resistance to the occupier. This again is not to suggest that resistance by Belgians was simply mythological. There was resistance and there were resisters, non-Jewish and Jewish alike, just as there was collaboration and there were collaborators. Instead, one of the mechanisms through which Belgian responsibility in the exclusion, persecution, pillage and killing of Jews in that country has been elided is through the creation of a myth structure, often or perhaps most powerfully, a legally created myth structure, of resistance against Nazi (or German) anti-Jewish measures.

In the cases of local government this mythology demands that the story which is (and has been) told be one in which local administrators and officials, forced by the occupying military power to identify, register and exclude individuals and businesses classified as "Jewish" in the foreign, anti-Belgian taxonomical structure of Nazism, resisted as best they could, through delay, obfuscation and reliance on the Constitution of Belgium and its guarantees of equality and freedom of religion. This mythological structure of local resistance has been embedded in Belgian legal discourse about the fate of the Jews from the earliest times. A report by the Allied governments issued in 1943 praised the Belgian population for its lack of enthusiasm and resistance to anti-Jewish measures imposed by the Germans.[14] More centrally for the construction of a legal memory of resistance and Belgian non-collaboration in the persecution of the Jews, the postwar *Report* on antisemitic persecution by the official War Crimes Commission established by the newly restored democratic Belgian government added to this narrative. This *Report* embodies and embeds not just the construction of the legal edifice of amnesia and amnesty which characterizes Belgian historiography of the past sixty years, but also the elements of proof which, in a legal dialectic largely ignored until the present, undermine that very edifice. The Commission, after outlining the first set of anti-Jewish Decrees[15] issued by the Germans, wrote: "These various decrees affected only a limited number of Jews. Moreover, their application came up against either open hostility or the bad faith of the Belgian public bodies which were to enforce them."[16]

In a passage more directly relevant to the question of the role played by municipal institutions in implementing anti-Jewish measures on Belgian soil, the Commission declared:

> Thus, a number of municipal administrations systematically sabotaged the creation of a Register of Jews, under the pretext of overwork, lack of material or manpower. On this point, it is useful to note that the majority of Jews invited to register themselves, obeyed. Forty-two thousand gave their names.[17]

This *Report* replicates the case presented about the Holocaust in Belgium by the French prosecuting authorities at the International Military Tribunal at Nuremberg. There, however, the lawyers representing the official Belgian position added an important analysis. They said:

> On this point, it is useful to note that the majority of Jews complied, when invited to register themselves, either because they were motivated by a renewed pride in their status as Hebrews, or because the moderation of the Germans blinded them to the grave consequences that registration could have for them in the future.[18]

These official government records establish as a matter of constitutional and constitutive legal discourse the continuing mythology of the role played by local officials in the administration of the preliminary phases of what became the Shoah in Belgium. First, the measures were imposed by the Germans. Second, there was passive compliance accompanied by active resistance to attempts to register and exclude those identified as Jews. Third, the semiotic deployment and use of the passive voice and similar constructions, usually exemplified by the invocation of reflexive verbs, not only reinforces the first two pillars of the myth structure but adds the final crucial element. The municipalities did not register Jews. The Jews registered themselves. They presented themselves for registration. They were "invited" to register and remarkably they did so. Tens of thousands of Jews, many of whom had fled pogroms in Poland and Russia, or who had left Germany after Hitler's rise to power, according to the predominant official legal texts of historical memory of the Holocaust in Belgium, proudly declared themselves. There is no compulsion, there is no threat and there certainly is no Belgian responsibility.

There is almost, as far as the Jews are concerned, no German military occupation. The Germans compelled Belgian cooperation while the Jews, grammatically at least, simply cooperated. This is the official story of the Holocaust in Belgium as told by the War Crimes Commission and the prosecutors at Nuremberg. This is the legal history of the Shoah in Belgium. There was a Holocaust in Belgium, but no Belgians, except for fanatical adherents of the New Order, were actively involved.

This in essence summarizes the official and unofficial popular memory of the Belgian historical position. Anti-Jewish measures were imposed on a reluctant and resisting Belgian public and officialdom by the Germans or more strongly in myth, the "Nazis". Compliance was minimal and largely at the behest of the victims. In the loop of traditional Holocaust taxonomical structures, perpetrator/victim/bystander, the first two categories are filled easily by the Germans (Nazis) and the Jews. The Belgians were either passive observers or active resisters. At worst their activities could be classified as falling into the self-created legal category of "passive collaboration".[19] It is this somewhat bizarre historical, juridical category, "passive collaboration", which characterized the myths about local participation in the persecution of Jews. And this passivity is a direct result of the construction of the limits of permissible, lawful, constitutional, conduct by the highest legal instances, from the Permanent Council on Legislation, made up of the country's pre-eminent jurists, to the top level of government, the SG, which in turn resulted in this mythology. In other words, what need to be more carefully and fully studied are the ways in which legal, constitutional discourse and practice served to limit (or not?), if not the actions, then at least the ways those actions were understood by the actors, when the local administrations throughout Belgium began to implement German anti-Jewish Decrees.

Emerging and competing counter-narratives which have recently become more readily available in relation to a more self-aware and critical assessment of Belgian complicity and involvement in the German attempt to destroy the Jews of that country can now be found. While dominant myths have supported the story of resistance and reluctant, begrudging, minimalist compliance by Belgian officials in implementing anti-Jewish Orders, a newer historiography has also begun to counter-balance this version of "passive collaboration". In February 2007, an official report on the role of Belgian authorities in the persecution of Jews by expert historians commissioned by the Belgian government was published.[20] The title of the report summarizes and semiotically embodies the findings of the commission of experts. Belgian officials exhibited "docility" when faced with German anti-Jewish Orders; they caved in; they failed to invoke in a vigorous and necessary way the provisions of the Hague Convention to prevent the implication of the structures of the Belgian constitutional state in the mechanisms of persecution. "Passive collaboration" has begun to give way to a more complex understanding of the realities of the fate of the country's Jewish population.

The Belgian state therefore adopted a docile attitude by collaborating, in a diverse but crucial variety of areas, in a manner unworthy of a democracy, in a policy which was disastrous for the Jewish population (both Belgian and foreign).[21] While one might argue that La Belgique docile does little more than synthesize the findings of other historians who had heretofore been a distinct historiographical, or in the eyes of the dominant majority, an ideological minority, even this mainstreaming of a more critical appraisal of Belgian state complicity in the Shoah and related events must be accepted as an important, if insufficient step forward. Yet, despite the historians' attempts to place the failures of the Belgian state apparatus in a wider context, there are still hints of the pre-existing historiography in the report. The question of the Jewish Star is treated as a clear example of resistance by the mayors of Brussels and Liège.[22] The Yellow Star story is characterized and highlighted as the moment of "rupture", the time when Belgian officials began explicitly to reject German antisemitic persecution policies. Not surprisingly, press coverage of the release of the report in Belgium focused not on the broader picture of collaboration but on this moment of "resistance" by the Belgian state since this characterization and this event fit more comfortably into the still dominant public perception of the story. An almost reflexive reaction to any attempt to deal with the reality of active Belgian state participation in the persecution of the Jewish population is the invocation of a counter-narrative of resistance and rescue. A more critical examination of the Judenstern episodes in Brussels and Liège reveals nothing more than a mere reluctance to participate in a process which seemed to offend the bourgeois sentiments of the Belgian officials involved, accompanied by a suggestion that either the Jews themselves or the German military authority would be better able to deal with the matter.[23]

Whatever its weaknesses and failings, La Belgique docile does begin a process of situating the local nature of the early phases of anti-Jewish Belgian government involvement in the enforcement of the German Decrees.[24] The structure of the Belgian state and the legal architecture of the synergies between Belgian constitutional law and the first anti-Jewish Decrees led inevitably to this detailed involvement of local authorities in the first stages of legalized antisemitic persecutions. In some municipalities, German demands for local participation in the process of identifying Jewish individuals and businesses preceded by some time the introduction of the first two Decrees.[25] The evolution of the attitudes of some local officials can be traced even in these early days of the occupation.

In Verviers, for example, the Germans demanded a list of all English citizens and Jews resident in the municipality in July 1940. The local police official charged with providing the information required for a response to the request informed the mayor on 1 August that there was no way for the police to identify Jews and therefore it was absolutely impossible to meet the German demand for information in this regard. Several ways of interpreting this early response to a German demand in relation to a local Jewish population can be imagined. One could see this as an act of resistance to German antisemitism. Or one could see it simply as a statement of the operational constitutional and constitutive facts of life in Belgium at the time. The category "Jew" was officially unknown and unknowable under Belgian law at the time. In addition, it might be possible to read this response as an early example of delay and obfuscation through the deployment of standard bureaucratic mechanisms and responses. It might then be read as resistance.

One might add further complexity to the interpretation of this incident by pointing out that the police officer added that the "Hebrew religion is not officially practiced in Verviers".[26] The police official in his report mixes the German request for "Jews" with the more traditional official Belgian understanding of "Hebrew", a lexical confusion which comes to characterize other Belgian official attempts to deal with the "Jewish question", particularly in the earlier stages of anti-Jewish persecution. At the same time, one might hypothesize that, had there been a synagogue in the town, the police would perhaps have made further inquiries about the membership of the congregation to fulfill the occupier's demand for information. The constitutional impossibility of identifying "Jews" in Belgium would, were this to be the case, give way to a simple factual impossibility or significant difficulty in obtaining the relevant information in the absence of a practicing Jewish community in the town. By the beginning of October, however, the Verviers police were able to report that, following the introduction of anti-Jewish measures in Luxembourg and the flight of many Jews from that country to neighboring countries, no Luxembourg Jew was present in the town.[27]

What had apparently been impossible in the summer, the identification of Jews, now appeared to be within the realm of local police competence. Of course, the existence of a complete police system of surveillance and registration of all foreign nationals would have made the identification of Luxemburgers a simple task. Determining their "Jewish" identity should, in theory, have been somewhat more difficult, indeed impossible, before the introduction of the First Order. The subsequent efficient application of anti-Jewish Decrees in Verviers bears witness to the adaptability of local officialdom.[28] On 2 January 1941, the chief police officer in the town could report to the mayor that his force had "scrupulously conformed" to instructions concerning the application of the first anti-Jewish Order, posting public notices requiring Jews to register and establishing a series of files for all Jews in the city.[29] What is revealed in local archival records of Brussels and Liège, to which I now turn in some detail as case studies of the mechanisms of legalized persecution in occupied Belgium, is a collaboration which was neither "docile" nor "passive".

Chapter 6

Brussels

Passive collaboration and the Jews of the capital

As Belgian historian Thierry Delplancq underlines, research into municipal records and the "Jewish question" during the occupation of Belgium is beset with numerous practical problems which make any exploration of the fundamental factual and ideological questions which are so important to our understandings of the Holocaust in Belgium all the more difficult. Many archives are closed and require special permission for access; the "hundred year rule" prevents scholars from identifying the subjects of many records from the Second World War; files are incomplete or missing, etc.[1] The situation in Brussels exemplifies many of these problems. The files relating to the years of occupation found at the Archives of the City of Brussels from the Mayor's Office (Cabinet du Bourgmestre) are incomplete. Indeed, the Inventory and finding aid at the City Archives summarizes the state of the holdings as follows:

> The part of the holdings relating to the war 1940–1945 is much less interesting. The documents, especially the correspondence with the Occupying Power were found in a state of extreme disorder, which could only be remedied to a small decree … Moreover, it appears that many of the files have been destroyed or removed.[2]

Indeed, the file concerning the Register of Jews bears the following note from the 1970s "The Register of Jews for Brussels has disappeared."[3] Even the appellation (Cabinet du Bourgmestre) under which the various files are held in the Archives is itself somewhat of a misnomer. Many of the documents come not from the records held and maintained in the office of the mayor himself, as his files, but from copies maintained by M. Gries, the translator. Communications between the mayor, as well as other officials and departments of the city administration, and the German authorities came to Gries to be translated into German. Likewise, communications originating with the occupiers also came to him to be translated into French before being distributed to the appropriate department or official.[4] Thus, many of the extant documents are carbon copies, not strictly speaking originals. The files are in fact incomplete copies. They tell part of the story and not the whole story.

Nonetheless, the story they reveal is a detailed one of bureaucracy and legality in anti-Jewish persecution in Belgium. There are no doubt counter-narratives, subtleties of distinction and real stories behind the documents. For example, it no doubt is the case that in Brussels as in other parts of Belgium, some local authorities aided Jews by supplying them with "real false papers", i.e. official birth certificates, or nationality papers, with non-Jewish origins or food ration coupons under a false identity for Jews in hiding. These acts of resistance and rescue will appear nowhere in official written communications between departments or with the German authorities. Documents speak for themselves, but they do not always or necessarily speak beyond themselves. This chapter is about bureaucratic and governmental action as embodied in the writings of the bureaucrats and elected officials themselves, nothing more and nothing less. They do not tell the whole story or reveal the whole truth, even assuming that this is the function of narrative, but they do offer evidence of and about law and of our understandings of bureaucracy, legality and legitimacy in implementing anti-Jewish measures in Belgium.

They evoke the ways in which bureaucratic and governmental practice grew up and flourished in a juridical framework in which a new legal subject, a subject for bureaucratic governance and surveillance, "the Jew", was created, identified, subjugated, expropriated and finally killed. The bureaucrats and other officials who participated in this system in the city of Brussels may have done so reluctantly. Some, as the official discourses and legal histories have it, may have resisted. Most may have been merely "passive" collaborators. They may well have been Belgian patriots. They almost certainly believed their actions were legally justifiable and justified. Few, especially in the earliest stages of the anti-Jewish Orders were real collaborators or adherents of Rex, the VNV or other Nazi allied organizations.

A complex jurisprudential edifice legalizing collaboration which was not *participation* had been constructed for their reference by some of the leading jurists in Belgium. Moreover, their acceptance, however reluctant, of the new subject, "Jew", embodies and exemplifies the fundamental importance of a legal framework for the operation of Nazi antisemitism which led to the Shoah in Belgium.

Protest, with one notable, but historically exaggerated exception, reiterated with great fanfare in *La Belgique docile*, over the imposition of the Yellow Star to be worn by all Belgian Jews, based in the fundamental principles of the Belgian Constitution guaranteeing freedom of religion and equality of all, did not arise.[5] This absence of protest, in part at least, is attributable to the legal framework established by the Conseil de Législation and the SG, under which the municipal officials found themselves. The jurists and highest-ranking officials of Belgian government had removed the Constitution from the equation through their complex legal interpretation. This point is underemphasized in much of past and current Belgian scholarship on the fate of the country's Jewish population. Discussion focusing on the unconstitutional nature of the anti-Jewish orders underplays the centrality of the other, competing and in this case, overriding legal norm, i.e. the interpretation of the Hague Convention, under which relations between the occupiers and the SG had been regulated since the agreement of June 1940 and the secondary legal role of the Constitution itself, as interpreted by the Conseil de Législation. Multi-factored analyses are obviously necessary but in carrying out these inquiries the legitimating impact of a clearly established legal framework for persecution must never be underestimated or overestimated.

As Vivian Curran so forcefully established in her study of Vichy France, the Constitution is not a sterile text but a document which lives in the hearts and minds of those who live under it, and who enforce and apply it.[6] It is no doubt true that there are multiple factors which must be understood in order to place the Shoah in Belgium not just in its domestic but also in a comparative context. The status and nature of the German occupation regime and its internal struggles, strengths and weaknesses; the bureaucratic machinery of antisemitism; relations between the occupier and the SG; the vexed and ongoing controversies surrounding the role of the official Association des Juifs en Belgique (AJB);[7] all of these factors and more must be remembered and considered.[8]

At the same time, we must never forget, as lawyers and as citizens, the unavoidable truth that subversion of constitutional normativity by and through the very same structures of that constitutional normativity remains, as Curran emphasizes, and as current events highlight, a real and present danger for us all. The example of the city of Brussels offers us an excellent opportunity to explore in microcosm the daily, lawful, routine practices and bureaucratic discourses through which Belgian officials participated without *participation* in the implementation of the early stages of the Holocaust. We must examine not just the facts of participation/not-participation but the professional, legal and ethical practices and rhetorics which were invoked to legitimate and legalize the exclusion of their fellows from the body politic. The processes of persecution in the city of Brussels demonstrate the ways in which legality, bureaucracy and governance operated within normal and accepted means to achieve the unacceptable. This combination of normalcy and legality is at the center of any understanding of the concept and practice of passive collaboration. The lesson from what has preceded and what will follow is

> that the object of social theory is not just other theories or theories about theories, but the ongoing and contingent practice that shapes, actively or by default, concrete events, underlying material processes and relationships, together with their intended and unintended consequences.[9]

The very notion of passive collaboration embodies and reflects key social and material practices, acts and actors, i.e. legitimation through legal norms which was the historical and juridical precedent for all the bureaucratic actions which followed in Brussels and elsewhere. As administrators and elected officials became accustomed to the new area of legal and bureaucratic life, "Jewish affairs" became a recognized and recognizable part of daily, lawful practice. This bureaucratic routinization of racial/religious exclusionary practices became normalized because law created the conditions in which such practices were made legitimate and binding. Law was itself, in other words, the precedent to passive collaboration, while at the same time serving as a limiting function only to a degree recognized and recognizable to bureaucratic necessity. In Brussels a legal and governmental regime was created which provided a legitimating framework combined with real, day-to-day, law in action as bureaucrats expanded legality to fit the practical needs of their work lives. What we do not find, in reality, is anything which can be justifiably characterized as narrow, passive collaboration as constructed in postwar legal history. The unanswered questions then become here, as elsewhere in the narratives and case studies which constitute the following chapters, why and how did even the potential limiting and justificatory functions of the Permanent Council's definition of acceptable and unacceptable collaboration seemingly collapse under the weight of daily governmental and legal practice?

"The system put into effect by the Brussels area towns and cities, must be adopted in the rest of the country": Brussels and its Jews, 1940

While the starting point of the history of involvement of the local administration in Brussels (and elsewhere in Belgium) is most properly situated in fall 1940 after the introduction of the two explicitly anti-Jewish Orders, any full understanding of the nature of the involvement of the city administration in "the Jewish question" would in reality need to begin much earlier, with studies of the policing system for foreigners or aliens (Police des Étrangers) and the phenomenon of waves of Jewish migration to Belgium and Brussels.[10] Such a detailed history of the prehistory of passive collaboration in Brussels is beyond the scope of this chapter. However, one incident of official correspondence in the time frame under review does provide an early warning, and serves as a harbinger of what would follow.

On 28 May 1940, in the earliest days of the occupation, the head of the city's public welfare agency wrote to the mayor. According to this note, two Germans sent by the Military Command had come to inform them that German citizens, including Austrians and Sudeten Germans, must henceforth be sent, should they need medical care or other help, to the German social assistance office.[11] Nothing appears on the surface of this recorded visit to be particularly noteworthy, if not perhaps for the imposed recognition by Belgian officials of the annexations of the Sudetenland and Austria. Germans are to be treated and cared for by Germans and within the German occupying power's bureaucratic and administrative structure. But one key word marks this document as the precursor for events which would follow in the autumn. Only "Aryan" Germans (les allemands aryens) are covered by the instruction given to the Brussels government employees.

At one level, none of this is still very surprising or particularly interesting. The discriminatory legal framework against German Jews by the German government had been in effect for several years and the extension as a matter of German law to the annexed territories was also consistent with long-standing practice.

Nazi antisemitism was well-known in Brussels at this time. That the German occupiers in Brussels should incorporate these anti-Jewish practices into their administrative structures and in their dealings with their fellow citizens was perfectly understandable and, it almost goes without saying, perfectly legal.[12]

Two interrelated points of bureaucratic inscriptive practices nonetheless are noteworthy. First, the Germans did not hesitate to address themselves to city bureaucrats to enforce and comply with these anti-Jewish practices. It is difficult to tell here whether the city employees were simply reporting on the German visit or were requesting further and better advice from the hierarchy and especially from elected decision-makers. There is no specific request for instructions and the document is simply entitled as a "note" for the mayor. It appears to be a document which passes on information with the strong implication by silence at least that the welfare agency would comply thenceforth with the German command. The document in question contains the handwritten notation that it has been seen (*vu*) but there appear to be no other documents which deal with the subject. Nonetheless, it is clear from this one inter-office communication that some officials, including the mayor himself, were aware that German anti-Jewish legal norms were being applied in Brussels and that they were expected in these cases to comply with them.

The second point which arises out of the memo to the mayor is again one of semiotic, interpretive import. The welfare office writes that "German Aryans" (*les allemands aryens*) are to be sent to the new address for assistance. The official correspondence of the Brussels administrations replicates, without hesitation, comment, or qualms, the language of Nazi antisemitism. *Aryen*/"Aryan" again was not a term recognized in the Belgian Constitution, a document and normative structure which continued to apply and to which the sender and recipient of this document had sworn allegiance. One might plausibly assert and argue that the writer is doing nothing more than replicating the language of the instructions which he received from the two German visitors to his office and not adopting the language as his own. But of course, that is precisely the point. This is a low-level, ordinary example of the "hermeneutic of acceptance" wherein the discursive and epistemological universe of Nazi antisemitism becomes legalized and normalized within Belgian administrative practice. The acceptance by the SG of a particular interpretation of the Hague Convention allowed the Germans to put into place a system of laws binding upon the Belgian state under which a new legal category, "the Jew" (and its necessary counterpart, "the Aryan"), became acceptable. Belgian officials in the first days of the German occupation came face to face with German antisemitism, which they were asked to apply and implement. For the most part, they did not resist; they did not refuse; they did not invoke constitutional principle. Instead they reiterated and transcribed the language of hatred of the occupier and noted that the document had been read. This may well be the first and most telling instance of bureaucratic neutrality and conformity as an exemplar of passive collaboration in Brussels. Worse was yet to come as the city of Brussels was charged with implementing the registration for local individuals and businesses identified as Jewish.

When the Ministry of the Interior circulated its letter of instructions about the duty to comply with the anti-Jewish Orders to local officials on 5 and 6 December 1940, it did so, as we have seen, against a background of legal and practical compliance with German anti-Jewish Decrees. The letter from Adam to the country's mayors and other local officials simply confirmed what had become the juridical reality of passive collaboration. Continuing the common theme of passivity, of non-*participation*, Adam made it clear once again that the registration process, in this case for Jewish businesses, was at the demand of the victims. Thus, local authorities were advised that

> It is also ordered that municipalities shall urgently publish a notice indicating that Jews are required to have themselves entered in the Register of Jews and that those in charge of Jewish establishments must request that the local administration proceed with the signs set out in the Decree.[13]

Jews are to have themselves entered on the register (*se faire inscrire*) and must request (*requérir*) the proper signs marking their exclusion from the Belgian body politic. Local officials are mere secretaries, transcribing the requests of the Jews to be registered, to be inscribed and marked as separate. They are passive receptacles, scriveners, automatic writers and fillers-in of forms. They do not *participate*.

Local authorities in Brussels took the grammatical structure and rhetorical formulations of the constitutionally and legally sanctified exclusionary process of registration one step further. They consistently invoked the passive voice to identify themselves publicly as mere followers of lawful and legitimate orders from above. For them, the legal obligation under which they submitted to the process came not just from the superior authority of the Germans, but from the powers vested by Belgian law in the SG. The notice published by the city of Brussels reads in part: "The Honorable Secretary-General of the Ministry of the Interior and Public Health orders that by command of the German Military Authority, municipalities must urgently publish this notice."[14]

But the beginnings of the process of registration and exclusion of the Jews of Brussels also evidence a certain ambiguity which since the occupation has been invoked to demonstrate the politics and practices of resistance and obfuscation which have been said to characterize the actions of the city administration. Adam wrote

> In order to facilitate the task which has fallen upon their administration, the municipalities of the Brussels region have decided to adopt the type of card (*fiche*) which is attached for the register.
>
> The German Military Authority has decided that unless enforcement measures have already been taken, the system put into place by the towns of the Brussels area must be adopted in the whole country.[15]

The response from Brussels to the content of the Adam letter was vociferous and apparently unambiguous. Georges Pêtre, mayor of the district of Saint-Josse-ten-Noode, wrote to the mayor of Brussels, Van de Meulebroeck, the day after Adam's missive, to protest at the dangerous misunderstanding of the position of the city on the question of implementing the anti-Jewish Orders. Pêtre characterized the Orders as blatantly unconstitutional (*ordonnances dont le caractère anticonstitutionnel est évident*).[16] At its meeting on 10 December, the regional Mayors' Conference (Conférence des Bourgmestres) discussed the issue and decided to write to the Secretary-General. In their reply to the central government, Van de Meulebroeck distanced himself and his local colleagues from any implication of *participation*.[17] In his capacity as leader of the Conference of Mayors for the Brussels region, Van de Meulebroeck sent an angry reply to the SG attacking the wording of the 6 December letter. He wrote:

> Without question, certain municipal employees have together drawn up a model card (*fiche*) for the eventuality of the application of the German Decree … but the Mayors, meeting together in Conference, have in no way adopted the model, nor have they taken a decision for its use in their area. On the contrary, taking into account that Paragraph 16 the German Decree of 28 October stipulates that "the head of the general military administration will decide the necessary provisions in order to carry out and to complete this Decree", the Mayors decided to wait until the necessary provisions for the application of the Decree of 28 October had been set out, to decide on their position. They have become aware of the publication of these provisions only by way of your aforementioned letter. They wish to underline that they will only apply these instructions because they are compelled and forced to do so.[18]

The objection of Van de Meulebroeck and his colleagues is first and foremost over the impression left by the Adam Circular that the Brussels region's officials had rushed to enforce the anti-Jewish laws. Second they objected to what they saw as a denial of authority and the possible abdication of decision-making power by the SG themselves. From the point of view of Brussels, the SG seemed to be asserting that the only position taken by them was that other municipalities should follow Brussels' lead. The elected officials from Brussels were careful to point out that the authority and order for compliance came from both the SG and the Germans and that the city of Brussels was simply complying with the commands of the hierarchy. The mayor put on the record the official Brussels' position, one which again sought to position the city as acting merely in the form of passive collaboration and under instruction and compulsion. Intriguingly and perhaps tellingly, Pêtre's clear position in his letter to the mayor that the Decrees themselves violated the constitutional order disappeared in the interval between his missive to van de Meulebroeck and the latter's response on all his colleagues' behalf several days later.

There is, and there was, no doubt that the Decrees violated any number of provisions guaranteeing equality and liberty under the Belgian Constitution. But that was never really the legal question facing either the SG or the local officials once the Constitution had been finessed by the Hague Convention. The opinion of the Permanent Council, if the need arose, put paid to that question. The real issue, at both the jurisprudential and practical levels, was what consequences, if any, would flow, from Belgian implementation of or participation in such measures. To put it another way, the legal framing of relevant inquiry had been shifted from one about what the Constitution said about anti-Jewish measures to one about what limits were placed by Belgian law and the national interpretation of the Hague Convention on the collaboration of Belgian officials in the application of legally binding anti-Jewish Decrees. Where did "participation" become *participation* punishable by law? The issue was one as to the consequences under Belgian law for Belgian officials involved in the practical consequences of such anti-Jewish measures, which, it was assumed, were legal in the international sense of being within the powers of the Germans, as occupiers, to introduce with full force and effect. The constitutional question of first import, the violation of guarantees of judicial independence, of equality and religious liberty, was as a practical matter by this time of no importance or relevance whatsoever.

As Thierry Delplancq convincingly and overwhelmingly demonstrates, it is almost impossible in the context of all the other events which surrounded the sending of this reply to the SG to read it as a protest grounded in general principles against anti-Jewish laws.[19] Instead, the letter can be understood and placed in its proper context most probably and convincingly as a document in line with the creation of the official mythology of passive collaboration. It is an act the result of which was intended to be an exculpatory piece of evidence. The local officials constructed themselves in their official correspondence with their hierarchical superiors as mere followers of lawfully binding orders from the Germans and from the SG. Up until the letter of 5 and 6 December, according to their own account, they had not taken any position on the registration of Jews, or on the nature of the file cards (*fiches*) which would serve as the bureaucratic entry point in the process of identification. Events and other documents from the same sources, however, betray a more complex, living, symbiotic bureaucratic process at all levels of Belgian government, including the administration of Brussels, in relation to which our understanding of passive collaboration in implementing anti-Jewish measures must now become more contextualized and nuanced.

As early as 21 November 1940, i.e. well before the Adam Circular and before, according to Van Meulebroeck's defense of his administration, any real action had been approved, city employees were confronted with a practical dilemma involved in implementing the First Order. On that date, a Mr Jacques Levy wrote to the city administration to lodge a complaint about the way he had been treated when he had gone to the Palais de Midi to register as a Jew.[20] The employee, he said, had been very friendly (*très aimable*) but a disagreement had occurred when the city's representative had asked Levy about the religion of his child.

Because her mother was of non-Jewish descent, according to Levy, his daughter was equally non-Jewish.

Levy had then replied to the bureaucrat's query that his daughter belonged to no religious denomination. The employee insisted that this answer was not acceptable and that the child, according to the instructions he had received from his superiors, had to be included either as Catholic or as Jewish. In his letter of complaint, Levy asked the city officials to issue instructions which were in strict conformity with the German Decree and to admit a "no religion" response. Councilor Verhaeghe de Naeyer informed the city's public servants, after a meeting of the Collège (Council) on the same day that they should henceforth engage in a bureaucratic holding pattern. From that time, city officials should simply inform individuals who came to register that their name would be noted and they would be contacted as soon as a uniform policy and practice had been decided by the Collège.[21] In late November, the city's administration and elected officials appear to have operated in a state of bureaucratic and legal confusion as they confronted the practical realities of passive collaboration and their obligation to create a Register of Jews. Mr Levy appears to have taken them by surprise, although the employee's position itself was evidently based upon instructions received from his hierarchical superiors. Despite the councilor's instruction that the actual registration process be held in abeyance, practical bureaucratic steps to implement the Decree were already under way in Brussels.

On 22 November, Mr Joostens of the office of Births, Deaths and Marriages (État civil) sent to Adam, at the latter's request, 100 copies of file cards (*fiches*) which were to be used in the registration of Jews. He also promised to provide copies of the signs to be posted in Jewish businesses as soon as they were received from the printer.[22] The city administration was once more clearly positioned in relation to its hierarchical superior in the central government, Adam, as providing information requested. The file cards had already been printed, obviously at the behest of the city's administration. The bureaucracy was ready to proceed with the registration of the city's Jewish population. At this date, before the Permanent Council advice, the city was already well on its way to full, complete and active compliance with the anti-Jewish Orders. Such activities as drafting a form of card for a possible application (passive) of the anti-Jewish laws was, according to the mythological constructions of Van de Meulebroeck's subsequent letter in reply to Adam's Circular, the work of employees, who might, we can infer, have been either overenthusiastic or simply efficiently preparing for an eventuality as good forward-thinking public servants. What remains indisputable for the mayors as they seek to establish an exculpatory record is their subaltern position as mere appliers of superior will and lawful obligations. They embody Belgian passive collaboration.

On the same day as he wrote the letter of "protest" to the SG, Van de Meulebroeck had posted, with his signature and approval, the public notice to all Jews about the registration process. At the very least the temporal coincidence of the two documents must go some way to undermining the mythological and contemporaneous claim of mere passivity and compulsion. As was the case with Joostens's ability to provide 100 copies of the file card for the Jewish Register two weeks before the Adam Circular established the formal and legalized institutional arrangements for the process, the administration in Brussels was pursuing activities which would enable it to comply with its obligations under the First Decree. Indeed, still other documents produced at around the same time shed new and intriguing light on the claims of compulsion and on the ways in which "participation" may or may not have been understood as *participation*. Van de Meulebroeck claimed in his protest letter to the SG that the Conference of Mayors had taken no decisions as to the registration process and more specifically that, conscious of the wording of the Decree itself, they awaited the pronouncements of the Military Command in order to comply with its prescriptions.

Official documents clarify and highlight the nature and degree of involvement by Brussels area officials in the preliminary preparatory steps for implementing the anti-Jewish Decrees by way of the registration of businesses and individuals. They indicate the manner in which issues were raised, debated, considered and decided. They again draw into question the historical construction in legal and other discourses about the role of local administrations in Belgium, of passive collaboration under compulsion. On 12 November, one week after the publication of the Decrees in the *Verordnungsblatt*, the Director of the Office in Charge of the Register of Births, Deaths and Marriages wrote to the Conference of Mayors, raising for their consideration a series of practical legal questions relating to the ways in which the Decrees were to be applied. Those questions were:

> what department will be charged with keeping the Register of Jews? Will it be the Police, Religious Affairs or the Registry of Births, Deaths and Marriages?
>
> Is it appropriate to invite Jews by public notice, to present themselves for registration to the office of the competent department?
>
> On the other hand, given that the Decree in question says in Article 16 that the Head of the Military Administration will issue edicts containing the necessary rules for the application and completion of this Decree, should we ask for complementary instructions from the German Authority?
>
> If need be, can the designated department call together delegates for the towns of greater Brussels in order to transmit to them any information compiled in order to ensure uniformity in applying the Decree?[23]

This document further clarifies and establishes the real context of the Pêtre letter, the discussions at the Mayors' Conference and Van de Meulebroeck's letter of protest. While the Conference of Mayors may not have made a formal binding legislative or quasi-judicial decision on the technical points relating to the Register of Jews, it seems quite clear that there was intimate involvement at all levels of local government in the construction of the bureaucratic processes and mechanisms under which the Jews of Brussels were to be registered by Belgian civil servants. Municipal employees, elected councilors and all of the mayors of the greater Brussels area were deeply implicated in the decision-making process, at a time well before, in many cases, the limits of passive collaboration and the extent of permissible participation which was not illegal *participation* had been firmly established by the Permanent Council. The Germans themselves subsequently indicated that the Brussels bilingual formula for registration was to be adopted throughout the country unless registration had already begun in a given municipality. The record throughout Belgium is one in which in many instances, municipalities were well ahead of the Adam Circular in the process of putting into place the bureaucracy for the identification and exclusion of Jews.

A review of registration documents from other Belgian municipalities indicates that different forms in fact were used throughout the country. These local governments had preceded instructions from both the SG and the occupying authority in order to ensure that they would also be able to comply with the deadline for the registration of Jews set out in the First Decree. Again, while further research is required to clarify the deep history of registration in each Belgian municipal area, these documents indicate, *prima facie*, that steps to register Jews in various municipalities everywhere in Belgium were already well under way before the Permanent Council issued its verdict on the legal limits of local compliance.

On 12 November, the Conference responded to most of the issues raised in the Joostens Report. The mayors decided not just which administrative department would deal with the matter but that waiting for the Germans to decide or to issue more specific instructions was not necessary. This arguably constitutes the foundation of firm evidence of active participation, in what could be characterized as a statement against interest, in an official memorandum to the mayor of Brussels, which puts the lie to the position expressed by Van de Meulebroeck in his "protest" several weeks later. The Conference had already taken steps for the registration process and did not feel, at this stage, compelled to await German instructions. This internal bureaucratic correspondence might also serve as a useful starting point for future and further interrogations of the traditional taxonomy of collaboration and resistance. The Note for the mayor begins by stating:

> The Conference, in its meeting of 12 November, decided that the Register of Jews will be, as you know, kept by the Office of the Register of Births, Deaths and Marriages. The Conference was of the opinion that it was not necessary to request complementary instructions from the German Authority, and that the opening of the Register should take place in any event.[24]

Not only does this record of the active decision-making by the Mayors' Conference throw a shadow of real doubt over the content of the 13 December letter to the SG and over the concept of passive collaboration by reluctant and recalcitrant local Belgian officials in the cities, towns and villages of the country, but it also again demonstrates the strength of Vivian Curran's insights into the phenomenon of democratic suicide. Two weeks before the official juridical framework of the legal limits of participation had been set forth by the Permanent Council, the assembled chief elected officials of Brussels and environs had decided to proceed, as ordered, with the registration of the Jewish inhabitants of the capital, and without further reference to the Germans. The historically dominant image of a passive, non-compliant, resisting local government structure must always be understood in this context. The deliberations and participation of local administrations did not end there.

Six days later, on 16 November, the Mayors' Conference met again to establish in still more detail the ways and means through which the identities of and information concerning the Jews for Brussels would be entered into the Register. Eleven separate decisions concerning the registration process were taken at this meeting.[25] I shall outline only a few of them here, but the number of decisions on individual "Jewish" issues alone serves once more to indict the legal mythology of passive collaboration in its own words and on its own terms. The decisions themselves demonstrate how five days before the elaboration of the limits and extent of unlawful participation by the Permanent Council, the highest elected officials of the Brussels region were going far beyond what was permitted under the law. At the very least, they showed initiative if not in substantive terms, then clearly in establishing the mechanisms of registration in a practical and functional way.

Inter alia the assembled mayors decided that, as a matter of policy and practice, they would immediately put the Decree into effect without involving themselves in its application in any way. In other words, they begin with an attempt to delimit the actions which they would take in order to position the Belgian administration as merely passive appliers of the German will. They attempted on their own to deliberate and decide the difference between participation and *participation*. They confirmed at this time that they would not "send away for a later date, Jews who present themselves for inclusion on the ad hoc register. The Administration has not at this time the task of determining who is considered a Jew according to the Decree."[26] On this issue, the city decided to comply with the impending deadline imposed by the Order and in the absence of further and better particulars or instructions from the German military administration or from the SG. They planned to produce and create an "ad hoc register" in which all of the information required by the Order would be entered.[27] Without official guidelines as to the procedure and format to be followed and used in the Register of Jews, ad hoc measures which complied with the Order would be taken by the city administration and officials.

> For each Jew who presents himself and comes to declare himself, a provisional file card (*fiche*) will be established. This file card will be completed later in the manner indicated by the occupying authority. The Population Offices will take no other initiative.[28]

Again, the mayors are anxious to comply without participating. They attempt to strike the fine line identified subsequently by the Permanent Council between mere compliance and active participation. The consistent use of the reflexive verb structure and the apparently purely administrative nature of the measures to be taken – ad hoc, provisional forms until official lawful orders were taken – all reflect the way in which the local administration and the elected officials of Brussels from the very beginning of their part in the application of anti-Jewish Orders positioned themselves as "administrators" of lawful orders and of the will of the Jews themselves. Any idea of responsibility, ethical or legal, is eliminated as passive collaboration takes root and Jews in Brussels are identified by city officials at the request of the victims. The Conference at its 14 November meeting clearly decided that this grammatical construction was essential to ensure its position on the question of the Register of Jews.

Moreover they would "await the declaration of the interested parties and have them sign".[29] City officials again become in this official process mere transcribers of the will of the Jews. They await the declaration and have the interested party sign the declaration identifying himself as a Jew. No one is to be sent away either because the final procedures for the official version of the Register have not been confirmed or because there might be some question as to whether they are individuals to whom the Order applies. A Jew is simply someone who registers himself as a Jew. The city has no other function than to enter that expression of free will into the Register. The matter is one, as always, in which the city takes no active role. This is confirmed in a literal fashion by the formal inscription which the officials decide must appear on every identity card of every Jew who presents themselves for registration.

> Place on the front of the first page of the identity card "Has requested his entry in the Register of Jews". (Bilingual text)[30]

Registered Jews will carry forward, thanks to the mayors and bureaucrats of Brussels, the graphic reminder of their new status as Jews, the new lawful category of non-citizen entered into the official records of the municipality. The simple inscription "Jew" however was completely out of the question. The identity card had to carry absolutely no connotation that the administration had played an active role in naming, labeling and classifying anyone as a "Jew". Passive collaboration had to be the practice literally and figuratively inscribed in all legal bureaucratic practice.

> ... as a result, the inscription placed by the Municipal Population Office on the identity card must not allow it to be believed or to be asserted that the administration has classified someone as a Jew. It must appear clearly that it is the interested party who has come to declare himself.[31]

While § 4 of the Jewish Order required the marking of the identity card of registered Jews, it set out only that the registration itself be mentioned. The subtle but crucial distinction in the approach adopted by the city officials in Brussels is the step whereby the Jews are made, by bureaucratic fiat, to accept responsibility for their own registration, thereby once more literally absolving the city of any participation before *participation* became the operative legal and constitutional limiting marker.

No matter how carefully the city officials may have wished to construct themselves as mere passive collaborators, active steps above and beyond the terms of the Decree were taken.[32] Decisions made at the 16 November meeting also involved the unification of the records of Jews who "entered themselves" at the Municipal Records Office and those whose files were found in the Aliens' Office (Bureau des Étrangers) into one register.[33] This clearly involved at some level of bureaucratic activity an investigation into Jews found in the files of the administrative office dealing with foreigners. Since, insofar as citizenship and equality as guaranteed by the Belgian Constitution were concerned, no one would be entered in these files as a Jew, a category unknown to a country the fundamental and founding principles of which recognized the equality of all, some form of participation or investigation for the improved efficacy of the Decree was required. Moreover, the assembled mayors also decided that in the records of the Municipal Registry of Births, Deaths and Marriages and in those held by the Aliens' Office, the files of these individuals who had been identified (not who had in every case identified themselves), should be marked with the letter J.[34]

Nowhere in the German Jewish Order is such a step required as a matter of law. Instead, this is a spontaneous measure undertaken and decided, without instructions from the German Military Command or the SG, by the highest elected officials of the local governments of the Brussels region. For what appears to have been the sake of complete and accurate up-to-date bureaucratic record-keeping, consistency and efficiency, the city of Brussels inscribed, literally and figuratively, their official files with the mark J which identified and, by defining, excluded the Jewish inhabitants of the city.

All of this decision-making seems to have occurred in an atmosphere of urgency and with a desire to efficiently set up the machinery for the imminent registration of Jews in the city. Not only were the mayors concerned about the rapidly impending 30 November deadline for the completion of the registration of Brussels' Jews, but they were anxious to find out what the situation was as far as the SG were concerned. The "protest" about the 6 December circular from Adam again takes on a different and more interesting light.

> As a result, since the declarations must be made before 30 November ... one of our civil servants telephoned the Ministry of the Interior, in order to learn if any decision or instructions were to be given. The response was negative. Today however it would appear that that Department has decided to take an interest in the question because M. Warans, head of the Population

Department, was requested to send a copy of the model card which was designed by your Departments and adopted by the delegates of the various towns of the region, at a meeting at the City Hall last Saturday, presided over by Councilor Verhaeghe de Naeyer.[35]

Again, the historically constructed and narrated passive city of Brussels, with its elected officials and employees, sitting idly by, doing as little as possible to comply with the odious German anti-Jewish Order, seems a somewhat bucolic and distorted image in light of the documents issued and circulated by these officials and employees. Instead of the mythological resistance by obfuscation, delay and bureaucratic lethargy, the records are full of memos, meetings, debates, concerns about bureaucratic methodologies and decisions; the daily bread of administrative structures everywhere. **J** marks the spot.

At some point in time after this flurry of activity, however, the mayors of the Brussels region had an apparent change of heart. At their meeting of 21 November they decided that they should, before making any definitive decisions, await further instructions from the occupying authority. Indeed, instead of entering Jews in an ad hoc register, it now seems to have been decided that it would be best to grant to any Jew presenting himself for registration a note indicating that he had done so, but that because no instructions had been received from the occupying authorities, he could not be registered.[36] This marked change of attitude by the Conference of Mayors, backtracking from their previous decisions to create provisional and ad hoc registration documents and procedures, to not seek further instructions from the SG or the occupying authority, coincides with the constitutional opinion of the Permanent Council by something more than mere chance. From the active steps, the meetings, discussions, debates, agreements on wording and process, to the sudden halt in proceedings, only one intervening factor can be found in the official, legal and constitutional framework under which the city and its elected officials and public employees were acting. The idea of participation was now being defined and enshrined as the hermeneutic framework within which passive collaboration was to be understood and practiced under law.

The idea and ideal image of the mayors waiting further instructions from their hierarchical superiors, the SG, as set out in the letter of "protest" is nonetheless belied by their own parliamentary record. The idea of resistance by legality, of the assembled mayors standing on a literal interpretation of the anti-Jewish Orders by insisting that the Order itself required the Military Command to take decisions about the practical modalities of the registration process, is, to put it mildly, absurd. It is rendered unbelievable by the initiative shown in this period between the publication of the Orders and the Permanent Council's constitutional hair-splitting; initiative which was clearly outside the strict limit of participation as non-*participation* as outlined by the Permanent Council days later. At some level, bureaucratic routine and administrative efficiency were now apparently being formally restrained by a new legally informed understanding of the limits on acceptable collaboration. Temporarily at least, the bureaucratic process of registration for the city's Jewish population appears to have come to a halt out of concern for the rule of law.

Indeed, this appears to have been the real legal reason which informed the letter of protest sent by Van de Meulebroeck on 13 December. Once the official constitutionally recognized taxonomy of unlawful participation had been established and clarified, it must have become evident to the elected officials that there would be, at the very least, serious legal doubts about their decision-making processes as evidenced at their meeting of 12 November, and the subsequent events and steps undertaken in pursuance of a policy and practice of ad hoc registration for Jews. They had, on their own records of activity, taken the initiative by rejecting the idea of referring any further questions to the Germans and setting up their own administrative structures and arrangements for the registration process. If that were the case, their actions were arguably in clear violation of their oaths of office and of their legal obligations as elected officials. Penal sanctions, the Permanent Council had made clear, would be imposed on any Belgian official found to be in such a breach of his constitutional duty to the nation.

The fine jurisprudential line between criminal participation and passive collaboration, Bauman's gray area between bystander and perpetrator, the distinction between resistance and collaboration, all come into stark contrast when examining and understanding these documents, from the memo to the mayor to the letter of protest which would follow two weeks later. The hierarchical dynamic set out in the 13 December reply seems the mirror opposite of everything the municipality had actually done heretofore. The local authorities were concerned about the position of the Ministry of the Interior. They contacted the central authorities who requested the registration form which already existed. The form, established by the Brussels area governments, was sent at the request of the Interior Ministry and its subsequent use as the template in the 6 December circular from Adam can hardly seem surprising in the circumstances. Even more important for a proper understanding of the events in Brussels, and for weighing of the evidence, historical, ethical and legal, on the question of passive collaboration, are two other elements of the memo to the mayor and the inscription of the mythology of resistance, reluctance and compulsion in the protest to Adam.[37]

First it emerges that the standard and standardized form for the registration and exclusion of the Jews of Brussels and of Belgium was constructed not just by "certain municipal employees" as Van de Meulebroeck asserted on 13 December, but by employees more directly responsible to the mayor himself (your Departments, *vos Services*) and following detailed discussion by the Conference of Mayors. The drafting of the model form for the registration process was not simply the work of overzealous or efficient, forward-looking municipal employees acting on their own initiative. Instead it was created by city workers responsible to the Mayor's Office. Nor is Van de Meulebroeck's assertion on 13 December that the Conference of Mayors had not approved the form the entire story. If it were, the narrative of resistance, reluctance and compliance by compulsion might have at this early stage of the legal history of the registration process more persuasive power and appeal.

As the memo clearly sets out, while the Collège des Bourgmestres may not have approved the model registration form, representatives of all the municipalities of greater Brussels, in a meeting chaired by the elected member of the Council with special responsibility for population matters, at the City Hall, had given their stamp of approval to the form. Other documents in the official records establish beyond any doubt that the mayors were ready, willing and able to proceed with an ad hoc registration form using provisional documentation. They had had careful discussions about how to construct the formulation for the stamp to be entered into each registered Jew's identity card, which would indicate that the registration had occurred but only at the behest of the Jews themselves. The elected officials had decided, over and above what was required by the German Order, to identify Jews in the files and records of the Aliens' Office in a unified way. They had further decided to mark the files of Jews there and elsewhere in the bureaucratic record-keeping system of the city of Brussels, still operating under the Belgian Constitution, with a **J**. Again, this was a step not required by passive collaboration nor was it consistent with the legal discourse of obfuscation, refusal, objection and resistance used to portray local governments in postwar proceedings and records. Thus, while Van de Meulebroeck is technically correct in his assertion that no decision had been reached by the Conference of Mayors, the fact remains that a variety of levels of municipal officials in Brussels, all ultimately answerable to the mayor himself, had been, and continued to be, actively involved in constructing the mechanisms for the registration of Jews in Brussels before the Permanent Council of Legislation had established the acceptable legal and constitutional framework of non-collaborative "collaboration". It is at least arguable on the historical record that the mayors of the Brussels region had every interest in protesting any implication in Adam's letter to authorities throughout the country that they had taken any steps which might fall outside the line of acceptable, constrained and legally justified collaboration. They needed to construct a documentary record, if only a *post hoc* one, which would establish that they had not done anything which might have constituted participation as now defined by the Permanent Council, precisely because they had clearly acted unlawfully up to that time in their rush to set up the mechanisms and structures necessary for the establishment of the Register of Jews.

One final, explicitly legal point comes out of the memo of 21 November to Van de Meulebroeck. It serves to highlight the historical fact that on the very day on which the Permanent Council was handing down its formulation of constitutionally appropriate behavior, the mayor was continuing to cover himself and his administration in the blanket of legally permissible passivity. This is another example of the early and uninterrupted construction of the Jews themselves as the active parties in the legal sense. They request their registration and the municipal authorities merely comply. Thus while there was perhaps some overzealous and "active" elaboration of the practical aspects of the registration process by local authorities in Brussels, activity which needed to be reinscribed in a more acceptable juridical framework by the 13 December letter to Adam, the Brussels officials from the very beginning shared in the broader jurisprudential understanding of the Jews as responsible actors in their own registration.

> From the legal point of view, the Population Department which has studied it, is now in a position to answer any questions which might be asked of it, but I believe that, as am I, you will be of the opinion, in accordance with the Decree, that it is up to the sole interested parties to decide, yes or no, if they must request their registration.[38]

The municipal officials and elected officers had already reached the conclusion that the question of who was or was not a Jew was not for them to decide and that they would limit their employees' activities and functions to entering details of individuals who identified themselves as Jews by the simple juridically binding act of presenting themselves for registration. Indeed, as a matter of fact and of law, Van de Meulebroeck would continue to assert the position that the registration process was always up to the Jews and that it was on this basis that he agreed to set up the Register in the first place. Questioned in the framework of postwar investigations into possible illegal collaboration by government officials during the occupation, the mayor of Brussels stated for the legal and historical record:

> As far as my own case is concerned, I consented to the opening of the Register on which Jews had to enter their names pursuant to the Decree, because I considered that they had the choice of registering themselves or not. They had this choice of complying or not complying with the Decree. I had received requests from several Jews wishing to register themselves in order to be in compliance. Only one Jew wrote me a protest letter.[39]

Not only is this the typical and consistent invocation of Jewish responsibility and agency which typifies the non-Jewish Belgian official position throughout the occupation and beyond, with the concomitant and necessary reflexive verb forms characteristic of these legal self-justifying documents, but here Van de Meulebroeck goes one grammatical step beyond. He uses, when explaining his "consent" to the opening of the Register of Jews, the past perfect tense *j'ai consenti*. When attributing active agency to Jews, however, he employs the pluperfect, "I had received" *j'avais reçu*. Thus, at the level of the semiotics and rhetorical construction of the legal history of passive collaboration, Van de Meulebroeck sets out the creation of the Register of Jews in Brussels under his administration and aegis as, in part, the result of requests from Jews who were anxious to comply with the German Order. Not only was it up to the Jews themselves to decide whether to register or not, the traditional formulation of passive collaboration, but the Register was established at their behest. In such circumstances, the actions by the mayor and the various city employees involved in the registration process could in no way be understood or defined in terms of *participation*. But is his postwar reconstruction of the historical record accurate?

At the point in time up to the Permanent Council's letter of 21 November, there is abundant evidence which indicates two patterns of bureaucratic self-legitimating behavior and practice. On the one hand, there was a long history of preparation and decision-making in relation to the registration process and the Register of Jews. On the other, there is also a consistent rhetorical and semiotic construction of the process as one in which the Jews actively participate and the bureaucrats and elected officials of Brussels simply concretize their wishes to be identified for the Germans as legally defined Jews. What happens after the letter of 21 November from the Permanent Council is that many of the preparatory acts are put on hold pending lawful instructions from the Germans. The construction of passivity continues in official documents as does that of the active and voluntary participation of the Jews. The subtle change which is required after 21 November is that all the preparatory acts must appear to have been merely administrative in nature. If they fit into a more active taxonomical structure, then the Brussels area governments would have been guilty of collaboration in the anti-Jewish measures. At the heart of the letter of early December in reply to Adam's missive and Van de Meulebroeck's postwar testimony appears to have been this awareness that the month of November 1940 was characterized by overzealousness and perhaps illegality on the question of registering Jews. The Conference of Mayors is anxious to go on the record in order to negate any inference which might have been drawn from the Circular to officials in the rest of the country that they had taken the initiative in registering Jews or even in constructing the registration form, since "any initiative, all investigations or complementary steps, with the aim of ensuring the full efficacy"[40] of the anti-Jewish Orders would have been a clear violation of Belgian law.

The Van de Meulebroeck letter (and his postwar testimony) can only be read as an attempt to "salt" the judicial files by creating an official correspondence between the Brussels' officials and the SG putting on the official record written evidence of their non-compliance with the German Order and their status as mere passive collaborators as permitted by Belgian law. The Permanent Council had confirmed the SG's argument that anti-Jewish Decrees could not be incorporated as such into Belgian law. It had also drawn a line between collaboration and participation. This is the juridical framework into which the Van de Meulebroeck letter must be placed, because it appears to have been the juridical framework into which the author wished to place himself and his elected colleagues.

The Jews of Brussels "register themselves": passive collaboration continued

Whatever the historical conclusion about the pre-21 November record may be, once the Permanent Council had rendered its "decision" and given its constitutional imprimatur to participation which was not *participation* in the implementation of German anti-Jewish Orders by Belgian officials, the process of identifying, excluding, expropriating and ultimately killing Belgian Jews could proceed in a lawful, constitutional and Belgian fashion.

The correspondence and other files for the post-21 November 1940 period offer an intriguing record of the continuities and discontinuities which marked bureaucratic and legal practice on the problems surrounding the implementation of the First Jewish Order. On the following day, M. Joostens, Director of the Office of Births, Marriages and Deaths, wrote to the College of Mayors requesting clarification about the actual registration process.[41] In his report to the College, the bureaucrat in charge of much of the practical implementation of the process of creating and maintaining the Register of Jews underlines the confusion between the position adopted on 12 November and subsequent clarifications and the position adopted the previous day, following the Permanent Council's decision, about the state of operations to be carried out by the city employees. Did they send Jews seeking registration away or did they register them, albeit in a provisional fashion? What was to be done about entering the appropriate notice on identity cards and in the various files of the Aliens' Office and the Office of Births, Deaths and Marriages? In other words, could they register Jews as the law required or should they wait further instructions from the appropriate authorities as the law also indicated? How could they do so, in either case, lawfully? In addition to concern over the status of the legal process for registration itself, M. Joostens underlined for the College of Mayors the practical impact of the question and the response thereto.

> The above question to the College has a particular practical interest, in the sense that if no entry can be made at the present time – contrary to the provisions of the Decree itself – the Office of Births, Deaths and Marriages would not be able to continue to place, on the identity cards of Jews who come to make a declaration, the notice: "has requested his entry in the Register of Jews" and could not moreover place the initial J., at the time of the registration of interested parties, in the Registry of the Office of Births, Deaths and Marriages (an indication which is indispensable for the proper functioning of the Office).[42]

Otherwise, the bureaucrats would only be able to rely on the decision of the mayors and proceed by way of taking a note of the name and address of Jews who might come to declare themselves and nothing more. The Jews, he adds, could be summoned later on, once the proper instructions of the German military authority had been received.

This letter from one of the principal bureaucrats in charge of the registration of Jews in Brussels to his political masters is highly instructive and informative. It demonstrates at one level that the conflict between pre-21 November decisions and actions to be taken subsequent to the clarification of the proper legal framework for passive collaboration had troubling practical implications for the bureaucrats of the city of Brussels. Second, it also gives a strong indication that the registration of Jews, the stamping of documents with the formula indicating that the individual had requested his entry into the Register and the use of the **J** in other city files, was already under way in Brussels before the Permanent Council had reached its legal conclusions on the question of participation and well before the official notice of 13 December had been posted throughout the city.

According to the note, bureaucrats could not continue (*ne pourrait pas continuer*) the processes of registration and marking. Given the tenses employed here by the civil servant to describe the current situation, and his concerns about them, he was clearly worried about having to stop a process of registration and inscription which was already under way. If this is the case, the mayor's subsequent assertion in his letter to Adam that, while some employees had taken preliminary measures to prepare for the obligations for registration under the Decree, there had been no actual active steps taken by the city is further subverted. It seems almost certain that, as far as those in charge of the Office of Births, Deaths and Marriages in Brussels were concerned, identity documents had been inscribed and files had already been stamped **J**.

A third point which emerges is the air of ambiguity and uncertainty which continued to surround understandings of the meaning and extent of unlawful participation apparently elucidated by the Permanent Council. The Director wrote that if the process as practiced were to be stopped, the city employees would have to note the names and addresses of anyone presenting themselves for registration and await German instructions before "summoning" (*convoquer*) the Jews to return. Such a course of action, as set forth here by the head of the administrative agency of the city of Brussels charged with ensuring the registration of Jews, would probably have violated the terms of acceptable action set out by the Permanent Council which explicitly placed "any initiative, all investigations or complementary steps with the aim of ensuring the full efficacy" of the Orders outside actions which would be acceptable under Belgian law. Summoning individual Jews, who had already been identified, to return to the offices of city employees to complete the registration process would in all likelihood fall within these areas of prohibited conduct. The conflict here which would haunt the entire process of the application of anti-Jewish Orders throughout the occupation was one between the limits imposed by Belgian law as interpreted by the Permanent Council and the exigencies of daily administrative practice. Again, this is the reason that the Public Notice issued by the City under the signature of Van de Meulebroeck on 13 December was 1) addressed to all Jews, 2) couched in terms which indicated that the order came first from the Germans and second from the SG for the Interior and 3) used the passive verb constructions which are by now familiar.

The inscription of the letter **J** in the files of the Aliens' Office and in the Office of Births, Deaths and Marriages was a step beyond that which was required by a reluctant, resisting, literal adherence to the letter of the anti-Jewish law which is the key component of postwar narratives. In this letter to his elected superiors,

Joostens highlights not just the fact that the practice was probably already under way in municipal offices in Brussels, but that it had been undertaken for the sake of internal bureaucratic efficiency. In other words, not only was this step not taken as part of the reluctant compliance with oppressive German military commands, but it was not taken as part of any process other than one of the inherent logic and functioning of an office of the city of Brussels administration. "What bureaucracy needed was the definition of its task. Rational and efficient as it was, it could be trusted to see the task to its end."[43]

The designation, the marking, **J** of the Jews of Brussels, not only on the identity documents they carried with them, but in addition in the other records of the city administration, not identified or required in the German Orders, is a process which marks and inscribes, literally and figuratively, a semiotics of bureaucratic, legal and legitimate classification and exclusion contrary to the founding principles of the Belgian Constitution but perhaps not contrary to the jurisprudential framework of constitutional government and law operating in Belgium at the time. Jews are marked by the bureaucracy, **J,** categorized and more fundamentally, differentiated from their fellows through and by law. And all, according to a top official, recorded in his unselfconscious bureaucratic style, for the "efficient operation of the Office" (*pour la bonne marche du Service*).

Meanwhile the bureaucratic wheels continued to turn, albeit in a slower and more obviously passive way, in part at least. On 27 November, a letter was sent to the Governor of the Province of Brabant, Baron Houtart, informing him that the "Jewish Undertaking" signs had not yet been printed as the city of Brussels awaited further details for the implementation of the anti-Jewish law from the Ministry of the Interior.[44]

This did not mean, however, that bureaucrats remained idly by while central authorities set about their work. On 13 December, the day the notice to Jews about the registration of individuals and businesses was finalized, the city Registry Office contacted the City Secretary about the content of the notice. Among other queries and suggestions, the Office asked "Do you not think that the notice could usefully include an indication that the identity card of all Jewish persons over the age of fifteen must be presented?"[45] Once again the bureaucracy is concerned not with issues of ethics, or even of constitutional principle, but about the efficient functioning of the Registration Office. If the file card which is to be used is the form already developed by the bureaucrats of the city administration in every case and if the identity cards of all Jews must carry the notice that a Jew "requested his entry in the Register of Jews", it would be much less onerous and much more efficient if the people who had to "register themselves" were notified that they must come equipped with their identity cards. As with the question of the **J** on internal files, this appears to be a classic case of bureaucratic structures engaging in their own internal processes and logics regardless of content, in order to ensure compliance with the law to the extent that the compliance in question also fulfills the bureaucratic imperative. The Belgian Constitution's guarantees of equality and religious freedom, even, it would appear, the opinion of the Permanent Council, take a back seat to the inherent logic of the administrative structures and practices of the city. Jews need to be identified and they need to register themselves, City employees need to stamp their identity cards. It would be in everyone's interest if the Jews were put on notice to bring the cards along for their self-registration.

The Office of Births, Deaths and Marriages was a busy place from mid-December 1940 until the end of the month. The SG had obtained an extension from the original 30 November registration deadline until the end of the year from the occupying authority. Jews were told on the public notice that the registration would proceed by alphabetical order from Monday 16 December until Friday 20 December. Monday and Tuesday, 23 and 24 December, were set aside for all latecomers. Registration would be complete in time for the (Christian) holiday. The bureaucratic structure had been making ready (and indeed appears to have begun the process itself) for some time. Certain details remained to be finalized. In the middle of the week of the registration, two documents circulated in the Office of Births, Deaths and Marriages refining and clarifying the administrative processes for registration.

In the first of these, dated 18 December, the Director referred to the provisions of § 3 (2)(a) and (b) and (3) of the First Order concerning Jews. The Decree required the registration by the head of each household of all members of his family. Everyone who subsequently reached the age of 15 had three days after that date to present themselves for individual registration. The three-day declaration period also applied to all changes in relation to the information entered in the registration form, and to births and deaths. When a registered Jew changed abode, the competent authority in the former place of residence was required to forward the file card (*la fiche de juif*) to the Registry Office in the new area of residence. In the first change in procedure adopted by the city of Brussels, the inscription "entered in the Register of Jews" was to be recorded in all birth, death and marriage records (*y compris sur les minutes d'actes de marriage*) held by the city.[46] Whether deliberately or by slip of the bureaucratic typewriter, the formula had changed in a significant way. No longer did the entry indicate that the individual had required his own registration, but instead it relates the simple fact of his registration.

Perhaps more importantly, this note for employees dealing with the records of the registration process highlights again that, despite the constitutional prohibition on initiative, the city bureaucrats were already extending the arm of classification and exclusion. Marriage records were to be marked with the notice that the person was a registered Jew even though the Order itself refers specifically only to birth and death records. Once more, bureaucratic processes, efficacy and completeness, thorough record-keeping and efficiency, *la bonne marche* of the Office, extends by a self-legitimating process the evil consequences of Nazi racial taxonomy. Jews are marked, inscribed and excluded not by German law, or Gestapo thugs, but by Belgian civil servants, employed by the city of Brussels; civil servants who take it upon themselves to extend, clarify and make more efficient the process of separating the Jews of Brussels from their fellows. The mythological structures of a historical memory inscribed with official narratives of resistance and refusal come face to face with a set of bureaucratic practices, internal to the Brussels administration and with no relation to German compulsion, under which the ideals of Belgian constitutional guarantees of liberty and equality are eliminated by the new Belgian legal practice of categorizing "Jews" in a bureaucratically comprehensive manner.

The next day, the Director of the Registry again clarified and expanded upon the role of Brussels and its employees in the registration process. In addition to reiterating the goals and nature of the process and its detailed requirements, he once again evidenced the requirements of bureaucratic efficiency which required him, for the internal purposes of the city of Brussels, to exceed the strict limits of what was demanded of him by the Decree. He informed his subalterns charged with the process that they must "indicate in the column 'previous registration' in the population registry the letter **J** in red for every person for whom a file card (*fiche*) has been created".[47]

The Director of Births, Deaths and Marriages also required his subordinates to take official notice of any change of residence by Jews within the city of Brussels. In such cases, "indicate in the observations on change of residence column a **J** in order to allow for a change in the file card".[48] The absurdity, when faced with this historical record, of the myths of resistance, of passive compliance, of obfuscation by local officials is confirmed once more by the internal records of the administration. This marking of the file of residents of Brussels with a red **J** is not part of the demands of the German military authority. Nor do the Germans require that internal change of residence documents and records be marked with a **J**. The Jewish Order, § 3 (2)(a), sets out that any change of relevant information, including here the address of a registered Jew, must be declared to the relevant authority within the three-day period, and § 3 (3) requires that on changes of residence or domicile the card should be transferred to the newly competent municipal authority. The Decree is silent insofar as the change of address of a registered Jew within the same Registry District is concerned, except by providing that change of address information be recorded. The Decree therefore was not relevant at this level to changes of address inside the same administrative area. In any event, the entry of the **J** in a document relating to change of address was simply not a requirement imposed by any German Decree. This marking is a Belgian act, a Brussels decision, writing by local officials of the Jew as a subject apart, a legal pariah, a new category of legal subject, "the Jew".

It matters little if any of these bureaucratic acts were motivated by evil intentions, by overt or even latent antisemitism. Collaboration at some level, or at least on one understanding of the taxonomy, like its opposite, resistance, does not require ,intentionality or motive. The creation of the new legal subject "the Jew". inscribed **J** throughout the record-holding structures of the administration of the city of Brussels, itself is an antisemitic act, or an act with antisemitic effect. The "Jew" is now the bureaucratic and legalized Other, created, marked, disciplined throughout the large machinery of the state at the local level in Belgium's capital city. This does not mean that actual anti-Jewish sentiment did not exist or, more cogently here perhaps, that the construction of "the Jew" as a new legal subject outside understandings of citizenship, membership in the body politic and beyond the protective norms of constitutional guarantees, was not a complex process which was indeed always informed by an underlying broadly understood construction of the Jew as somehow not Belgian. Indeed, in the next set of documents relating to the registration process the intimate connection between overt antisemitism and bureaucratic and political discourses of compliance and legality becomes clearer.

On 16 December 1940, in the middle of the administrative process of registering Jews in Brussels, Van de Meulebroeck received an anonymous letter signed by "a group of Brussels citizens" (*un groupe de Bruxellois*) informing him of an unacceptable bureaucratic inconsistency.[49] According to these concerned citizens, while the stamp used to mark the identity cards of Brussels' Jews was easily noticeable because of its size, the officials in the town of Schaerbeek were using a stamp which was only three centimeters long by one centimeter in height. This smaller stamp was for them much too discreet to allow for the quick and easy identification of Jews.

The letter was sent to the Director, who replied to the city councilor with special responsibility for the Registry of Births, Deaths and Marriages, Verhaeghe de Naeyer, and eventually forwarded to the mayor.[50] The letter contains a copy of the stamp used by the city of Brussels and again underlines that the wording is that approved by the Conference of Mayors. He concludes by offering the opinion that: "If at Schaerbeek they have been able to reduce the format of the stamp, it is presumably because they have not respected the required formulation."[51]

After making further inquiries at the behest of the mayor, the Director could subsequently confirm that two different stamps had been used by the authorities in Schaerbeek. The first, which measured four centimeters and not three as the original anonymous letter had asserted, was no longer in use. In fact, he went on to explain, the authorities had abandoned the first stamp when it became clear that the inscription needed to state clearly that every entry in the Register of Jews had been requested by the interested party.[52] The stamp used in Brussels proper was nine and a half centimeters long and the letters larger.[53] Even these few probably incomplete documents offer some evidence not just of the fact that the mayor, councilors and top-ranking civil servants in Brussels in the midst of the registration process were willing and able to take the time to investigate the assertions of anonymous letter-writers about the size of the official stamp used to mark the identity cards of registered Jews, but that they did so in a routine fashion.

The councilor in charge of the administrative agency was informed, the head of the department was charged with the investigation, officials at the level of local town administration in Schaerbeek were contacted and the story of the stamps was told with examples as proof. Nowhere is there any indication that the officials at any level treated this case with anything but the utmost seriousness and vigor. Uniformity in the use of the formula indicating that the person in question requested his entry into the Register of Jews was vital. Jews, registration, stamps etc. were by December 1940 just a matter of bureaucratic routine and daily practice. This is not the overzealous inclusion of a **J** in a variety of files, nor is it obstruction, obfuscation, delay or resistance. Instead it is the proper functioning (*la bonne marche*) of local government.

As the registration in its first phase drew to a close in late December 1940, other administrative documents from the city continue to evidence one of two operative characteristics. First there is the practice of bureaucratic normalcy in which the "Jewish question" simply becomes another issue with which the employees of the city of Brussels had to deal. The second pattern is one in which, despite the constitutional prohibition on any initiative in enforcing or perfecting the anti-Jewish Decree, public servants in the capital nonetheless made apparently independent decisions about matters which arose in the course of dealing with the implementation of the Order. What these phenomena of bureaucratic normalcy and occasional administrative spontaneous decision-making share is that neither fits nicely and without question into the postwar legal myths of Nuremberg and investigations of the Belgian government which constructed a history of non-compliance, slowdowns, overwork and understaffing as forms of collaboration which was really passive resistance.

Files from the mayor's office for the occupation period include the "List of Temporary Agents Employed for the Creation of the Register of Jews (Population Office) and Released from Employment on 28 December".[54] The list of the fourteen employees let go after the first phase of the registration process was terminated offers on its face some foundation for the assertion that understaffing was an issue, as postwar arguments would have it. But the list indicates as well that the city did not hesitate to engage temporary workers in order to complete the task. This was not subversion of the Nazi racial policy but compliance. Unless of course one wants to read into the reasons for dismissal of the fourteen an idea that subversion of the process took place through the indirect means of hiring incompetents to register Jews in the city's records. Such an argument might be based on the fact that one employee was dismissed because of extreme slowness, one was dismissed because of a complete lack of education and one because they could not write properly. The others were released because they were generally mediocre employees. Of course, such an argument about subversion would be somewhat more persuasive if the registration process had been slowed or stopped but that was not the case. Brussels completed its registration of local Jews and Jewish businesses even when encumbered with these dim-witted incompetents. Five of the temporary employees were allowed to remain in their posts, obviously because the work of processing all the information on Brussels' Jews was not yet fully finished. On 24 February 1941, in reply to a German letter, city of Brussels officials were able to confirm M. Joostens's assertion that "the City has accomplished its mission. The municipal administration of Brussels is unaware of any Jews living within the city limits who have not registered."[55]

By way of contrast and comparison, the reaction of the city and its officials when they were faced with a request to provide the German authorities with a list of those of its residents who were from the region of Alsace-Lorraine incorporated into the Reich is instructive. In that case a form of resistance or refusal to comply based on its surface at least in bureaucratic impossibility and insurmountable practical obstacles can be found in city files. The mayor of the district of Saint-Josse-ten-Noode stated to the local police that such information was impossible to produce because the population registers simply contained the place of birth without any indication of the region.[56] M. Joostens of the Office of Births, Marriages and Deaths, who had no difficulty just five months earlier compiling the Jewish Register, informed Chief of Police Gilta that it was impossible to comply with the German request. He explained that city officials would have to review all the records for every inhabitant of Brussels for their place of birth, since a search of French or German citizens would not catch those who, while born in Alsace or Lorraine, might have acquired another nationality. Three other difficulties also arose. First, a large number of employees would be required for the task. Second, except in cases involving well-known towns, employees would need to refer to an atlas of some sort in order to determine if a birth place in fact was in Alsace-Lorraine. The Aliens' Office possessed only one atlas, rendering the task practically impossible. Finally, Joostens identified one further obstacle. A simple cost-benefit analysis made the job a waste of time. Considering the resources involved, the number of individuals in question would in all likelihood be small.[57]

In the Alsatian case, a series of practical bureaucratic roadblocks was thrown up by local administrators to "refuse" to comply with an order from the German authorities. This is either the triumph of pragmatism or an example of the administrative resistance so exalted as part of the mythology of the local government history of Belgian patriotism under occupation. It stands as a stark contrast to the attitude adopted by the same officials to the task of registering Jews. In that case, there was no thought of offering objections based, for example, on the number of employees who would need to be involved, let alone on an assertion that the Belgian Constitution prohibited any such categorization of the city's residents. Instead, extra help was hired. Alsatians were too hard to register and the pay off was too small. Jews on the other hand "register themselves" and the question of the result and its benefit was either self-evident to Joostens and others or such a consideration was simply beyond them.

Another part of the registration process also sheds some useful light on the postwar, historically dominant narrative of obfuscation, refusal, delay, etc. The list of establishments which now carried the appropriate and legally compulsory "Jewish Undertaking" sign compiled at the end of the registration process, on 24 December, and transmitted through the bureaucracy of the Population Office and Department of Births, Deaths and Marriages, listed only eight restaurants or drinking places.[58] All but one now carried the appropriate signage. Only the restaurant of Jacob-Israël Rubenstein, rue du Midi 61, was exempted by administrative decision from being identified as a Jewish undertaking. City employees continued (unlawfully?) to exercise their discretion as to how to apply the Decree. M. Rubenstein's restaurant was in fact spared the imposition of public labeling not out of any subversive intent by the bureaucrats in charge of the registration process, nor out of some sense of solidarity for a small businessman singled out for discrimination and possible humiliation because of his religion or race. Instead the motivating factor for the bureaucrats was the inconvenience the signage might cause to non-Jews.

> This restaurant is installed on the second floor, it has no sign or written indication of any kind which could make the public aware of it. Placing the placard would be such as to cause harm to the non-Jewish firms which are situated in the same building and for which the signs are announced on the entry door.[59]

This decision not to require the "Jewish Undertaking" sign in the Rubenstein case is without doubt an initiative taken by city employees in interpreting and applying the terms of the anti-Jewish Order (§ 13) which required all restaurants of which the owner or lessee was a Jew or a Jewish commercial enterprise to carry the appropriate sign. The only further clarifications or specifications found in the Decree itself are that the sign must be in three languages, German, Flemish and French, and that it must be easily visible (*bien visible*) in the French-language version under which the employees were operating. There is no exception or exemption for any reason set out in the Order. The justification given by the city is clearly an explanation which is outside the strict wording of the law. The city officials in Brussels charged with the implementation of the anti-Jewish Order exceed at their own initiative the strict limits and obligations imposed by the German authorities on the Belgian state apparatus. Moreover, the concept of a legal taxonomy in which there are Jewish businesses and non-Jewish businesses is accepted as a fact of bureaucratic life. Indeed, this distinction becomes one which the officials themselves actively enforce in exempting M. Rubenstein's establishment. Once the law imposed on them an obligation to enforce anti-Jewish measures, the bureaucrats of Brussels adapted themselves to the epistemological worldview of the occupiers without objection, qualms or moral dilemmas. This is not the world of bureaucratic obfuscation and resistance to German anti-semitism of popular and dominant myth. Instead, this is a city administration in which officials not only accept the pernicious categories of the Nazi system, but adopt them and adapt to them with alacrity. The world in which there are Jewish businesses and non-Jewish undertakings and in which this is a valid, operating and legitimate difference, became part of the world of Belgian civil servants. This had become for them, in the earliest days of applying the anti-Jewish Decree, a world of bureaucratic implementation, of an understanding of the politics of mere passive collaboration, in which the pernicious distinction becomes a norm which they enforce with their own inventiveness. They innovate here, not just by adopting the distinction and difference between Jewish and non-Jewish businesses, but as they give new substantive content to the rule and make the Jewish/non-Jewish divide a determining factor in policy application. No harm must come to non-Jews by the literal enforcement of the anti-Jewish Order. Belgian officials in this case made Nazi antisemitism an operative and operating part of the daily lawful existence of Belgian government administration. They could only do so, however, by choosing to ignore the apparently clear legal distinction between acceptable and unlawful collaboration set down by the Permanent Council.

Jewish employees, the city of Brussels and passive collaboration

Meanwhile, the ambit of the involvement of the bureaucrats of the city of Brussels extended beyond the registration of individuals and businesses and the creation of the Register of Jews. The Second Order of 28 October had banned Jews from the public service and from certain professions. They were also banned from newspaper editorial positions and from similar positions in radio.[60] As we have seen, § 4 of the Order placed the responsibility for the enforcement of the provisions excluding Jews on the relevant organs of the public administration, especially the Ministry of the Interior which had the special duty of issuing instructions for the carrying out of the Decree. On 3 January 1941, the National Institute for Radiobroadcasting (Institut National de Radiodiffusion) asked the officer in charge of public records in the First District of Brussels to supply him with the birth certificates of six named employees "in order to permit me to comply with the enforcement of the present legislation concerning Jews".[61] The city employee to whom the inquiry was made rejected the Radiobroadcasting Institute's request for free copies of the birth certificates by insisting that there could be no exemption from stamp duty and other administrative charges. The hunt for Jews and the rush to comply with the German Orders proceeded unimpeded but at the same time standard procedures had to be followed and general rules applied. Administrative fees had to be charged. It is this juxtaposition of bureaucratic routine and normality on the one hand, and zealous extension of authority and cooperation in the execution of the anti-Jewish Decrees on the other, which emerges from and characterizes the documentary record relating to the application of anti-Jewish Orders by the administration in the city of Brussels.

There were at the same time gray areas of legal application for which the city sought further and better particulars and official, lawful instruction from the central Belgian authorities. One of the vexing areas for the local bureaucrats was that raised in part by the letter from the National Institute for Radiobroadcasting. The Second Decree listed a series of professions and types of employment from which Jews were to be excluded. Several legal issues relating to the interactions between the registration of Jews and Jewish businesses under the First anti-Jewish Order and Second Decree targeting Jews immediately arose, particularly around the mechanisms for determining whether someone was or was not a Jew. How for example could one who believed that they were not a Jew prove it? The Order, which defined the legal category "Jew", provided only in § 1 (1) that someone with three Jewish grandparents was a Jew; § 2 (2) of the Second Order stated that in cases of doubt about an individual's Jewish origins they would be treated as a Jew until the question could be determined definitively. How could a person, asked to establish their status, who did not possess adequate information about their grandparents, for example, go about proving their non-Jewish legal identity? What kind of evidence was required?

It was possible that someone who entertained doubts about their "racial" origins might have registered as a Jew because they believed they were by implication obliged to do so through the interaction of these provisions in the two Decrees. As a result, they might then lose their job. In addition to the technical legal question about how one was to prove one's non-Jewish origins, two subsidiary questions also arose.[62] To whom did one offer this proof and how did one go about, if one successfully established their non-Jewish status, getting one's name off the list of registered Jews?

In France a complex bureaucratic system for dealing with such questions under the jurisdiction of the Commissariat Général aux Questions Juives was established as a part of French law. Investigations were carried out, requests were made and the CGQJ issued certificates attesting that an individual was not Jewish (*certificat de non-appartenance à la race juive*).[63] The French system could operate as it did because the anti-Jewish laws in that country were pieces of domestic legislation. In Belgium, as was evidenced in the Dietz case in Liège, the question was not as easily solved. The legal regime under which Jews were registered and defined in late 1940 and early 1941 was established by German Decrees and then administered by the Belgian state apparatus in accordance, in theory at least, with the norms of acceptable participation as set out in the opinion of the Permanent Council.

The question of who should determine, in doubtful cases, who was a Jew, was left open at the time of registration and exclusion. The Decrees were silent as to any notion of administrative mechanisms dealing with cases of legally problematic Jewishness. All that was stated in the First Order was that the head of the military administration could make any decisions necessary for the proper application of the Decree and that he could render final and compulsory decisions in any case where there was some doubt about the applicability of the Decree (§ 16). The Decree also indicated that any individual or business about whom some doubt persisted concerning the applicability of the Order nonetheless was legally obliged to comply and register. There was no mechanism established under which these doubtful cases could be adjudicated and, for example, someone who was incorrectly entered into the Register could have themselves removed (*radié*) therefrom.

Indeed, this legally ambiguous situation was the result of a deliberate decision by the occupying military administration in Brussels. In the early winter of 1941, as the registration process was terminating its first phase, the Military Commands in Belgium and France engaged in correspondence about the issue of apparent discrepancies in the operative legal definition of who was a "Jew" in each juris-diction and differences in administrative arrangements for dealing with these perceived problems. On 28 January 1941, German officials in Belgium explained their position to their Parisian colleagues as follows:

> The above definitions have been left out of the Jewish Decree of the Military Command in Belgium and the North of France, because they are not relevant to the implementation of the Belgian Jewish Orders, and because, in the interest of facilitating their implementation by Belgian authorities, every unnecessary complication of the "definition of Jewishness" should be avoided.[64]

The dilemmas which arose in January 1941 were related to questions which had been specifically evaded by the Germans in large part to avoid complicating the more important broad-based implementation of the anti-Jewish Orders by the Belgian government and local officials. But in the second week of January 1941, the problems and legal dilemmas could no longer be shunned. The question of who was or was not a Jew and what to do about it was now firmly part of the bureaucratic reality in Brussels.[65] While § 4 of the first Jewish Order permitted any person, upon a simple request, to consult the Register of Jews, the various municipalities in Brussels soon found themselves with not just a line of visitors wishing to see the Register but with a multitude seeking the Belgian equivalent of a French *certificat de non-appartenance*. Not only was such a procedure not part of the anti-Jewish legal regime imposed by the Germans, but arguably any compliance with such a request by municipal employees would actively enhance and encourage the implementation of the Orders in such a way as to constitute participation in the collaborationist and therefore illegal sense of the term. Indeed, the Population Bureau in Brussels had specifically decided that, while it had made a careful study of the issue and could reply to any inquiries at the registration stage as to who was or was not a Jew and therefore required to register, it would not and could not engage in such a process if the position of passive collaboration were to be maintained. Jews needed to register themselves and part of that process was that each individual, without guidance from the municipality, had to decide if he or she was covered by the legal definition found in the Order. A central element in the early stages of the registration process had been this "principled" refusal by municipal employees to involve themselves in any activity which could have been interpreted as in any way being concerned with determining who should register. Passive collaboration always meant that such a definitional process was a German prerogative.

On 10 January the Conference of Directors of Births, Deaths and Marriages wrote to the SG of the Interior outlining the situation in which they and their employees found themselves. They explained

> But since the coming into effect of the Order individuals and especially notaries, lawyers and bailiffs have requested certificates of registration or non-registration in the Register of Jews. At the same time, certain public bodies demand that every request for employment be accompanied by a certificate of

non-registration in the Register of Jews. This demand is apparently based on the interpretation of the 2nd Order furnished in your circular of 6 December 1940 which states on page 4 "whenever new nominations occur, proof must be given by way of an official document that the candidate is not a Jew under the Order."[66]

Multiple layers and insights into the daily functioning of the lawful regime of antisemitism as administered in Brussels emerge from this document. The legal system and its principal actors, notaries, lawyers and bailiffs were actively involved in their professional capacity in the hermeneutic of acceptance. They were seeking official confirmation, in records held by a Belgian state agency, of the status of individuals as "Jews". They also appear to have been seeking confirmation not just to exclude people from the list of Jews but to have been after proof that an individual might be a Jew.

Various organs of the Belgian state itself sought official proof that actual or potential employees were not Jews. The historical record on the question of just what, both legally and psychologically in the minds of those implementing the law and drawing the taxonomical boundaries, constituted aggressive enforcement of the anti-Jewish laws and therefore *participation* also raises important questions about the practical limits of the category collaboration. As this letter points out, the law itself was silent on the question of issuing such statements or certificates. What, ask the civil servants, is to be done?

Can they issue such certificates of registration or non-registration to lawyers, notaries and bailiffs? Must they issue non-registration certificates to those seeking civil service jobs and, if so, can they charge for the research necessary for the issuance of such certificates as they do for other searches in municipal records and for issuing official documents? In addition, of course, the municipal officials would face another or perhaps more precisely the same problem. Their employees were also covered by the Orders. How would agencies of the city of Brussels proceed when faced with the question of "Jews" in municipal employment?

In early January 1941, the newly appointed medical inspector for the schools of Brussels requested a certificate of non-registration in order to take up his new post and conform to the requirements of the anti-Jewish Decrees. M. Warans of the Office of Births, Deaths and Marriages wrote to the councilor in charge of public education informing him that the Conference of Mayors had indeed written to the SG of the Interior seeking instructions on how exactly to proceed in such circumstances.[67] Warans also informed the councilor that Doctor Marcel Jean Marie Vanhoevorst had not in fact requested his inscription in the Register of Jews. At the same time, Warans wrote to the good doctor that he had sent the desired information to the councilor in charge of public education for the city of Brussels. He indicated that the "temporary difficulty" of having no procedure to follow in such cases had been solved by this simple expedient of sending a letter to the official in charge of the doctor's employment.[68] The next day a similar letter was sent from the Office of Births, Deaths and Marriages to M. De Tollenaere of the City Secretariat informing him that Jean Robert Leemans, who was seeking employment in the Parks and Gardens Department, had not requested his inscription in the Register of Jews.[69] While the legally binding instructions issued under the Decree required proof of non-Jewish status in the form of an authentic, official document, no such legal instrument existed. Indeed the correspondence on these matters is quite carefully worded in order to avoid any implication that the city would or could produce such a document. The city does not decide or declare who is or is not a Jew as a matter of law. It offers a simple declaration of a nil return from city files. It says instead that the candidate has not asked to be included in the Jewish Register, a statement of fact with a legally different character. The city officials, above and beyond what was required by the letter of the law, in an attempt to meet legitimate citizen demand, as well as their own internal staffing needs, acted on their own initiative to fill the legal void. Again, this is arguably an action which in fact and in law violates the express limitation imposed by the Permanent Council that "all investigations or complementary steps, with the aim of ensuring the full efficacy of any of the provisions of the Decrees by Belgian public servants is forbidden".[70]

The picture of delay and obfuscation, of refusal under the pretence of the absence of specific and legally binding instructions from a higher authority on how to proceed, is replaced by one of bureaucrats creating their own procedures to deal with practical matters as they arose on a daily basis. If there was no such legal document as a certificate of non-registration in the Register of Jews, a letter to the effect that the person was not registered as a Jew from the bureaucratic department in charge of the Register of Jews would suffice. As in the case of Mr Rubenstein's "Jewish" restaurant which was exempted from the operation of the posting requirement, city officials appeared to operate in such a way as to not interfere with the rights of non-Jews who might be adversely affected by the operation of anti-Jewish legal measures. Both Dr Vanhoevorst and M. Leemans were non-Jews who needed an attestation to that effect to take up their posts. The simple absence of a procedure to comply with a legal requirement incumbent upon the potential employee to prove his non-Jewish status should not stand in the way of their employment. In any event, this is yet another case of city officials acting at their own initiative in relation to the operation of the anti-Jewish Orders. They do so even while waiting for instructions from their legal hierarchical superiors. At worst, this is an instance of steps taken to protect the new category of Belgians, the concomitant counterpart of the "Jew", the legally recognized "non-Jew".[71] At best, this is bureaucratic routine and even initiative in which the idea of the classification of inhabitants of Brussels as "Jews" and "non-Jews" is as unproblematic as any other task.

But bureaucracy and law each still abhor a vacuum. The situation of ad hoc written confirmation by way of letter for each new employee could not continue if the rule of law and orderly practice of bureaucratic routine were to be followed. City officials wrote to ask that a mechanism for dealing with such requests be put into place. The Conference of Mayors and Councilors decided that in order to undertake the recruitment of personnel in a reasonable and orderly fashion, they would specifically "Authorize the Office of Births, Deaths and Marriages to deliver declarations attesting that interested parties had not requested their entry into the Register of Jews".[72]

This is undoubtedly an action which goes beyond the mere passive application of anti-Jewish measures. In order to ensure that the city itself complies with the Orders, or at least that potential city employees can provide the documentation required by the Decrees, and by the Belgian Ministry's supplementary instructions, the city of Brussels, through the highest organ of its elected, legislative officials, creates the very means for compliance where the law was itself silent. This is a legislative/administrative filling in of a gap in the legal apparatus of German antisemitism allegedly imposed on a reluctant Belgian state apparatus. This is the embodiment of a version of "passive collaboration" which appears never to have troubled city officials. The law was the law; city administrative offices had to continue to function; orderly lawful compliance is better than ad hoc decision-making while awaiting the arrival of a decision from the SG. An initiative which was not psychologically perceived to be an initiative in the legal sense of collaboration was required. Declarations confirming that a Belgian citizen seeking employment in a public agency of the Belgian state was not a "Jew" became part of the legal, documentary and documented discourse of the city of Brussels. Technically the city did not offer any conclusion, legal or otherwise, that the individual in question was or was not a Jew. Instead it stated that the person had not requested that s/he be included in the Register of Jews. While this fine distinction may have served as a psychological balm for all those involved, in the absence of a direct instruction from the occupying authority, even such a letter which required investigation and confirmation by way of an examination of the city's Jewish Register appears to have exceeded the limits of permissible participation as set out by the Permanent Council. Once more, the practical requirements of efficient daily bureaucratic practice trumped strict constitutional legality.

The continued invocation of traditional rhetorical devices was deployed to elide the most pernicious implications of the practice and with them perhaps avoided official responsibility. The declarations stated that the person in question "had not requested their entry into the Register of Jews", not that they were non-Jews or that, in the phrase created by French bureaucrats and law, they "did not belong to the Jewish race". In Brussels, the city officials do not directly classify anyone as a Jew or non-Jew; they simply report a bureaucratically recorded fact. The person has not requested that their name be entered in the Register of Jews. They thereby avoid direct involvement in any direct definition of who is or is not a "Jew" by limiting themselves to reporting an official, verifiable bureaucratic fact of non-registration. Indeed, they leave open the theoretical possibility that the person requiring such a declaration from the city could be a "Jew" who is not registered. All they are asked to certify again is the fact of non-registration. On such semantic legal arguments rests the distinction between participation and *participation* and a foundational myth of the Holocaust as part of national memory in postwar Belgium.[73] The apparently arcane legal issue of whether the creation of a mechanism which allowed for the better practical application of the German anti-Jewish Orders violated the limits of permissible compliance as set out by the Permanent Council simply passed into oblivion.

All Jewish employees of the city would need to "declare themselves" and as a result be dismissed. On 6 December 1940, the Ministry of Labor wrote to the city informing officials there of this obligation to gather details concerning its Jewish employees, to fill in the forms relating to the names, places and dates of birth, nationality of the parents and maternal and paternal grandparents of the employees in question. The last category to be filled in on the form created by the Belgian government, to be implemented by government departments and by the municipal authorities, simply contained the mention "Jew or non-Jew" (*Juif ou non Juif*) for each relevant family member.[74] This was not, at this stage, a form which could be completed without reference to the operative provisions of the Orders. The statement required by the Belgian government was not whether an employee is registered as a Jew. Instead, the Ministry required Belgian employees of the Belgian state to identify themselves and their ancestors according to criteria established under the Nazi legal order and to forward this information to government officials. The line between passive collaboration and illegal participation here became very fine indeed.

In February and March of 1941, the governmental hierarchy swung into place in order to determine the success of the measures aimed at removing Jews from the Belgian civil service. The Germans made a request for information to the SG; they in turn asked the Provincial Governor to furnish the information; the Governor wrote to all local administrations in the province; and the City Secretary wrote to all heads of department in the government of Brussels asking them to provide him with information concerning "The number of Jewish persons under the jurisdiction, direct or indirect, of the city and establishments under its power, who have had to leave their posts pursuant to the Order dealing with the cessation of functions and activities carried on by Jews."[75]

This file in the Archives of the City of Brussels contains an extensive set of documents recording the number of municipal employees who were removed from their jobs because they were identified and registered as Jews. The litigation department informed the City Secretary that a Miss B., a lawyer, stopped work (*a cessé ses fonctions*) on 31 December. A journalist, Mr C., who had been hired as a temporary employee by the Municipal Food Service also left on that day. One worker in the Police Department was let go. Five employees of the Public Education Department lost their jobs because they were Jews. Dr H., who worked in the anti-venereal disease clinic, left his post. Thirteen employees of the Municipal Welfare Agency were removed. M. Joostens charged with ensuring the successful completion of the registration process was able to report a nil return in so far as Jewish employees of the Office of Births, Deaths and Marriages were concerned. In total, 22 employees of the city of Brussels were dismissed because they were identified as Jews. The city administration, which in its postwar mythology, resisted anti-Jewish measures, objected to the hardships and immoral treatment which resulted from the Orders, offered multiple forms of bureaucratic lethargy, incompetence and obfuscation to alleviate or negate the impact of Nazi antisemitism, in fact, in the words and writings of its own administrative hierarchy, dismissed 22 human beings in its employ because they were "Jews". Only the Director of Religious Affairs, Burials and Funeral Transport (Direction des Cultes, des Inhumations et des Transports funèbres) did anything other than mechanically and heartlessly apply the German law. He stated that while technically the Boards of the Jewish Synagogues fell within his field of responsibility, he did not deem it appropriate to apply the German Orders to such bodies.[76]

Other municipal governments in the Brussels area acted in a similar fashion. Thierry Delplancq has carefully documented these cases. He concludes that the attitude of local authorities "vacillated between passive execution and a certain form of disguised participation".[77] Delplancq also offers a salutary word of warning about the state of the historical record. He notes and underlines the fact that not only is the documentary record incomplete, but that it may also be the case that "official" compliance with the Order was accompanied by unofficial "resistance" or at least by steps meant to alleviate the harshest consequence of the dismissals. He argues that, perhaps owing to a sense of social solidarity among members of the bureaucracy, there may well be hidden evidence of such resistance.[78]

This then is not a written record of resistance, nor at the most basic level does it appear to fall within any possible definition of passive collaboration, but caution about the incomplete record may be required. However, at this stage, there is little or no evidence at all that the city did anything other than fully comply with the letter and spirit of the German Order and the executive decisions of the SG in relation to the legal status of the employees in question. Technically the employees were not fired because they were Jews. Instead they, like the national civil servants, were "*mis en disponibilité*", i.e. made redundant or laid off. Indeed, the only real debate and discussion which existed at the municipal level about the fate of their Jewish employees was a technical legal issue as to the applicability of the Order-in-Council of 30 March 1939 dealing with civil servants subjected to such lay offs. In fact and in law, it appeared from the correspondence on the matter that a special and different legal regime of compensation applied to teaching staff.[79]

Nowhere in the correspondence relating to the dismissal of the Jewish employees of the city administration is there any evidence of resistance. Employees are referred to in official responses from departmental heads as Jews or persons of the Jewish race, not as Hebrews. There is no indication that this language, this bureaucratic process of constructing a new category of governmental employee, one who is a Jew or of the Jewish race, is extraordinary, un-Belgian, worth protesting. As in the registration process itself, the government of the city of Brussels comported itself as law-abiding and norm-enforcing. Civil servants complied with the law and saw their fellow employees leave because they were Jews. They wrote memos identifying the employees in question. They passed the information to their superiors and that information was then transmitted along the line to the Germans.

Quite simply, the bureaucrats and elected officials of the city of Brussels identified and dismissed 22 of their fellows because they were Jews. No amount of postwar myth building or collective amnesia can remove this historical and legal fact from the case against enshrining the concept of passive collaboration as a form of resistance practiced by Belgian officials. The true story is not only different but there are few, if any, real exceptions. The tale of collaboration, of persecution, of willing, unresisting compliance must always be seen to be a Belgian story.

Chapter 7

Communicating, informing and deciding

The city of Brussels and passive collaboration 1941–1944

The flourish of activity, innovation and compliance which characterized the stages of registration and its early sequelae did not abate in 1941 and in subsequent years. The Germans continued to seek full compliance with their anti-Jewish Orders and the municipality continued to comply with German instructions. In May 1941, the mayor transmitted a list, compiled by his employees, of all German Jewish men with their names and addresses.[1] Other questions arose in which the city and its officials did more than simply comply with German commands.

In June 1941, as new anti-Jewish measures began to take effect, and to have a direct economic impact on Jewish individuals and families, municipalities were faced with the issue of Jews moving into their area.[2] The issue was exacerbated by the internal exile of some Jews from Antwerp who were forced by the Germans to move to the Province of Limburg.[3] Several of those Jews had obtained permission to move again, this time to Brussels, but on the condition imposed by the Military Commander in Hasselt that they provide a written authorization from the appropriate mayor of the suburb or district in the Brussels area to which they wished to relocate. The question for determination was whether permission to reside in the new home needed to be provided by the mayor since the Order imposing the obligations on mayors, cities and towns to create the Register of Jews and to transfer the appropriate records to the new locality in the case of registered Jews who subsequently changed residence did not include any mention of such an authorization. Once again, the silence of the law and the practical exigencies of the system of occupation posed another legal and practical dilemma for the local authorities.[4]

At the same time, city officials continued to receive specific instructions from their Belgian superiors and the Germans. The new SG for the Interior wrote to all provincial governors and local mayors informing them that all identity cards of registered Jews now had to carry the bilingual stamp, in red ink, **JUIF-JOOD**. Once the new inscription process had been completed the municipal officers were to forward a new copy of the list of all registered Jews with a special mark indicating which Jews had presented themselves to have their identity documents marked.[5] This time the list of registered Jews, including by definition recalcitrant registered Jews who had not had their cards stamped, was to be forwarded directly to the German Security Police (Sicherheitspolizei) office on Avenue Louise.

City officials began, at some level, to attempt to strike a distance between themselves and the process of marking Jews. Unlike the case of the registration process itself, the administrators at first took a passive stance, insisting that no posters announcing the stamping requirement be issued or displayed. Instead, they relied on SG Romsée's circular in which he stated that the new process would be announced by way of a notice in the press. The circular did not state that the city could not proceed by way of public notices themselves but in this instance no innovation or self-motivated actions were forthcoming. Contrary to normal practice (*contrairement à l'usage*), the city officials would simply prepare themselves for any Jew who would choose to comply.[6]

This mere passive reluctance of Brussels officialdom was quickly replaced by rigorous bureaucratic compliance above and beyond the call of duty. Postwar assertions would have it that the lack of manpower was consistently invoked as an excuse, a delaying tactic and a way to avoid implementing anti-Jewish measures. In the case of the **JUIF-JOOD** stamp, the Office of Births, Deaths and Marriages, in order to proceed with the process of stamping identity cards and then to comply with the construction of a list with special markings indicating which registered Jews had had their cards stamped, borrowed five employees from the Public Procurement Agency (Service de Ravitaillement) and maintained the temporary employees from their own service to assist in the tasks.[7] On 29 August 1941 the College of Mayors forwarded the list of registered Jews to the German Security Police, marking the names of those who had presented their cards with a cross in red.[8] Contact with the Security Police continued in the fall of 1941. Romsée informed the mayors that, in future, information compiled under the Jewish Orders relating to the change of address of registered Jews was to be sent to the Avenue Louise headquarters of the Sicherheitspolizei.[9] The appropriate services within the city administration were kept abreast of their new obligations.[10] At the same time, this information took on ever more sinister overtones as the Germans decreed that Jews were henceforth forbidden from moving anywhere other than the four cities of Antwerp, Brussels, Charleroi and Liège.[11] The process of concentration and control was tightening and the local officials, including the police, continued to play their role by transmitting vital information locating and naming Jews for the Security Police.[12]

At around the same time, the administration of Brussels, like their colleagues in other cities and towns, had to deal with other practical aspects of the application of the Decrees concerning Jews. The question of the applicability of the Decrees to Italian and Spanish Jews, for example, required the intervention and interpretation of the Military Command before any change to the Register of Jews could be made by local officials.[13] Brussels' bureaucrats created a special form dealing with cases of those "Jews" who had died before 28 October 1940 so that some form of official proof that an individual had not been registered as a Jew could be produced in such a case.[14]

In the mean time, the various municipalities of greater Brussels had been compiling their own lists of Jews, i.e. employees of municipal government and related agencies who had been identified or had identified themselves in the Belgian formulation as Jews. That information was forwarded by mayor Coelst to the German authorities on 24 October 1941.[15]

Local administrators also dealt more specifically in the "hermeneutic of acceptance" in this context. While the questions surrounding the definitional taxonomies of "Jewishness" had been deliberately sidestepped by the German Military Command in Belgium in an effort to ensure general compliance with the registration procedures, this did not mean that the issues of the parameter and content of the new legal category "Jew" did not arise to trouble municipalities in the Brussels region.

Later in the autumn of 1941, as we saw in the introductory chapter, the German authorities in Belgium introduced an Order stripping Jews outside of Germany of their German citizenship.[16] The city administration had already handed over, at the request of the German *Ortskommandantur*, a list of German Jewish men figuring in the Register of Jews.[17] The new Reich provision quite naturally led the local German authorities to seek from the Belgian officials all information from the records of their administrations concerning former German Jews. While waiting for other departments to decide how they would deal with their obligations under the Order, the Offices of Births, Deaths and Marriages, which were obviously directly concerned with the Order, decided to take a joint position on the question on how, *inter alia*, to deal with the question of the statelessness of those who were now former German Jews in Belgium.[18] Among the practical questions to be resolved were how to deal with requests for travel documents and requests to marry by newly stateless Jews. The Brussels officials revealed

> In order to cover ourselves, we have demanded that the parties of German origin concerned produce:
> an extract from the Register of Jews
> an extract from the Population Register(s) as required
> Without a doubt, the real guarantee would be found in the production of a document originating with the German Authority itself stating that the person in question has lost German nationality through the application of the November Decree.
> *It does not appear that for the present at least it is possible to obtain such a declaration.*[19]

Bureaucratic innovation in order to ensure compliance not just with both the spirit and letter of anti-Jewish legality, but also for the sake of the continued efficient running of the bureaucracies of the city administration charged with their implementation was once again in evidence. While from the perspective of Belgian bureaucracy it would be preferable if the Germans established a system of duly certified documents identifying former citizens, the city could make use of the Register of Jews for its own purposes of administrative efficacy. This was not simple compliance. This was innovation in the face of legislative silence and the absence of a decreed solution. Bureaucrats once more found their own solution and the solution they found involved them treating the Register of Jews as a valid, binding and authentic source of documentation on the vital question under Belgian law as to who was a registered Jew.

At the same time as they bemoaned the absence of an official attestation by the German authorities dealing with the loss of citizenship by former German Jews, the officials of the Passport Office and the Registry of Births, Deaths and Marriages were quick to underline the distinction between measures which involved them as Belgian bureaucrats doing their legal jobs and activities undertaken by the Germans for German purposes. The memorandum sets out the jurisdictional debate. The Order, § 8, required that the Sicherheitsdienst play a vital role in order to establish the loss of citizenship as the essential condition precedent to the forfeiture of all property belonging to the now stateless Jews to the German state. However, for the Brussels officials, the question of their power to act as they had been could not be determined by what the Security Police did in relation to the seizure of Jewish property.

> ... it is when it is a question of executory measures to be taken by the *Reich* that it is established that the dossier of the party in question must contain as a basic document a declaration from the Security Services. This text can not bind us when it is a matter of delivering a passport, or of marriage ...[20]

The Belgian bureaucrats were perfectly willing to use the Register of Jews for their own domestic purposes but they would not be bound by the prescriptions of the 11th Order which was seen to be a purely German measure. This attitude of drawing a distinction between the powers of the occupiers under their own domestic laws and the jurisdiction and practices of local officials under Belgian law and administrative structures was consistent with the idea of a continuing Belgian state apparatus with the power and ability to act within its own domain. It invoked a strict delimitation between the Belgian state and its agents and the Germans acting as occupiers and acting in relation to its own subjects. Yet at the same time, the Brussels officials proceeded to establish under their own rules a kind of ad hoc system of record-keeping and official documentation concerning stateless, former German Jews for the purposes of creating Belgian records in relation to marriage and travel documents. They established this new category of bureaucratic subject with specific reference to the Register of Jews which, no more and no less, should have also been considered to have been created solely for German purposes dealing with matters of German concern. Instead, while drawing distinctions between German anti-Jewish measures and Belgian administrative emergencies and exigencies, these officials voluntarily used the Register of Jews for purposes well beyond those demanded and imposed by the Germans. They made use of information which under the Belgian Constitution they were forbidden to have, for Belgian purposes. Yet, because they used this information for domestic ends, it might well have been argued that they did not participate in investigations or other activities aimed at completing or complementing the German Decree as forbidden by the Permanent Council. Anti-Jewish laws here became incorporated into the daily, legal and perhaps legalized activities of Brussels bureaucrats under the guise of an extended "passive collaboration" which did not involve the German authorities except tangentially.

At the same time municipal authorities were still being called upon to comply with the anti-Jewish measures themselves. The language of the 11th Order as published in Belgium imposed no obligations of Belgian authorities to do anything.[21] The Germans nonetheless insisted that the Conference of Mayors ensure that for all entries in population registers, the Register of Jews itself, on identity cards and other documents serving as valid ID, all mention of German nationality for Jews who had been stripped of their citizenship was to be removed (à biffer). All other documents such as nationalization papers, passports, identity cards dealing with German nationality were to be withdrawn from the Jews. In addition, the names and addresses of all registered "German Jews" (who legally were no longer "German" Jews) were to be sent in two copies by local officials in Brussels to the Office of the Chief Administrator (Verwaltungschef).[22]

The question of the effect of the 11th Regulation in Belgium and in Belgian domestic records continued to trouble local officials. The Mayors' Conference for greater Brussels met on 20 August 1942 to take official notice of the instruction from the German military authority that changes in all official Belgian documents, the Population Register, the Register of Jews, identity cards and any other type of document, had to be modified so that any mention of German nationality was struck out and all German identity documents (proof of naturalization, passports, etc.) were to be surrendered.[23] Belgian officials insisted on their own lack of jurisdiction over substantive definitional issues under the Regulation and on the sole German power to issue documents required by individuals. In one typical case, the SG of the Interior, for example, inquired as to whether the Aliens' Police would enter Wilhelm Loeb in their records as a stateless person pursuant to his loss of German citizenship as a Jew residing outside the Reich. The Aliens' Office representative, M. Standaert, replied that the question was beyond the jurisdiction of the Belgian authorities and that M. Loeb should address himself to the appropriate German authorities. The Aliens' Office position was also that once he was in possession of an appropriate document identifying him as someone who had lost his citizenship, he could be entered into the Belgian files as a stateless person, following the normal and existing procedures of Belgian law from the prewar period.[24]

Another typical example can be found in the 7 October 1942 case of Benjamin Billa. On that date, the Population Bureau of the municipality of Ixelles compiled a supplementary list of German Jews and included Benjamin Billa, who had registered himself as a stateless person.[25] Belgian officials not only complied with the letter of the German law, but with its spirit. In the case of Billa, like the others in his situation, as a matter of German law itself, he was not in fact, a "German" Jew. At best, he was a former German. Yet the municipal officials in Ixelles passed on his name as a German Jew, in part at least, because that is what the Germans themselves wanted. They, like officials all over Brussels, used the Register of Jews: they classified individuals as Jews; they classified them as Germans; they compiled lists and supplementary lists; they had little difficulty, once the jurisdictional framework was established, in managing their information within the broader, antisemitic legal parameter established by the Germans, distinguishing as a matter of law and of bureaucratic practice between Jews and non-Jews.[26]

In the autumn of 1942, the mayor of Etterbeek, following inquiries from his subordinates, sought legal advice from his colleagues in the Conference of Mayors.[27] With the view of arriving at a uniform approach in each municipality in Brussels, he asked a series of questions on the legal operation of definitions of the idea of "Jew" as found in the Orders to determine, *inter alia*, who was or was not liable to be entered into the Register of Jews. He wanted to know if 1) a Catholic woman marrying a Jew became a Jew? 2) a Jewish woman marrying a Catholic became an "Aryan" (*aryenne*)? 3) a Jewish minor adopted by a Belgian Catholic became an Aryan and if they became by the fact of adoption a Belgian citizen if they are a foreigner? 4) the non-recognized child born out of wedlock to a Jewish woman and subsequently recognized by a Belgian Catholic father, does that child become and Aryan and can they be removed from the Register of Jews? and finally 5) if a Jewish person dies, can their name be removed from the Register of Jews?

There is still some obvious confusion about the religious nature of the taxonomy of German law as opposed to its racial basis (Aryan, Jew, Catholic). The notion of equality of all Belgians as found in the Constitution has gone by the wayside to be replaced by the signifiers of the Aryan/Jew dichotomy of Nazi law as local officials in the Brussels area attempt to grapple with the various thorny legal and practical issues which arise out of the anti-Jewish Orders.

The reply from the College sets the record straight.[28] The very first paragraph states in no uncertain terms that the reply which follows has replaced the term "Catholic" with the word "Aryan" since the determination of a subjects "Jewishness" is based in birth and consanguinity and not religion. There is no confusion about the basis of German anti-Jewish law. The highest deliberative body of elected officials in the capital city of Belgium knows just how important the term "Aryan" is and they do not hesitate to use it as intended by the Germans. They then proceed to address *seriatim* the questions relating to who is and is not a Jew for purposes of the uniform municipal application of their legal obligations, despite having earlier always asserted that such questions were beyond their jurisdictional competence. The interpretive matrix and jurisdictional competence which had from the beginning, in theory at least, informed the Belgian position have been replaced. The interpretation of anti-Jewish Orders as a legal matter, heretofore within the exclusive remit of the occupying authority, in part as a necessary consequence of the Permanent Council's definition and delimitation of participation, now becomes part of the normal functioning of the Belgian Conference of Mayors

In so far as the Aryan woman (*femme aryenne*) who marries a Jew is concerned, assuming she is not herself descended from two Jewish grandparents, in which case she would by marrying a Jew, be considered a Jew under § 1(2)(2), she is not a Jew and her identity card must not be stamped **Juif-Jood**. Likewise, a Jewish woman who marries an Aryan is still a Jewish woman and the **Juif-Jood** inscription must remain on her identity card. In any event, the reply points out, reiterating the traditional line, it is up to Jews to request their registration and there is still no place for the town's administration to act on its own initiative.

The question of the adoption of a Jewish child is a bit trickier from the legal point of view. Technically, nothing about the child's ancestry has changed and a strict interpretation of the Decree would mean that the child is still a Jew. Given the effect of Belgian adoption law on the concept of full integration into the adopting family and into rights of consanguinity, however, this is a question on which legal advice must be sought from the Ministry of the Interior.[29] In the mean time, pending such an opinion, the identity card must remain marked. On the nationality question, the result is simply a matter of Belgian nationality and citizenship laws which do not confer nationality by the simple act of adoption.

The issue of the illegitimate child is also a simple and straightforward one for the College. As long as the child has not practiced the Jewish religion and become a Jew by virtue of the operation of § 1(2)(1) of the Jewish Order, then that child is not a Jew under any other provision of the Order. If they have been entered into the Register of Jews, they must follow the procedure of requesting a certificate authorizing their removal from the Register from the appropriate German authority. As a result they will be removed from the municipal records marking them as a Jew and a new identity card will be issued. Finally, since the Decree itself is silent on the subject, the file of the deceased Jew must remain in the Register of Jews with the appropriate mention of death being entered.

Legally speaking, there is not too much which is remarkable about this document. The Germans themselves took charge of the process of striking off individuals from the Register, whereas the municipalities of their own initiative produced documentation verifying that someone was not a registered Jew.[30] The interpretation of both the anti-Jewish Orders and Belgian law are solid and legally correct. In the one case of doubt about the effect of the interactions between Belgian adoption law and the anti-Jewish Order, advice from a higher authority is recommended, especially since the adoption matter, as we have seen, was controversial and involved high-level legal and political actors. In the one case where the Decree is silent, the effect of death on the presence of a name in the Register of Jews, the College opts for strict compliance and non-independence of action. The Register must remain intact and no file can be removed just because the individual has died. At some level, there is a small contradiction with other practices in which local officials filled in the gaps left by silence in the Order by following their own course of action, for example, in completing other municipal records with an annotation relating to the presence of the individual's name on the Jewish Register. But in those cases, the Register of Jews itself remained unchanged and that is no doubt the crucial difference in this instance. Moreover, this is an attitude which is perfectly consistent with the idea of the Jew as the proactive self-registering individual and with its counterpart, official municipal passivity. Jews register themselves and the local officials simply make a note of the wishes of the individual. To remove a name from the Register, in the case of death, on their own initiative, would resemble, in their minds, participating in the process of registration.

Of more interest is the document as an embodiment of the hermeneutic of acceptance. This is a text which gives legal advice about who is and who is not a Jew and what needs to be done, if anything, in the cases under examination. Uniform action on the Jewish question across the municipalities of greater Brussels must be the norm. Legal provisions are compared and analyzed. The situations of Belgian and German law are considered. Reference is had to hierarchical superiors in case of doubt or conflict of authorities. There is no idea in evidence that a discourse in which the Aryan/Jew distinction becomes the operative juridical matrix in which Belgian mayors and their subordinates exercise their jurisdiction is somehow problematic, let alone un-Belgian, or illegal. Instead, the collective mayors once more invoke their own passivity and underline Jewish agency in the registration process. For the rest, Aryan and Jew are simply legal categories the limits of which need to be understood for the uniformity of all administrative practices throughout Brussels. The reluctance as a matter of legal principle to enter into the definitional issues raised by the Orders which was present from the beginning of the registration process in Brussels is replaced by bureaucratic uniformity. *La bonne marche* and nothing but *la bonne marche.*

The Yellow Star Order and passive collaboration: Brussels and its Jews 1942

On 27 May 1942 the German Military Command for Belgium and Northern France introduced the so-called Yellow Star Order.[31] All Jews over the age of 6 were forbidden to appear in public without wearing the "Jewish Star" (§ 1(1)). The Star was to be six-pointed in yellow cloth with black markings, palm size with the letter "J". It had to be worn in a visible fashion and sewed permanently on the left side of the breast (§ 1 (2)).[32] The Second Order relating to the Star was passed the same day and set out in its § 4 that Jews covered by the obligation to wear the Star were required to obtain them from the same municipal authorities where they were registered.[33]

The mayor of Brussels, after meeting with his colleagues from the various towns and municipalities of the region, wrote in the name of the Conference of Mayors of Greater Brussels to the Germans on 4 June 1942.[34] This letter marks an apparently radical departure for the city of Brussels in its previous unbroken record of implementing anti-Jewish Decrees and, as we have seen, is still portrayed as the moment of rupture with the policies and practices of Belgian docility in relation to anti-Jewish Orders. M. Coelst wrote in part:

> It is not incumbent upon us to discuss with you the expediency of this measure taken against the Hebrews, but we do have the duty to inform you that you cannot demand our collaboration in its enforcement.
>
> A large number of Jews are Belgians, and we cannot resolve to associate ourselves with a prohibition which damages the dignity of every man, whoever he may be.
>
> This prejudice is all the more grave as it carries with it, for those who are subjected thereto, a prohibition against wearing the insignia of our national honors systems.
>
> We are convinced that you will recognize the legitimate nature of our feelings …[35]

The letter from the Conference is a key document in any understanding of the history and myth of the city of Brussels and its Jews under the occupation, and remains central to present-day constructions of issues of Belgian complicity in anti-Jewish persecution. This is, on the current and dominant reading, a letter of refusal and resistance. It is a letter of refusal grounded in ideas of basic human dignity (*une atteinte aussi directe à la dignité de tout homme*). It is an act of resistance wherein the city of Brussels categorically refuses to implement or to play any role in implementing this particular anti-Jewish Order.[36] This is Belgian resistance grounded in conceptions of human dignity and what we would now call human rights. This is the hermeneutic of rejection and is a bright and shining moment in the history of resistance. Indeed, after a meeting with a delegation of the Conference on the following day, the German authorities yielded in the face of the Belgian refusal and undertook the coordination of the distribution of the Stars by the AJB. They asked only that a notice be posted in the place where the Register of Jews was held informing Jews of the time and place for the distribution of the Stars.[37]

Again, however, as lawyers and historians concerned with context, accuracy and nuance, we might offer another reading of the same text which allows us to adopt the more nuanced position that the moral high ground on which the Conference of Mayors situated itself was not as unambiguous as dominant renderings of this event would have it. An undated document, but one clearly written at around this same time, compiled by the Mayor's Office in Brussels, entitled "Number of Stars of David" (*nombre d'étoiles de David*), meant for distribution to the mayors of each of the municipalities of Greater Brussels, lists the number of Stars of David by locality, from 6,500 for Brussels down to 12 for Ganshoren.[38] Preparations for compliance were under way for the municipal distribution of the *Judenstern* at exactly the same time as the principled protest was being made. Indeed on the day the College of Mayors met, M. Warans of the city's Office of Births, Deaths and Marriages had written to the mayor raising issues relating to the practical implementation of the Yellow Star Order, without any mention of a principled protest.[39] Warans asked the mayor if the distribution of the Stars of David should be the responsibility of the Population Service which kept the Register of Jews. If the mayor was in agreement, Warans went on, should they not contact the Germans to obtain detailed information concerning the manufacture of the Stars according to the dimensions and description contained in the Decree and more particularly about the exact meaning of the reference to "limited numbers" of Stars in the Order. In conclusion he requested that the mayor consider consulting the College of Mayors to address the question, not as a matter of principle, but in order to ensure that "uniform practices are adopted by the entire city".[40]

A careful reading of these texts subverts at least part of the claim to a superior moral status attributed to the missive refusing to implement the *Judenstern* Order. At the very least, such a reading calls to our attention the importance of a closer second look at all parts of the historical record. The position of the mayors is not unambiguously good, nor is it necessarily irredeemably bad.

The mayors begin their "protest" by deploying a particular semiotic strategy which had not heretofore been encountered either in their correspondence with the Germans or the SG, or in internal writings. The letter begins by employing the French *Israélites* instead of the term *Juif(s)*, although they do return to the latter in the next sentence. This is not an unintentional slip. Instead it should be seen to be an intentional invocation of a term which is meant to distinguish the Nazi policy of identifying "Jews" by way of a distinctive marking and the Belgian concept of not identifying Hebrews at all. The term *Israélites*, in the context of the protest letter, carries with it Belgian understandings of equality and dignity inherent in the Constitution, and of the place of Hebrews as full bearers of the rights and entitlements of Belgian citizenship. Indeed, one might also read this letter as an embodiment of a rediscovered sense of the centrality of the Constitution by the mayors who had been shocked into this realization by the widely perceived vulgarity of the Yellow Star Order.

In the next sentence which invokes the concept of human dignity which will not be interfered with by Belgian officials, the mayors while reverting to the term *Juifs,* also invoke their central argument. "A large number of Jews are Belgians" – this phrase is the key both to our understandings of the first part of the act of resistance embodied in this letter and to the failings and limitations inherent in this and many other so-called acts of resistance by Belgian officials. What is invoked in the range of objections issued by the mayors to the *Judenstern* Order is a basic and limited, and in the end fundamentally flawed, conception and understanding of citizenship and constitutional order. They link together "dignity", "*Israélites*", "Belgian" and "insignia of national honors" in their argument about compliance and human rights. What has struck the mayors is the potential of witnessing eminent, brave, decorated war heroes, Belgians, men who fought in the blood and gore of the First World War, for their country Belgium, reduced to the status of spectacle, of marked men, men marked by the same occupier who had inflicted untold misery on Belgium in the First World

War, the Germans. In addition to the visceral revulsion which seems to have characterized public reaction to the introduction of the Yellow Star in much of Western Europe under German occupation, there is at work here a particularly Belgian sensibility and national identity forged under the horrors of the brutal First World War occupation and the increasingly harsh German regime. "A large number of Jews are Belgians".

Herein lie the strength and weakness of the protest. The mayors use the term *Israélites*. The term encapsulates for them their understanding that citizens are being targeted for particularly odious measures. Jews are strange and foreign and perhaps deserve to be marked and separated, registered. Hebrews, on the other hand, are Belgians, like us. They deserve protection and protest because we deserve protection and protest. Why, when Belgian Jews were registered, was there not a similar protest? Why, when Jewish businesses with Belgian Jewish owners or officers, were registered and identified, was there no protest? Why now, why the Yellow Star Order?

Some preliminary, albeit speculative, issues might be highlighted. We could advance our historical understandings by examining for example what else was happening at the time, now two years into the occupation and by looking at public reaction and opinion to the Order. In any event, we must always bear in mind that for the mayors, at some level at least, the distinction between Belgian and foreign Jews was of some key importance. This we know from the very language they used and the arguments they constructed. What is brought into question here is what was meant and understood at the time by Belgian officials by the term "Belgian".

The process of implementing the Yellow Star Order was not entirely outside the ken and practice of municipal officials in Brussels. The German request that notices be placed in the offices in which the Register of Jews was kept informing Jews of the time and place for obtaining the Stars was passed through the various municipalities with some haste. The contents of the letter from Dr Gentzke to Coelst, received at 5:15 in the afternoon of 8 June 1942, were communicated the next morning by telephone to all the municipalities represented at the Conference. Given that the distribution was to begin on 9 June and that the letter itself was marked "urgent" and hand-delivered to Coelst's office, we can reasonably infer a certain degree of compliance with the German request as evidenced by the series of telephone calls from the Mayor's Office.[41] Furthermore, the police of Brussels assured a presence at the offices of the AJB every day the Stars were in fact to be distributed.[42]

There is also extensive correspondence in the mayor's files involving Coelst seeking, at the behest of Jewish citizens, exemptions from the obligation of wearing the Star – § 1(a) and (b) of the Second Order on the implementation of the Yellow Star Order permitted requests for exemption for those who were Jewish husbands living in mixed marriages in which there were non-Jewish children and for Jewish wives in a childless mixed marriage. In at least one case, Mayor Coelst intervened in favor of an 80-year-old woman whose late husband had had connections with the Belgian royal family and who had been a local mayor. She refused to leave her house out of fear and embarrassment if she had to wear the Star.[43]

Coelst intervened on what would appear at one level to be grounds based in human sympathy. The letter of the law, the exemptions permitted under the Order, did not apply in this case. A frightened old lady appealed to the mayor to exercise his powers of persuasion with the German authorities and he did so. However the argument presented by Coelst was not that the law is somehow offensive to basic principles of human dignity (the hermeneutic of rejection) but rather that within the parameter of an acceptable and accepted legal order, an exception should be made (the hermeneutic of acceptance). Not only must the letter from mayor Coelst requesting an exemption for Widow W. be seen and read and interpreted against this ethical and legal interpretive grid, but it must also be read for its actual content.

The Widow W. was born in the United States; she belongs to a "very honourable family" (*une très honorable famille*). Her late husband's background included connections to the royal family and elected office. In other words, at some very central level, this is an intervention in behalf of a "good Jew", an *Israélite*, not a *Juif*. This reading would make the mayor's intervention on her behalf consistent with the line he had adopted in his "letter of protest" only a few days earlier. Once more, narrow and restrictive understandings of citizenship and Belgianness appear to be at play. In similar subsequent cases, the mayor of Brussels, by this time M. Grauls, intervened on behalf of a Mr B. to write a letter which would serve as an attestation of good morals because B. was a man of upstanding reputation and well-known in the right circles, particularly those related to Belgium's colony in the Congo.[44]

In later stages of anti-Jewish persecution in Brussels, the mayor also dealt with requests for housing and rent assistance for prominent Jews who found themselves in a state of penury under the occupation. He and his officials were asked to intervene on behalf of the Widow K., whose late husband had "left in the history of Brussels a famous name".[45] The mayor's help was also sought for financial assistance for Mrs R., of a famous Jewish family, some two years later.[46]

The stories these interventions tell are ambiguous except in so far as they speak of the mayor's personal involvement in the hermeneutic of acceptance throughout the same period in which he was objecting, as a matter of principle, according to the dominant mythology, to anti-Jewish measures. Again the Conference did not object to the *Judenstern* Order as such. They objected to being compelled to distribute the Yellow Stars. They in fact suggested that the matter might be better left to the Jews themselves, under the auspices of the AJB which could distribute the *Judenstern*, a solution quickly accepted by the Germans. While the letter relating to the Star of David Order might be as close as the administration of Brussels came to outright protest or "resistance", it is in fact a highly attenuated form of rejection. In the end, the solution for the distribution of the odious signs was one which was perfectly consistent with the overarching idea that the administration was always passive and that in fact the Jews were themselves responsible for complying with German measures.

Some of the later correspondence from the mayor's office intervening in behalf of individual Jews also demonstrates that Jewish citizens and their plight were part of the conscious awareness and daily professional existence of municipal leaders. Sometimes the mayor was asked to intervene on their behalf with the Germans to seek exemption from the Yellow Star Order. On other occasions he was asked to intervene within the municipal bureaucracy to apply exceptional measures on behalf of impoverished Jews and on still other matters he was asked to provide documentation about a Jewish individual's good character and reputation. "The Jewish question" was on the agenda in the Mayor's Office but it appears to have been on the agenda in these cases only if prominence, reputation and social class were at stake or in play.

Photographs of occupied Belgium reveal innumerable scenes of Jews wearing the Yellow Star. All Jews, regardless of origin, family connection or history, etc., were liable to deportation to the killing factories of the east. The letter of "protest" must always also be placed in this context.

Other laws, other Jews: the city of Brussels and the legalized exclusion of the Jews

As the German occupiers expanded and extended their processes of excluding Jews from Belgian society, they continued to call upon the officials of the city of Brussels to assist in the implementation of the steps towards the Final Solution. As part of the separation of Jews into their self-contained life-world, the Germans targeted educational structures. The 1 December 1941 Decree on Jewish Education set up a system of distinct Jewish schools, thereby excluding Jewish students from the public education system.[47] The Ministry of Public Education was given overall jurisdiction under § 3 of the Order and local education officials in the towns and cities of Belgium were called upon to implement the exclusion of Jewish students.

In Brussels, the mayor had already been asked to supervise the census of all Jewish students in public secondary schools and to enter into contact with private educational institutions in order to obtain the relevant information from them.[48] Three weeks later all but one of the towns and suburbs of Brussels had completed the census of Jewish students and the report was sent to the German authorities.[49] At this stage the municipal authorities continued to implement the bureaucratic efficiency with which they had completed their other tasks in relation to compiling and passing on information about the Jewish residents of Brussels.

A little over a year later, and at about the same time as the Yellow Star Order was raising serious doubts about Belgian complicity in the implementation of anti-Jewish Decrees, in April 1942, the city was informed by the Germans that the AJB had complained that it was having difficulty in some municipalities in obtaining buildings and other facilities for the establishment of Jewish primary schools.[50] Mayor Coelst replied in the name of the Conference, in language which would find an echo a few days later in the protest over the Yellow Star Order and the German decision that the distribution of the Stars would be run by the city.[51] Coelst informed the Germans of the local administrations' inability to comply with the demands for space for primary schools. He wrote:

> We must tell you that the assistance which until now has been given to the Hebrews by local governments for the creation of kindergartens has resulted in numerous expressions of satisfaction.
>
> A large number of the children who attend these schools are Belgians, and many among them are unhappy. On this ground, they deserve our concern. Please rest assured that we have done, and will continue to do, everything possible to alleviate the harshness of the measures taken against them.
>
> But it is important that you also know that what we have done for the kindergartens we cannot do for the other types of schools.[52]

The language and ideas deployed in this letter from the mayor of Brussels indicating his and his colleagues' unwillingness or inability to comply with the creation of a separate system of Jewish schools are now recognizable. The term *Israélites* is invoked and in this instance *Juifs* is nowhere to be found. The mayor asserts that many of the children are Belgians and they are unfortunate. The next sentence is somewhat more ambiguous. "On this ground they deserve our concern". Is it because they are unfortunate children or because they are unfortunate Belgian children? Is this a general humanitarian declaration by the mayor and the Conference, or is it again a humanitarianism informed by a limited and deforming understanding of Belgianness and citizenship? Are the measures against them harsh because they are children who suffer or because there are Belgian children who are suffering? It seems at least to be implied here, in the entire context of administrative compliance in legalized anti-Jewish persecution that something has changed. It may be that the city officials are shocked to their ethical and humanitarian senses because they see, as they may not have seen through the simple act of registration, the real human suffering imposed by Nazi antisemitic law. It may also be that they see suffering by Belgians, *Israélites*, and that is what has shocked them. The concepts of suffering and misery are to some degree, in the very discourse deployed by the mayor, always connected to concepts of Belgianness and the concomitant understanding of the term *Israélites*.

The various administrations of the Brussels region had not hesitated to assist in establishing these separate Jewish schools, in which Belgian children are now, according to the mayor, suffering.[53] Their protest, if that is what it is, comes about not as the result of an ethical awareness that the separation of Jewish children is wrong in principle, but from a realization that the practice of separation, which they implemented, carries with it certain cruel consequences. This is, in a practical nutshell, the distinction between the hermeneutics of rejection and acceptance.

The concluding remarks in Coelst's letter again render the stance undertaken by the Conference morally and legally ambiguous. The last paragraph indicates that what has been done for one type of educational establishment cannot be done for the primary schools about which the AJB has apparently complained to the German authorities. The French-language construction of this part of the mayor's letter is vital. The French verbs deployed make the characterization of the letter as one of protest or refusal subject to some qualification. Coelst says that *nous ne pourrons le réaliser*, i.e. we will not be able to do, to accomplish, to achieve, (*réaliser*) what we have done for the other schools. This becomes perhaps less a protest grounded in principle than a complaint or statement that adequate resources are simply not available to give a practical effect to the desired outcome. Of course, this does not mean by definition and by the exclusion of all other possibilities that this is the real or only reason for non-compliance. The postwar construction of local resistance always placed a strong emphasis on obfuscation and pleas about being under-resourced as defining elements of official refusals to implement anti-Jewish laws. The use of the verbs *pouvoir* and *réaliser* in this context may simply be a way of obscuring the real reasons for non-compliance by placing that failure to act under the rubric and guise of a lack of resources. This letter of 30 May 1942 may be seen to have been a letter of refusal and protest, or as a letter of protest and refusal disguised in terms of practical impossibility, or it may have been a letter informed by a pernicious hermeneutic of acceptance and narrow, unacceptable and ultimately antisemitic constructions of Belgian citizenship. It may be all of these things at once.

The Germans stubbornly replied after receipt of the Coelst missive that they interpreted his letter as assuring them that the city of Brussels would see to it that Jewish pupils in the forthcoming school year would attend only Jewish educational institutions.[54] Once again, in consultation with his fellow mayors, Coelst attempted to outline to the occupying authority with precision and care the position of the city of Brussels in so far as the question of establishing Jewish schools in and by the city was concerned.

After insisting that the German official Callies had obviously misunderstood the previous letter, he wrote

> In our letter of 30 May, we said that because of the harsh measures taken against the Jews of whom many are our compatriots and of whom many are unhappy, they were deserving of our concern.
>
> But, we have neither the desire nor moreover the ability to create for them any kind of education which is reserved solely for them.
>
> The only spaces available which we have immediately made available for the Hebrew Association and those which will become free in the future will not be sufficient to shelter the thousands of primary pupils who have been prohibited access to our schools.[55]

Again this protest letter contains the lexical ambiguities which informed the previous document it is meant to clarify. While the term *juifs* is used, the qualifier *Israélite* is also deployed. The argument about Belgian students and their state of unhappiness is repeated in the same ambiguous formulation. Coelst continues to combine ethical, political protest with practical concerns. The city has neither the desire nor the resources to create a separate Jewish education system. The physical facilities available are insufficient to provide access for the thousands of children subjected to the process of exclusion and segregation. Is this principled protest or practical objection or both? Once more, how does a narrow understanding of Belgian citizenship inform the objections voiced by the Conference? How does the fact that facilities for segregated teaching of some Jewish students have already been made available to the AJB by the city fit in with understanding Coelst's declaration as principled protest and resistance? Can Brussels' officials at one and the same time comply and resist? Is this letter an embodiment of the ambiguities which sit at the heart of Bauman's gray area and of our troubled relationship with the categories of collaboration and resistance as they must be understood in the context of considering the status and nature of "passive collaboration" in Brussels?

How are we to understand resistance in the Belgian context and in the context of Belgian municipal administrators? Against whom and against what are they protesting? They have set aside some facilities for the exclusive use of the AJB and Jewish children but they will (or can) not provide any more. They had already produced lists of Jewish pupils in February 1941, but when asked to provide the same information to the Department of Public Education of the central Belgian administration, Coelst offered the Conference's regrets that they could not compile and pass on such information. He informed the representative of the Ministry that, instead of providing a list of buildings set aside for the AJB and Jewish education, he was attaching a copy of his letter to the Germans.[56] The city and its officials seem to be taking a firm stance, whatever the grounds, in refusing to hand over any more facilities for the creation of Jewish schools pursuant to the German Decrees.

The Military Administration then did what it had almost always done in the face of refusal and obfuscation by Belgian officials – it finessed the situation. The Germans acknowledged the letters from Coelst and again drew his attention to the provisions of the relevant Orders. Dr Oesterheltt (*Kriegsverwaltungschef*) then simply washed his hands of the matter. He declared that as far as the military administration was concerned, the matter was closed and that the implementation of the legal obligations in relation to Jewish education was henceforth a matter between the city and the AJB, upon whom the juridical burden in relation to the establishment of separate Jewish schools was placed by the Decree.[57] The problem was now a uniquely Belgian one in which the Belgian Jewish organization faced the legal compulsion to comply with the German Order and the national Education Department was given overall responsibility for the practicalities. In such a situation, the Conference of Mayors was informed that the municipalities had decided "to assist the Jews to the greatest extent possible".[58]

Protest and principled objection then become transformed into bureaucratic compliance. The organizational genius of the German occupation of Belgium was always in large part attributable to its ability to co-opt the local Belgian government agencies and representatives into doing what it wanted them to do. By the simple expedient of saying that the matter was closed as far as they were concerned and turning the question of Jewish schools into one in which the AJB dealt with the local authorities under the regime still governed by the Decree system, the Germans had achieved a kind of legal alchemy. They transformed the operative taxonomy from a German/Belgian question into a Belgian/Belgian (or a Belgian/Jewish) issue. This did not automatically mean that compliance was forthcoming in a complete and unambiguous fashion. But it did mean that the situation which now faced the Brussels' administrators and officials took place within the boundaries once more of a hermeneutic of acceptance. Resistance, if any, now had to come in a practical context of the implementation of the overarching legal order of separate and segregated Jewish education.

On 10 July 1942, local government officials in Brussels, yielding in principle but not yet in practice, to the combined pressure from the Germans, the AJB and the Ministry of Public Education, wrote to the Military Command again pleading that they simply did not have the space available for Jewish schools. They asked that the Germans think about handing back for the purposes of Jewish education the school building at 62 Rue du Vautour which had been taken over by the Organization Todt.[59] Two weeks later, on 24 July, city officials again wrote to the Germans reiterating their request that they hand back buildings which they had expropriated for their own use to be transformed into Jewish schools. School space, they argued, was already at a premium because the Germans had requisitioned so many buildings. They explained that the removal of Jewish pupils from the public school system did not make any space available for exclusive Jewish education because these students were spread throughout the system. The departure of a few students here and there from a number of schools did not free up entire classrooms. The Belgian officials, faced with the finessing tactics of the Germans, appear to have attempted to turn the tables back on them with a double bluff, both by insisting on their good intentions and desire to comply with the lawfully binding Decrees of the military occupying authority and by trying to play on institutional rivalries within the ranks of the German structures under occupation.[60]

> The school buildings situated at 68 Rue Du Vautour, were requisitioned not for the purposes of the occupying army, but for the Organization Todt. No school or other large space being available in this district where the Jews are specifically concentrated, to allow us to comply with your order, we are obliged to ask for the return of the building at 68 Rue du Vautour, for Jewish schools.

We are certain that you will understand this need, and that you will want to issue the necessary instructions so that this school can be made available to us, in order that we will be able to follow your commands. This question, according to the letters we have received, needing to be resolved quickly, I ask you for a quick reply to the request for the vacating of the building on Rue du Vautour.[61]

Despite their original "humanitarian" objections to aiding the AJB in finding premises for their primary schools, local officials then decided to offer their assistance to that same body. They also continued to comply with other aspects of the anti-Jewish German educational regime, by for example identifying pupils who were permitted to continue their attendance at particular institutions under the provisions of general Belgian educational laws, and identifying those pupils as "Jews" (élève juive).[62] Resistance, if there was resistance, was patchy, incomplete, ambiguous and finally ineffective.

Jewish matters: "passive collaboration" continued

In other "Jewish" matters there is more evidence not just of the response of the local officials in Brussels to German demands for assistance in implementing anti-Jewish Decrees but indications of an evolving Belgian attitude to the measures and their role therein. As the grip of the Germans over the Jews of Belgium was extended and expanded, the use of compulsory work orders became the method of choice for excluding and exploiting Jews. The Jews of Belgium by this time had begun to resist the German system and many refused to present themselves when summoned for "labor duty". In June 1942, Brussels police refused to participate in a German round-up of "recalcitrant" Jews. Yet some officers did give directions to the Germans. Police agents of the city force served as interpreters for the Germans who arrested Jews. Agents in other local municipalities may have been somewhat more actively involved.[63] Mayor Coelst protested that the German Lieutenant Phillipp by his actions had compelled Belgian officials to "arbitrarily collaborate in a purely political operation which cannot be covered by our national laws".[64] Coelst demanded an investigation by the German authorities into these events and that instruction be given that in future Belgian police would not be called upon in such actions.

In July 1942, the Military Command expressed its annoyance in a letter to the Chief of Police of Brussels, wherein he was ordered to compel his men to take Jews summoned for labor either for the compulsory medical examination to determine if they were fit to work or to the employment office for their assignment.[65] On 6 July 1942, Coelst replied by informing the Germans that the role of the Belgian police was governed by Belgian law and that the provisions of Belgian law in fact prevented them from acting as the Germans wished.[66] On 15 September 1942, councilor Verhaeghe de Naeyer, again explained to Oesterhelt that the Belgian police could not, as a matter of Belgian law, assist the Germans in enforcing compulsory labor measures against Belgians. The Brussels police existed only to maintain law and order in the city of Brussels. Should trouble arise, this force would quite naturally assist the German police in restoring calm. However, they were not permitted to forcibly compel Belgian subjects (*sujets belges*) to comply with compulsory labor orders, and should they do so, they could find themselves charged with false arrest. The King's (Crown) Attorney had made this fundamental legal point explicit and had already threatened prosecutions. At the same time, political realities also affected the practical questions. On 16 July 1942 the German Military Command had contacted the governor of the province of Brabant, in which Brussels was situated. The Germans insisted that they had every right under the operative provisions of the Hague Convention to call upon the Belgian police to assist in the arrests in question since they were necessary to protect and maintain public order. The Germans requested that the governor inform the mayor of Brussels of the legal error under which he appeared to be operating.[67]

Instead the governor handed the juridical ball to the SG for the Interior.[68] At the same time, the governor set out a legal argument which would support the mayor's, the Attorney's and the police refusal to cooperate with the Germans in making the arrests in question. He first underlined that in reality the arrests were being undertaken pursuant to the Decree of 8 May 1942 outlining a system of forced labor for the Jews of Belgium.[69] This Order embodied the detailed implementation of the previous Decree of 11 March which simply established a special regime for the employment of Jews.[70] Under this second Order relating to Jewish labor, Jews were compelled to take up any "job" assigned to them by the (Belgian) Labor Service (§ 7). They could be employed only in a group and had to be kept separated from the other employees (§ 8). The Germans insisted that their request for Belgian police assistance in enforcing these provisions fell under the scheme established pursuant to an order issued on 24 July 1941, requiring Belgian police assistance in all arrests relating to penal matters. That order however admitted that some instances were particularly sensitive and recognized that, in those cases, German security officials would act alone. The governor insisted that the SG would no doubt agree that "the arrest of Jews in order to compel them to report for work falls under these exceptional cases included in the order".[71] Because the matter was one of general interest across the country as a whole, the governor encouraged the SG to enter into direct talks with the occupying power.

These refusals by the mayors of Brussels, the police, the Crown Attorney and the governor, have often been invoked as proof of local resistance to German legalized antisemitism. The Brussels police, unlike their counterparts in Antwerp, did not round up Jews at the request of the German authorities. In fact they refused to participate.[72] Compulsory labor was a particularly sensitive issue for Belgians given the experience of mass deportations in the First World War.[73] It would become even more problematic as the system of voluntary work introduced in May 1941 was replaced by a system of obligatory labor in the service of the Reich for all able-bodied Belgian men in March 1942. The second refusal to lend police assistance clearly occurred in a time frame marked not just by the oppression of Jews but more importantly by the oppression of Belgians. Each of these refusals also occurred in the further complicating context of Belgian police interactions with German forces more broadly. Benoit Majerus has convincingly argued that the objections to the use of Belgian police in rounding up Jews were not grounded in objections of principle to anti-Jewish measures but were more immediately informed by the politics surrounding Belgian policing issues as they reflected a clear and strong desire for maintaining local police autonomy.[74]

At around the same time as the city was perhaps obstructing (or complying with) demands for space for separate Jewish schools and while the mayors were refusing to allow local police to help in arrests for compulsory labor, the Conference issued a formal protest concerning deportations for "military labor" outside Belgium. The Conference of Mayors did intervene in this instance in an unambiguous fashion. After expressing their profound emotion at hearing stories of compulsory deportations, the Conference requested that the SG, who had jurisdiction over these questions of national importance intervene with the Germans in order to bring a halt to the deportations. They invoked apparently for the first time in any official correspondence, the limitations imposed on the Germans by the provisions of the Hague Convention.[75] Why did they wait until this late date, when the machinery of death was put into motion, to invoke the provisions of the Hague Convention against the Germans?[76] Why this act of resistance, of legal objection, and not before? Why this resistance in 1942 when the job of registering and marking, identifying and separating had already been completed within a world of bureaucratic and administrative self-understanding in which the question of legality had never arisen? Can we at this point, and in this context, call this "resistance"?

The police force of the city of Brussels, from its own activity reports, had previously gone beyond mere translation and guide service in implementing German measures against individuals identified as Jews. The story of resistance and the invocation of Belgian legal autonomy told by those who might recount the story of mayor Coelst's protests without this important historical contextualization and caveat serves to mask and elide the true and more complex record of police involvement in German anti-Jewish measures.

In the last week of November 1940, as the first Decrees against the Jews began to take effect, the Belgian police commenced what would be a practice followed throughout the occupation, of assisting the occupying power in tracking down and identifying individual Jews. On 25 November 1940, the police chief, Gilta, in his bulletin to all police divisions in Greater Brussels, indicated to his colleagues that the Germans had requested the address of one S., described by Gilta as "a Jewish subject" (*un sujet juif*), a journalist, born in Vienna. No other information was provided by the German police. Gilta informed the police of Brussels that in the circumstances they should seek and return to him any information on all those individuals with the surname S., registered in Brussels.[77] In the earliest days of the occupation and of the German anti-Jewish legal order, the police of the city of Brussels went out of their way to compile a list of individuals as the Germans searched for someone they had identified as a Jew, a description simply reproduced by the police chief as if such a description were an ordinary and accepted part of the vocabulary of the police of the city of Brussels. The police force was still operating under the founding principles of the Belgian Constitution and was subject to the clear limitations on "participation" in enforcing such measures.

Similar practices of overzealous compliance can be found throughout police records of the period. When in the following year the police received a request to track down a Mr W. (a Jew), or his wife, Mrs K. (a Jew), they were told that the German information showed him as residing on Avenue Armand Kugsmann in Brussels.[78] The police themselves helpfully volunteered that the street name was more likely to be Avenue Arm Huysmans.[79] The police of Ixelles were then able to confirm that the wife did in fact reside at the address on Avenue Arm Huysmans and for the sake of completeness attached a copy of her registration document carrying the red stamp JUIF-JOOD.[80]

Throughout the occupation, the Brussels police followed a similar practice of self-defined "passive collaboration" which clearly exceeded that which was permissible according to the Permanent Council under Belgian constitutional and criminal law. Like the city's bureaucrats, the police appear to have adopted an attitude that efficiency in their daily operations required them to engage in activities which would have the effect of assisting the German hunt for Jews. In April 1941, they went on the look out for "a Jewish family" (une famille juive) who had left their residence in Courtrai to come to Brussels without the proper permission.[81] In July, they began searching for a Mr S. and a Mr B., each described as a Jew (juif).[82] In October of the same year they were put on alert to discover the whereabouts of a Mr Z, a Jew (Juif).[83] Similar reports and actions in pursuit of individuals can be found in each year of the occupation. The police of Brussels actively sought out individuals identified as Jews on behalf of the German authorities. While they did not in most cases arrest these individuals, they did provide the information required for action by German police officials. This was the limit and nature of "passive collaboration" as practiced by the officials of almost all branches of Brussels municipal government. They did not do the dirty work of arrest, torture, deportation and killing.[84] Instead, they provided the detailed information on which such practices could be based. The Jews registered themselves; the German police requested information. The officials of Brussels, loyal as always to the Belgian Constitution, simply kept the records and provided the facts.

Even this brief tale of passive collaboration à la Bruxelloise does not reveal the true depths of anti-Jewish activity by local police officials. Clear evidence emerges from a variety of police files and documents that the Brussels law enforcement authorities soon adopted and adapted to the new Nazi legal nomenclature according to which a new category ("Jew") of criminal was created. Police reports on alleged black market activity describe, for example, three subjects arrested as being of "German Jewish nationality" (de nationalité allemande juifs [sic]).[85]

The same police force reported on its surveillance of a cake shop at which it was believed that "Jews" (*des Juifs*) gathered to conduct illicit transactions.[86] Following an anonymous denunciation about a Mr W. who allegedly violated the curfew regulations, the police of Saint-Gilles described the suspect as "of Polish nationality, entered in the Jewish Register" (*de nationalité polonaise, inscrit au registre des juifs*).[87] The fact that someone known to the police is a registered Jew became a relevant and cogent consideration in official record-keeping practices within the police bureaucracy itself.

Not only did the police consider the identifying trait of being a registered Jew as relevant to their internal identification practices, procedures and discourses, but they also actively policed the presence of individuals as registered Jews for the Germans. They pursued the request from the *Oberfeldkommandatur* to identify Mrs R. and to verify if she was a registered Jew.[88] Police from around Brussels responded to the circular seeking this individual and her whereabouts within two days. From Saint-Gilles came a list of three individuals with the surname R., each of whom was described as being a registered Jew.[89] The Aliens' Office (Bureau des Étrangers) also provided the name of an individual who was not at this time a registered Jew (*Ne figure pas inscrite au registre des Juifs*).[90] The police of Schaerbeek finally offered information concerning another individual who had come there in 1940 and had been entered on the refugee register before disappearing from view.[91]

Again and again, the Brussels police, like the rest of the local administration, participated on an ongoing basis in implementing Nazi anti-Jewish legal measures in the Belgian capital. They did not originate the Orders or the requests for information, but they pursued them with vigor and enthusiasm. They volunteered information on individuals identified as Jews; they expanded on the information requested to include more names and more details; they took the initiative when information about Jews was incomplete or inaccurate; they began describing those under suspicion, surveillance and arrest in the language of antisemitism in internal documents. At the same time, they refused to participate in rounding up Jews; the chief protested against German attempts to involve his police forces in such actions. There was "resistance", however belated.

This resistance appears on the available record to have been far outweighed by the number and breadth of instances in which the officials complied not just with the letter of the German law but expanded upon it for their own administrative purposes. In the final section of this chapter I want to turn briefly to an examination of the most understudied areas of Belgian municipal involvement in the implementation of anti-Jewish measures, their role in relation to the Aryanization process.

Bureaucratic routine, administration and Jewish property in Brussels

The city administration played its role in late 1940 and early 1941 in registering Jewish undertakings and in ensuring that the law in relation to compulsory signage was carried out, in compliance at least with the spirit of the anti-Jewish legal regime. While the city was charged with ensuring compliance with the signage regulations in relation to restaurants, cafes and bars (§ 14 of the First Jewish Order), the vast majority of actions and legal measures involving Jewish businesses, their registration, administration and Aryanization were left in the hands of the Germans.[92] This did not mean however that the city administration was completely insulated from having to deal with aspects of the Aryanization process. Municipal officials were not called upon to administer the German laws or to participate in the process of appointing an administrator (*Verwalter*) for Jewish businesses, or in running or terminating and winding-up their businesses. Instead, they had to deal with those normal and routine aspects of city administrative functions involving for the most part the provision of utility services such as gas, electricity and water and in the determination of city charges owed by the businesses in question.

In August 1943, for example, the accounts department of the City Gas and Electricity Board wrote to the German administrator Karl Schneider concerning premises owned by Mr C., a Jew. The administrator had sought to recover, as a Jewish asset now Aryanized, the unspent amount paid by C. as a deposit to the Gas and Electricity Board. The city officials insisted that, because the account had been opened by Mr C. and he had not cancelled his subscription, they could not release the monies. The operation of contractual relations between a client and the City Gas and Electricity Board, under general provisions and principles of Belgian contract law, appears to have been invoked in the defense of monies belonging to a Jew, to shelter them temporarily at least from German demands. The next two paragraphs of the correspondence with the administrator tell a somewhat more complex tale. The Gas and Electricity Board asks for permission to seal the meters opened in the name of Mr C. Once a date has been fixed for such a technical procedure and the operation completed, the officials inform the administrator that they will be happy to free the funds in question and pay them into the *Verwalter's* bank account.[93]

A similar letter concerning Widow G. was also sent to the *Verwalter*. The Board informed him that 252.75 BEF had been deducted from the account for consumption until 31 May 1943, when the account was closed. Upon receiving written confirmation of this from Widow G., the monies would be handed over. In the mean time, the remainder of 447.25 BEF would be held for the administrator.[94] Similar correspondence continued to flow between administrators and the Gas and Electricity Board. Accounts were closed, meters read and sealed, payments deducted, and remainders placed by the city of Brussels into bank accounts of Jews whose assets were controlled by a German *Verwalter*.[95] Conversely, the Gas and Electricity Board did not hesitate to demand payment from the *Verwalter* when an account was closed in arrears.[96] It helpfully referred questions relating to accounts for water bills to the Brussels Intercity Water Company (Cie Intercommunale Bruxelloise des Eaux) when approached by administrators.[97] On occasion several issues were dealt with at once. On 26 July 1943 for example the Board wrote to *Verwalter* Schneider concerning Joseph W., the Michel Lourie Company, the

Samuel Cwiren Company and the Niecheiski Company. In two cases, money was deducted from the deposits in payment for utilities used and the remainder given over to the nominated Aryanized or frozen bank account. In one case there was no record that an account was held in the name of the company in question and, in the final instance, the city requested that the account be closed by the subscriber before any payments could be made.[98]

This correspondence between city utility boards and the German administrators is the textual embodiment of the overriding concepts of administrative efficiency (*la bonne marche*) and participation which is not *participation*. Clearly the city employees operated in these cases as if they were under some kind of legal obligation to correspond with and obey the requests of the *Verwalter*. They did not think that there was anything contrary to Belgian law or to the limits of legal power under the Hague Convention which might render the Aryanization process legally, let alone morally, suspect. They ignored the government-in-exile's declaration that the Aryanization process was a form of unlawful expropriation. They did not follow the attitude adopted by the Commercial Court that the *Verwalter* had no lawful authority to act on behalf of an Aryanized company. They did insist in some instances that contractual terms be respected but once the appropriate authorization was forthcoming they did not hesitate to turn over money deposited with them by Jewish customers to bank accounts controlled by German administrators for the sole purpose of expropriating Jewish property for the benefit of the Reich. They felt no legal fiduciary duty to insist that the money, under Belgian law, belonged to the clients upon termination of the contract. Instead, they recognized the legal fiduciary power of the *Verwalter*. Indeed, they exceeded, as city employees had done from the earliest days of the registration process, the strict limits of that which was asked of them by the German officials.

When faced with a request for monies held as a deposit in the name of the Michel Lourie Company, they informed *Verwalter* Schneider that they had no account in that name at the address given. Bureaucratic resistance and obfuscation, or a sense of strict legality, or of minimal compliance, or of the permissibility of only passive collaboration, or some sense of fiduciary obligation to the client, or a combination of any of these factors, might have led the Board to stop with the simple statement that they held no such account in that name. Instead, the divisional chief added that the account at the address in question was in the name of Widow G., obviously here a Jew, and an individual then targeted for expropriation. The city of Brussels Gas and Electricity Board voluntarily identified a Jew whose assets were then handed over to the German *Verwalter*. Likewise in early August 1943, after assuring Schneider that the monies remaining on account for Mr S. had been paid into the nominated bank, they also passed on a copy of Schneider's letter to the town of Schaerbeek and to the Brussels Gas Company (Société Bruxelloise du Gaz) so that they might proceed to terminate accounts held in that locality by S. and have any remaining monies paid over to the *Verwalter*.[99]

This is passive collaboration in its Belgian version as practiced by the agents of the city of Brussels, a year after the protests by the mayor about the use of

Belgian police, about the treatment of Jewish school children and about arrests and deportations of Jews. This does not appear to fit easily within a narrated history and historiography which portrays municipal employees as using tactics of delay and obfuscation to counter German attacks on the city's Jewish population. Like the city officials who decided that a special entry was required in all municipal records just to ensure the efficient operation of the registration process and its possible *sequelae* for the bureaucracy itself, this is compliance over and above the letter of the law.

The Brussels police also participated in the processes of Aryanization. In the autumn of 1941, for example, the police of the district of Saint-Gilles mounted a special surveillance operation at the open-air market on Boulevard Jamar following reports that the requirement for Jewish businesses to carry a sign pursuant to the Order was not being respected. The report to the German *Ortskommandantur* indicated that the problem was in fact caused by the wind blowing the merchandise on display, momentarily covering the Jewish Undertaking signs. The police undertook to ensure that such events did not occur again.[100]

The following year, the Brussels police force was charged with delivering liquidation notices to Jewish businesses when the occupying authority decided that all such undertakings were to be wound up by the end of March. The police had to obtain signed receipts of notification. The task was divided up by the central police authority of the city and distributed to each police district. The order from the Chief of Police Van Autgaerden also carried a specific indication that should service be impossible because the business had changed address, the notices were to be returned to headquarters with the relevant information so that they could be served by the police authorities in the appropriate district.[101]

The Permanent Council specifically forbade as contrary to Belgian law, under which the police continued to operate, any investigations or similar measures meant to ensure a more perfect compliance with the Decrees. Yet in each case, the Brussels police in fact conducted inquiries and surveillance, and provided further information, in order to enable more complete adherence to measures aimed at Brussels' Jews. The line between passive collaboration and *participation* appears to have been crossed without having had any impact on a police force which throughout the occupation and afterwards portrayed itself as loyal to the Belgian Constitution and to its legal duties thereunder. Indeed, the mythology of police resistance to the Germans is still predominant.

This brief examination of the ways in which the utilities services and police in Brussels became involved in the day-to-day functioning of the process of Aryanization through the ordinary processes of bureaucracy embodies all of the elements which characterize the role played by the municipality in the persecution of the Jews of that city. There was compliance and there was innovation; there was legality and there was excessive zeal. Jews were identified and Jewish businesses were signposted, unless such an act would have an adverse effect on surrounding non-Jewish businesses. Schools for some Jewish children were created but objections were raised to the creation of other Jewish schools. Lists of Jewish municipal employees were compiled and provided to the Germans. Lists of Jewish pupils were drawn up and passed on.

On the one hand, the Brussels officials, as was the case for the SG, operated in a system in which law continued to exist, in which the Belgian Constitution still had effect and in which the powers of the occupier were in theory limited by the terms of the Hague Convention. Yet there was no principled protest about the registration and marking of Jewish cafes and restaurants. There was no invocation of constitutional and international law principles when Jewish property was expropriated or when Jewish schools were imposed. None of this struck the Belgians, the Brussels administration, as particularly problematic in basic terms as long as the Jews registered themselves. Belgian democracy and concepts of equality, as Vivian Curran argues so forcefully was the case in France, killed themselves, with little or no help from the Germans.[102]

In addition to law's inability to serve those in need of its protection because the exclusion was to some extent always experienced as itself being lawful, the hermeneutic of acceptance played a key role. Once the lawfulness and legitimacy of registration, identification, exclusion, separation, expropriation, etc. come to be accepted, principled objection was almost automatically impossible. Instead, from the very beginning "Jews" and "Aryans" begin to appear in official documents, correspondence and daily administrative practice. It is at this level of stark bureaucratic routine that what happened in Brussels and elsewhere in Belgium might find a partial explanation. The "Jew", the "Jewish question", like rationing, or like education, became new administrative categories and practices to which the bureaucracy adjusted itself without a second thought.

This bureaucratic routinization which characterized much of the history of the fate and treatment of the Jews of Brussels throughout the occupation is exemplified by the question of the Star of David. Objections based in humanitarian concerns apparently expressed by the leading officials in Brussels at the very idea of marking Jews with the Yellow Star, setting them apart in such a graphic way, can be found, however problematically. Yet several documents found in the City Archives holdings from the Mayor's Office include a mark like this ✡, sometimes alone, sometimes with the letter "J" inside, in ink of various colors and sometimes in pencil, marking the documents concerned as ones dealing with "Jews". It appears that the marking with the ✡ was contemporaneous with the creation and filing of the document itself. The documents which are so marked are found in the general files of the Mayor's Office, not in those labeled as dealing explicitly or exclusively with the "Jewish question". They are found in general correspondence files, on copies of letters to and from the German Military Administration. Those officials who took the time to inscribe "Jewish" files with a ✡ need not have been antisemites. Instead what the ✡ marks, graphically, both literally and figuratively, is that "Jews" or matters pertaining to "Jews", became a separate issue of bureaucratic, legally justified and justifiable categorization. They serve as a quick reference in general correspondence to a specific subject matter, the Jews. Anyone looking for letters dealing with "Jewish" matters in the ordinary mayoral correspondence could easily find them among all the other general correspondence. The constitutional equality of all Belgians was replaced in daily practice, no matter the motivations or personal sentiments of the actors involved, by a common, accepted and understood discourse of exclusion. At a very practical level of bureaucratic compliance, of passive collaboration, the ✡ marks the new Nazi legal category of the "Jew" as part of routine in the office of the mayor of Brussels. The road to Auschwitz to no small extent begins at the point at which a file can be marked, by a patriotic and loyal Belgian civil servant or municipal employee, with a ✡. This is the mundane reality of the concrete material practices of the Brussels bureaucracy. *Participation* is this semiotic participation in the worldview of Nazi taxonomy. Collaboration in Brussels is written ✡.

Chapter 8

Liège and its Jews

"Hebrew and Polish stores", June 1940

In Liège, as in every other Belgian city and town, in May 1940, local officials came into direct contact with the occupying authority. These Belgian mayors and other elected officials were faced with a crisis and with a new political reality. Life had to be returned to normal as quickly as possible, but this would be a new normality. Daily existence and the business of local government would now take place in a context in which the Germans would play a regular and overriding role. Notwithstanding the new legal and administrative ordering in the country, local officials nonetheless had to deal with the immediate and pressing needs of the population. Citizens had to be fed and housed. The duty of the city of Liège, its mayor, the Socialist Joseph Bologne, its elected councilors and its administrative staff, was to return life to its ordinary routines in these exceptional times as quickly and as painlessly as possible.

Two immediate concerns occupied the minds and actions of the city officials in the earliest days of May and June 1940: public procurement (food, housing and other daily necessities for the population) and the perilous state of city finances to allow normal functioning of municipal government to continue. The central government had fled, the King was powerless. Daily administrative responsibility for governing the country had fallen to the SG, but the budgetary state of the nation remained chaotic. On 17 May, a few days after the fall of Belgium, Bologne wrote to the occupying authority and informed the Germans of the "very precarious" food and housing situation of the population of his city and of all the municipalities in the surrounding region.[1]

The city officials were in fact no strangers to these extraordinary circumstances. In addition to the still acute memories of a brutal German occupation in the First World War, the government of Liège had some more recent experience. As the German Army advanced through the Low Countries, thousands of Belgians, including many from the region of Liège, had fled towards the Belgian coast and south to France. According to a contemporary report from the chief of police, "approximately 20 to 25,000 inhabitants fled before 10 May".[2]

Among these evacuees were many of the city's merchants, for the most part small-business owners. Their absence meant that many perishable items, especially precious food stocks, were at risk of being ruined as they sat in abandoned premises. There was also a heightened risk of civil disorder, break-ins and theft, not to mention the subsequent black-market sale of these goods. On 13 May, Bologne issued an executive order requisitioning all primary foodstuffs and subjecting them to a system of rationing. For those goods held by owners who were now absent, Article 6 authorized their seizure.[3] Two days later, on 15 May, the councilor in charge of the Department of Public Procurement, the Liberal Jennissen, granted authority to the Chamber of Commerce of Liège to take over the management of the properties of all absent business owners. The representatives of the Chamber of Commerce in turn proceeded to name individual trustees for these businesses. These trustees were then empowered to lawfully enter the abandoned premises, accompanied by a police officer who produced an official account of the visit (*procès-verbal*) and an inventory of goods. Following this, the trustees could administer the business. All proceeds from the sale of goods were handed back to the Chamber of Commerce who then deposited them in the Caisse Communale.[4] Half of these proceeds would be made available for public welfare purposes, the other half, in theory, would be held for the owner.[5]

The public procurement crisis in Liège was clearly governed within a pre-established legal framework. The mayor issued an emergency executive order; the councilor in charge of the Department of Public Procurement acted to apply that order and delegated the practical aspects to local experts, the Liège Chamber of Commerce. During this period, councilor Jennissen contacted all the local police commanders and asked them to provide him and the Chamber of Commerce with a list of abandoned stores and warehouses in their districts.[6] The goods were inventoried and then sold, with the proceeds placed with the Caisse Communale. The city receiver-general examined all such deposits and reported to councilor Jennissen every morning.[7] Everything occurred within a strictly local political and legal framework. The crisis in Liège was managed by municipal government officials and others with special expertise drafted into the rescue effort. City officials (mayor, councilors, the receiver-general, the police, together with the Chamber of Commerce) ensured that normal economic activity and the needs of the citizenry of the city were looked after, all according to the principles of Belgian and public international law. While they maintained daily contact with the occupying authority, in Liège it was local officials, Belgians, who oversaw the commercial and political life of the city and the surrounding municipalities. Perishable goods were saved and put to good use, for the public benefit. Citizens were fed and normal life began again. These emergency measures taken by Bologne and the city council, with the goal of protecting the owners against looting and at the same time of feeding local citizens of a city once again under German occupation following a defeat of the Belgian Army, proved successful. The mayor and the councilors, municipal employees, the Chamber of Commerce and the police had together fulfilled their duties to their fellow citizens in extraordinary and difficult times.

Yet, on 24 June 1940, the feast day of St John the Baptist, this normal, legal Belgian world underwent a change which, although it passed virtually unnoticed at the time, would forever change the city of Liège. On this day, more than four months before the First and Second Decrees concerning the Jews would be introduced by the German military authority in Belgium, elected Belgian officials and their agents took the first steps in establishing an anti-Jewish legal order in that country. In the Liège City Archives, in the files relating to the mayor's office during the occupation period, the legal smoking gun of legalized antisemitism in occupied Belgium lies innocuously amid thousands of ordinary, daily administrative documents. On 24 June, the Chamber of Commerce, which was intimately involved in local government steps to save and to re-establish the local economy, wrote to councilor Jennissen: "Following your wishes, we enclose herewith the list of Hebrew and Polish businesses, already liquidated or in the process of being liquidated by the Chamber of Commerce."[8]

The municipal and other archives in Liège give no other indication about what might have motivated Jennissen's request for such a list. Was it in response to a German inquiry or demand? In any event, such a motivating factor should have been irrelevant in practice and remains to this day legally inoperative. The Germans could well have asked for the information, but Belgian officials, including councilor Jennissen, remained bound by and loyal to the country's Constitution. The most important question surrounding these events of late June 1940 is the question about the reactions and actions of the local Belgian authorities and officials to an unconstitutional and illegal process of identifying inhabitants of their city as "Jews" or "Hebrews". The Belgian Constitution guaranteed religious freedom. This Belgium of the national Constitution, which remained in force throughout the occupation and to which officials like Jennissen swore an oath of allegiance, knew nothing of stores which were Catholic, Protestant, "free-thinking", atheist or Hebrew. Such labels were completely foreign to the Belgian constitutional order. Yet the archives reveal no protest from the representatives and officials of the Chamber of Commerce or from Jennissen himself. The documentation merely contains the letter with the attached list of "Hebrew and Polish businesses, already liquidated or in the process of being liquidated by the Chamber of Commerce".

The representatives of this trade organization, established according to Belgian law, had in theory no legal basis upon which to compile this list. Did they consult the files of the Aliens' Police in order to establish the nationality or citizenship of each absent owner? On what basis, according to which data, using what criteria could they have established the religious faith of these same absent owners? Jennissen asked for a list of "Hebrew and Polish" businesses. The question is framed in an operative Belgian linguistic framework. The Chamber of Commerce refers to the owners (or the businesses, although it is difficult to imagine how the Chamber of Commerce would have defined a "Hebrew" business according to any criteria other than the single one of the owner and his religion) as "Hebrews" (*Israélites*), not as Jewish (*Juives*). Whatever the origin of the request for the information, the response is clearly written in the language recognizable in intra-Belgian correspondence of the period. *Israélites* are not *Juifs*; Hebrews are not (yet) Jews.

The list is also described and compiled in terms which are sometimes written in the conjunctive, sometimes in the disjunctive, i.e. describing or detailing businesses which are both Hebrew *and* Polish, and others Polish *or* Hebrew. At this stage not all Jewish businesses are included. Only those which are both Jewish-Hebrew and Polish seem to have interested the councilor and the Chamber of Commerce. Whatever the answer to the underlying questions which must inform any further examination of the 24 June 1940 letter and the list attached thereto, one underlying truth remains and it is uncontested and incontestable. The sad reality is that this remains, whatever the original demand, a Belgian letter, written by the Liège Chamber of Commerce to the city councilor in charge of the Department of Public Procurement. It deals with a matter of ongoing concern, the legal and practical state of play relating to the process of liquidating the interests and businesses of absentee owners. But it singles out "Hebrew" businesses for particular attention. A separate list has been constructed and it is in reality a list of "Jews" and/or "Jewish" businesses. The list has been compiled and communicated by Belgians to Belgian elected officials. The list of Jews or Hebrews attached thereto was drawn up by the Belgian administration, by and for local officials in Liège. The construction and circulation of such a list should have been in practice and was in theory a constitutional and legal impossibility. But it became a practical reality in Liège in June 1940. It would also return to haunt the entire subsequent history of Aryanization in Liège.

In the mean time, the legal and administrative world of public procurement in Liège continued its normal course. The city council had authorized the receiver-general to use half the proceeds from the liquidation process for public welfare purposes. Creditors of the absent businesses had sued to realize their debts and registered their claims against any proceeds held by the city. The council agreed to release the sums owed to several of these creditors.[9] The council also asked for advice from its legal department as to whether it could withhold 5 per cent of the monies held and administered for absent owners.[10] The receiver-general wrote to the council on 16 July to obtain a list of all business owners whose goods and property had been sold. His purpose in seeking this information was to ensure that he was able to make his claim as a preferred creditor against any proceeds for unpaid taxes on the amounts in question.[11]

During the summer of 1940, life in Liège slowly returned to normal. The sale of seized goods from abandoned businesses drew to a close. Creditors and their lawyers took all necessary steps to ensure that they could protect their legal interests and the city made sure its taxes would be paid, even if the owner/taxpayers were no longer present. And, of course, the Chamber of Commerce drew up a list of Hebrews/Jews without batting an eyelid. This was the perfectly ordinary way a legal system of antisemitic norms and practices gained a foothold in Liège. It was Belgian officials who first established a partial list of Hebrew businesses, a "Jewish Register", four months before it became compulsory under the German Decrees.

At the same time, the occupying Germans constructed an ever-more-complete form of control over the country, and especially over the Belgian economy.[12] A series of Decrees formalized the process of German command and control in economic matters. The most important of these for the future fate of the Jewish population of Belgium and of Liège were those regulating enemy property.[13] The two supplementary Decrees of 2 July and 23 August set the stage for the involvement of a new element in the processes and mechanisms already in place in Liège. The German military authority now became intimately linked with the operation of the local Belgian apparatus. After these Decrees, all "enemy" property became the object of an administrative system which required that the property be declared. In addition, restrictions on the sale or other types of disposal of the property were introduced. According to the 23 August Decree, the definition of "enemy" now included all Belgian subjects or residents who had fled the country and were now present on "enemy" soil, i.e. in France (§ 2). Every trustee or administrator of such property, or of property belonging to someone whose whereabouts were unknown, was now obliged to complete a declaration form and submit that declaration to the German authorities (§ 4).[14] Any doubtful case was to be presumptively one in which a declaration was required (§ 7). The city of Liège therefore found itself subject to these compulsory reporting requirements in relation to all the properties and businesses which it had liquidated or was in the process of liquidating, where the owner fell under the operative definition of an "enemy".

On 9 September 1940, the Public Procurement Department of the city of Liège wrote to the German Office of Enemy Property, in Brussels, informing the occupier that the city held the amount of 1,970,788.25 BEF as the result of the winding up of businesses falling under the Decrees.[15] They further informed the German Office that formal declarations required under the Orders were in the process of being completed. Finally, the city authorities asked for permission to return the proceeds to those owners who had in the mean time returned to Liège.

Ten days later the Germans authorized such payments to any returned Belgian subjects. As far as any monies owed to foreign or enemy subjects were concerned, however, they had to be deposited in a frozen account in a Belgian bank. While they were perfectly willing to comply with the German system relating to enemy property, despite the Hague Convention provisions limiting the power of an occupying authority to interfere with private property rights, the city officials faced a practical problem. They could not obtain copies of the official declaration forms from Brussels or from the local *Feldkommandantur*. They were concerned that in the circumstances it would be impossible for them to comply with their legal obligations *vis-à-vis* the occupying authority.[16] Finally, on 2 October the appropriate forms were sent from Brussels to the Liège *Kommandantur*.[17] Throughout the month of October, the relevant civil servants and elected officials in Liège went about their duty. Monies were returned to those business owners who had returned from temporary exile and the appropriate declarations of enemy property were returned to the German Office in Brussels.

The routine involvement of the local government officials in Liège in these first steps of what would eventually become the unlawful process of the expropriation of Jewish property is exemplified in the letter sent by councilor Jennissen to the Chamber of Commerce on 29 October, at exactly the moment at which the anti-Jewish Decrees were about to be published and enforced.

> Because the Chamber of Commerce has sole possession of the accounts of the relevant parties, I am passing on to you with this letter a packet of forms which will need to be filled in by you, bearing in mind that the completed form will be signed by the municipal Receiver who holds the funds or by a Councilor.[18]

Jennissen wrote to the President of the Chamber of Commerce again on 9 November, underlining that time was of the essence and that the Germans had in fact set the final date for the submission of all declarations relating to enemy property on 1 December.[19] The legal system established by the city administration in Liège, under which administrative powers were delegated to the Chamber of Commerce at the very beginning of the occupation in order to put into effect the mayor's emergency measures, was still functioning at this date. As an integral part of the administrative system of the city of Liège it now operated within the dynamic of relations between the city government and the German authorities. And then a new legal order, the First and Second Decrees concerning the Jews, took root in Belgium and in Liège.

As we have seen, the First Order of 28 October established the operative legal definition of the new juridical person "the Jew". Article 2 forbade the return of Jews who had fled Belgium. For many Jewish business owners, then, the entire history of the administration, expropriation and sale of their operations would occur in their absence. The administration of these businesses, which had now become "Jewish" businesses, would fall to the lawyers, bailiffs and civil servants in Liège. The city of Liège itself, with its political, legal and administrative structures, became, as trustee of the sums realized from the liquidations of these businesses following the conquest of Belgium, intimately involved in dealing not just with the German bureaucratic apparatus in Brussels, but with the returning owners, as well as with the lawyers representing either the absent owners or their creditors. On a daily basis throughout the occupation, these Belgian elected officials and civil servants participated in the legal processes surrounding the expropriation of Jewish commercial property in the city of Liège.

Chapter III of the First Decree concerning the Jews established a procedure for the declaration of "Jewish" undertakings. Article 6, as we have seen, set out the operative legal definition for determining when a business could be characterized as Jewish. Chapter IV prohibited any act aimed at the sale or other form of disposing of a Jewish undertaking.

It was on this last legal question about the "disposal" of Jewish property that the first practical and legal issues arose for the city and its civil servants. They apparently had no difficulty with the idea of the declaration and registration of Jewish businesses under the administration and trusteeship of the city.[20] There was no hint that the Hague Convention might be of any relevance, let alone an assertion that the Belgian Constitution protected religious freedom and guaranteed the right to private property. Nor was there any idea that permissible "passive" collaboration must be strictly limited. Instead there was inter-office cooperation, and added information, all probably illegal if the position of the Permanent Council on what constituted unlawful collaboration were to be applied. Nonetheless inter-agency cooperation allowed for a more efficient system of declaring Jewish property held under the trusteeship of the city of Liège. The city and its officials already had in their possession a partial list of "Jews" and their businesses provided four months earlier by the Chamber of Commerce. At that time, the owners possessed Hebrew businesses. Now their stores had become Jewish.

Several of these business owners, like many other inhabitants of Liège, had trickled back from their brief period of exodus and exile. They now requested the return of their property or, if that was not possible, the payment of the funds held by the city from the sale of their assets. But Chapter IV of the anti-Jewish Order barred any sale or disposal of Jewish property. Would handing back the remaining monies to the Jewish owners of the businesses constitute a breach of these provisions? On 15 November 1940, while other city bureaucrats and elected officials were finalizing the necessary steps for the establishment of the Register of Jews, councilor Jennissen sent a letter to the German Office for the Declaration of Enemy Property in Brussels seeking a legal clarification from the occupying authority on this question. This elected Belgian official, loyal to the principles of the country's constitutional order, wrote:

> But now business owners, whom we had supposed to be Hebrews are coming to our Office and are stating that they returned to the country before the Decree of 28 October. I would be grateful if you could let me know as soon as possible if I can hand over the funds belonging to these persons.[21]

This letter reveals the state of mind of an elected Belgian official, Jennissen, at this crucial time in the history of "la Belgique docile". In effect, Jennissen fulfilled three different roles in the governmental, legal and administrative structure of occupied Belgium. He was an elected local councilor, loyal to the Belgian Constitution and subject to the provisions of the country's criminal laws relating to dealings with the enemy. At the same time, his official status as councilor in charge of the Department of Public Procurement put him in direct contact with the German authorities and imposed certain legal and pragmatic obligations on him to ensure the smooth operation of an important aspect of municipal governance. Finally, he had a fiduciary duty to the owners whose funds he administered. The letter reveals much of how he attempted to juggle these often mutually conflicting roles.

Jennissen still used the more restrained and traditional Belgian terminology to refer to the returning owners: Hebrews (*Israélites*). He did not employ the

Nazi racial terminology and describe them as "Jews" (*Juifs*). At the same time, however, he does identify, for administrative and legal purposes, a group of his constituents, taxpayers in the city of Liège, according to a single criterion, religion (or perhaps race/ethnicity), unknown to the Belgian legal and constitutional order. While he did not use the Nazi terminology in his letter, he does their bidding nonetheless and engages in a practice of identifying his fellow inhabitants in what might be considered, even under the lax interpretation of his duties according to the interpretation given by the Permanent Council two weeks later, a blatantly illegal way. How did he, or his subordinates, identify these returning merchants as "Hebrews" in the first place? They had, according to his correspondence with the Germans, some reason to suppose that they were Jews? What reason? What constitutionally identifiable criterion could these Belgian officials have invoked to justify their supposition?

The Decree of 28 October did contain the provision which required all cases of doubt to be resolved by registration. But for there to be doubt, there had to be both an acceptance of the normative suppositions which informed the anti-Jewish Decrees and some unarticulated basis upon which the supposition was formed. Yet the assertions found in Jennissen's letter to the Germans in Brussels flew in the face of the limits that would be placed on "passive" collaboration by the Conseil de Législation's November letter. Any measure meant to supplement or to complete the registration and identification process under the Jewish Order would be strictly forbidden. Whatever the basis of the councilor's supposition in fact, in law, this inquiry is something more than docile acquiescence.

This is the crucial moral and legal question which informs any reading of the letter seeking further and better particulars about the interpretation of the anti-Jewish Order and the obligation incumbent upon the city of Liège in relation to monies held in trust from the sale of property. Belgian officials were forbidden to undertake any investigation, inquiry or supplementary step which would complete or perfect the application of the anti-Jewish Decrees. They could "apply" the Decrees but any and all other actions were strictly contrary to Belgian law. Jennissen appeared to request a legal opinion from the Germans, a legal opinion which he sought in order to protect himself, to cover himself and his civil servants from any allegation that they were somehow preventing the complete and efficient application of the anti-Jewish measures. Or else his goal was to complete and perfect the application of the antisemitic provisions of the German occupation law. He was either dangerously close to crossing the line from the permissible to the unacceptable and the illegal or on another interpretation he had clearly transgressed the fundamental principles of his nation's constitutional order. He did not merely and meekly, in a docile manner, ask for information. He asked for information concerning individuals whom he had, as he himself put it, reason to believe were Hebrews.

The basis upon which these suppositions, suspicions, beliefs were formed remains a mystery. Did he, for example, consult a list of "Hebrew and Polish" businesses constructed in July for him by the local Chamber of Commerce? Did he, like many citizens at the time, draw the conclusion that there was in fact a direct inevitable synonymy between "Polish" and "Jewish"? Did he know these individuals? Did he base his suppositions on the "un-Belgian" sounding surnames of the returning owners? In the end, the answers are of little importance. This was the second time that a Belgian official identified Jewish individuals on his own initiative. This was not a response to a direct German request, order or demand. The initiative was Belgian in origin. Why did the city officials not simply hand over the money to the returnees? Instead of acting in a manner consistent with Belgian legal norms, these civil servants and elected officials opted instead to refer all questions concerning "Hebrews" to the authority with jurisdiction in such matters, the Germans. Jennissen chose, not passively, but actively and with full knowledge, to submit his legal question to German jurisdiction. But the Germans only had jurisdiction here because Jennissen and his subordinates insisted on identifying the individuals in question as persons they had some reason to suppose might be Hebrews, and because they now accepted that these Hebrews would be from this time forth Jews. This was an act, on the sole initiative of Belgians, of the identification of Jews. It was also an act which rendered the application of the anti-Jewish Orders more efficient and complete, contrary to Belgian constitutional and criminal law.

But these legal and moral issues appear to have been far from the minds of these Belgian officials and civil servants. What they concerned themselves with were the practical consequences and aspects of their twin duties as liquidators and administrators of the sums realized from the sales of properties and businesses on the one hand, and their legal duties as administrators of property which fell under the provisions of the anti-Jewish Orders on the other. The proper balance between these two duties was struck for them in a letter from the Brussels *Kommandantur* when the German legal adviser replied on 22 November. The German lawyer indicated that payments to the supposed Jewish owners, who had returned, were acceptable "because it is not a matter here of a disposal of Jewish properties in their entirety".[22]

The city of Liège and its civil servants now entered squarely into the German machinery aimed at the removal of the Jewish influence in the Belgian economy. On 21 November the Caisse Communale held 182,363.10 BEF remaining to be liquidated.[23] On 25 November Jennissen informed the municipal receiver of the German decision which permitted him to return the funds to the owners, owners who the city still suspected of being "Hebrews".[24]

Meanwhile the city continued to meet its legal obligations towards the occupying power. On 20 November 1940, Jennissen sent more than 20 completed "Enemy Property" declaration forms to the Population Bureau, again so that the civil servants there could complete the entries for "given name" and "nationality".[25] The councilor submitted the duly completed forms to the Office for the Declaration of Enemy Property in Brussels on 24 November. Of the 23 names on the list of declarations, 21 are Jews.

Those charged with the financial affairs of the city administration continued to administer the accounts of the abandoned businesses throughout the occupation. The list of "Stores/Sums to be Liquidated as of 30 April 1941" included a clear majority of Jewish names, as did that drawn up on 30 June of the same year.[26] Other organisms within the city administration also dealt, on an almost daily basis, with the fiduciary administration of Jewish property. The legal service had to be involved in those instances in which claims for preferred creditor status were lodged and liens had been lodged by creditors of the Jewish business owners.[27]

On 31 May 1941, the Germans introduced the "Third Order concerning economic measures against the Jews".[28] This Decree increased German control over Jewish property and businesses. Article 1 granted to the Military Commander for Belgium the power to name an administrator (*Verwalter*) for every Jewish business. These companies could no longer enter into any contract or assume any other legal obligation without the prior agreement of the German authorities (§ 1). Under Article 17, which granted plenary powers to the Military Commander on all matters concerning the Jewish presence in the Belgian economy, each registered owner of a Jewish undertaking would receive, as we have seen, at the beginning of 1942, a notice requiring the liquidation and closing down of the business.[29] In the spring of 1942 more than 100 Jewish business owners went to the office of the Business Registry in Liège to have their name struck off the list of operating licensed businesses in the city. Each owner paid the Belgian government costs of 12 Belgian francs for the privilege and right to have their business come to a legalized end, according to the standard forms and practices of Belgian administrative and commercial law.[30]

Once again, Belgian administrative and governmental officials in Liège became key players in the process of eliminating their fellow inhabitants, Jews, from the economic, social and political life of the city and region. This antisemitic task became a matter of simple bureaucratic routine for these state and city employees. All costs associated with this elimination of "Jewish" businesses from Belgian economic life were borne by the Jews themselves. The payment of 12 francs in regular administrative fees went to the Belgian state. This does not appear to sit easily beside traditional renderings of "passive collaboration" or *la Belgique docile*. Instead it taints the hands of the Belgian state with the blood money of Aryanization. This is not *Référendaire* Vandeperre's refusal to allow Belgian courts and Belgian law to be sullied by involvement in the legalized theft of Jewish property. This is the administrative routine of the Shoah and it is a Belgian routine. All acts the effect of which was the removal of a business from the Business Registry cost 12 francs.

All these acts through which the Belgian officials in the city of Liège entered into intimate contact with the German anti-Jewish legal order continued to form part of administrative routine. In a letter dated 12 January 1942, the Liège *Kommandantur* informed the mayor that the Military Commander for Belgium required a full declaration of all property belonging to Jews who had left the country for France and who had not returned. The mayor was to provide this list of

exiled Jews to the Germans in very short time. Woolen or fur products belonging
to Jews were to be seized to help equip the Flemish and Walloon Legions.[31] These
volunteers in the battle against the Soviet menace, part of the larger struggle to
establish the New Order in Europe and in Belgium, were to be the beneficiaries
of the removal of the Jewish presence in Belgium. And the goods which would
benefit these fine Belgian patriots would be identified by Belgian officials.

But these Belgian officials, the civil servants in Liège, had a problem. On
13 January, the receiver-general wrote to the mayor to inform him of the visit of
a German officer who was following up on the request for the list of all goods
belonging to Jews who had failed to return. The receiver had told the German
representative that he could only provide a list of all business owners who had
not yet come back to Liège but that this was unacceptable to the Germans. The
Germans wanted a list of all the exiled Jews and reserved for themselves the
right to verify the "Jewish" status of all names provided by the city. The receiver
complained to the mayor: "I tried in vain to explain to him, to the best of my
abilities, that the city had no way of knowing individuals who belonged to the
Jewish religion."[32]

Was this an example of a calculated refusal to collaborate in the German
hunt for Jews and Jewish property? Was it an act of resistance hidden behind a
bureaucratic explanation that such information was simply not available under the
rules of Belgian constitutional government? Did the receiver not know of the list
of "Hebrew stores" already drawn up by the Chamber of Commerce at the request
of councilor Jennissen? Did he not know about the Jewish Register established and
maintained by the city of Liège? Was he not aware of the official declarations of
Jewish businesses completed and submitted in December 1940 by city officials? If
he were aware of these events, as he probably was, then this is the first public act
of resistance by obfuscation and delay in the implementation of the anti-Jewish
Decrees by a municipal employee in Liège.

Whatever the case may be, the matter did not disappear with this apparent
complaint about the impossibility of the task from the receiver. The mayor
requested that the chief of police furnish him, "in duplicate", with a list of
Jews, with their given names, addresses, professions and their chattels and real
property. Neither the chief of police nor the Socialist mayor Bologne tried to
hide behind a self-defined inability to determine under Belgian law who was
a Jew. Bologne underlined that he was asking the police for a list of property
belonging to JEWS by employing block capitals in his letter *(JUIFS)*.[33] Bologne
knew about the city's Jewish Register. He no longer referred in his official
correspondence to "Hebrews" (*Israélites*). For him, from now on, the question
would be one of JEWS. There is no evidence of any thought of resistance, of
invoking domestic constitutional law or public international law. Bologne was
not unaware of the provisions of the Hague Convention limiting the powers
of the occupying authority. He did not hesitate on numerous other occasions
to invoke its provisions with passion. It simply was never relevant in dealing
with JEWS.

Bologne provided the list of "abandoned" Jewish property with the help of the Belgian police. The purpose of the list was to provide the Germans with further information about Jewish property in Liège prior to expropriation and in the shorter term to equip Belgian fascist legions. The local government authorities in Liège, the police and the mayor himself, all acted in such a way as to provide direct assistance, by way of police investigations, in the compilation of information on the identity and property of Jews in that city. The goal and effect here were none other than the more complete, more perfect application of German measures against the Jews of Belgium. This was not docility, this was not passivity. This was collaboration pure and simple, headed by Joseph Bologne, the first Socialist mayor of Liège, imprisoned by the Germans and almost executed as a Belgian patriot in the First World War and hero of the Resistance in the Second War. These actions of the highest political and police officials in Liège were flagrant violations of Belgian criminal law and of the Constitution. They were also part and parcel of daily bureaucratic, police and political life in occupied Liège.

This occupying authority's battle against the enemy presence in the Belgian economy continued in early 1943. The German officials wrote to the mayor on 19 January asking for information concerning monies deposited by the Chamber of Commerce for the benefit of "Polish subjects".[34] City employees immediately began the hunt for the relevant information. The councilors in charge of city finances, the Office of Births, Deaths and Marriages, and the Public Procurement Office engaged in correspondence on the matter. On 23 January, the Office of Births, Deaths and Marriages sent the list of declarations filed by the city in November 1940 in respect to "enemy property" to the Public Procurement Office. The list contained handwritten annotations which give the nationality of each owner, the amount in question and some supplementary information. An analysis of this document reveals that of the twenty-three names found in the declarations of "enemy property", fourteen were Polish or stateless, formerly Polish. One was Dutch, four Belgian, two French, one Romanian and one had Spanish citizenship.

On 29 January, the Caisse Communale forwarded further supplementary information to the Office of Public Procurement.[35] This list included the names of the fourteen Polish proprietors (all Jews) with an indication of the amounts still owed by the city. Nine of these had a nil account, their assets having already been completely disbursed by the city. For the remaining five, four accounts indicated that formal legal claims by creditors had been filed against the monies held by the city. All of this information was duly passed on to the German authorities in Brussels by letter on 1 February. The councilor in charge, Jennissen, in order to complete and explain the information provided, added that two of the accounts in question also owed unpaid municipal taxes. In this case as in others, all of the resources of the municipal government organization were put to work to meet a German request for more information on a group of individuals who were in the majority Jews. Once again, the city of Liège sent what was in effect a list of "Jews" to the German authorities in Brussels. Ostensibly, the list was a list of

"Polish subjects" but from the earliest days of the summer of 1940, at the heart of City Hall in Liège, the logical path for the connection Jew–Pole, Hebrew–Pole, Maison Israélite et Polonaise, was an unerring one. Finally and once again, the city also made sure that its own interests were protected. Unpaid taxes were due to be paid by some of the absent owners. The city of Liège had to position itself in relation to any claim so that it would get its fair share of any Jewish property. *La Belgique docile* was never docile in making sure that Belgian administrative fees and local taxes were extracted from expropriated Jews.

Six months later the occupying authority asked for yet more information on eight of the "Polish" business owners, all of whom were Jewish.[36] The mayor responded: four of the required declarations had already been lodged with the Office of Enemy Property. The remaining properties, worth 73,325.50, 6,805.50, 65,180.50 and 14,370.50 BEF respectively, were in the hands of liquidators, the details of whom were passed on to the Germans. During December 1943, the BTG wrote to the municipal officials demanding more details about the sums belonging to five *Juden*.[37] A representative of the BTG came in person to Liège on 24 January and once more asked for more details concerning the amounts still held by the city for the five Jews. The Germans demanded information on the total amount realized by the city as well as a detailed accounting of any and all payments made from these accounts.[38]

The BTG was hot on the trail of Jewish money. Everything took place two years after the liquidation of all Jewish businesses at the end of May 1942. This was the final mopping up exercise for Jewish property still in Belgian hands, the final stages of Aryanization in Belgium. The city, now under the collaborationist Rexist mayor Dargent, took up the German request without hesitation. In this there was no discernible difference between the attitude and practices adopted under a *Résistant* Socialist mayor like Joseph Bologne or a blatant collaborator and traitor like Dargent. Any request for information, detail or assistance in relation to "Jews" was always met with full and often excessive compliance in Liège, except perhaps when the receiver and the Caisse Communale attempted some kind of delaying tactic, only to be stymied by the rest of the administration's ready and willing compliance.

Under Dargent's rule, Nazi antisemitic discourse dominates the correspondence between local officials and the Germans, although this differs little from Bologne's JUIF. The letter dated 21 December 1942 from the mayor of Liège to the BTG was headed "Jewish Assets" (*Avoirs Juifs*) and the text itself refers to "the assets of the Jews Hofman, Lindenberg, Litman and Wajnberg".[39]

On this occasion, the full city council took responsibility for the matter. At this point, all pretence of Belgian constitutional order in Liège disappeared. The city council under Dargent's collaborationist leadership became the legislative and legal agent for the process of Aryanization in Liège. On 18 February 1944, the council authorized the Finance Office of the city of Liège to pay over the remaining amounts in the "Jewish" accounts to the BTG.[40] In this instance, the council was complying with a request relating to "funds held in the Caisse Communale for the Jews", followed by the same list of names. The council in the full throes of collaboration did not seek out a more subtle formulation for its actions. The sums which were to be paid to the Germans were those monies owed to the "Jews" (*Juifs*). In February 1944, as the end of the dream of a New Order was in sight, after almost four years of occupation, of deprivation, suffering, and resistance in the heart of Belgium, the city council of Liège simply handed over Jewish assets to the Germans, but with a proviso. Even the Rexists had some properly Belgian priorities: "Given that the named parties Lindenberg and Hofman still owe certain sums to the City for taxes."[41]

While they ordered the Finance Office to make the payment to the BTG, the councilors and the mayor also ordered the payment to the receiver-general of the city of Liège "the amount of 1,385 francs for taxes due".[42] Once more the administration guaranteed its own small portion of the elimination of the Jewish influence in the Belgian economy. The city of Liège, its council, its Finance Office and the receiver-general "Aryanized" these Jewish assets. Gone were the often subtle and potentially difficult questions of the permissible limits of a "passive collaboration". In their stead, this was a municipal administration, from top to bottom, actively involved and implicated in chasing after its own share in the German policy of the elimination of the Jews of Belgium. Taxes had to be paid by these Jews before any monies went to the Germans.

The BTG continued to call upon the cooperation of the city officials. On 14 June 1944, a week after the Normandy landings, it wrote to the receiver-general seeking information on the deposit of funds ordered in February.[43] In the heart of the civil service in Liège, a jurisdictional battle between the receiver and the Office of Public Procurement appears to have broken out over the subject of Jewish assets. The BTG was forced to send another letter on 11 August to the Public Procurement Office, once more seeking clarification on the fate of the sums from the sale of Jewish properties which were due to be paid, but which had still not entered the BTG account in Brussels.

What emerges from beginning to end is the story of the daily involvement of the administration of the city of Liège, its elected officials and its employees, its mayor and its police force, in the hunt for Jewish economic assets. There was no act of resistance. Mayor Bologne unapologetically asked time and again for a list of JEWS. Well before the first German Decrees concerning the Jews, the city of Liège with the Chamber of Commerce identified "Hebrew and Polish stores". Lists of "Jewish" undertakings were compiled by civil servants in Liège without hesitation or objection. They were then passed on to the Germans. Bookkeeping concerning Jewish assets under the administration of the Caisse Communale was regularly kept up to date and then handed over to the Germans. The city's legal department looked after liens and freezing orders obtained by creditors in order to ensure the orderly and lawful administration and liquidation of all assets identified by the city itself as "Jewish". This occurred within the framework of the normal application of domestic Belgian legality. The city council agreed to the payment of Jewish assets to the BTG but only after ensuring the payment from these funds of municipal taxes. The city of Liège identified Jewish undertakings and their Jewish owners. They ensured that every German request for information concerning Jewish properties or Jewish owners was met with quick, efficient and complete answers. On a regular and ongoing basis, the city of Liège, its elected officials and its civil servants, like their counterparts in Brussels, violated the basic principles of the Belgian Constitution. But only, to be sure, when they were dealing with "Jews".

"Hebrew and Polish" merchants

Who were these Hebrew and Polish merchants identified by the Chamber of Commerce for councilor Jennissen in June 1940? Who were the owners of other businesses in Liège declared to the occupying authority in Brussels in November 1940 and subsequently as possessors of enemy property? Who were these men who owned the Jewish assets liquidated for the benefit of the BTG in 1944, but only after the city administration extracted the sums necessary to pay outstanding taxes? A brief history of some of these "Jewish businesses" illuminates the processes of Aryanization in Belgium and more particularly focuses on the intimate involvement of local, Belgian officials at the heart of these measures taken against the country's Jewish population. It also reveals a heretofore unmentioned possible act of bureaucratic resistance to the Aryanization process in Liège.

Bloemendael and Sons

Together with tens of thousands of other Liègeois, Aron Bloemendael and his son Henri fled Liège in May 1940. The Chamber of Commerce named a liquidator-administrator for the family business, Bloemendael and Son, wholesalers in confectionary. The liquidator and a police officer entered the store, drew up an inventory of candies and other delights worth 9,420.25 BEF, of which 8,505.25 BEF remained to be deposited with the city after liquidation.[44] The Bloemendael family business is not found on the famous first list of "Hebrew and Polish stores" drawn up by the Chamber of Commerce, nor does it figure on the two lists of 27 August and September sent by the Caisse Communale to councilor Jennissen concerning liquidated merchandise. But the Bloemendael business does appear in the month of November, on the list sent on the 26th, containing the declarations sent to the German authorities in Brussels pursuant to the Decree on enemy property. The Bloemendael family was of Dutch origin and they had fled to France, placing them clearly in the enemy category. The remaining sum of more than 8,000 BEF figured in this report as well as that sent on 30 June 1941.[45] In February 1942 the family and its business were also on the list of commercial enterprises the owners of which had not returned to Liège.[46] The same situation obtained on 23 January 1943 as the city of Liège and its civil servants continued to administer the funds deposited in May and June 1940 and to keep the German authorities up to date on the state of the accounts.

Up to this point, the story of the Bloemendael confectionary business and its assets of 8,000 BEF is fairly typical and uninteresting. The Bloemendaels were Dutch and exiled in France and as a result their assets clearly fell under the operative definition of enemy property found in the various German Decrees on the subject. The obedient services of the city of Liège reported to the competent German bureaucrats in Brussels. However another document found in the archives reveals more clearly the deep involvement of the Belgian officials in Liège in the hunt for Jews. On 5 March 1941, the "liquidator mandated by the Chamber of Commerce" reported that the assets of the Bloemendael business operation had been liquidated and that the business had ceased trading. Again, at one level, this fits into the standard pattern of the process of administration and liquidation of business assets in the cases of absentee owners under the aegis of the Chamber of Commerce in Liège. What marks this declaration as different and important is that the document in question is a "Declaration of a Jewish Undertaking" pursuant to the First Order concerning Jews.[47]

The reason the Chamber of Commerce continued to administer the Bloemendael property was that the family was not in Liège. They were in France – the factor which made the property enemy property. That is also the reason why the declaration was signed by the liquidator. Precisely because they were not in Liège, the Bloemendaels did not figure in the Register of Jews. The question in this case of a Jewish business and the processes of Aryanization in Belgium is how and why did this representative of the city of Liège and the legal apparatus set up to deal with the assets of those inhabitants who had failed to return, register and declare the business as "Jewish"? What was the basis, in fact and in law, for this declaration? A "Dutch" business somehow became in the eyes of the city government and its administration "Jewish"? Were the Bloemendaels known to be Jewish before the war? Did "Bloemendael" sound Jewish to the "Belgian" liquidator? Did the given name of the elder Bloemendael "Aron" somehow indicate that the family might have had Jewish ties?

Article 6 of the First Decree concerning Jews defined a Jewish business, a definition which required the identification of physical persons associated with the undertaking as "Jews" according to the operative definitions of the preceding sections of the Order. Article 17 of the Decree, as we have seen, provided that all doubtful cases were to be subject to declaration.

The declaration was itself three months late, coming in March 1941, well after the December 1940 deadline. Was the liquidator simply obeying the legal duty imposed on him by the provisions of the Order? What was the technical legal interaction between Article 17, which placed an onus to act in case of doubt on Belgian officials, and the rule of domestic law which forbade any measure or steps to complete or to perfect the application of anti-Jewish measures? There was in many cases an inherent contradiction between these two legal norms, each of which operated in such cases. The liquidator for an unknown reason waited three months to declare the business. The system of the Register of Jews and the clear impetus of the rest of the First Order clearly indicated that the Germans intended to operate a system of control over the Jewish population and over Jewish economic assets. All of these measures were contrary to Belgian domestic law.

As was the case with the list of "Hebrew and Polish" stores, in the instance of the Bloemendael family, the city of Liège and its agents took it upon themselves to identify Jews. The statement in an official document declaring the Bloemendael confectionary business as Jewish was made voluntarily by the agent of the Chamber of Commerce. There was no resistance; nor was this a case of hesitant and passive collaboration. The Belgian Constitution, the Hague Convention, a sense of social solidarity, none of these can be found here. What can be found is a hunt for Jews, at the heart of the municipal governmental structures, in forms and written statements, the paperwork of exclusion and hatred.

Juda Littman (Litman)

Juda Littman's name, unlike that of Aron Bloemendael, did figure on the list of "Hebrew and Polish stores" drawn up by the Chamber of Commerce in June 1940. The Chamber had named a liquidator on 29 May 1940 and taken possession of his men's clothing store on 31 May.[48] The Chamber paid the outstanding gas and electricity bills, 41 BEF, the locksmith's bill for allowing access to the police and the liquidator, 28 BEF, the unpaid wages of the Littman's employee, named as administrator, Mme Liègeois, 850 BEF, stamp duties on transactions 19.80, and finally its own administration fees of 2 per cent, 605.80 BEF. The remaining amount of 28,745.40 BEF was subjected to three liens filed by creditors. Juda Littman was Polish and like many of his compatriots from Liège he had left the city in May 1940. As a consequence, his goods became enemy property and the city of Liège followed its legal obligations in November 1940 by including his name on the list of enemy property under administration by the city.[49] The property of another Polish Jew was identified for the Germans by city officials who were simply doing their duty.

In October 1941, a full year after the first anti-Jewish Orders, the city of Liège sought the permission of the German authorities to disburse the sum of 682 BEF from Littman's account. Pursuant to the provisions regulating enemy and Jewish properties, permission was granted.[50] On 12 December, councilor Jennissen agreed a draft motion for the Council which approved the disbursement four days later. The amount of 682 BEF was duly deposited into the city's coffers, in payment of Littman's tax bill. Through the channels created by the German legal and administrative system for dealing with Jewish property, the city of Liège again guaranteed its own rightful share of Jewish assets. The city requested permission for the payment from the proper (i.e. German) authorities in Brussels. For the city officials, the process appears to have involved nothing more than making use of the available and necessary legal structures to ensure that Belgian debts, owed to the Belgian municipal apparatus, were paid as they fell due. They simply adapted their bureaucratic routine to the system of German legal administration over Jewish property for their own domestic, Belgian purposes. The initial identification of

Juda Littman's business as a "Hebrew" one appears to have led quite naturally to this state of affairs under which a Belgian municipal administration requested permission from the German authorities to make the payment of taxes due from the sums of the absent Jewish owner.

Throughout the occupation, civil servants and elected officials in Liège had dealt with various matters concerning the business assets of Juda Littman. They knew he was a Jew even though he was not present in Liège and not entered in the city's Jewish Register, since they had included him in the Hebrew list of June 1940. On 3 and 4 December 1941, the municipal authorities were busy pursuing Jews at the behest of the Germans. The Public Procurement Office demanded to see the file relating to the liquidation of Juda Lissman (*sic*) and the Office of Births, Deaths and Marriages returned the relevant file with appropriate additional information concerning his nationality, etc.[51] Later, in January 1943, the Caisse Communale once more drew up a complete statement of account for the councilor for Public Procurement, indicating that the unliquidated amount was 28,063.80 BEF.[52] Towards the end of 1943, on 18 November, as we have seen, the BTG sought to lay its hands on all unliquidated "Jewish" assets still in the hands of the city of Liège. In its letter to the Caisse Communale, the BTG sought all financial information concerning the administration of goods belonging to Juda Littman, "the Polish Jew".[53] After the visit of its representative to Liège to inspect the accounts, we know the BTG wrote again on 24 January 1944 to the Public Procurement Office seeking complete details on four accounts held by the city, all for Jews, of whom one was Juda Littman.[54]

Leyba (Léon) Miklacsky

This is another story of a merchant from Liège who took the exile route in May 1940. As in other such cases, the Chamber of Commerce took over his affairs, naming an administrator for his shoe store on rue St Séverin. After payment to the locksmith, back wages to the sole employee and, to be sure, stamp duties and administration fees, the remainder of 164,782 BEF was credited to M. Miklacsky's account. Another 15,000 BEF was claimed by creditors who placed liens on his assets.[55] Standard liquidation measures were taken in relation to the Miklacsky business and his name appeared a month later on the list of "Hebrew and Polish businesses". The Miklacsky files highlight and explain the interactions between the operations of the series of special legal regimes set up by the Germans to deal with enemy and Jewish property on the one hand, and the continuing operation of the normal systems of Belgian civil and commercial law on the other.

Throughout the occupation, the Belgian courts continued to sit and to hear all types of matters. While they only rarely dealt with cases in which the anti-Jewish legal regime was directly before them, as examined elsewhere in this book, Belgian courts and court officers, particularly bailiffs (*huissiers*), and Belgian lawyers, all dealt with matters in which Jews and their property were involved in civil disputes.

On 15 October 1940, SICO, a shoe-manufacturing company, informed the Liège Receiver's Office of its lien against the Miklacsky business. They also sought information as to whether the Caisse Communale held sufficient funds in Miklacsky's account to satisfy his debt. The receiver started correspondence with the councilor in charge of Public Procurement, Jennissen, on 17 October, in which it was suggested that any further communication with SICO be limited to a request that notice of the lien be formally served on them in accordance with the normal procedures of Belgian law. Jennissen not only informed SICO of the need to act according to the normal procedural requirements of Belgian civil litigation, but added that Miklacsky was considered an enemy because he was presumed to be still in France. As a result his assets were subjected to the German legal rules dealing with such cases. On 29 October, a bailiff formally served the city with SICO's claim.

Two weeks later, on 13 November, the bailiff Emile Mylle informed councilor Jennissen that a judgment in favor of his clients, Bral-Donego Ltd, and against Miklacsky had been rendered by the Belgian court. He was thereby authorized under Belgian law to seize goods or assets in the possession of a third party, in this case the city of Liège. However, Belgian law also prevented complete satisfaction of the judgment, entered by default, by means of the sale of such goods. Instead, only the sale of the household goods of Miklacsky would suffice in law. Given the potential hardships arising from the circumstances as a consequence of this procedural regime of Belgian law, Mylle pleaded with the city to act to avoid the seizure of household goods, as well as subsequent, and costly, ancillary proceedings by the expedient of paying him 5,000 BEF from the monies held by the city. Jennissen handed on the file to his subordinates for follow-up.

This case from the relatively early days of the occupation, but after the publication of the anti-Jewish Orders, demonstrates how the normal workings of the Belgian legal system continued in relation to the goods and other assets of exiled Jewish merchants in Liège: default judgment, service of the judgment by bailiff, negotiations about payment mechanisms to make everyone's life easier (except perhaps M. Miklacsky's). The matter was handled like any other involving the Belgian justice system in Liège. Many Belgian Jews lost property "legally" as a result of this entirely domestic process which coexisted with the direct anti-Jewish German legal regime.

One or two complications did arise in the Miklacsky case. Jennissen revisited the Miklacsky file and replied personally to bailiff Mylle. He was more than willing to pay the sum as suggested by the bailiff but, as he explained, his hands were tied.

Because he (Miklacsky) has not returned, the sums we hold in his behalf are considered as enemy property and perhaps as Jewish property. We cannot hand anything over and we have to declare all the property to the Office for the Declaration of Enemy Property.[56]

The city filed its declarations several days later, including information concerning the Miklacsky assets.[57] Again Jennissen anticipated the classification of the Miklacsky property as "Jewish". Miklacsky was still absent from Liège, as the councilor himself noted. Indeed, as with Juda Littman and Aron Bloemendael, it was this absence which made him an enemy for the purposes of classifying his property. At this date, 18 November, the Register of Jews was still in its infancy in Liège. The Adam circular establishing the formal procedures to be followed throughout the country for establishing and maintaining the Jewish Register was still more than two weeks away. The only official indication of Miklacsky's status as a Jew was the 24 June list of Hebrew businesses drawn up at Jennissen's own behest by the Chamber of Commerce. But Jennissen did not hesitate, in his capacity as councilor in charge of Public Procurement for the city of Liège, in official correspondence with a legal officer acting under a judgment of a Belgian court, to indicate that he had reason to suspect that Miklacsky was a Jew and his property might be classified as such. Since June, when the owners were still Hebrews (*Israélites*), they have already become, for internal Belgian purposes, two weeks after the First and Second Decrees concerning Jews, "Jews" (*propriété juive*).

Meanwhile the administrative processes continued to function as normal. City employees operated at first within the framework established by the German rules dealing with enemy property. When other potential creditors of Miklacsky attempted to have the debts paid from monies held by the city, Jennissen simply repeated the line that the monies were considered enemy property and that he could not dispose of the assets.[58] Three creditor companies sought judicial recognition of their claims.[59] Bral-Donego decided to pursue its interests according to the German legal system. It made a request for access to the funds to the competent German Office in Brussels and received authorization to have the city pay the amount of Miklacsky's debt.[60] Councilor Jennissen then asked that bailiff Mylle send him a copy of the court judgment so that he could begin the bureaucratic process leading to payment according to the rule of law.[61] The bailiff sent the judgment on 21 December and Jennissen responded on 26 December. Christmas vacation did not stand in the way of legal process in Liège when it was a matter of handing over Jewish assets to Belgian creditors.

Jennissen was ready and willing to pay the amount authorized but he could not deposit, as Mylle wished, the money directly into the bailiff's account without a power of attorney from Mylle's client.[62] Belgian law, after all, had to be respected, and such a direct payment to a person who was not the legally recognized creditor but a mere representative for limited purposes was illegal. On 4 January, Mylle forwarded the appropriate power of attorney and the money was paid into his account.

But it was not only the system of Nazi legality and the rules and procedures relating to enemy property which regulated the Miklacsky assets. On 18 December, the clerk (*greffier*) of the Court of First Instance in Liège, M. Glineur, was appointed by a judgment of that court as Miklacsky's official provisional administrator. He wrote to the city in an attempt to determine what steps he had to follow in order to gain legal control and custody of the Miklacsky assets. The receiver forwarded the letter from Glineur to Jennissen for action on 27 December.[63] The receiver also included information bringing the accounting for the assets up to date. The city controlled 158,201.75 BEF. In addition to the debts already brought to their notice, the receiver also underlined that Miklacsky owed 3,113 BEF in various municipal taxes. Typically, the city was interested not just in identifying and managing Jewish assets, but also took great care to extract its part before all other creditors. The double system of German occupation Decrees and the administrative structures thereunder and normal Belgian civil and commercial law systems and procedures continued to operate mostly side by side, always as long as the city got its taxes. There was no resistance in evidence nor was there any indication of principled insistence on the primacy of the Belgian legal and constitutional order. Instead, there was accommodation to a legal system which classified some assets as "Jewish" at the practical level.

Glineur wrote again to the receiver, this time on 29 December. He explained that, as provisional administrator appointed by the Belgian Court, he had a legal duty to act in M. Miklacsky's interests. He added that he could not do so unless he could obtain access to the monies held by the city. Miklacsky's creditors were threatening further legal proceedings for unpaid debts. Associated costs, including interest, were beginning to add up.

In the mean time, Léon Miklacsky had returned to Liège. On 27 December 1940, his lawyer, Me Terfve, visited the offices of the Public Procurement Department and requested the reimbursement of the sums owed to his client. Councilor Jennissen informed the lawyer that he too would have to gain the permission of the German Office for the Declaration of Enemy Property in Brussels before any monies could be handed over. On 30 December, Jennissen informed *greffier* Glineur, the provisional administrator, of the return of M. Miklacsky. On 5 January, 1941, Léon Miklacsky submitted his form declaring his business as "Jewish". He indicated that his business no longer functioned as a going concern because "The business was liquidated in June 1940 by the Chamber of Commerce of Liège, by order of the city of Liège."[64] The suspicions about the Miklacsky business in November 1940 by Councilor Jennissen proved correct. He was a Jew.

The existence of the parallel and sometimes intersecting German and Belgian legal systems continued to cause problems in settling matters relating to the Miklacsky assets. On 10 January 1941, Dufrane & Minon, creditors of the now defunct Jewish business, informed Jennissen that they had received permission from the occupying authority to realize their debt against the sums held by the city.[65] On 22 January the receiver wrote to Jennissen concerning the number of liens and other claims he had received against the Miklacsky assets. He wanted Glineur, as the Belgian provisional administrator named by the court under the terms of the Civil Code (Arts 112 et seq.), to take responsibility for all these matters.[66] Meanwhile, Miklacsky's lawyer, Me Terfve had received permission from the Germans to proceed with the complete liquidation of the affairs of his client. He was given permission to pay all of Miklacsky's debts from the monies held by the city and to return any remainder to Miklacsky.[67] The interactions between the two legal systems were complex. Some of the creditors had obtained the appropriate permission to have their debts paid from the Germans. Miklacsky's own lawyer had also received the consent of the occupying authority to deal with his client's assets. Meanwhile, Glineur continued to be the sole person acting pursuant to the powers and jurisdiction of the ordinary Belgian court system.

In the following weeks, correspondence arrived at the city offices from the creditor companies complaining to the civil servants about the continuing inaction in relation to their claims. On 3 February, Jennissen, in an obvious attempt to wash his hands of the whole matter, informed Mylle and Dufrane & Minon of all the relevant facts: M. Miklacsky had returned, and a Belgian provisional administrator had been appointed by the Court. Permission to proceed against the assets from the German Enemy Property Office did not appear to trump, at this stage at least, the appointment of a court-sanctioned Belgian administrator.

Mylle was unimpressed, to say the least. He wrote to Jennissen on 6 February indicating clearly that neither the return of M. Miklacsky nor the judicial appointment of an administrator could stand in the way of his seizure order. Me Terfve also began to lose patience with the city, which still held M. Miklacsky's money. He wanted to pay his client's outstanding debts, have the administrator's appointment terminated by court order and get whatever remained for his client.[68] Jennissen finally took decisive action. He wrote to the receiver on 27 February and instructed him to take the necessary steps – payment of the creditors by deposit of the sums with *greffier* Glineur, a request for the termination of the administration of M. Miklacsky's assets and the handover of the remainder to the rightful owner of the monies. The receiver however, objected, informing the councilor that what he was asked to do was beyond both his abilities and his field of expertise. He suggested handing the entire matter and monies over to the provisional administrator who would take charge of determining the final amounts, including costs and legally accrued interest from each creditor.[69] Jennissen agreed, since this took the matter out of the jurisdiction of the city. He informed Me Terfve that M. Glineur would take over the entire process of obtaining the necessary permissions from the German authorities and of making the appropriate payments to creditors and finally of reimbursing any remaining amount to M. Miklacsky.

The legal and financial problems facing M. Miklacsky did not stop there. Glineur wrote to Jennissen on 5 March 1941 informing the councilor that M. Miklacsky was now "in a very precarious situation".[70] The *greffier* as provisional administrator wanted to proceed as quickly as possible to the settlement of all outstanding debts and the release of all remaining funds. He asked Jennissen what exactly he had to do to put an end to the intolerable situation in which M. Miklacsky found himself. Jennissen fell back into his apparent default position and told Glineur that the solution to the matter lay with the German authorities in Brussels. The earlier permission granted to Me Terfve was not legally sufficient according to Jennissen because it gave Miklacsky's lawyer access only to "the net amount remaining after all debts were covered".[71] The elected representative of the people of Liège constructs the situation in a manner which is literal in its adherence to a strict and limited legal frame.

The suffering of the Polish Jew Miklacsky is of no apparent concern. The law must be obeyed, but the law is something of a mess. In this instance, this means that in order for Belgian law to apply reference must be made to the superseding German legal system. For the city of Liège, the dual legal system under which its elected officials and its civil servants had to operate was one in which primacy was given to the German Decrees, despite a normative structure of Belgian and international law in which private property interests, such as those of the Polish Jew Miklacsky, should have had primacy. The hardship suffered by this inhabitant and taxpayer of the city of Liège was of little if any apparent relevance.

Not for the first time in the history of legality and the Jewish question in occupied Belgium, it was the German legal regime which offered a glimpse of a more flexible approach to the operation of the rules relating to enemy property. Of course, what might be characterized as flexibility may equally be categorized and understood as a strict interpretation of the legal provisions. For the German legal officers in Brussels, it was clear that because M. Miklacsky had returned to Belgium before the end of 1940, he could no longer be considered to be an enemy under the operative legal definition of the term. As a result, the Office for the Declaration of Enemy Property would no longer concern itself with his property. "It follows that only the provisions of the Belgian Civil Code are to be followed for this liquidation."[72]

The city of Liège was aware of the provisions of the German Decrees relating to enemy property. The administration already knew therefore that the German legal regime did not operate in relation to property or assets belonging to those who had returned to the city. But they continued nonetheless to refer M. Miklacsky's legal representatives to the German authorities. A rigid, unthinking attitude to the German legal system and to the fate of Jewish inhabitants of Liège appears to have been the position adopted by the administrative officials of the city later portrayed as having been at the heart of Belgian national resistance to the German occupation. This Polish Jew, who was perhaps now a Russian Jew since he was born in that part of Poland then under Russian rule, gained possession of his assets not because of the good will of the city of Liège and its employees, but because at this point in time German legal officers were concerned with the efficient and correct operation of the legal system regulating enemy property. The actions of the city and of councilor Jennissen in particular evidence something more again than mere passive collaboration or "docility". They attempted at every turn to avoid any direct responsibility for the application of the legal rules relating to enemy or Jewish property, referring creditors, bailiffs, judicially appointed administrators and members of the Belgian Bar to German officials in Brussels. That strategy however ignored the basic fact that the reporting about Miklacsky's business began in June 1940 with the Chamber of Commerce identifying him for Jennissen as a Hebrew merchant, a designation which gave way to Jennissen's subsequent speculation in correspondence that Miklacsky was possibly a "Jew".

Glineur informed Jennissen of the German legal decision that Miklacsky was no longer to be considered an enemy in a letter dated 17 March 1941.[73] After Glineur forwarded a copy of the court decision appointing him as provisional administrator to Jennissen, the council issued an order permitting the transfer of funds to the *greffier*. Among the debts to be paid by the administrator from these monies, naturally, are city and state taxes as well as costs and interest accrued during the city's administration.[74] Throughout the summer of 1941, the city continued to forward any correspondence from creditors seeking payments of their debts to Glineur.[75]

Two years later, in 1943 and 1944, as the German hunt for Jewish assets in Belgium reached its peak they looked again at the Miklacsky case. In a letter to the city dated 26 June 1943, the German authorities asked for his complete file, since he was considered to be a Polish subject. Almost a year later, a week after the Normandy landings, on 14 June 1944, the BTG in its urgent hunt for the last Jewish assets in Belgium demanded the payment of the entire amount credited in earlier reports to Miklacsky's account, and declared originally to the Office of Enemy Property by the city of Liège, i.e. 158,210.75 BEF.[76] The Rexist mayor of Liège, as we have seen, then asked the receiver for the necessary information to permit him to comply with the BTG demand and deposit the Miklacsky funds, along with other "Jewish" monies, to their account.[77] He reiterated his request in another piece of internal correspondence on 27 July.[78] Finally on 3 August, the receiver reminded the councilor for Public Procurement that all the monies in the Miklacsky account had been, with the permission of the relevant German authorities, handed over to *greffier* Glineur. There was nothing left in the Caisse Communale. The BTG was informed of this on 11 August, days before the final liberation of Liège.

Moïse Goldberszt

The penultimate story about Polish and Hebrew stores in Liège highlights other key aspects of the Belgian side of the history of Aryanization. Moïse Goldberszt, born in Warsaw, became a Belgian citizen on 8 July 1937. His wife Rebeka (née Horenblas) obtained Belgian citizenship on 2 December 1937. Like thousands of their fellow residents of Liège, the Goldberszt family found refuge in France in May 1940. In July, Brucha (also known as Brogna) Horenblas, Moïse's sister-in-law, who had worked as a seller in the family hat store before the war, came back to Liège to take care of the family's affairs.[79]

Before her return, however, the city of Liège had taken possession of the store and goods found therein.[80] The hat store, Chez Maurice, situated at number 64, rue Puits en Sock, had become, in June 1940, a "Hebrew" establishment when it figured on the list of such stores drawn up by the Chamber of Commerce. On 19 and then on 27 July the receiver indicated that liens had been placed by unpaid creditors on the proceeds from the sale of goods from the Goldberszt store.[81] Even though Moïse Goldberszt was Belgian, because he had fled the country and was presumed to be in France, his property fell under the operative German definition of enemy property. As a result, the Goldberszt assets figured on the Declaration of Enemy Property submitted by the city of Liège on 26 November 1940.[82] Brucha Horenblas found herself entwined in the dual legal system, German and Belgian, when she returned and attempted to put the family's affairs in order.

The Goldberszt files are important because the story of the involvement of the legal system(s) operating in Belgium at the time is in fact one in which the domestic legal system appears to have played by far the more significant role. The struggle for the protection of the assets of this Jewish family in occupied Liège played itself out largely in the forum of the Belgian legal system. Belgian officials, civil servants, lawyers and courts dealt with the Goldberszt–Horenblas case. This Hebrew store figured in a system of domestic legality in which the Germans hardly appear at all, especially in the earliest days of the dual legal system's operation.

Thus, on 14 October 1940, the municipal receiver wrote to councilor Jennissen asking for a statement of account for the Goldbertz (*sic*) file. The reason was straightforward. The government had issued a tax notice for amounts owed by Moïse Goldberszt and this debt was first in line to be paid from the individual's assets.[83] The councilor in charge of Public Procurement replied that while the amount in question was 9,380.35 BEF, the absence of the account's owner would pose certain problems for any payments from the account or any final liquidation of assets.[84]

Mme Horenblas informed the city of her return in early November. She wrote to the mayor and to the city councilors but her correspondence was referred to the Caisse Communale. She told them that her brother-in-law's return from France was delayed because of the serious illness of some of his children. She went on to explain that she was in possession of a power of attorney, duly sworn before a French notary, from Moïse Goldberszt. She requested the handing over of the monies held by the city and added: "I wish to point out to you that the City Receiver is insisting on the payment of taxes, something I cannot do without gaining access to the monies held by the city."[85]

Mme Horenblas was in her own words simply trying to get access to the money held in trust by the city of Liège in order to pay her brother-in-law's tax bill. There was no question here of a demand from the Germans. This was the case of a debt owed to the Belgian state, by a Hebrew business, identified as such by other agents of that state, the city of Liège. But once again, the administration proved itself to be rigorously obstinate. The receiver referred the matter again, as was the usual practice in such instances, to the councilor for Public Procurement. In his letter he not only underlined the fact that a mere power of attorney could not have the same effect as the actual return of the owner of the business, but he added an extra detail so that Jennissen was fully informed about the state of play and the stakes at play in the matter: "At this time, I would also like to bring to your attention the recent Decree from the German authorities concerning Jews."[86]

This is another clear instance of the normality of bureaucratic antisemitism which appears to have been embedded in the municipal administration in Liège. The receiver took the time and effort to signal the recent Decree concerning Jews to the councilor. Chez Maurice had already been identified as a "Hebrew" business in June. The receiver in all likelihood saw in the names "Moïse Goldberszt" and "Rebeka Horenblas" something not quite Belgian. But the Belgian Constitution which still operated in Liège strictly forbade such identifications. Moïse Goldberszt was a Belgian citizen, entitled to the full protection of that country's laws. But of course, the process of identification of Goldberszt as a "Hebrew" in June 1940 clearly set the groundwork which allowed the receiver to commit the unconstitutional but practical calculation Hebrew = Jew (*Israélite* = *Juif*) in November of the same year, only a few days after the official publication of the First and Second Decrees concerning the Jews. Bureaucratic antisemitism became a central and uncontroversial part of official practice and discourse in the city administration under the Socialist mayor Bologne. These were not in June and November 1940 officials acting under the openly collaborationist, New Order Rexist regime of late 1943. This was Liège, the city of Resistance, but never of resistance to anti-Jewish Decrees or actions.

In this case, a high-ranking city official, the receiver, wrote to a high-ranking elected official, councilor Jennissen, identifying not just a Jew and a Jewish business, but highlighting the fact that any thoughts of making payments from the monies held in trust by the city had to be informed by an awareness of the recent anti-Jewish Decrees. Again all of this occurred a full month before a centralized and agreed practice had been developed on the proper procedures to be adopted by Belgian officials in relation to the anti-Jewish Orders and communicated to government agencies throughout the country. In Liège, the initiative was taken at the local level and it was an initiative the result of which was the more efficient working of the German Decree system. Since 24 June 1940, the city administration had been well ahead of any German request or demand in relation to Jews and Jewish businesses in the city. Each letter in the liquidation files simply marks another step in a bureaucratic antisemitism found in the routine paperwork of the municipal administration.

On 8 November Jennissen wrote to Mme Horenblas, He explained apologetically that he was not in a position to hand over the funds held by the city for M. Goldberszt because he himself was subject to the wishes of the occupying authority. The continuing absence of M. Goldberszt meant that he was classified as an enemy and his property subjected to a special legal regime. The city was compelled in the circumstances to lodge a Declaration of Enemy Property with the German authorities in Brussels. On 7 December, acting according to her power of attorney, Mme Horenblas herself filed a Declaration of Jewish Property under the First Decree.[87]

At the same time, Brucha Horenblas was busy with other matters under Belgian civil law concerning the family business. Local lawyer Me Raymond Mottart continued to act for her. The owner of the building in which the business was situated wanted to repossess the premises for non-payment of rent. Me Mottart suggested to Mme Horenblas that this might be for the best. "I also believe that it is in your own interest, given the recent measures adopted by the authorities, to finish this matter as soon as possible."[88] These recent measures to which the lawyer makes reference are doubtless the Decrees concerning Jews and Orders relating to Enemy Property. Mottart found himself faced with a moral, ethical and professional dilemma. He was a lawyer. He represented a woman and business which were both Jewish under German legal norms. He had to act under the normativity established by various German Decrees and other provisions of the occupying power but at the same time he was bound by his oath to uphold the law and the Constitution of Belgium. The two were clearly in conflict. His client was Jewish. She clearly fell under the provisions of the First Decree. At the same time, the very idea of identifying a client as Jewish for legal purposes was contrary to all the basic principles this leading lawyer had been trained to cherish as part of his professional culture. In this case, Me Mottart opted for a pragmatic approach and advised his client to settle matters as quickly and presumably as quietly as possible. In this part of the Goldberszt/Horenblas file, Me Mottart appears to have recognized the harsh reality of the existence of a pernicious legal normativity which defined his client as a Jew and which then imposed certain consequences on her as a result.

Other matters continued to arise under Belgian law and Me Mottart attempted to deal with them. At the end of 1940, after Brucha Horenblas had completed and submitted the declaration that Chez Maurice was a Jewish undertaking, Jules Glineur, *greffier* at the Court of First Instance in Liège, once more entered the picture as the domestic legal system dealt with the flow-on effects of the persecution of Belgium's Jews. On 31 December he wrote to Me Mottart informing the lawyer that he had again been appointed to the role of provisional administrator, this time in relation to M. Goldberszt's affairs. When he had visited the store, he explained, he had found Mme Horenblas on site with her power of attorney signed and witnessed before a French notary. He asked that the lawyer speak to his client about matters so that the proper legal state of affairs could be established in this case of apparently dueling mandates.[89] Me Mottart had already busied himself with attempting to put the affairs of the business in proper order, trying to pay off creditors and to obtain an order putting an end to Glineur's provisional administration since M. Goldberszt's duly empowered representative was now present.[90] In the interval, Glineur, as administrator duly appointed by a Belgian court having jurisdiction in the matter, had contacted the German officials dealing with enemy property as well as the city of Liège in his own attempt to gain access to the funds held for M. Goldberszt at the Caisse Communale.[91]

But these steps taken to reinforce and confirm the legitimacy of his status under Belgian law as the provisional administrator of M. Goldberszt's assets had another effect. In addition to the Declaration of Enemy Property already lodged by the city of Liège, the Germans now demanded that Mme Horenblas make a separate similar declaration.[92] Glineur nonetheless continued to do what he saw as his duty under Belgian law. On 11 January he had written to Mme Horenblas informing her that he was in fact and in law the official provisional administrator appointed by the Belgian court. Despite this, he went on to say, she continued to carry on the business and refused to provide him with a proper inventory as required by law.[93] He also fulfilled his official functions and wrote to the city of Liège who then requested a copy of the judgment appointing him as administrator and of the written permission from the German authorities granting him authority to obtain the assets held by the city.[94] The accounting provided by the Caisse Communale revealed a number of liens by creditors against the monies held, as well as a tax lien, legal costs and the fees of Glineur himself.[95] Yet again, this Hebrew undertaking, transformed into a Jewish business, was subjected at one and the same time to the legal requirements imposed by the occupying authority and by the ordinary operation of the Belgian legal system. As in the other cases briefly explored in this chapter, it was this Belgian legal system which ensured that the appropriate payments of fees and taxes were made first of all from these Jewish assets.

On top of all this, Me Mottart had to ask Mme Horenblas to pay his legal fees. Representing this Jewish client had not been easy and in any event it could not be free.[96] He was obliged to continue his correspondence with Me Burthoul, representing one of M. Goldberszt's creditors, as well as carrying on further communication with his client and with Glineur through the winter months of 1941.[97] He requested that Glineur suspend his request for a full inventory pending the outcome of various matters then before the courts.[98] He served a motion before the Commercial Court to end Glineur's provisional administration and sought to have the Court recognize the power of attorney. Mme Horenblas, according to her lawyer, was at all times prepared to satisfy all creditors of Moïse Goldberszt, including the payment of all costs and fees arising out of Glineur's administration.[99]

But at this stage, the civil servants of the city of Liège and *greffier* Glineur were the ones who continued to deal with the Goldberszt file. Glineur received the consent of the occupying authority to disburse part of the monies held at the Caisse Communale.[100] Among the debts to be paid were national and local taxes and interest accrued for non-payment while all of the procedural and jurisdictional matters were being worked out within the mechanics of the dual legal system.[101] Any responsibility on the part of the city for having seized the assets of Moïse Goldberszt, making it impossible for his representatives to have made any debt payments, was completely elided in the process. This owner of a Hebrew store later identified as Jewish in official correspondence within the administrative hierarchy of the city of Liège continued to owe his duty as a taxpayer to the Belgian state which was in the process of betraying him.

Mottart succeeded in obtaining a court order ending his term as provisional administrator of Goldberszt's assets, but Glineur continued to act as though nothing had changed.[102] At this point, following the decision of the Belgian court relieving him of his status as administrator, if Glineur continued to act in some legal capacity in relation to the Goldberszt case, it can only have been as an individual authorized by the Office for Enemy Property to disburse 9,380.85 BEF from the account held by the city. He could no longer pretend to act as an agent of a Belgian judicial process.[103] This officer of the Liège court continued to act in relation to property identified as Jewish under the orders of, and only by authority granted by, the German occupier. He became at this point a German agent, a collaborator. He was also a German agent with a difference since one of his primary tasks was still to make sure that all Belgian taxes were paid. The double-edged legal system operating at this time in Belgium became in this instance a unified Nazi system, voluntarily administered by Belgian officials.

Jennissen had requested in his letter of 19 March a copy of the judgment which named Glineur as provisional administrator in order to be able, according to Belgian law, to free up the funds in his name as authorized by the occupying authorities. On 5 April Glineur sent a copy of the original judgment and on 9 April the city council authorized the payment to him.[104] But by this point the Belgian courts had ended his powers as administrator. Under Belgian law, Glineur had no authority whatsoever in so far as M. Goldberszt was concerned. Goldberszt had granted a power of attorney to his sister-in-law, who at this time therefore held the only recognized power to act under Belgian law.

On 28 March, Glineur explained in a letter to Mottart that things had been slowed down in the whole of the matter by the lack of personnel at the Court.[105] Me Mottart, despite Glineur's lack of continuing Belgian legal authority and legal legitimacy, did not protest that Glineur was not permitted to continue as he had been doing. Mottart appears to have been yielding to the authority granted to Glineur by the Germans. The occupying authorities had informed Mme Horenblas that Glineur had been granted access to the funds to pay the creditors. Yet, in another case, when the Director of the Postal Checking Office informed him that Moïse Goldberszt's account had been closed at the request of Glineur, Me Mottart quickly informed the Director that Glineur no longer acted pursuant to a Belgian court order and had no authority to ask for the closure of the account.[106] Whatever may have motivated Me Mottart's decisions to intervene or not in cases involving Glineur at this point in time, one thing is clear. Glineur acted legally only by virtue of the authorization given him by the Germans and not under any power granted by Belgian law.

In the following months, Me Mottart continued his efforts to free the sums held by the city so that Mme Horenblas would be in a position to pay the taxes attributable to Moïse Goldberszt for 1941.[107] In order to reduce the amount of accrued interest at least, Mottart suggested to his client that she ask the receiver to pay the taxes due out of remaining funds.[108] Instead, the receiver simply made a payment of 9,000 BEF to Glineur with a list of outstanding liens and debts, including taxes.[109] On 31 May 1941, Glineur again wrote to Mottart, informing him that he was now in possession of the funds and that he had to pay off the outstanding taxes and other debts. He sought legal advice from the attorney as to whether he was within his rights under Belgian tax legislation to ask for a reduction of city taxes in the form of abatement (*dégrèvement*).[110]

The lawyer took up the case and entered into correspondence with the city tax office and with his client, who informed the lawyer that she had become ill (*malade*) as a result of "all these hassles" (*tous ces tracas*).[111] Glineur also kept busy and contacted all the competing tax offices who insisted at a minimum that they should each receive an equal payment. He also indicated at this time that his fees "would stand at 800 francs, to which would be added some disbursements".[112] Me Mottart again declared that the judgment of the Belgian court had ended Glineur's administration of these matters and insisted on a full and proper statement of account. Mme Horenblas saw to the payment of all other creditors.[113]

At around this time, Mme Horenblas was also summoned to the local tax office where she was told that Glineur had still not paid the outstanding amounts.[114] She then made a partial payment herself.[115] Later that year, in October, she again paid 552.80 BEF to the city of Liège in part settlement of Moïse Goldberszt's outstanding tax liabilities. The city continued to write to her throughout this period in pursuit of Goldberszt's unpaid taxes.[116] In January and February 1942, she was visited by city tax inspectors and had to ask Me Mottart to contact Glineur in order to get copies of the necessary receipts to prove her payments to the city and to put an end to the harassment she was suffering.[117] While the hunt for Jews in Belgium by the German authorities was intensifying, in Liège it was the hunt for Jewish taxes. The ongoing exclusion and removal of Jews from Belgian society in no way relieved them from their obligations as Belgian taxpayers.

Finally, the German authorities reasserted themselves. All Jewish businesses were wound up and placed in the hands of a German *Verwalter*. Mme Horenblas sent her accounts and the monies received every month to the *Verwalter* Robert Müller in Brussels.[118] The Goldberszt business, Chez Maurice, was Aryanized, but its taxes were kept up to date.

Joseph Lindenberg

One final narrative from the archives of the city of Liège serves to reinforce the key role played by Belgian officials and Belgian law in the process of identifying and expropriating Jewish assets, even after the war ended. Joseph Lindenberg was among those who fled in May 1940. The Chamber of Commerce appointed a liquidator for his fabric store, 22 rue Chaussée des Près, and realized 17,798.10 BEF from the sale of merchandise. After paying various expenses (water, gas, employee salary, stamp duty and of course, administration fees), the Chamber deposited a balance of 16,688.45 BEF with the Caisse Communale.[119] On 24 June, Lindenberg's store was identified in the list of Hebrew undertakings and towards the end of November 1940 it figured on the list of Declarations of Enemy Property filed by the city with the German authorities in Brussels. The by now familiar internal inquiries at the Office of Births, Deaths and Marriages confirmed that Joseph Lindenberg was "stateless of Polish origin".[120]

As in the other cases of absentee owners in Liège, the standard rules and procedures of Belgian civil and commercial law continued to operate. Creditors brought legal proceedings against their debtors and attempted to gain access to the funds held by the city.[121] Some managed to obtain the necessary authorization from the occupying authority to have their claim paid from these monies.[122] Others like the firm Novita sought information from the city about how to proceed in such cases.[123] Jennissen proved to be most accommodating. In his reply to Novita on 24 January 1941 he explained that he was treating their letter as an informal lien against the funds. In order to proceed lawfully, he told them, they would need to obtain a judgment from a Belgian court, as well as an authorization from the German authorities and then have both documents officially and formally served on the city.[124] As a postscript he provided the address in Brussels of the German office dealing with claims against enemy property. The dual legal system was put in motion and it was the elected councilor from Liège who greased the wheels of justice. On 8 May 1941, the Germans authorized Novita's lawyer to claim 585.60 BEF from the Lindenberg funds. Subsequently, the amount increased to 690.10 BEF when registration fees, postage and bailiff's charges were added, and the lawyer for the company, Van Raemdonck, filed his request with the city. On 14 May, Jennissen informed the lawyer acting for Novita that the city had to be served with the Belgian court judgment and the German authorization before any payment could be made.[125]

This dual Germano-Belgian legal system continued to create both practical and legal problems for the employees of the municipal government. They were more than willing to make the appropriate payments to creditors but the formalities of both Belgian law and the German system had to be followed to the letter. In relation to the Lindenberg case, the head of the Public Procurement Office wrote for advice to the city legal department on 23 July 1941. He wanted to know if the city could act when served with a default judgment, or alternatively, whether the employees needed to await a final judgment from a Belgian court. In addition, he sought clarifications on the rights and duties of city employees on the question of the German authorizations. These only referred to the principal of the relevant debt, and did not refer to supplementary costs such as legal fees, etc. In the instant case, could he authorize the payment of 4,110.25 BEF, an amount which included these additional costs or should he limit the disbursement to the 3,801.75 BEF explicitly authorized by the Germans?[126]

The answer from the legal department did not directly address the technical issues raised in the director's letter. As far as the city's lawyers were concerned, it was always simply a matter of referring to the principles of the Belgian legal system. The city was not a party to any legal actions between creditor and debtor. Belgian law laid out the appropriate procedures to be followed in such a case. "This ministerial officer (the bailiff Debatty) must be invited to follow the rules of procedure laid down in Articles 557 et seq. of the Code of Procedure."[127] In his reply of 25 August, Debatty expressed his shock (*je suis étonné*) at the city's position. He emphasized again that he had already done everything the city had asked of him. He objected to the imposition of yet another technical bureaucratic legal burden, especially given the small amount involved.[128] The legal department sought further legal advice from the city's legal counsel, Me Charles Fincoeur.[129] Once again, the city's legal advice hinged on the application of Belgian law. This, according to Me Fincoeur, "is consistent with the position we adopted a number of months ago, and I can see no reason to change it. We cannot hand over funds to a third party, without completing these formalities, in the absence of the agreement of our creditor."[130]

The rules and norms of Belgian law upon which the city relied offered some temporary respite to M. Lindenberg. But they were in reality designed to protect the city of Liège which found legal shelter behind the formalities of the Code of Procedure. What the city could not hide behind any legal barrier was the fact that it had identified M. Lindenberg as a Hebrew in June 1940 and all subsequent events flowed to a greater or lesser extent from that first unlawful and immoral act.

Following this legal advice, various creditors of M. Lindenberg undertook proceedings pursuant to the Belgian Code. At the same time, however, the city did not always in this period attempt to shelter behind the strictures of Belgian domestic law. After a lengthy, complex and difficult correspondence between various departments, the administration decided that it could permit the release of funds for the payment of insurance premiums on M. Lindenberg's store.

> Technically we could oppose this payment and demand a regular procedure.
> However, given the small amount, it is a good thing, even for the client (M Lindenberg) that the premium be paid. The legal theory of agency (*gestion d'affaires*) can be used to justify the payment.[131]

It is perhaps not completely accurate to argue that the city ignored the application of legal principles to find a pragmatic solution. In fact, the Legal Department found another, more flexible, legal solution. The doctrine of agency or in the civil law version in Belgium *negotium gestum* was based in the law of quasi-contract. It permitted a third party to intervene in certain circumstances in favor of a property owner who was unable to act in his/her own interest. The rules required that the intervening party act in a reasonable manner (*en bon père de famille*). The city in this case was paying the insurance premium owed by Joseph Lindenberg and meant to protect his business. This goal of protecting and preserving the property of another was clearly within the standard application of the rules relating to *negotium gestum*. In so acting, the city placed itself in a solid legal position in relation to any subsequent action in case of damage to the Lindenberg premises.

But it was not just the Belgian legal system which continued to operate in relation to Joseph Lindenberg's assets. The dual German/Belgian juridical axis still had its effects. In October, the fire insurance premium came up for renewal. The legal advice from the city Legal Department this time did not refer to Belgian civil law but instead to the German regime regulating enemy property. In his advice of 13 October 1942, the councilor in charge of the Legal Department pointed out that, while the operative German Decree provisions prohibited all acts aimed at disposing of such property, they also permitted ordinary acts of management or administration in relation to such property as well as any related act which did not constitute a "disposal" thereof. He also underlined, in case there was some doubt on the matter, "This is the property of a Polish Jew."[132]

The advice then went on to consider in some detail the Third Order concerning Jews and the role of the municipality as holder of Joseph Lindenberg's assets. According to the city's lawyer, Liège is not "the manager of the deposit. Its role is passive" (*gérante du depot. Son rôle est passive*). This legal advice contradicted in part at least the previous opinion which had asserted that the city could actively intervene under the doctrine of *negotium gestum*. More important, perhaps, is what this legal opinion did in fact contain. The question was not whether the city could or could not pay the insurance premium. The German part of the dual system had to be given precedence. The person whose goods and assets were being discussed is "a Polish Jew" and as a result Belgian law became for all practical purposes inoperative. The Polish Jew had become a subject to be treated only according to German law. At the same time, it should be noted, the city's legal officer did not hesitate to offer a considered interpretation of the operative German legal provisions relation to "enemies" and to "Jews".

The process of declaring Polish and Jewish businesses and assets as we have seen continued apace. On 1 February 1943 the city following the German request for such information sent a list of Polish businesses administered or liquidated by the Chamber of Commerce.[133] On the list figures the business of Joseph Lindenberg with its remaining assets of 10,604.55 BEF. The Germans were also informed that several liens and other claims existed against the Lindenberg monies – among those other claims, city taxes.

The administration engaged in further accounting in relation to the Lindenberg monies. The receiver reported on 9 February that the amount indicated to the occupying authority had been reduced to 10,312.75 BEF since the city had paid the fire insurance premium of 291.80 BEF.[134]

As we have already seen in the other cases from Liège, after November 1943, the BTG became intimately involved in hunting down Jewish assets. But one element further complicated the Lindenberg matter in the minds of the German authorities. There was, according to them, an indication of unauthorized payments from the account. While awaiting the deposit of the Jewish funds into their account, the BTG wrote to the city on 14 June 1944 seeking clarification about this issue.[135]

This revisits in effect the lengthy prior correspondence between the city and bailiff Debatty on the question of judicial and other costs, as well as the administrative payment authorized by the city to itself. There was, as we have seen, some doubt about the strict legality of paying to Debatty an amount which included extra fees and charges and which therefore exceeded the amount technically authorized by the German authorities in Brussels. The mayor sought an answer to the BTG query from the receiver.

Could you inform me of the reasons which led to the difference between the payment made to M Debatty and the German authorization?

How could we justify the transfer of 1,350 francs made following the details provided by M Boelen of your Office (these were taxes)[136]

These minor thefts of Jewish property committed by the city of Liège, apparently either for the pragmatic purpose of making everyone's life a bit easier (except perhaps Joseph Lindenberg) or else to make certain it received its rightful share of these Jewish assets, had come back to haunt the city. The receiver replied in a typically bureaucratic manner that he had done nothing without the express authorization of his superiors and that all such authorizations in the form of powers of attorney or resolutions of council were already in the hands of the mayor.[137] All of this again was taking place in July 1944. After the Normandy landings, when the writing was well and truly on the wall, the city of Liège continued to argue and debate over the proper disposal of Jewish assets, as it attempted to offer a full and complete accounting to the BTG. On 27 July, the mayor wrote to Debatty himself asking him to justify the excessive payment he received, even though as we have seen, the answer to these questions was to be found in the files and correspondence of the city itself.[138] The administration finally offered its explanation to the Germans on 9 August 1944. The payment to bailiff Debatty they explained was in the form of normal costs and fees associated with official proceedings and the payment made to the city's own coffers could be characterized as "public debts" (*dettes publiques*).[139] There was no longer any question of the theft of Jewish assets. Instead these were all payments made according to the normal practices and rules of Belgian law.

The postwar period: Aryanization light?

On 18 May 1945, Robert Bloemendael wrote to the Councilor in charge of Public Procurement asking for the return of the monies held by the city.[140] Robert had found refuge in France with his wife and his parents. He came back to Liège after the war but his father Aron had died after being deported in the seventy-second convoy from Drancy. Faced with this request, the Public Procurement Office sought advice from the Legal Department. A particular difficulty in the mind of city officials was that following Liberation the re-established Belgian government had introduced legislation blocking certain bank accounts relating to assets under German control. The Legal Department found an elegant legal solution. Robert Bloemendael was not asking for the return of monies held in a bank account. Instead he had a credit in his name for an amount held by the city. On 31 March, 1946, the council ordered the payment of 8,505.25 BEF to M. Bloemendael.

At this point the city still obviously held non-liquidated amounts of money deposited in the Caisse Communale. In addition to the money belonging to the Bloemendael family, other "Jewish" money was still unclaimed at this point in time. In 1947, the city reported that it still held 10,020.95 BEF credited to Joseph

Lindenberg and 28,068.40 BEF belonging to Juda Littman.[141] In these two cases, these were in fact the amounts which were to have been handed over to the BTG in early to mid-1944 and about which the Germans had sought more details in the summer of that year, having not yet received the money. These monies were never sent, despite the council's approval of the transfer of funds and its instructions to the receiver and the Caisse Communale to act in accordance with the council's decision. For two years after the war, the city of Liège continued to hold "Jewish" money, most of which had been in its possession since May or June 1940.

The administration had obviously been aware of the situation relating to unclaimed Jewish assets from the end of the war. Robert Bloemendael managed to get his family's money back. On 12 February 1945, Eagle Star Insurance had written to the councilor in charge of Public Procurement in relation to the Lindenberg matter. The company had received payments for insurance premiums throughout the occupation and the current year's amount was now due. To underline the type of matter with which the city was dealing, Eagle Star indicated that "Mr. Lindenberg, Joseph, Jewish subject, still absent" was the policy-holder.[142]

In January 1947, the Caisse Communale had informed the city council that it still held monies from the liquidations carried out by the Chamber of Commerce in 1940, including the cases of Littman and Lindenberg. The city administration, its elected officials and bureaucrats, knew at this point as they had all along that the money in question in each case was Jewish. On 13 January 1947, the city council of Liège simply voted to expropriate the assets of another Jewish resident it held in trust. The council decided

> Given that Mr. CYNGLER did not wish to retrieve the whole of the sum and that a balance of 2,194.20 francs remains provisionally consigned with the Receiver; the situation must be settled
>
> Following the proposal of the Councilors in charge of Finance and of Public Procurement;
>
> We authorize the Receiver to carry over into the receipts under Article number--- of the budget if 1946, the amount of TWO THOUSAND ONE HUNDRED NINETY FOUR FRANCS AND 20 CENTIMES (Frs. 2,194.20)[143]

The Aryanization of Jewish property continued in Liège two years after Liberation, and to the benefit of the city of Liège. The story of the Hebrew and Polish stores continued well after the war ended.

The Lindenberg saga offers a final summary of the history of the Hebrew store owners in Liège. Having returned after the war to Liège, Joseph Lindenberg attempted to get his property back. At the end of 1947 he went to the offices of Me Jean Libon, lawyer and member of the Bar of the Court of Appeal. Me Libon entered into communication with the Chamber of Commerce and contacted his client on 2 September 1947. According to his lawyer, M. Lindenberg could have his money simply by going himself to the offices of the Caisse Communale, and proving his identity. Me Libon also told M. Lindenberg that there were still some outstanding debts owed and that he should contact his creditors to settle matters.[144]

However, things did not go as smoothly as the lawyer led his client to believe. City officials at the Caisse Communale told M. Lindenberg that they no longer held his money which had been handed over to the Germans.[145] This was clearly untrue. Several months earlier, as we have seen, the receiver in an official report had identified monies held by the city for M. Lindenberg. Yet after several inquiries within the bureaucracy, the Legal Department referred M. Lindenberg to Brussels. According to them, the money in his account had been sent to the BTG in February 1944. Of course, we also know that this was incorrect and that the Germans themselves had protested in the summer of 1944 that the monies had not yet been deposited despite the city council's instructions to the responsible bureaucrats. Lindenberg was told that he would have to avail himself of the complex procedures established by the Belgian government in the post-occupation period concerning claims against German organizations or agencies and assets held by them.[146]

Information about Jewish assets was circulating between and among a number of departments and even to the council in the period before M. Lindenberg sought the return of his monies. In January, the Caisse Communale had identified the Lindenberg account and specified that 10,020.95 BEF remained unliquidated. At some level, other representatives of the city appeared to have been hiding its Jewish accounts from their rightful owner.

In 1950, ten years after the system for administering and liquidating Hebrew and other assets had been instituted in Liège, the city once again dealt with the Lindenberg file. This time however it did not concern itself with a claim for the return of monies it held in trust for a Jewish victim of Nazi persecution. Instead, it acted to protect its own interests. This time, it recognized that it did in fact still hold monies in the Lindenberg account. It was not seeking to reimburse these monies wrongfully withheld from their Jewish owner, the existence of which it had denied some three years earlier. The receiver wrote to the city council on 10 January 1950 as follows:

> Mr. Lindenberg has left the country for the United States, when he still owes several unpaid taxes, of which the detail follows. 1940. art. 60186 194
>
> 62411... 784.
> 1941 60206... 244.
> 65034... 64.
> 1946 63037 116.
> 1947 63037 155
> total... 1557.
>
> A resolution is required to "clean" M. Lindenberg's account.[147]

The elected representatives of the city of Liège, the city at the heart of the Belgian Resistance, reopened the Lindenberg file. On 17 January, councilor Renotte asked the receiver for more details on the authorization given on 26 February 1944 permitting the payment to the BTG. After inquiries, the receiver replied on 9 February, informing the councilor that the Caisse Communale had apparently not followed up on the matter and had not made the payment to the Germans. Some bureaucrat either through oversight brought about by disorder and disarray as the occupation neared its end, or deliberately as an act of resistance and defiance of the Rexist mayor's collaboration in Nazi attempts to finalize the legalized theft of Jewish assets, had ignored the order to transfer the funds to the Germans in Brussels.

According to the city accounts, there was still money left over in the Lindenberg account, indeed enough to satisfy all outstanding tax debts. The archival file ends on 21 February with a handwritten annotation that the receiver could simply deal with the remaining questions himself, making sure that the limitation period in relation to some tax debts had not run. What may well have been an act of bureaucratic resistance by city bureaucrats in 1944, when someone failed, or refused, to make the final payment of Jewish assets to the BTG, served as the basis for this final stage of Aryanization of Jewish assets by the city of Liège in 1950.

Chapter 9

Hirsch & Co.

A case study of Aryanization in Belgium

The process of Aryanization, the legalized removal of all "Jewish influence" in the Belgian economy, began, as we have seen, before the introduction of the first anti-Jewish Orders at the end of October 1940. A series of measures concerning enemy property had already been introduced by the occupying power. The first of these came into effect a few days after the defeat, on 23 May 1940.[1] The Second Order of 8 July extended the definition of enemy property to include property belonging to Belgians who had fled the country and who found themselves in France or England.[2] In addition to establishing compulsory registration and a formal declaration system for enemy property, the Germans set up a regime for the appointment of an administrator (*Verwalter*) for such enterprises. Because many Belgian Jews had joined their countrymen in fleeing the German onslaught in May 1940, these first Orders dealing with enemy property were applied to property which would, from October 1940, be considered Jewish.

While this system of identifying and administering enemy property was created and functioned under the legal regime of the occupying power by way of Orders or Decrees, another central part of what would become the system of Aryanization in Belgium was created under the provisions of Belgian law, again before the first anti-Jewish Orders of 28 October 1940. The Brüsseler Treuhandgesellschaft (BTG) was created on 12 October pursuant to the basic provisions of Belgian partnership law. With its head office at 1 rue de Louvain in Brussels, the BTG had as its primary business purpose "all civil and commercial transactions relating to the management, administration, liquidation and control of property belonging to individuals or companies as well as all other financial or industrial activities relating directly or indirectly to these purposes".[3] The chief unwritten goal of the BTG at the beginning of its life was to investigate and detect the presence of enemy and Jewish influence in the Belgian economy.[4] The legal and bureaucratic apparatus, under both German and Belgian law, for the process of Aryanization was therefore already in place when the first anti-Jewish Orders came into effect at the end of October 1940. Hirsch & Co., the story of which is the focus of this chapter, had already been identified as a Jewish company.

Léo (Lévi) Hirsch was born in Altena, Westphalia, in April 1842. Joining a wave of German Jewish immigrants who established themselves in Belgium in the second half of the nineteenth century, Hirsch married another German Jew,

Johanna Freudenberg in 1869.[5] That same year, he founded Hirsch & Co. The company, in the prestigious rue Neuve, would become one of the leading women's fashion stores in Brussels.[6] Léo Hirsch became a naturalized Belgian citizen in 1879. Throughout his life he remained an active member of the Jewish community, serving as a member of the Consistory, of the Jewish burial society (Hevra Kadicha) and on the board of the Hebrew Community of Brussels (Communauté Israélite de Bruxelles). He was also active in various charitable works, most notably in the founding of the Villa Johanna, a vacation camp for underprivileged children, Jewish and non-Jewish alike.[7]

By the outbreak of the Second World War, three of Léo's grandchildren, Lucien, Robert and Jean-Paul, ran the family business.[8] The eldest, Lucien, was mobilized at the outbreak of hostilities, and fled to France as the country collapsed. He spent the rest of the war in exile in Rio de Janeiro. The middle brother, Robert, was wounded in battle and evacuated from Dunkirk to England where he spent the war years. Only the youngest brother, Jean-Paul, who also served in the Belgian army, returned to Brussels after the fall of his country. He was the only family member involved in the operations of the company during the first years of the occupation. In 1942, like thousands of other Belgian Jews, as the German net closed around them, Jean-Paul and his family went into hiding. With false identity papers, he and his family spent the rest of the war in France, where he joined the Resistance.[9]

The story of Hirsch & Co., like the story of the various members of the family, embodies a set of complex elements which offer, as a case study, insights into the operation of the mechanisms of the German efforts to Aryanize the Belgian economy. In addition to the Jewish aspect of this company history, we find a Belgian side to the story of Hirsch & Co. During the early days of the war, in May 1940, the three Hirsch brothers were absent, called up for military service in defense of their country. In these circumstances, the family's lawyer, Henry Botson, an eminent member of the Brussels Bar, at the behest of the employees of Hirsch & Co., ensured the continuing operation of the business.[10] He appointed Albert Ghislain, a foreign exchange officer and friend of Lucien, as *pro tem* head of the enterprise.[11] Upon his return to Brussels, Jean-Paul Hirsch insisted that Ghislain remain in place and second him in running the family business. Ghislain accepted and took charge of many of the operations in partnership with Jean-Paul.[12] When the youngest Hirsch brother fled to France in 1942, Ghislain took over the running of the business until June 1944.[13]

Among the first documents in the Hirsch & Co. archives is one entitled "The Racial Situation of Hirsch & Co."[14] The document, which comes from the company itself, was signed on 22 June 1940, four months before the first anti-Jewish Orders. As we have seen, under the watchful eye of the German authorities, leading businesses in Belgium fell under a system of control by the appointment of a *Verwalter*. The German process of Aryanization in Belgium was being prepared from the earliest days of the occupation.

This racial history of the company is a fascinating and important document in the unfolding of the process of Aryanization in Belgium. After establishing in the first paragraph that the company was legally established under Belgian law, the text in paragraph two, entitled "Blood" (*Sang*), sets out that the three brothers run the company. Their father, Arthur, son of Léo, is described as "100% Hebrew" (*100% israélite*) while their mother, Clara Van Campenhout, is "100% Aryan" (*100% aryenne*).[15] The document underscores the confusion about the exact nature of Nazi antisemitism which existed in the early days of the occupation in the minds of many Belgians. The categories chosen to describe the father and mother of the three siblings are a mixture of the religious (Hebrew) and the racial (Aryan). At the same time, while the taxonomical difficulty continues, the consequence of this combination of parental blood is clearly set out in the final phrase of the second paragraph. "The Hirschs therefore have 50% Aryan blood and have nothing to do with the Hebrew religion."[16]

Even before the legal framework defining the new juridical category Jew was established in Belgium, the assertion produced in this document prepared by Hirsch & Co. clearly goes to creating a legal argument which would technically allow the business to escape being characterized as a Jewish undertaking. Jean-Paul Hirsch and his associates sought to create a situation which would protect the business from the worst effects of the German occupation. The narrative "General Remarks" (*Remarques Générales*) which follows the company accounts concludes the presentation of Hirsch & Co. as an operation which sits on the margins of Jewishness. The argument set out by the company is that, while the capital is marginally more Hebrew than Aryan, on the question of blood, the level of corporate control by Jews falls below 50 per cent. When the employees are taken into account, the Hebrew presence is "negligible". On the other hand, the company not only employs numerous Aryans but a number of business opportunities for a lucrative trade with Germany can be identified. Finally, according to the document, the liquidation of the business should not occur since it would not result in any return to the Aryan shareholders.

Despite these arguments, the business would clearly fall under the provisions of the First Order concerning the Jews of 28 October 1940. On 11 July, Hirsch & Co. had produced an extended argument in relation to the German Orders dealing with enemy and "Jewish" property.[17] In that document, the company asserted *inter alia* that only one-third of the company's stock was held by an enemy, Robert, who was in England. Lucien was in Brazil, a jurisdiction arguably not covered by the Orders concerning enemy property, and Jean-Paul was in Brussels.

On the Jewish question, Jean-Paul both for himself and acting on behalf of his brothers invoked their previous legal strategy. They asserted that all three brothers had the same Catholic mother and thus two Catholic grandparents, "all from an old Brussels family" (*tous de vieille famille bruxelloise*). It was only the marriage of two of the brothers to women considered Jews that allowed the business to be characterized as falling under the Orders. Jean-Paul's wife was not to be considered Jewish, since there was evidence only that two of her four grandparents were Hebrews. Again this type of argument falls into the dangerous, but perhaps pragmatically necessary, strategy of invoking Nazi legal categories in order to prove that certain individuals were not Jews. Robert's and Lucien's marriages to Jewish women clearly made them Jews under the First Order since a *Mischling* who married a Jew was thereafter considered to be Jewish. Therefore two-thirds of the company was controlled by Jews, one of whom was in enemy territory in England. While the argument about the doubt concerning Lucienne Van Praag, Mme Jean-Paul, succeeded in buying some time and assuring the third brother's participation in the running of the family business, the strategy of this "hermeneutic of acceptance" was doomed to fail in all senses.

The German response was swift. Lucien and Robert Hirsch were considered to be Jews because they had two Jewish grandparents on their father's side and because each was married to a person considered to be a Jew (§ 1(2)). Dr Wilhelm Pée was appointed as *Verwalter* of the Jewish undertaking. But the full force of the anti-Jewish Orders was not brought to bear on the company. Pée confirmed that Jean-Paul was not a Jew because he had only two Jewish grandparents and that the Jewishness of his wife had not yet been sufficiently established.[18]

Jean-Paul was therefore permitted to retain his functions at the company. At the same time, *Verwalter* Pée decided that, even though the company was Jewish under the operative Orders, signs indicating that it was a "Jewish undertaking", and an indication of the Jewish nature of the business on all bank accounts, need not figure on the company's premises or in their banking records.[19] Employees were informed of the decision and were instructed to send any Belgian officials or German authorities who might seek to question the absence of "Jewish undertaking" signs to the *Verwalter*.[20]

The reasons for this exceptional treatment are obscure. Hirsch & Co. quite clearly fell under the operative legal definitions of a "Jewish undertaking". German officials in Brussels were vigorous in their enforcement of the signage provisions of the Order, as we have seen, calling on the local police to enforce them. The *Verwalter* appears to have acted without formal legal authority in exempting the store from these signage requirements. The note of 10 July confirming the interview between Pée and Jean-Paul, signed by Pée, which became part of the company records, carries the following introductory note. "This document can never be referred to with third parties. If necessary, reference must be made to the confirmation note which I sent on 11 July to Dr. Wilhelm Pée, the administrator named for Hirsch & Co. by the Military Commander."[21] Pouillard in her company history speculates that Pée may have reached his decision either as a result of certain advantages he might have received or because he decided that the placing of conspicuous "Jewish undertaking" signs as required under the Order would have had a negative effect on the economic activities of the company which he was charged with administering.[22] Another important factor comes from Pée's own letter of 10 July. Therein he underlined that the exemption from the signage and bank account provisions of the Decree was a merely temporary measure since the two main Jewish interests in the company, those of Lucien and Robert, were soon to be sold. In such a case, the company would no longer be Jewish. Perhaps the decision was simply a pragmatic one, seeking to avoid unnecessary or unprofitable measures which would be rendered null in the very near future by the sale of the Jewish parts of the business. Whatever the motivating factor(s), the case of Hirsch & Co. underlines the key role played by individual German administrators in the daily operation of anti-Jewish legal measures and in the processes of Aryanization and highlights that they enjoyed a certain degree of discretion in dealing with the minutiae of business affairs.

The period of exemption as far as the bank accounts of the company were concerned, however, was short-lived. The Bank of Brussels was informed of the exemption on 11 July. The bank replied on 14 July, acknowledging receipt but requesting further clarification and proof as to the basis of the exemption, expressing concern over the bank's own legal position in such a case. A week later Pée withdrew the exemption concerning the bank accounts and Hirsch duly informed the bank of the renewed obligation to label the company's accounts as Jewish.[23]

Throughout the early part of 1941, Jean-Paul Hirsch worked on a plan to Aryanize the business himself, by selling the company to Albert Ghislain. In April of that year he met with his bankers at the Bank of Brussels to discuss the length of the new lease arrangement for the business premises which would remain in family hands and various technical aspects of the necessary sale and mortgage arrangements. The bank was careful to underline that Lucien and Robert were classified by the Germans as both enemies and as Jews. Therefore, the approval of both German bureaucracies would be necessary for any and all transactions. The bank's legal officers had other concerns about the proposed transactions. According to their technical analysis of the deals, the actual parties to the sale were the three brothers, rather than the company itself. In such a case, since two of them were enemies and Jews, there was a strong possibility that the Germans would require that any and all amounts owing to the two brothers be placed in a special blocked account. If the sale were to take place through the company as a legal person, the bank's lawyers thought this risk would be lessened. How they came to this conclusion, given that the company itself was Jewish is unclear, unless they thought that the funds would remain whole and Jean-Paul would retain some control over them, although this seems less than probable. This was also the opinion apparently shared by Me Botson and Jean-Paul Hirsch. They felt that the entire amount, rather than only two-thirds, would be frozen by the Germans if the sale took place with a Jewish company as the vendor.[24]

Furthermore, Me Botson was acutely aware of the delicate legal position surrounding such a transaction. He decided that any deal between Hirsch & Co. and M. Ghislain should take place before a notary and be legally certified by him. While Belgian law permitted a transfer such as the one contemplated in this case to take place by way of a simple written contract, Botson held firm to the belief that a notarized "authentic" exchange offered better protection and notice to third parties. Furthermore he offered his legal opinion that such a safeguard was important given the scale of the deal itself. Botson also expressed the clear desire to the bank that he no longer figure on any relevant documentation as a party representing the brothers Lucien and Robert. He pointed out that Jean-Paul now had full and binding legal authorization to act on their behalf. Botson's participation, even as a representative of the absent siblings, was for him contrary to his professional obligations as a member of the Bar. The transfer of a business undertaking such as Hirsch & Co. was a commercial transaction and lawyers were barred from participating in any way in such a contract.[25]

Pée continued to keep a close eye on the operations of the company. With the proposed sale to Aryan interests in mind, he asked Jean-Paul to clarify the circumstances surrounding Ghislain's role in the business. Hirsch responded in detail on 21 July 1941, outlining the circumstances which led Me Botson to seek Ghislain's help in the days following the collapse of Belgium.[26] Hirsch also explained that the planned sale of the business was motivated by several interconnected factors. The Jewish nature of the business made its future in German-occupied Belgium precarious. In addition, the business had been suffering diminishing returns for some time and this had been exacerbated by the war and occupation. Retail fashion in his opinion was not likely to flourish under the current circumstances. Finally, he informed the *Verwalter* that he was aware of the cases of the Philippson Bank and the foreign exchange operation of Pels and Goldsmit, which had recently been Aryanized by way of sale to high-level employees. In light of all these circumstances and factors, Jean-Paul had consulted with the firm's legal advisers, Me Botson and Me Thoumsin-Saintenoy. Because Jews, even in Germany, were still permitted to own real property and to live off the income therefrom, it was decided as a result of all these factors to sell the business while keeping ownership of the building itself. While M. Ghislain's name was mentioned as a possible purchaser, because he had only recently come into the business, they were unsure if he had any real interest in running the company in the longer term.

After further consultations, according to Jean-Paul's explanation to the *Verwalter*, M. Ghislain expressed his desire to purchase the business. Thereafter, there followed a number of consultations by all parties with both Belgian and German legal authorities in order to finalize the transfer of the business pursuant to all legal formalities and obligations. In other words, Jean-Paul Hirsch sought to explain to the *Verwalter* that the proposed sale to Ghislain was an above-board, legitimate sale based in all relevant circumstances and not a sham transaction meant to preserve Jewish property in the hands of an Aryan straw-man.

The involvement of the *Verwalter* in the Hirsch affairs extended to the personal property of Lucien and Robert, for which he was named administrator on 29 September 1941. As Jean-Paul explained in a letter to the family's notary, Camille Hauchamps, the initiating factor appears to have been the desire expressed by the German occupants of Robert's house to purchase the wine cellar. A legal representative for this Jewish wine had to be found before it could be lawfully disposed of.[27] The nomination of Dr Pée as *Verwalter* for Robert's personal property also raised legal issues concerning Robert's interest in the estate of Clara Van Campenhout. The notary's assistance was called for.

At the same time, Jean-Paul informed his two lawyers, Thoumsin-Saintenoy and Botson of these legal developments.[28] Botson replied the same day, suggesting to Jean-Paul that he inform the *Verwalter* that he held a power of attorney for his brothers only in so far as the business of Hirsch & Co. was concerned. The following day, 4 October, Botson added to the legal mix by explaining that the nomination of the *Verwalter* would have a complicating effect on several legal matters concerning the brothers, including the fate of the sum of 700 BEF remitted to him from the estate of their mother from an unspent deposit for telephone taxes. He entered into contact with Dr Pée to obtain his permission to deposit the money.[29]

The complexity and intricacy of the legal regime then operating in Belgium concerning Jewish property is highlighted by the family affairs of the Hirsch brothers. Two of the siblings, Lucien and Robert, were Jews, while the third, Jean-Paul was not. The estate of their mother, which the brothers inherited in equal shares, was already being dealt with under the normal provisions of Belgian law.[30] On top of this was layered German anti-Jewish occupation law, with which Belgian lawyers, notaries and financial institutions had to deal. The estate of the brothers' mother held an account with the Bank of Brussels. On 11 October 1941, the bank was informed of the appointment of Dr Pée as the *Verwalter* for the personal property of Lucien and Robert, the two Jewish brothers. As a result, two-thirds of the estate's accounts were now under the jurisdiction of the administrator while one-third remained the personal property of the non-Jewish brother, Jean-Paul. Any future transactions relating to these monies would require the signatures of both the *Verwalter* and of Jean-Paul as long as the estate remained legally undivided.[31] The bank had also held in a safe deposit box silver objects which had belonged to the mother. These objects had been removed and inventoried, pursuant to Belgian law, by the notary dealing with the estate, M. Mourlon-Beernaert. On 22 October, Jean-Paul wrote to him asking urgently for an inventory to be handed over to the *Verwalter*.[32] That same day, Jean-Paul also wrote again to Me Thoumsin-Saintenoy informing the lawyer that the German administrator required the drafting of a document, constituting a power of attorney, permitting M. Ghislain and Jean-Paul to complete all necessary acts and to pay all taxes and charges, insurance premiums, etc. on behalf of Lucien and Robert and the mother's estate.[33] In other words, while the *Verwalter* had legal authority over the properties and estates in question, he wanted to delegate the tasks of daily administration to Ghislain and/or Jean-Paul. In order to do so, he felt that it was appropriate that the mechanisms of Belgian civil law be used. Jean-Paul who held power of attorney for his absent brothers apparently was limited to acts relating to the business of Hirsch & Co. He could not, absent a new power of attorney, act for his brothers in relation to their personal property, nor could he act for the estate, two-thirds of which was Jewish and therefore under the control of the *Verwalter*. In this case, he would be acting not according to a power of attorney drawn up with the consent of his brothers but instead with a Belgian legal instrument created in effect at the behest of the German *Verwalter* of his brothers' private property. Once more, the system of mixed German and Belgian law was brought into the service of German anti-Jewish measures.

Belgian law, the Hirsch family, Jews and Jewish undertakings

Belgian law as we have seen in other cases continued to function, albeit in the shadow of German occupation law and practice. The demands of normal business required that Jean-Paul continue to use all means necessary, including ordinary civil law norms to ensure the continued and proper operation of the family's affairs, all of which occurred under the surveillance and ultimate decision-making power of the *Verwalter*.

In February 1942, Jean-Paul sought the advice and assistance of Me Thoumsin-Saintenoy concerning a contract between the Hirschs and one Samuel Cahn, relating to two Brussels cinemas, the Lutétia and the Cigale. At this date, Cahn was behind in his rental payments to the Hirschs, but Jean-Paul indicated that they had information to the effect that Cahn was in fact receiving monthly rental payments from his sublessees for the two establishments.[34] Jean-Paul Hirsch wanted a legal opinion as to whether the lease signed by Cahn had been extended by the effect of law. He also informed the lawyer that should Cahn continue his recalcitrance in paying his debts, the services of the legal adviser would be called upon. The legal opinion which was received on 27 February was that the lease would be terminated on 31 December and could not in the circumstances be extended under operative Belgian law.[35]

In the mean time, other legal matters continued to affect the running of Hirsch & Co. as well as the affairs of the family itself. On 2 March 1942, the company, like all other registered Jewish businesses in Belgium, received a notification from the Military Commander that as of that date it was forbidden to continue to operate as a going concern. It was to be removed from the Commercial Register and was required to liquidate its stock by the end of the month.[36] The full-bore process of Aryanization of Jewish business in Belgium was coming to an end. Meanwhile the *Einsatzstab* Rosenberg, charged with the expropriation of property of cultural significance belonging to Jews, informed *Verwalter* Pée that it was taking possession of a number of paintings and books belonging to the two Jewish Hirsch brothers.[37]

Jean-Paul continued his judicial attack on Samuel Cahn for unpaid rent. He wrote to Me Thoumsin-Saintenoy on 7 March, five days after being notified that the family business was to be closed as a Jewish undertaking. He informed his lawyer that he had written to Cahn, without response, informing his debtor that he now owed over 200,000 BEF and that the matter would be handed over to his lawyer for further action. Intriguingly, Jean-Paul informed his legal adviser that he knew that the rental payments owed to Cahn by his sublessees had been placed in a blocked account.

In other words, Hirsch knew that Cahn was a Jew, that his property was Jewish and that as a result of the various German measures targeting such property, Cahn had no access to any funds which would have permitted him to meet his contractual obligations to the Hirschs. Jean-Paul knew this not just because he had been informed that all payments to Cahn were placed in a blocked account, but because of his intimate dealings with the affairs of his two Jewish brothers. Nonetheless Hirsch & Co. pursued its legal rights against Cahn the Jew with vigor. The lawyer not only shared his client's view, but added to the case a patina of legalism which justified and authorized the continued pursuit of the Jewish debtor.

In his expert legal opinion, Cahn was without any possible defense which he might seek to raise as a result of the circular of 2 March closing down all Jewish businesses. For Me Thoumsin-Saintenoy, Cahn could not invoke the German action against his creditor Hirsch because as matter of law, i.e. Belgian law, he did not operate a business which was subject to the closure Decree. According to the Belgian jurist, Cahn sublet the two cinemas and therefore he was not himself engaged in a commercial activity covered by the German measure. He was acting as a landlord not as a cinema operator. He did not directly run the cinemas, an activity which was forbidden to him in any event.[38] Therefore, the legal argument went, he was not obliged to close down a business because he did not operate a business. He remained bound by his contractual arrangements with the Hirsch family.[39]

M. Cahn's counsel disagreed. He paid a visit to the competent German authorities and obtained from them an official legal finding that his sublease did in fact and in law constitute an "economic or commercial activity" covered by the 2 March Circular.[40] Once more, the dual system of law operating in Belgium in Jewish cases worked in an intriguing fashion. Even if we assume that Hirsch's lawyer's opinion was correct as a matter of Belgian civil and commercial law, that advice was clearly understood by all parties to have been trumped by an official legal designation of the business by the competent German authorities.

As Me Thoumsin-Saintenoy then went on to explain to his client, this meant that Cahn was unable to continue to enjoy and use the property as a result of an "act of God" (*cas fortuit*). Under Belgian law, to which the case returns as the operative normative system under which the contract was to be interpreted, this meant that Cahn no longer owed any rent. Indeed, this was the case even though the lease provided for the payment of 300,000 BEF in rent on 1 January 1942. Under Belgian law, this anticipatory payment was contingent upon M. Cahn being able to enjoy the use of the premises until the end of the lease on 31 December of the same year. This was now no longer possible. Indeed, had he paid in January, he would have been entitled to reclaim most of the money back. On 30 March, the day before his business was to be liquidated, Cahn served official notice by bailiff upon Hirsch & Co. that he was obliged to stop trading but that the business would continue to operate through the sub lessees and that Hirsch could now deal directly with them.[41]

The day after being served by Cahn, Jean-Paul Hirsch wrote to Pée asking permission to enter into a contract directly with the Messrs Gerrebos and Mestdagh, the two Belgians who continued to operate the cinemas. He also provided the contact details for Dr Wilhelm Offergeld, the *Verwalter* for M. Cahn, in order to ensure that all interested parties could be informed. Pée followed up almost immediately. He wrote to Offergeld on 7 April passing on the relevant details and asking for his agreement for the new lease with the Belgian tenants.[42]

Things became more complicated still with the appointment of a new *Verwalter*, replacing Dr Pée, in the person of Karl Schneider. Schneider cancelled all powers relating to business matters given by Pée to Jean-Paul Hirsch and Albert Ghislain by letter dated 18 May 1942.[43] At the same time, Schneider insisted that Hirsch and Ghislain remained legally obligated to continue to deal with business matters in good faith and competently, perhaps as a result of an equitable duty imposed by the doctrine of *negotium gestio*. All powers of attorney relating to the personal matters of the two absent brothers, Lucien and Robert, Robert's wife and their mother's estate remained in force. Confused by the apparent contradiction contained in Schneider's missive, voiding the authority given by Pée to run the business but maintaining a legal obligation to do so, Jean-Paul again sought legal advice from Me Thoumsin-Saintenoy.[44]

The Belgian lawyer found himself in a difficult position since part of any legal answer to his client's inquiry would be grounded in German occupation law and not Belgian law relating to *pouvoirs* and *mandats*. He asserted in his response that it was impossible to reach any conclusion about the powers vested in Jean-Paul and Albert Ghislain based on the terms of Schneider's letter. The lawyer confirmed that the letter appeared at one and the same time to remove all authority to act from Hirsch and Ghislain while imposing on them a duty to continue to act. For Thoumsin-Saintenoy, it was arguably the case that no power or authority at all was given by this letter. According to the overall effect of operative German Decrees, the appointment of a *Verwalter* suspended all legal powers vested by Belgian law in officers and representatives of the company affected. The *Verwalter* could delegate some of his powers to the existing company officials but only pursuant to a proper and binding power of attorney, as Dr Pée had done.[45]

Meanwhile Dr Schneider sought a solution to the cinema rental imbroglio by following up on Pée's attempts to ensure a new lease with the Belgians who continued, under their agreement with Cahn, drawn up under Belgian law, to actually run the theaters.[46] In order to complete the legal formalities for the new lease, an expert opinion and survey of the premises was required. According to this report, work needed to be undertaken to correct the damage and dilapidation of the building. Under the lease conditions and the operative provisions of the Civil Code, M. Cahn was obliged to make good the damage to the building caused during the term of his lease.[47] The lawyer contacted his client a week later.[48] He informed Hirsch that he had received no reply from Samuel Cahn, but had run into his lawyer in the court house and had been informed that his representative had no information about his client's current whereabouts. Pursuant to the standard steps of Belgian civil procedure, Me Thoumsin-Saintenoy suggested that a bailiff attempt to perform a legal service of documents and notify the court of his inability to locate M. Cahn.

The handwritten annotations from the client on the lawyer's letter are instructive. Across the top half of the letter he has written in large script 'non non non'. A note is added about contacting the expert to determine the exact amount of damage to the theaters. More intriguingly, we find the following annotation in handwriting: "Cahn is a dangerous person. He does not even reply to his lawyer. Don't do any new business with him."[49]

Samuel Cahn was a Jew. Arrests, round-ups and deportations of Jews had begun and many Belgian Jews were going into hiding. It is hardly surprising, then, that in mid-June 1942, Samuel Cahn was making himself scarce. Jean-Paul Hirsch, who would himself go into hiding a little over two months later, must have known this, yet the internal documentation of Hirsch & Co. demonstrates that the company was carrying on business as usual and condemning Cahn as "a dangerous person".

Schneider, like his predecessor Pée, took charge of various matters relating to the personal property of the two Jewish Hirsch brothers. Like Pée, he also allowed Jean-Paul to continue to deal with questions of daily concern. Thus, the youngest brother had to look after the family house on rue de Suisse, ensuring the payment of taxes, insurance premiums, etc. Schneider also insisted that Jean-Paul report every trimester on the accounts relating to this matter and required him to deposit two-thirds of all excess amounts flowing from this building into a blocked bank account.[50] He likewise insisted on receiving detailed information on the rue Neuve business premises.[51]

In September 1942, just before the disappearance of Jean-Paul and his family, the *Verwalter* imposed still more restrictions on the affairs of the family and the company, insisting that all correspondence from the company carry the indication "'Jewish Undertaking' in German, Dutch and French" as well as the indication *Unter Kommissarische Verwaltung*.[52] At the same time, the cinema affairs finally came to an apparent conclusion. *Verwalter* Robert Müller, now in charge of Samuel Cahn's property, decided that, confirming the previous German opinion, and notwithstanding the opinion and legal advice of the Hirschs' family lawyer, the lease between Cahn and the Hirschs remained valid until 31 December 1942. They therefore requested the payment of the sums due into their account. At the same time, they sought and gained permission to have the rental for the Cinema Lutétia paid into the account in the Continental Bank.[53]

After the departure of Jean-Paul in search of safety in France, Albert Ghislain took over sole responsibility for the management of Hirsch & Co. In October 1942, he wrote to the company's lawyer, Me Thoumsin-Saintenoy, informing him of the latest meeting with the *Verwalter* dealing with Samuel Cahn's properties, and with Müller. After what Ghislain describes as a "difficult and stormy" (*une discussion difficile et orageuse*) meeting, he managed to persuade the administrators that a clause in the proposed new rental arrangement for the Lutétia, pursuant to which it was made clear that Ghislain was not acting as a guarantor for the ratification of the contract by the Hirsch brothers, would be inserted into the contract.[54] Ghislain also managed to get the occupying authority to revisit its previous decision as to the existence of the lease between Cahn and the Hirsch family and to accept the previous legal opinion that under Belgian law the lease had been terminated by an Act of God on 31 March.[55]

Meanwhile, he continued to pursue, as had Jean-Paul Hirsch, the monies, some 3,443.35 BEF, still owing from Samuel Cahn. He asked *Verwalter* Müller to deposit the sum from the blocked monies held for M. Cahn at the Continental Bank of Brussels. In other words, Ghislain continued the policy of treating this as a simple case of debt, while at the same time being compelled as far as the practical details were concerned to recognize that the entire process was implicated from start to finish in the mechanisms of the Aryanization of Jewish property in Belgium. At this point, the Company and Ghislain appear to have had little choice given the presence of *Verwalteren* for both the two-thirds Jewish interest in Hirsch & Co. and for Cahn's economic assets. Instead of an ordinary intra-Belgian question of contract and debt, the real legal stakes in the lease dispute were simply which Aryanized pot of money the disputed sum would enter.

The dealings with Müller continued into the next year. Concerns were expressed by the *Verwalter* about the amounts requested by Ghislain from Cahn's monies to pay for the refitting of the Lutétia. On 3 February 1943, Müller informed Ghislain that the refurbishment expenses claimed were excessive and that the next 50,000 BEF in expenses would be taken out of the Hirsch account.[56] Ghislain in turn attempted to receive Müller's authorization to pay for changes in the fire insurance policies covering the cinema.[57]

In fact, various aspects of the dispute concerning the Lutétia continued through-out the war and even thereafter. In October 1944, Samuel Cahn returned and began legal proceedings against the two sublessors, MM. Gerrebos and Mestdagh. The facts are similar to other cases being adjudicated at the same time in Brussels pursuant to Belgian legislation which permitted Jewish individuals who had been removed from their real property because of German actions to demand a return to the *status quo ante*.[58] In this case, Gerrebos and Mestdagh alleged that Cahn had in fact ratified the new lease signed by them with the agreement of the *Verwalter*. They also alleged that he had been paid money by them in return for his ratification, money which was handed over and not declared to the *Verwalter*.[59] In their complaint to the Crown Attorney they sought to open a criminal investigation concerning Cahn and his associates who they alleged had attempted to blackmail them into renouncing any claim to the cinema. The disagreement between the parties continued in November 1944 with claim and counter-claim.[60] The next year, in February 1945, Hirsch & Co. wrote to the tenants informing them that they now were in possession of information indicating that neither one of them was legally permitted or licensed to run a cinema and that they had in fact sublet the Lutétia to MGM.[61] Hirsch & Co. then proceeded to file suit against Gerrebos and Mestdagh. In the course of these proceedings and negotiations aimed at settling the movie theater dispute once and for all, the two defendants recognized that the lease signed in October 1942 had been drafted under the pressure of the German *Verwalter* and had not established a fair market value for the rental. They further recognized that this was the real reason Ghislain had refused to guarantee the subsequent ratification of the lease by the Hirschs and had insisted to the *Verwalter* that a clause to that effect be appended to the agreement. They also confirmed that an oral arrangement between the parties had been made to the effect that a realistic rental would be fixed and paid upon the return of Lucien Hirsch.[62] The Aryanized business arrangement, which could only have had some equitable *de facto* effect in any event under Belgian law, was not, therefore, in fact or in law, the true contract between the parties. The Hirsch brothers signed a new lease with Gerrebos and Mestdagh on 14 June 1945, the object of which was to settle any and all disputes arising out of the continued uncertainties surrounding the premises of the Lutétia.[63]

This brief case study of the fate of Hirsch & Co. under the Nazi legal regime leading to Aryanization in Belgium embodies many of the important legal aspects of German anti-Jewish policy in Belgium and its daily operation in a real context. A dual system functioned under which German Military Decrees identifying the new juridical category Jew could only really be put into practical effect in many cases pursuant to the operation of standard and normal rules and procedures of Belgian civil and commercial law. As a result, Belgian lawyers dealt with their clients on an almost daily basis in ways which implicated them deeply and inextricably in the acceptance of Nazi antisemitism. At the same time, behind the scenes efforts were made in many cases to obviate if not to negative entirely the Aryanization process.

In order to keep some form of control or involvement in the family business, Jean-Paul Hirsch had to argue, or at least accept and acknowledge that legally, that his two brothers had become Jews while he himself was not legally Jewish. The Bank of Brussels and its legal advisers had to attempt to ensure that any monies paid as a result of the Aryanization of Hirsch & Co. would not end up in a blocked Jewish account. In the mean time, Jean-Paul had to make sure that legal actions were undertaken to protect the family's business interests, even if this involved dealing directly with the *Verwalter* at the heart of the Aryanization of Samuel Cahn's affairs, invoking as necessary Belgian law of contract and German Decree laws regulating the disposal of Jewish assets. As always, the dual legal system operated in a hierarchical fashion so that German anti-Jewish legal norms always formally trumped Belgian law or else served as the basis upon which Belgian law acted.

Chapter 10

Belgian lawyers, Belgian judges, Jewish cases

The arrangement between the SG and the German Military Command in the fall of 1940 whereby all anti-Jewish Decrees would be German in origin and nature and would merely be implemented by Belgian official state structures had a clear effect on the operation of the Belgian legal system under occupation. Unlike their French counterparts, Belgian legal officials were never directly confronted with a domestic system of antisemitic law.[1] But a combination of the mechanisms of passive collaboration and the inevitable effects of the various anti-Jewish German Decrees meant that, in some instances, Belgian lawyers and judges had to confront the new realities of the legal category Jew in their daily practices. We have already encountered instances where the dual legal system implicated Belgian state and judicial officials and lawyers in direct encounters with Nazi legal antisemitism. In this chapter I explore those cases where the Belgian legal system and its actors were even more intimately confronted with the normative effects of anti-Jewish Decrees on the Belgian juridical order. What follows is a brief history of how the Belgian legal system coped with "Jewish cases".

In addition to those instances in which official legal authorities within the Belgian state hierarchy and judicial apparatus had to confront and deal with these broad issues of principle and come face to face in practice within the national legal system of the potential impact of anti-Jewish Decrees, Belgian courts also encountered cases when they were directly asked to construct and apply the effects of the Orders in relation to basic and continuing principles of ordinary legal rules. Again, unlike France, anti-Jewish laws were not directly introduced as part of domestic law, so that the Belgian courts were faced with a different problematic than their southern neighbors. They had to adjudicate in those instances where the dual existence of a system of legal rules imposed by the occupying power (rules which were always assumed at some level to comply with the Hague Convention) and ongoing domestic norms appeared to clash. While the empirical base of reported cases is extremely limited in comparison with the French example, unsurprisingly perhaps given the exceptional nature of those instances in which a clash of legal systems could manifest itself, these few decisions shine an important new light on the way in which the Belgian legal order confronted German anti-Jewish Orders.

The first reported case of the application of German antisemitic norms actually slightly predates the first two Decrees concerning Jews. On 29 October 1940, the Conseil de Prud'hommes in Brussels considered a case in which an employee, a Jew, was dismissed from his post by his Belgian employer as the result of an order given by the German authorities.[2] The employee sued for unlawful dismissal and sought to recover unpaid wages, as well as an amount in damages due to the failure of his employer to respect the legal notice requirement before firing him. He was awarded his unpaid wages but on the damages issue the tribunal was clear. It found that the circumstances surrounding the dismissal constituted a case of sovereign command (*fait du prince*) which the employer was compelled to obey and for which no legal redress was available.[3] The reported version of the case in Theodor Smolders's occupation law reports is not particularly helpful. Because of German censorship control, most of Smolders's reports are mere paragraph-length summaries, although it should be noted that they constituted an invaluable service to Bench and Bar during the occupation, given the lack of other sources.

The archival file in the case provides more detail and further insight.[4] The plaintiff was Friedrich Rotmann (Rottmann in some renderings), an employee of Théo Van Den Borre, proprietor of Ready Garage in the Brussels suburb of Anderlecht. Rotmann was engaged to keep the books at the garage. Van Den Borre worked primarily for the Heeres-Kraftfahr Park repairing vehicles for the Wehrmacht. Ironically, perhaps, Rotmann, a German, was an invaluable employee because he could translate bills and invoices into that language for submission by Ready to its customers. The file does not indicate how the Germans discovered Rotmann's background or indeed even how they discovered he was working for Ready. According to Van Den Borre, he was dismissed on the orders of the Germans who would not tolerate a Jew working for the Wehrmacht.[5] Rotmann maintained that he had been assured that he was being paid from the employer's own funds and was not listed as having any involvement with the German organization, Heeres-Kraftfahr Park. Be that as it may, the tribunal accepted that Rotmann had been dismissed as a result of the German demand contained in the letter of 9 October and that this *fait du prince* removed any liability on the part of his employer for failing to provide notice.

This case raises some interesting points from the perspective of a legal history of Belgian law and Nazi antisemitism. First, it offers clear evidence that the Belgian judicial system was dealing with Jewish cases even before the introduction of the First and Second Orders. At one level this might be classified as a purely German case, involving the Wehrmacht and a German citizen. At another level, however, this is also an unequivocally Belgian case. The employer is a Belgian (involved in unlawful collaboration with the occupier by rendering direct assistance to its military force). The Conseil de Prud'hommes is clearly dealing with the dispute within a framework of applicable Belgian employment law. Secondly, the case shows that, from the very beginning, Belgian legal officials seemed content to accept, without further inquiry, the idea that German anti-Jewish measures were somehow legitimate and should be recognized as such. It was open, in theory at least, for the tribunal to assert that the German demand that Van Den Borre dismiss Rotmann was both contrary to Belgian law and to international law under the Hague Convention. It instead simply accepted the sovereign act of the German military and allowed the occupying authority to interfere with lawful domestic contractual relations. After all, Rotmann was not asking to be allowed to resume his job at Ready. He was merely seeking full compensatory damages for what he characterized as an unlawful dismissal. The German desire that *Der Jude* Rotmann be dismissed was a *fait accompli*. The only question for determination was whether he was entitled to a small monetary compensation (5,070 BEF) for the lack of legal notice. The dispute was clearly one which took place within the framework of Belgian employment law. The tribunal was faced with a Belgian employer who was collaborating with the German Army and repairing vehicles used to conquer and oppress the country, on the one hand, and a Jew removed contrary to basic norms of equality under the Constitution, and contrary to the limited powers of an occupying authority under the Hague Convention, on the other. The court chose to refer to an exceptional legal rule, *le fait du prince*, in order to allow the employer/ collaborator to escape any further liability. The Belgian courts were not off to a good start in their defense of the rule of law.

They would, however, redeem themselves to a great extent as the real nature of Nazi legalized persecution became apparent. One might begin to explain the Brussels Prud'hommes decision in the Rotmann case by situating it temporally in the earliest days of the occupation, as all Belgian state organs were attempting to feel their way in their dealings with the Germans. Memories of the misery caused by the breakdown of Belgian law during the First World War and its replacement by a German legal order no doubt influenced locals to be extremely cautious in their dealings with the Wehrmacht, even indirectly. Moreover, in the presence of an overwhelming military occupation it is perhaps not surprising that the notion of a fully sovereign state of exception, *le fait du prince*, might have had a highly significant impact on the judicial consciousness in October 1940.

As time went on, however, the nature of the occupation became clearer. In particular, the introduction of anti-Jewish decrees, particularly the Second Order which directly affected the Bar and the judiciary shocked the conscience of the legal elite. After October 1940, the Belgian judiciary appears to have adopted, for the most part, an attitude and jurisprudential practice of resistance. This resistance was nuanced, as we have seen, in order to allow participants to shelter behind basic principles of Belgian law. At the same time in cases involving *de facto* Aryanization through the normal application of Belgian domestic creditor/debtor law, the legal system of the country did become intimately involved in the removal of the Jewish influence in the Belgian economy. The judicial record of resistance is without doubt complex, nuanced and on occasion double-edged.

Nonetheless, the series of Jewish cases which took place after the Decrees concerning Jews became part of the legal landscape is characterized by a firm resolve to refer to fundamental parts of domestic law in an apparent attempt to obviate the worse consequences of the new Nazi legal order. Judges hearing these

Jewish cases simply invoked the basic normative structures of a legal system which did not recognize the existence of a legal subject known as a Jew. At the same time, their adjudicative practices took cognizance of the factual reality of the situation of Jews in Belgium.

The first such reported Jewish case to be decided after the introduction of the anti-Jewish Decrees does not in fact concern itself with these provisions at all. It is a purely Belgian case. In *René Meyer v. Roger Wouters*, the Brussels Commercial Court (Tribunal de Commerce), was faced with a request for the dissolution of a partnership, under the provisions of Article 1871 of the Civil Code, on the grounds that the mutual trust between the partners had been destroyed.[6] The facts are simple. One partner was called up by the Belgian Army in May 1940 and after the defeat, returned to Brussels and the business in June. The second partner, Meyer, a Jew, had fled in the mean time to the Belgian coast and then to France, taking with him the monetary assets from the company's account. The first partner, Wouters, obtained a default judgment against Meyer in August 1940, and a liquidator was appointed. Upon his return, Meyer attempted to avoid the loss of the company. The Tribunal de Commerce took the position that only in exceptional circumstances, when the relations between the parties were irrevocably beyond repair, should the court order the definitive winding up of the business.[7] On the facts, the court determined that the actions of the Jewish partner had had a minimal impact on the commercial activities of the business. During the hostilities, in May and June, both partners were absent and the business was inactive. Upon the return of Wouters, other minor practical difficulties were overcome and by October the business was functioning normally.

The Court then reviewed the circumstances leading to the departure of Meyer, including the ambiguity of government instructions to all men aged between 16 and 35 in the build-up to hostilities. It also took into account the general state of disruption and panic in Belgium and northern France at the time. It concluded that the breakdown between the parties was not irrevocable or permanent. It was merely the temporary consequence of extraordinary circumstances flowing from war and the first days of occupation. It overturned the dissolution order and quashed the appointment of the liquidator. It based its conclusions in part on a plea to Belgian values: "people in this country generally act in a way which is more understanding, lenient and tolerant".[8]

While little is made in the text of the judgment of Meyer's Jewishness, it must be seen nonetheless to have played a key role. It is clear that one of the motivating reasons for him to have fled the country was the fact that he was a Jew. He joined thousands of others in the exodus of May and June 1940 as they faced an uncertain fate under German occupation. The Tribunal de Commerce emphasizes again and again the state of uncertainty and even panic which dominated the country at the time. This analysis is confirmed by the subsequent Court of Appeal decision rejecting Wouters's appeal. The very description of Meyer as a Jew really has no other meaning in the context unless it is meant to underline the justified nature of his decision to leave the country. It should be noted again that the choice of language is instructive. Meyer is referred to as both a "Jew" (*Juif*) and as a "Hebrew" (*Israélite*), indicating graphically the confused and confusing reality surrounding the facts of the case and the application of an appropriate Belgian legal rule. Nonetheless, the two courts in this case clearly invoke standard and normal legal provisions of the Belgian Civil Code, apply the legal principle to a set of facts and interpret those facts in a way which takes into account the real panic which overcame many Belgian Jews (and non-Jews) in May 1940.

Another factor may have been at work in this case, although this analysis is admittedly speculative. Under the provisions of Chapter III (§ 5 et seq.) of the First Decree concerning Jews, the business operated by Wouters and Meyer would have been classified as Jewish. It would have been subject to compulsory reporting as a Jewish undertaking and, of course, as the occupation went on, the Third Decree of May 1941 imposed further reporting obligations and attached still more onerous restrictions on such businesses and their assets, before proceeding to the liquidation of the operation itself. It was clearly in Wouters's interest, then, to have the business wound up and for him to gain access and title to as many of the assets as possible. After October 1940, it certainly was not a good idea to be involved in a business partnership with a Jew, and an appeal from a decision of the Tribunal de Commerce compelling one to resume commercial operations in such circumstances may have made from his perspective good business sense.

Notwithstanding the reality of German anti-Jewish measures, which by January 1941 had come into force in the Brussels area as far as the compulsory registration/declaration of Jewish businesses was concerned, the Brussels court simply treated the case, formally at least, as one involving nothing more complex than the interpretation and application of Article 1871 of the Civil Code.

Other cases presented starker confrontations between the Belgian legal order and Nazi anti-Jewish laws. A remarkable and unstudied example from the Flemish-speaking part of the country reveals a case of outright refusal by a Belgian court to be implicated in the enforcement or legitimation of the Nazi antisemitic legal order. The Commercial Court in Ghent found itself faced with just such an issue in 1941 and 1942. A *Verwalter* had been appointed in Germany to oversee the liquidation of the business of two German Jews, the brothers Selmar and Albert Windmuller. The brothers had been forced under German law to wind up their business and had subsequently fled to Brazil.[9] The *Verwalter* sought access to the Belgian courts to obtain payment of monies owed to the Windmullers by a Belgian debtor. The court refused to allow the *Verwalter* to use the Belgian judicial system to enforce such a debt on the grounds that Belgian private international rules prevented the courts of that country from recognizing any legal basis for such a debt.

Once again, a Belgian court invoked basic rules of Belgian law in a Jewish case. Unlike the *Meyer v. Wouters* litigation a year earlier in Brussels, however, the Ghent court was dealing directly with anti-Jewish legal norms. In this case, what was in dispute was not the enforcement of anti-Jewish Decrees passed by the Germany Military Command in Belgium, but German laws aimed at the expropriation of assets belonging to German Jews. The Ghent decision is worth quoting and examining in some detail because it is a clear example of the refusal and resistance by some Belgian courts to participate by way of legitimation in the persecution of Jews. It demonstrates that resistance was possible, that it did in fact occur and that all that was necessary to resist was for judges to rely on the formal rules of positive Belgian law. In this case, the Commercial Court in Ghent was able to analyze the issues as falling within standard conflicts of law principles. These basic private international principles and concepts led the court to conclude that the laws in question were political, penal and expropriatory, all categories of foreign law the enforcement of which is rejected as part of the normal application of conflicts rules in most jurisdictions. In addition, it made clear that Belgian public policy (*ordre public*), the principal and principled foundation of national conflicts of law jurisprudence, prevented Belgian courts from enforcing debts such as those involved in this case.

The Ghent court begins its taxonomical analysis by declaring that the laws used to force the liquidation and appointment of a *Verwalter* are political in nature and like all political laws are considered to be geographically limited to the borders of the state which enacted them.[10] While it identifies the German laws as targeting "Jews", it thereafter refuses to engage specifically with the language of Nazi legalized antisemitism. The court then adds to its analysis by arguing that there can be no doubt that the law in question attaches a penalty to the Windmullers. Nor for the Ghent court is there any dispute about the legal principle that it is either the law of the *situs* or the domicile of the debtor which determines the regime relating to property. In this instance, then, the court is faced with a foreign political law which is penal in nature and which seeks to affect the status of property, in the form of a debt, situated in Belgium. Again, conflicts of law rules under Belgian law are clear and no effect can be given to such a foreign law by a Belgian court: "the German legislature has no power to organize the expropriation or the seizure of this debt or to have these measures enforced by the Belgian courts based on the sole reason that the debts must be recovered against Belgian debtors".[11]

The court then goes on to invoke specifically and unequivocally the idea that such an expropriation is contrary to Belgian *ordre public*. The Constitution (Art. 11) and the Civil Code (Art. 544 and 545) enshrine the respect for private property at the highest levels of the Belgian legal order.[12] This protection of private property "is one of the fundamental bases of Belgian national institutions which we cannot bend when faced with a foreign law without profoundly upsetting the established order of the country".[13]

The next argument advanced by the Ghent Commercial Court is even more astounding. It tackles head on the existing and established political and legal order of occupied Belgium. It unequivocally and unashamedly asserts that while there is *de facto* German rule in the country which allows it to administer the territory, international law recognizes the continuing existence of Belgian national sovereignty. Neither the occupation itself, nor "even the Decree of 28 October 1940" has any effect on the continuation of Belgian law and national sovereignty.[14] The Ghent Commercial Court in February 1942, deep in the period of accentuated

German anti-Jewish actions, stood up and refused to allow legalized antisemitism to enter the Belgian judicial system. It invoked and deployed standard norms of private international law and characterized Nazi anti-Jewish measures as punitive, pernicious and completely contrary to Belgian *ordre public*. By way of simple legal positivism, by invoking and applying nothing more complicated than the provisions of the Constitution and the Civil Code, decided cases and doctrinal authority, it placed a *cordon sanitaire*, around the Decree of 28 October 1940. That was a German measure, it had nothing to do with a Belgian legal normativity, the confirmation and upholding of which was the sole task of the court.

Of course, this was not always the case within other bodies sworn to uphold and defend the values and rules enshrined in the Constitution when these Belgian officials and institutions were confronted with Nazi legalized antisemitism. Passive collaboration soon gave way to active and willing assistance in identifying, tracking, listing and expropriating Belgian Jews. But we ignore at our peril this example from the Ghent Commercial Court. This is a clear manifestation that traditional legal argument could be deployed in a technically proficient, positivistic fashion with the intended effect of going to the constitutional jugular of the German racial legal order by the simple expedient of the Belgian judiciary acting like Belgian judges.[15] The Hague Convention, the Constitution, even the Civil Code contained the seeds of judicial rejection of Nazi antisemitism and the Commercial Court in Ghent in February 1942 stood ready, willing and able to defend the basic principle of equality enshrined in Belgium's foundational normative legal texts. Finally, it is worth noting that this case did in fact take place in Ghent, in the heart of Flemish-speaking Belgium. For too long, the history and narratives of anti-Jewish persecution in particular and resistance and collaboration in Belgium have been colored and characterized by a folk-wisdom that the Flemish collaborated and the Walloons resisted. The truth is more complex.[16] One new, or at least heretofore unexamined, element in the ongoing construction of the history of collaboration and resistance of Belgian officials can be found in the corridors and chambers of the Commercial Court of Ghent, from December 1939, when the case was first brought, to February 1942 when this decision was rendered. Flemish judges are at the center of the first reported instance of judicial resistance to the Nazi antisemitic legal order.

A month later, the Commercial Court in Brussels revisited the same issue considered by the Conseil de Prud'hommes in Friedrich Rotmann's case, the breach of the required contractual period of notice before the termination of a contract of employment. In *Rosiers v. E.-D. Isidor Vranckx et Cie*, the plaintiff had been employed by the defendant as a salesman, paid on a commission basis.[17] A three-month notice period was part of the contract between the two parties. However, on 7 March 1942, the defendant notified the plaintiff that it was terminating his contract with effect from 31 March.

The defendant was a Jewish firm and had received notice from the German Military Command requiring it to cease all commercial operations at the end of March.[18] It claimed in its defense to the damages claim from its employee that it was acting under compulsion enforced by the German occupiers and that the termination of the plaintiff's contract of employment was attributable to a sovereign act *(fait du prince)* for which it could not be held liable.

While the court recognized the source of the defendant firm's decision to close its business and thereby to terminate the plaintiff's contract, it did not accept the defendant's legal characterization of events. It also refused to refer to the racial nature of the case except by citing directly the Decree in question. The Brussels Commercial Court also appears to have made an effort to scrupulously avoid the language of Nazi antisemitism or to give effect to its norms. Instead, like the Commercial Court of Ghent in the Windmullers' case, it invoked overriding principles of Belgian and international law. It made specific reference to Article 6 of the Constitution with its guarantee of equality for all Belgians and Article 128 which extended similar protections to aliens on Belgian soil. The court then referred specifically to Article 46 of the Hague Convention which specifically forbade interference with private property rights by the occupying power.[19]

In these circumstances, the court found that it could not sanction the defendant's position because to do so would be to give full force and effect to an attack on the sanctity of private property and to the basic provisions of Belgian constitutional law and to operative international legal norms. It also went on to elaborate the view that, in any event, the disruption to the defendant's business was not fatal or permanent but simply temporary because it was directly linked to the German occupation which the court stated should legally be characterized as temporary. In such circumstances, the defendant should have suspended rather than terminated its contractual relationship with Rosiers.

This case again illustrates the simple power inherent in a reliance on existing legal norms which were always available to the Belgian judiciary. Unlike the Windmuller case in Ghent, where the *Verwalter* sought to apply German law to collect a debt owed by a Belgian, this decision involved two Belgian parties to a Belgian contract which was interfered with by the Third German Order concerning Jews. The Commercial Court invoked the Hague Convention and the Belgian Constitution to find in essence that the German Decree was an effective legal non-entity as far as domestic law and domestic jurisdictions were concerned. Indeed, it might be argued that, on the terms of the oft-ignored Conseil de Législation's construction of the legal rules governing passive collaboration, this was the only solution available to the court in such a case. To recognize a legal effect such as that pleaded by the defendant would have *de facto* served the purpose of completing or perfecting the application of the anti-Jewish Orders. Moreover, as the court itself held, the Decree itself was contrary to the Hague Convention and therefore beyond the power of Military Command. It was not a legitimate *fait du prince.*

Still, the effect of the refusal to allow the defense presented in this instance meant that a Jewish firm which was in the process of being liquidated was subjected to potential liability under Belgian law to pay monies to the plaintiff which, after 31 March, it was potentially forbidden to do. All moveable assets of the business had to be liquidated before 31 March. The applicable Order (§ 24) established unspecified monetary penalties, imprisonment and confiscation of assets for any breach of the Decree. This decision of principle in defense of fundamental rights of equality may well have had serious consequences in practice for the defendant firm which was bound in fact if not in law by the German Decree.

The Commercial Court had little choice in the matter. The equities seem relatively even as between the parties and the principle of defending Belgian legal autonomy and asserting the juridical non-existence of Nazi anti-Jewish legal rules within that autonomous system cannot be underestimated in their rhetorical and ethical significance. While Belgium and its state organs remained either actively compliant in assisting the German attacks on Jews or docile in its attitude, the Tribunaux de Commerce in both Flanders and in Brussels rejected any path of collaboration in these cases.

Aryanization and judicial resistance

The next series of cases from the Belgian courts also directly engages with the impact of Aryanization measures in Belgian law. The Commercial Court of Brussels was confronted by attempts by German *Verwalteren* to bring actions before Belgian courts in the name of the companies they represented. The court used a variety of legal arguments, based in Belgian procedural and corporation law, to stymie these incursions by the legal agents of Aryanization into the system of Belgian legality.

In *S.A. Tannerie et Maroquinerie belges v. S.A en liquidation Peausserie et Couperie belges*, the court held that a corporation could only bring an action if the interested individuals representing the moral person, the company, are listed in the pleadings.[20] Pleadings entered in the name of the "board of directors and the *Verwalter*" were flawed on their face and therefore without legal validity.

Verwalter Eric Schwager did not abandon his efforts to realize all the assets of the company under his stewardship. He brought another action, this time in his name and that of the "Board of Directors composed of", followed by the names of the individuals.[21] The directors in this case were all individuals appointed by the *Verwalter* after he had taken over the company pursuant to the anti-Jewish Decrees. The Commercial Court again insisted that all such proceedings must comply with Belgian law. It must be assured that the named representatives of the company

> are vested, in order to act in the name of the company, with power which Belgian courts, organs of Belgian sovereignty in the domain given to the judicial branch, should recognize as valid, that is to say, in conformity with Belgian national legislation.[22]

The Tribunal de Commerce invoked its inherent power to demand further and better particulars concerning the exact constitution of the board in order to ensure that Belgian law was being followed. Once again, the Commercial Court invokes the standard provisions of domestic law and covers those provisions with a broader assertion of the constitutional function of the judicial branch in order to thwart, in so far as it can in the circumstances, any attempt to use Belgian law and legal institutions to legitimize the Nazi Aryanization program.

The *Verwalter* made one more attempt, instituting an action "at the request of the company, represented by its Kommissarischer Verwalter".[23] This too was doomed to fail. Faced with an open assertion of the legal standing of the *Verwalter* to act in the name of an Aryanized Belgian company, the Commercial Court stood firm. It characterized the claim of the *Verwalter* as follows:

> The Kommissarischer Verwalter is neither an organ, nor an authorized representative of the company in the management of which he intervenes. He is a third party imposed by the Occupying Authority at the head of the business. He is the delegate and the instrument of that Authority, which has given him the task of taking control of the business. He is responsible for his actions only towards that Authority. He in no way represents the owner of the business.[24]

It follows logically for the Tribunal de Commerce that, given the characterization of the *Verwalter's* role and status as a purely German agent, the Belgian company over which it has jurisdiction is not really a party to the action. The case therefore must be dismissed for want of jurisdiction. The Commercial Court relies on an interpretation of Belgian law to characterize the position of the *Verwalter* as completely foreign thereto. It cannot hear the case because it is not, on its own jurisdictional rules, properly vested with an action. There is no Belgian company before it, merely a creature of the military occupying power. Nowhere does it refer to Aryanization, to the Jewish nature of the company, to the specific content of the Decrees. It is sufficient to resist all of these aspects of the pernicious Nazi legal order to maintain and to assert an ongoing Belgian legality and sovereignty. Such resistance was always available, yet it rarely manifested itself in the "docile" elites of occupied Belgium.

Herman Van Goethem has argued convincingly that it is possible to trace much of the policy and practice of passive collaboration to the 1916 decision of the Court of Cassation interpreting the Hague Convention.[25] In this case the Court held that German occupation law could alter Belgian domestic law and that the courts of the country could be compelled to enforce that superseding norm. This precedent was argued in the *S.A. Tannerie et Maroquinerie belges* litigation. The Commercial Court specifically rejected the precedential value of the First World War case and asserted that this was no longer the view of the country's highest tribunal. The careful analyses offered by Van Goethem and Michelsen might indicate that the Commercial Court did not in fact correctly or completely analyze the actual state of the law in Belgium at the time of its decision.[26] Nonetheless, this series of decisions under which that court refused to permit the national legal system to be used to enforce and legitimize the takeover by German *Verwalteren* of companies identified as Jewish under occupation Decrees demonstrates the tools which were available to the Belgian authorities to resist the anti-Jewish Orders.

The Tribunal de Commerce continued to apply the general principles of domestic law in all such cases. In *S.A. Visseries et Tréfileries Réunies v. P. Gagliazzo*, that court once again refused to recognize that an action brought in the name of a *Verwalter* was a form of procedure recognizable by courts applying Belgian law.[27]

The courts also continued to resist the insertion of German anti-Jewish legal norms in other areas, again through the application of Belgian national legal principles of general application. The court in Bruges, for example, was faced with a request by the wife of a Jew, then under arrest by the Germans, for a divorce on the grounds that the husband had failed to disclose an essential and fatal personal flaw at the time of their marriage, i.e. that he was a Dutch Jew.[28] While there was an extensive case law in Germany recognizing such grounds as the basis for divorce or a declaration of nullity in marriage, it was unknown in Belgian law.[29] Article 231 of the Belgian Civil Code permitted divorce on the grounds of "serious excesses, cruelties or abuses of one of them toward the other".[30] The court found that such a case not only did not fall under the provisions of Article 231 but that it would be contrary to Belgian public policy (*ordre public*) to permit such an action. Here the court openly rejected an attempt to introduce Nazi antisemitism into Belgian marriage and divorce law. The Jew was not a category subject to legalized identification and exclusion in Belgian law.

For the most part, the record of Belgian judicial authorities, when faced with anti-Jewish legal norms is commendable. A variety of techniques and principles, mostly derived from the application of basic and fundamental rules and norms of domestic law, informed by an institutional self-understanding of the place of the judicial function in the Belgian constitutional order, permitted the courts to resist. They rejected attempts to insert German anti-Jewish principles into Belgian law, either directly or indirectly. Not all Belgian lawyers appear to have found a way to act in such a principled fashion. In the cases studied briefly here, the *Verwalter*, or the party asserting antisemitic legal principles, found a Belgian advocate to plead the case. There was no refusal by these members of the Bar to invoke an ethical impossibility to act as the representative of, for example, an illegally constituted board of an Aryanized business. One might possibly assert here a duty to represent any client to the best of one's ability as an argument in defense or at least in mitigation as far as these members of the Bar are concerned. On the other hand, one might perhaps more convincingly argue that a member of the legal profession has no right or duty to make an argument which is not just immoral and unethical but also unconstitutional and possibly criminal.

The Conseil de Législation had clearly set out the permissible limits of passive collaboration in November 1940. It indicated that any cooperation in applying or completing anti-Jewish Decrees would be illegal. The Bar, the Court of Cassation and the Attorney-General had, in their letter of protest against the exclusion of Jewish lawyers, invoked the basic foundational principles of the

Belgian Constitution. While none of this might directly affect or compel lawyers as independent actors and not agents of the state apparatus, each of them did swear an oath of allegiance to the Constitution and each of them was, like every citizen, subject to the general provisions of the criminal law which attached severe consequences, in theory at least, to collaboration with the enemy.

Indeed, in the first flurry of legislative provisions passed by the Belgian government-in-exile in London, we find, as noted earlier, ample evidence of the official position of the Belgian state on German measures attacking property rights. The Pierlot government, basing itself on the First World War experience of German violations of the Hague Convention, declared that all expropriatory measures taken by the occupying power were absolutely void and that Belgian courts would be obliged to take steps to establish the *status quo ante* when circumstances permitted.[31] The Commercial Courts' refusal to recognize the legal status of the *Verwalter*, for example, was therefore not just a reflection of the general principles of Belgian law, but an *ex ante* application of this Belgian Decree in anticipation of the country's liberation.

Belgian courts, Belgian law, "Jewish cases": the postwar law

After the liberation of Belgian soil, the courts of the country were faced with a myriad of claims seeking redress from the *de facto*, if not *de jure*, deprivation of the right to property under the German anti-Jewish Decrees. The decided cases demonstrate the various factual situations involved and narrate the Belgian judiciary's attitude in Jewish cases when the judges were no longer subjected to any threat from the occupier.

A series of cases dealt with returning Jewish tenants who sought to re-enter into possession of their premises in situations where they had been relet to Aryan lease-holders by the *Verwalter*. In one of the earliest decisions, the Justice of the Peace in the Brussels suburb of Ixelles held that any lease granted by the *Verwalter* was void. The current tenant as a consequence had no legally recognizable entitlement to remain in the premises.[32] In these early days after the Liberation, however, the Belgian courts experienced some linguistic difficulties in coming to terms with the translation of Nazi anti-Jewish measures in an environment of a re-established national Belgian legality in which the *Juif* was unknown and unknowable and the *Israélite* was back, in theory at least. Thus, the Justice of the Peace in this case refers to the fact that the plaintiff was "of the Jewish race" (*de la race juive*). Today we can recognize the cognitive difficulties which these Belgian judges must have experienced. They were faced with a series of measures which discriminated against "Jews" and which identified, defined and targeted individuals falling in this category. In order to describe the situation which they were meant to remedy, they needed to refer to German measures against the "Jews". At the same time however, they perhaps should have been more aware of the radical transformation at the ideological and jurisprudential levels inherent in this Nazi legal terminology and could perhaps have been more willing to carefully monitor their own discourse.

There was no doubt that at the substantive level Belgian judges recognized the inherent evil and illegality of the anti-Jewish Decrees. The Justice of the Peace in Ixelles gave voice to the newly re-established legal normativity when he wrote

> Given that it suffices to read the text of the various German Decrees to realize that all these provisions against Jewish subjects can be characterized as an expropriation of property; that the German authorities instituted deportations, incarcerations and confiscation of property, all without a legal basis and contrary to the provisions of public international law; that all German legislation against the Jews led to the confiscation of their property and to the extermination of their race; that these evil laws are contrary to natural law and to public international law ...[33]

The lease entered into by the current tenants with the *Verwalter* is non-existent. The court's moral and juridical outrage is expressed in terms of a bizarre mixture of legal positivism, natural law and a continued deployment of Nazi linguistic and legal taxonomies. The Nazi legal order is characterized as involving "legislation" and "Decrees" but is defined as entirely lacking in a legal foundation. The provisions are "evil" (*iniques*) and contrary to both natural law and positive public international law norms. At the same time, the court speaks of the targeting of "the Jews" (*les Juifs*) and extermination of their "race". The moral and jurisprudential outrage of the court is palpable but the rhetorical devices employed here are problematic.

In February 1945, a similar case came before the Justice of the Peace in Brussels.[34] In this instance, however, the lease had been entered into with the new tenants by the landlord who had previously rented the premises to the plaintiff, who had, because of his status as a Jew, fled Belgium. His property was placed under the auspices of a German *Verwalter*. In his absence, the landlord had re-leased the building. Upon his return at the end of the war, the original tenant sought the eviction of the current possessor. Once again the court recognized the nullity of all agreements relating to the defendant's property. In this case throughout the judgment the plaintiff is described not as Jew but as an *Israélite*. The pre-existing Belgian legal and constitutional order appears to have been recognized and affirmed.

The Court of the Justice of the Peace in Saint-Josse-ten-Noode in *Levy v. Jockmans and François* also dealt with an absentee Jewish (*Israélite*) tenant.[35] The Levys had signed a lease for their apartment in April 1939. They fled the country in May 1940 both because they were Jews and feared the Germans and because the husband had demonstrated his loyalty to Belgium during the First World War (*l'époux de la demanderesse ayant eu, au cours de la guerre précédente, une attitude patriotique*). He additionally feared reprisals based on his anti-German actions.[36] Upon her return the widow Levy sought to resume the lease. In the mean time, in January 1943, the owner had relet the apartment but had notified the new tenants of the existing arrangement with the Levys and added the stipulation "that the apartment must be made available to Mr. Levy as soon as he expresses his desire to return".[37] The legal rules applicable in such cases were set out in the government regulation of 12 March 1945.[38] A tenant was entitled to return to abandoned premises under a set of conditions. The decision to leave had to have been made under physical or psychological compulsion (*la contrainte matérielle ou morale*) which was the direct or indirect result of the German military authority (§ 30). The tenant had to pay his legally incurred debts to the landlord. Finally, the judge had to decide every case by applying principles of fairness (*équité*) and every case had to proceed first by way of a conciliation process.[39]

The court found that the Levys had left the country under a legitimate fear of persecution by the Germans and that they therefore left the country under compulsion and not of their own free will.[40] The court also held that the lease had been suspended during the period of the Levys' absence and therefore still had time to run. The current tenant had complete and adequate notice of the pre-existing relationship between the landlord and the Levys. The tenant was given a reasonable time to leave the premises.

On the other hand, the Justice of the Peace in Borgerhout decided in the case of *Meyer Hartog v. Aron Lesser and Union de l'Industrie du Bâtiment* that a Jewish lessee (*Israélite*) of vacant land who had left his domicile before the arrival of the German forces could not avail himself of the provisions of Belgian legislation suspending time limits and stopping the running of time in contractual agreements.[41] The court found that the decision to leave was voluntary. The plaintiff had not been compelled to undertake a course of action which adversely impacted on his contractual obligations. The different results in these cases might be explained technically by the characterization of the Levys' decision to leave as one which they were compelled to take and that of Hartog as one which was freely made. Yet this limited positivistic reading is neither complete nor satisfactory. The court in the Levy litigation placed a great deal of emphasis on reading the provisions of the legislation in question in light of the real circumstances obtaining in 1940, including the knowledge among the Jewish community of Nazi persecutions in neighboring countries. They used a liberal and equitable interpretive technique in order to characterize the decision of the plaintiff to leave Belgium ahead of the arriving Germans as one taken under "moral compulsion" (*la contrainte morale*). The Borgerhout court on the other hand paid no attention to the possible existence of such real danger and apprehension or fear of the consequences of waiting for the Germans to arrive. Instead it adopted another type of strictly positivistic approach. For the court, the Germans were not occupying the area militarily at the time Hartog abandoned the property. Therefore on the wording of the applicable regulation, no constraint was imposed on the Jewish lessee who simply chose to leave. In such circumstances, he had to accept the consequences of this free choice.

I do not wish to assert here that this decision of a Flemish-speaking court should be read and negatively contrasted with a Francophone jurisprudence which seems more sympathetic to the fate of Jewish parties on linguistic grounds. The attitude of the Commercial Court in Ghent adequately belies the traditional mythology of universal and unbending Flemish collaboration in anti-Jewish persecutions. It is interesting to note nonetheless that at this date, October 1945, the Borgerhout judge not only adopted a singularly narrow and positivistic interpretive position but he also deployed a similar linguistic strategy to that used by the Justice of the Peace in Ixelles in December 1944, eleven months earlier. The plaintiff Hartog is a "Jew", in Flemish *Een Jood*. The French rendition in the publication aimed at all Justices of the Peace in Belgium on the contrary adopts a translation which is perhaps characterized as more in conformity with the return of an acceptable constitutionally informed juridical discourse. Thus, *Een Jood* becomes in French *un israélite*, a Hebrew. Finally, one might also find an important distinction, in legal terms, between the cases in the fact that the widow Levy sought to return to her apartment while Hartog was asking to be reintegrated with a piece of commercial, vacant land. Perhaps the court's attitude in this case is influenced by the different equities which might have been seen to be at play in a residential as opposed to a commercial case.

In any event, a further reaffirmation by the Justice of the Peace Court in Ixelles of the party's status as an *Israélite* rather than as a *Juif* can be found in the case of *Cahen v. Roba*.[42] A Jewish (*Israélite*) landlord claims payments for rent due during the period of the *Verwalter's* administration of the premises. In his defense, the tenant asserted that he had in fact regularly paid his rent to the *Verwalter*. The court applied the consistent position adopted not just by the courts but as enshrined in the order-in-council by the government-in-exile in January 1941 that the expropriation or confiscation of property under German rule in occupied Belgium was void. Payments made to the *Verwalter* in such circumstances were themselves characterized as null and void and were therefore unrecognizable and unrecognized by a Belgian court. Under domestic law, rental payments must be made to the creditor himself or "someone having power from him or who is authorized by the courts or by the law to receive it for him".[43] A payment to a *Verwalter*, being null and void under Belgian law, is not a lawful payment of monies owed on the lease. Therefore the lessee still owes the amount of rent claimed to the landlord. It is open to him to pursue the sums paid to the *Verwalter* under operative war damages mechanisms. In theory at least, the Jewish landlord deprived of his property by the German authorities can be made whole by the operation of the general principles of the civil law as embodied in the Code Civil and the aggrieved tenant will be permitted to recoup the double payment under the operation of the system for restitution established at the end of the war.

By and large, the Belgian courts appear to have reverted relatively quickly to a semiotics of constitutionality in which they referred to parties as "Hebrews" (*Israélites*) and very rarely, if ever, as "Jews". At the same time, the application of the provisions of the Decree of 12 March 1945 did cause some difficulties in the practical implementation of a post-occupation Belgian legal system forced to deal with the effects of German anti-Jewish measures. An additional series of cases illustrates the ways in which a newly re-established Belgian judiciary, with the normative frame of Belgian national legislation and the country's Constitution, applied these principles of fairness.

The majority of cases followed the line that Jewish (*Israélites*) tenants who had left the country or who had gone into hiding during the occupation were acting under the type of psychological compulsion covered by the March 1945 Decree because both their person and their property were in real danger. Under such circumstances they could benefit from the right to resume their tenancies. This was the position adopted in *Muhlstein v. Putte and Roefs*, and *Klaynaert v. Halloy and De Rouckt*.[44] Two separate decisions in Brussels recognized that Jews in particular were indeed entitled to take special measures to ensure their own safety even before the actual invasion of May 1940.[45] While not everyone who had fled before the advancing German Army could lodge a claim for repossession, it was public knowledge that Jews were particularly threatened by the Germans. It was, the courts held, basic prudent common sense for them to have fled. In those circumstances, they could avail themselves of the right to return to their premises.[46]

In other cases, however, the courts found that the former tenants, *Israélites*, had left their premises in circumstances which did not justify the right to repossession. In *Benamon v. Dewael*, the court found that the equities in the case favored the current tenant because the plaintiff had, at the time of leaving the rented property offered to pay all damages caused during his tenancy, taxes which had fallen due during the time of the tenancy and had asked for the return of his deposit.[47] In addition, he had explicitly permitted the owner to rerent the property. In these circumstances, even if the events occurred under a compulsion envisaged by the Belgian Decree, the court held that the tenant instead of paying the amounts in question should have negotiated a payment in the form of a holding deposit. Having terminated the lease and given his permission to the landlord, this plaintiff had no claim.

In another case, the court found that the cancellation of a lease by a *Verwalter* could have a legal effect in circumstances where the Jewish tenant had consented thereto and had in fact been in contact with the new lessee without putting them on notice of the precarious nature of their title.[48] In this instance the court applying Belgian law seems to have been more willing to recognize that a *Verwalter's* actions could have a recognized status under domestic legality postwar than courts were willing to grant even in the presence of occupying German forces. In this case, the actions of the *Verwalter* seem identical to, or at least may appear to have had the same legal effect as, those of an agent, appointed specifically by a Jewish tenant, who cancelled a lease while the tenant himself was a refugee in America.[49] While throughout the occupation, the Tribunal de Commerce in Brussels took the unwavering position that a *Verwalter* was an agent of the German occupying authority and had no status in Belgian law, as the representative of the owners of the company in the name of which he pretended to act, this absolutist position was abandoned in the postwar period in order to apply principles of "fairness". Here, to some extent at least, the *Verwalter* is assimilated in his position to that of an agent of the Jewish tenant. In addition the court fails to offer any analysis based in concrete reality about a possible *vice de consentement*. It assumed that the consent given by a Jewish tenant to a *Verwalter* concerning the disposition of his property was an act of free will and therefore binding on the Jewish plaintiff who attempted to attack the agreement in the postwar period.

At the same time, the Commercial Court in Brussels continued to follow its established jurisprudential line. In *Lichtenschadt v. Manufacture Moderne de confections*, the court refused to recognize the validity of any transfer of shares ordered by the occupying authority and declared that any actions or votes undertaken by shareholders who had obtained their stake in the company as a result of Aryanization processes were null and void.[50] Similarly, any shareholders' meeting called by a *Verwalter* and any decisions made by that meeting were also unlawful and could be annulled at the request of shareholders who were not allowed to be present.[51]

The Commercial Court also found that a payment made by an insurer under a policy in the name of a Jewish client and placed in the hands of the BTG was without any effect on the rights of the policy-holder to claim the amount due under the contract. The Swiss insurance company pleaded in its defense that as a corporation doing business in occupied Belgium it was compelled to make the payment in the way it had by German legal Orders. The Court, consistent with its case law on the effect of any such transactions, found that the defense could not be invoked against the policy owner who was in Belgian law a stranger to any such transaction.[52] The court also refused to give any legal protection to transactions undertaken in relation to Aryanized property. Any resale of such goods and merchandise by a purchaser who was aware of the origin of the goods falls under the general provisions of the Code Civil Article 1382 which establishes the principle of delictual (tortious) liability.[53] In these circumstances, resale made it impossible for the true owner of the goods, the Jewish proprietor of the Aryanized business, to recoup his goods, thereby making the seller liable.[54]

Other Jewish lease cases tended to follow a path informed by the equities and factual circumstances of each case. For example, a tenant already occupying a three-room apartment in the same building was not permitted to avail himself of the right to have his former apartment returned since he could not show any real detriment had been suffered.[55] In similar circumstances where the former tenant had taken back possession of part of the premises in question and that part of the property was sufficient for all his needs, the court again decided that the equities of the case did not permit him to take possession of the rest of the premises covered by the original lease.[56] Finally the court decided to reject the defendant's objection that the plaintiff had found alternative accommodation which meant that he did not need his former premises. The court visited the new premises and decided that on the facts they were both insufficient for the plaintiff's needs and inferior to the originally leased property.[57]

With a few exceptions, the decisions of Belgian courts in postwar Jewish cases can be characterized as being situated in a continuous and unbroken line of principle with those decisions rendered during the occupation. For the most part, anti-Jewish legal provisions and German institutional arrangements meant to concretize their effects were barred from entry into the domestic Belgian legal system. Most cases where Jewish plaintiffs seeking redress did not win can be explained either on the basis of facts which took them outside the limits of standard domestic legal redress or of equitable decision-making in difficult circumstances. One final set of decisions perhaps illustrates these complexities and the continuities and discontinuities in the Belgian cases dealing with the "Jewish question".

MGM and the Belgian legal system

Throughout the occupation period and after, the film company Metro-Goldwyn-Mayer (MGM) featured as a party in a series of cases which highlights the issues, difficulties and concerns facing the Belgian judiciary at this time. At the outbreak of war and the fall of Belgium, MGM was at one and the same time a corporation under foreign control and one identifiable as having Jewish involvement in its capital and management. It was therefore subject to both the Enemy Property and anti-Jewish Decree system, which, as we have already seen, often operated in tandem. In addition, MGM fell under the German special legal regime for the control of film and other entertainment facilities introduced early in the occupation. Under the "First Decree relating to the Reorganization of the Film Industry in Belgium", all cinemas wishing to show movies to the public had to join the trade organization established by the occupier.[58] Membership and the necessary certificate of good character would be controlled by the military authority (§ 2). On 23 September 1940, the Military Command also issued a "Decree concerning the operation of theaters and amusement facilities" which subjected all such business to the specific permission from the occupying authority before they could reopen.[59] At the same time, MGM remained a legal person duly incorporated pursuant to Belgian law and therefore subject to its provisions and benefiting from its protections.

As a foreign, Jewish firm it soon became clear that MGM could not obtain the necessary authorization to continue its business operations.[60] This meant that its rental agreements for film theaters would need to be renegotiated and that some of its employees would be laid off. These two issues, the situation of contractual agreements, particularly leases and the termination of employment as a result of circumstances created by German legal Decrees, were among the most typical concerns in Jewish litigation during the occupation. In two large Belgian cities, Brussels and Liège, MGM operated major film theater operations. The local courts in each city dealt with these Jewish cases.

The first case to appear before the Belgian judiciary involved the rental contract for the MGM movie theater in Liège. In *S.A. Belge Métro Goldwyn Mayer v. Léon*

Beckers et al., the Court of the Justice of the Peace in Liège had to deal with the issue of the legal status and state of the lease for the movie theater premises.[61] The parties had entered into a ten-year contract in June 1939. In April 1940, MGM held back on the rental payment claiming that the international and national crises adversely affected its ability to operate its business. It paid the arrears after receiving a summons to appear before the court but subsequently sought to avail itself of the special measures contained in the Belgian emergency legislation of 22 March 1940 under which reductions in rent and suspended payments were possible in the specific unrest of prewar circumstances.[62] It sought a reduction of at least 35 per cent in its rent under the special statutory regime. MGM also availed itself of the general provisions of Belgian law, Code Civil Article 1722 under which a lease could be declared void or a reduction in rent could be ordered if the property were destroyed in whole or in part by accident (*cas fortuit*).[63]

The court found that these general principles of Belgian law had clearly established a rule when a lessee was faced with a situation where it was impossible to enjoy unfettered use of the property as the result of a sovereign act (*fait du prince*). This was synonymous with the situations covered by provisions of Article 1722. After listing the factual and legal circumstances which served to encumber the movie business in occupied Belgium, from German censorship and control, curfew regulations and the lack of reliable transport for customers, the court was faced with the question of the appropriate remedy. MGM requested a reduction in rent payments while the owners of the affected properties sought to have the lease voided. The court found in favor of MGM and ordered a reduction in rental payments.

In Brussels, the situation was somewhat different. The directors of MGM had left the country and essentially abandoned the business. One of the company's employees, M. Becker, found himself effectively without a job. An administrator restarted the business once the situation had calmed down and Belgian daily life returned to something approaching normality. Becker sued to allow him to resume his position and requested his back pay.[64] The Tribunal de Commerce rejected the defendants' claim that Becker had voluntarily left his employment.

At the end of the same year, MGM brought an action against the owner of the building which it rented in another part of Brussels because by then it had fallen under the regime of the anti-Jewish Decrees.[65] As a Jewish undertaking, it could no longer use the premises for the purposes for which it had entered into the contract with the defendant. The Germans ordered them to cease and desist and informed the Cinema Owners' Association of the withdrawal of the company's certificate on 28 April 1941. MGM sought to avail itself of a number of provisions of the Code Civil, including Article 1722, to obtain either a reduction of rent or the termination of the lease. It invoked the lessor's obligation under Article 1719 to provide the premises in a state fit for the purpose of the contract.[66] The question before the court then was that of the proper application, or even the applicability, of these general provisions of the Civil Code in circumstances in which a Belgian contractual relationship was rendered impossible by the acts of the occupying power against a Jewish company. The Belgian legal system in cases such as this had to face a *de facto* reality of an anti-Jewish legal regime and somehow translate the *de jure* effects of that legal system into domestic law.

The court in this case walked a very fine jurisprudential line indeed. It relied on the provisions of Article 1741 of the Code Civil which allowed for the cancellation of a lease in the case of the total loss of the rental property or by the complete failure of one party or another to meet its legal obligations.[67] In the circumstances, however, it would not and could not conclude that the inability to use the rented property was properly characterized as permanent or total because: "the ban can only be temporary and can only depend on the occupying power".[68] This is, as we have seen, an argument invoked with some consistency by Belgian courts in Jewish cases. The court invokes the purely temporary and arbitrary nature of the system of rule imposed by the Germans in order to maintain and preserve the application of the general rules and principles of the Belgian legal system. It adopts the juridical position that the occupation must be seen as legally temporary even at a time when Germany remained the superior military force in Europe and the end of the Thousand-Year Reich did not appear on the political horizon. The court then simply applied a standard form of judicial interpretation of the provisions of the Civil Code. It read Article 1741, a provision dealing with a specific form of contract, i.e. a lease, in light of the general principle for all contracts under the heading of contractual interpretation, that a failure imputed to a contracting party to seek the cancellation of a contract must be the result of some fault.[69] At the same time, it had to interpret the obligation for the owner to furnish the free enjoyment of the leased premises and MGM's argument that under Article 1732, the lessee was not responsible for any damage or loss to the property, including the loss of the right to enjoy access thereto, if they were not attributable to some fault on their part.[70]

The case therefore became one concerning the interaction between and among the various provisions of the Belgian Code Civil. The opposing sides raised arguments relating to general contract interpretation, various responsibilities of each party to a lease in case of loss or damage to the premises or the contractual rights to enjoy the benefits of the lease. These legal questions had to be resolved in light of the foundational fact of the "temporary" German anti-Jewish legal system. The court found that the respondent could not provide the peaceful enjoyment of the premises to the appellant MGM and that the only equitable solution was to suspend the contract during the period when the Germans made it impossible for the lease to be put into effect. The respondent was permitted to rent the premises to a third party but on the condition that at the end of the prohibition imposed on MGM, that agreement would be terminated within three months.[71]

The result was that general provisions and principles of Belgian civil law were applied and the Germans were not permitted by way of Decree to terminate contractual relations established under domestic law. At the same time, the court recognized the practical realities of the situation were such that MGM could not carry out its business and that it would be unfair to the respondent to force them to maintain an empty building and lose money.

Meanwhile in Liège, litigation concerning the fate of the premises leased by MGM in that city continued during and after the war. The notice of 28 April 1941 from the German Propaganda Office which had forced the closure of the MGM operations in Brussels also applied to the Forum cinema in Liège. The closure was scheduled for 2 May 1941 because the Germans had information that "the company – Metro Goldwyn Mayer – is a Jewish business".[72]

The owners of the building sought to compel MGM to continue its operations pursuant to the lease or, failing that, to cancel the lease with the payments of rent due and damages for the early termination of the contract. The lease was cancelled by judicial order on 18 November 1941 and MGM was given until 30 November to vacate the premises.[73] The owners, Beckers and Masereel removed MGM from the theater on 10 and 11 December. MGM had decided to continue to pursue the case by way of appeal but on 21 January 1941, as a Jewish undertaking, it was forced under the jurisdiction of a *Verwalter*, Herr Doctor Bruckhaus. Bruckhaus signed a memorandum of understanding with the cinema owners on 27 February, cancelling the lease and desisting from the appeal. On 3 March 1942 he informed the company's Belgian lawyer of the steps he had taken.

Beckers and Masereel then leased the premises to a German firm, Bruciné, which showed propaganda films. When that agreement came to an end the owners decided to run the business on their own, under the name of Mr Lombard who was able to obtain the necessary operating certificate from the German military authority. At the end of the war, MGM picked up where it had left off and recommenced its appeal to the Court of Cassation against the termination of its lease.[74] The court adopted a position contrary to that taken by the Brussels courts in parallel litigation concerning the competing and contrasting obligations of the lessor and lessee in the circumstances. The highest court in Belgium found that the inability of the lessee to access and "exploit" the premises and the consequent impossibility to pay the rent could not be blamed on the owner of the building, but instead had to be attributed to the German authorities. Since the fault was not personal to the lessor, the court held that the trial judge could not lawfully apply the provisions of Article 1722 of the Civil Code. Given that the proper legal characterization of the facts then became one in which the lessee failed to meet its contractual obligations to use the premises and to pay its rent, the lease could be cancelled. The Jewish enterprise was forced to pay the remaining rental for the period from 1 July to 30 November 1941 by the Court of Cassation of a free Belgium. The building's owners, who had gone into business with the German propaganda machine and who had derived a profit from this collaboration with the enemy, received an added bonus of more cash from the court. Belgian democracy and the rule of law had been restored.

But MGM did not stop there. Instead it found another means of litigating the injustice of its expulsion by bringing an action to restore its possession of the premises under the provisions of the special Decree of March 1945.[75] The defendants, the collaborators/owners, insisted that the action was barred by the application of the principles of *res judicata* (*chose jugée*) under Article 1351 of the Civil Code.[76] The lease, according to the defendants, had been legally annulled by the November 1941 decision and this had been confirmed by the Court of Cassation in its postwar decision. The Liège court rejected this argument. It asserted that the 12 March 1945 Belgian regulation had been created precisely to deal with the injustices caused by the rule of German occupation and the application of its pernicious legal norms.[77] The removal of MGM from its possession of the cinema premises was directly attributable to the control of the occupying authority over the movie theater industry and over Jewish businesses during the occupation. Its legal position in relation to the lease of the premises was determined by the action of the German *Verwalter* whose actions could not be recognized under Belgian law. The application of the equitable new legal rules under the March Order could not be neutered or prevented from applying by an appeal to the principles of *res judicata* since the Order was specifically intended to overcome such injustices and to deny *prima facie* the operative legal effect of the German antisemitic system.

The defendants then asserted that the lease had been terminated not under any physical or moral compulsion, as required by Belgian law, but due to the failure of the plaintiff to pursue its rights under the lease and to act in such a way as to preserve the contractual relationship even after German interference. On this point, the court simply decided that the defendants were hoist on a petard of their own making, i.e. *res judicata*.[78] The courts had already found in the original litigation, and the Cour de Cassation had confirmed the point, that the lease was terminated through no fault attributable to MGM and as a consequence of German occupation law.

> ... it is certain that the plaintiff tried in vain to find solutions reconciling its interests and those of the lessors; that it is clear that all these steps were doomed ahead of time to a certain failure, the Germans wanted to get their hands on this establishment to set up Bruciné there, and in any event to once and for all ... get rid of a Jewish business.[79]

Finally, the defendants/collaborators invoked, perhaps unsurprisingly, the general equitable provision of the Belgian Decree-Law. They claimed that the plaintiff was a powerful multinational corporation and they were simple Belgian small-business operators. According to them, the court should use its equitable jurisdiction and refuse the plaintiff's claim to take back the leasehold on the cinema. We might be thankful that they did not specifically invoke the specter of a return of Jewish dominance over the domestic economy.

The court was having none of it in any event. It took note of the fact that MGM had just entered into a long-term lease when the war intervened; that it had lost business and income following the outbreak of the war; that it had carried out improvements to the building; and that in the mean time, the defendants had profited from the rental and use of the building. The equities concerning

M. Lombard, the manager, did not weigh in his favor either, given that he owed his position to the fact that he was on a list of approved managers created by the Germans, a list determined in large part by the criterion of political reliability. He had more than adequate notice of the precarious nature of his position in a liberated Belgium. MGM got its theater back not under the operation of traditional general principles of the Belgian civil law which had otherwise been used to offer some form of legal protection to other Jewish businesses and individuals during the occupation but by invoking special post-Liberation legal measures. In Brussels it had been able, to some extent at least, to rely on the Code Civil and the courts' refusal to recognize the legality of measures undertaken by a *Verwalter*. In Liège on the other hand, the local court had adopted the opposite view of Belgian law under the Code Civil and this had been confirmed by the Cour de Cassation.

This brief survey of how the Belgian legal system sought to deal with the dilemmas of "Jewish" cases brings us back to a consideration of legal positivism as a source of resistance during the occupation. The court in Liège and the Cour de Cassation came to conclusions about the effect of German anti-Jewish Decrees on existing leasehold agreements and the operation of the relevant provisions of the Code Civil diametrically opposed to those arrived at by the Brussels' judges. Legal positivism on its own is clearly not sufficient either as a tool or indeed as an explanation for instances of judicial resistance to the German anti-Jewish legal order. Any competent lawyer will identify the strengths and weaknesses of the interpretive strategies adopted and deployed in the cases mentioned in this chapter. Lawyers from the Belgian Bar argued both sides of these cases without any apparent sense that they were being disloyal, un-Belgian or unprofessional. No legal positivist worth his or her salt would assert that one or the other position adopted in Brussels or Liège in the MGM cases was illegal or indeed normatively wrong. In the life-world of lawyers and of the normative parameter of legal positivism, both sides are clearly arguable as appropriate solutions. Neither can be said to impose itself. Within this frame, it might even be asserted that the Brussels jurisprudence was wrong because the hierarchical rules of recognition inherent and necessary to the positivist enterprise might easily lead us to conclude that the analysis of the highest instance, the Cour de Cassation, is the right and final decision in the matter.

These Jewish cases seem to indicate, by and large, that reliance on, and referral to, domestic Belgian legal normativity was what Belgian judges knew. There is also evidence that they were able, if they so wished, to deploy Belgian legal principles as a bulwark against the incursion of the legal regime of the German occupiers into the key national institution, the judiciary. In doing so, they protected, in many cases, the interests of those individuals and businesses identified by the German legal order as Jewish. While the practical result of refusing to allow the Belgian courts to be used to confirm and legitimize the actions of a *Verwalter*, for example, may not have prevented in the short-term the confiscation of property, in the longer term it may have had not only this effect but also served a strong symbolic signifier of Belgian resistance.

Chapter 11

Constitutional patriotism and the fragility of law

Beyond the obvious attractions of beer and chocolate, Belgium has much to offer as a site for legal historical research and lessons for any study of legality and the Holocaust. The two dominant linguistic and cultural groups, Flemish and Walloon, have lived in an uneasy peace since the country was founded. In late 2007, a general election resulted in a political stalemate which led to the country being governed on an interim basis, as the key political parties, divided in large part but not solely along the nation's linguistic border, were unable to form a stable ruling coalition.[1] For some, this was the inevitable result of the inherent instability of the country's constitutional structure and led many to conclude that Belgium/Belgique/België was in its last throes of separation and division.[2] Radical proposals for a new constitutional structure were advocated as the crisis endured.[3] Finally, in March 2008, months of negotiations led to a precarious and complex arrangement among the various parities which resulted in a political, constitutional compromise allowing for the creation of a ruling "permanent" but always fragile coalition government.[4]

The key to understanding the constitutional crisis of 2007–8 lies not in the linguistically determinist mythology of Belgium's struggle with nationhood but in the same circumstances which informed the Shoah in that country. The formal constitutional and political failure of the nation's institutions to create and maintain a system of governance and political life which would allow a sense of national and social solidarity to flourish exist today just as they lie at the heart of the tragic story of official Belgian collaboration and complicity in German attempts to destroy Belgian Jewry.[5] As is the case with Europe more broadly, there is in Belgium a case of constitutional and constitutive failure which lives at the heart of the nation state.[6] When the leading Brussels jurists Braffort, Gesché and Jamar wrote to von Falkenhausen to protest against the exclusion of their Jewish *confrères* in the autumn of 1940, they could confidently invoke the continuing existence of a Belgian nation to support their principled objection to Nazi legalized antisemitism. In 2008, at the heart of a vibrant and flourishing democratic, yet problematic, Europe, Belgium as a nation seems again to be in peril.

Constitutional crises can arise in any number of circumstances and the successful negotiation of these crises depends not just on political will and *nous* from the members of the political elite classes but on a broader shared social willingness to survive as a nation. The crisis in Belgium is symptomatic not just of that country's particular social and political history, but also of a broader *malaise* at the heart of the very notion of the nation state and sovereignty within Europe itself.[7] All of these difficulties find echoes in the period of German occupation 1940–5.

Werner Warmbrunn in his detailed study of the history of the occupation of Belgium during the Second World War concludes that the governance arrangements arrived at in the summer of 1940 between the military administration and the SG was a boon to the German regime. "It enabled the Germans to govern with a handful of men a territory containing twelve million people."[8] Only recently has a key consequence of this arrangement been brought under sustained scrutiny. Without the active compliance of Belgian officials, from the SG down to the lowest levels of local, municipal bureaucracies, the processes of identifying, excluding and expropriating Belgium's Jewish population would not have been possible. When in October 1940, the joint deliberations of the SG resulted in a refusal as a matter of constitutional principle to accede to German demands that anti-Jewish measures be incorporated into domestic legislation, the Belgian Constitution with its guarantees of religious liberty and individual freedom stood as a bulwark against Nazi Judeophobia. The legal opinion of the country's leading jurists under the organizational imprimatur of the Permanent Council on Legislation, despite its often Jesuitical analyses, offered a further layer of potential legal insurance to the SG and other levels of the Belgian government structure which might have permitted a firmer stance against the policy of the occupiers. The Hague Convention also served as a potential source of legalized resistance.

Very quickly, however, constitutional principle gave way not just to craven compromise but to pragmatic collaboration in the legal and bureaucratic processes of identification, exclusion and expropriation of Belgium's Jews. The leading Belgian historian Jean-Philippe Schreiber has recently argued that it would be incorrect and misleading to place too much emphasis on the advice of the Permanent Council since the document itself had no binding authority and was little known at the time.[9] Schreiber is no doubt factually correct but his analysis ignores two key points. The simple fact that the Permanent Council's opinions had no binding authority does not make that body's conclusions any less legally correct. Secondly, the fact that the advice did not itself circulate widely does not in the historical context of occupied Belgium and the elite structures and the role of leading personalities of the time mean that its content was not known where it could have played a key role. The members of the Council were the leading jurists of the country; Bench and Bar who, along with other high-ranking and prominent individuals, were in the time and circumstances of the occupation intimately connected both professionally and socially. The SG knew of the content of the advice which was drafted at their behest. They and top bureaucratic officials in all government departments were both clearly cognizant of the limits placed on Belgians by the Hague Convention and Belgian domestic law and at the same time responsible for the supervision of the application of all anti-Jewish Decrees by state and local government employees. Whether a civil servant in the Office of Births, Deaths and Marriages in Liège knew about the Permanent Council's legal opinion has absolutely no effect on the general issue of Belgian state complicity in the active, excessive and illegal application of anti-Jewish Decrees.

One caveat does remain however. Any suggestion that things would have been different had legal and constitutional resistance manifested itself consistently throughout the occupation regime must remain speculative. The counter-factual is intriguing but remains just that, counter-factual. There was no such generalized legal opposition to German juridical Judeophobia. On the other hand, we do know, as Warmbrunn and others have consistently pointed out, the SS presence in Belgium was minimal. The anti-Jewish German bureaucracy operated as efficiently as it did because it enjoyed the unquestioning cooperation and collaboration of the Belgian state apparatus. Had such cooperation been refused on constitutional grounds, a different manpower deployment would have been required of the Germans. But beyond this perhaps narrowly legalistic and positivistic debate about the state of knowledge of individuals and collegial bodies concerning the legal and constitutional limits on collaboration, two interrelated and more important issues remain for our understanding of the nature and practice of domestic legality in the Shoah in Belgium.

First, there is the question of the nature and functioning of a legal system in a time of crisis, more specifically in relation to legalized Nazi antisemitism. As the preceding chapters reveal, the record of Belgium is ambiguous. Early principled resistance by the SG ceded to pragmatic and overzealous application of anti-Jewish Decrees at all levels of the state apparatus. Belgian notaries and courts participated in the early stages of the Aryanization of Jewish properties, largely within the framework of ordinary Belgian legal principles, and in other official activities in compliance with the early anti-Jewish Orders. But these same notaries later refused to give legal status and legitimacy to any real property transactions during the key phases of the Aryanization program in Belgium. The Bar in Brussels refused to acknowledge the status of the Decree removing Jewish colleagues and actively resisted German attempts to compel them to provide lists of "Jewish" lawyers. After early similar refusals, the Antwerp Bar ultimately expelled its Jewish members. Throughout the occupation many Belgian lawyers and judges were faced with the effects of anti-Jewish Decrees in the ordinary course of domestic litigation. Some gave precedence to the German legal order, while others found ways to circumvent the invader's norms. Still other judges, from Ghent to Brussels, actively and overtly refused to recognize the status of German anti-Jewish Decrees in Belgian law.

In all of these instances, positive legal norms were analyzed and applied. The examples of the Commercial Courts in Ghent and Brussels indicate that legal positivism was available as a tool to those Belgian lawyers and judges who wished to resist the imposition of Nazi legality. This allowed them to reject Nazi antisemitic norms by invoking both the standards of domestic law and the limits on Nazi jurisdiction imposed by the international law norms of the Hague Convention.

These same norms, which should or could have served as a positivistic shield in relation to anti-Jewish Decrees, were not invoked by other levels of Belgian government as a result, as Herman Van Goethem has carefully argued, both of an overly rigid interpretation of First World War case law, and an intellectual failure of the spirit. The first point of Van Goethem's study, echoed by Schreiber more recently, highlights the potential fatal flaw in any argument which would rely solely or indeed primarily on positive legal normativity to serve as a protective bulwark in times of crisis. Simply put, positive law can and did cut both ways. What was required was an informing principled desire to subvert German antisemitic legality. Only then could legal positivism be invoked as a tactic within a broader strategic rejection of the underlying Nazi normativity.

This brings us to the second and crucial point for any discussion of the fragility of law in the particular context of occupied Belgium and the fate of that country's Jewish population. If legal positivism is never enough, some other normative or ethical principle needs to be uncovered if any idea of the rule of law is to be saved from the tragic historical record of legality and the Shoah. In recent times, Jürgen Habermas's "constitutional patriotism" has been deployed by some in an attempt to rescue or recover a core of normative essence from law's positive failures in relation to the Holocaust and indeed other more recent instances of legality's inability to save us from ourselves.

Of course, it is inherently problematic to invoke a subsequent philosophical and analytical concept or framework on prior historical and jurisprudential circumstances and events. Habermas has deployed his idea of constitutional patriotism in the particular historical contexts of debates surrounding first German national identity in a divided Germany, and later in an emerging European constitutional context. The place of the Holocaust in such debates was and is central to Habermas's political choice to develop and deploy the concept of constitutional patriotism.[10] The place of the Shoah must also remain central to our understandings of, and engagement with, any idea of a democratic, legality-bound Europe today and in the foreseeable future.[11]

Constitutional patriotism, as opposed to nationalism, depends as Habermas argues on a clearly enunciated and applied idea of constitutional citizenship which goes beyond narrow understandings of nationalism.

> Such generalized political cultures have as reference national constitutions: each of them contextualizes the same universal principles, popular sovereignty and human rights, differently from the perspective of their own particular history. On this basis nationalism can be replaced by what one might call constitutional patriotism. Compared with nationalism, constitutional patriotism appears to many as a bond too thin to hold together complex societies. So the pressing question remains: Under what conditions can a liberal political culture shared by all citizens replace the cultural context of a

more or less homogenous nation in which democratic citizenship was, once, in the initial period of the nation state, embedded?[12]

The experiences of the Belgian legal profession and governmental officials between 1940 and 1945 teach that constitutional order is always fragile and can be broken even by those sworn to uphold it. Equally, the Belgian record underlines and highlights the possibilities for constitutionally informed resistance to legalized evil. It does not stretch the taxonomy or the permissible limits of jurisprudential argument to assert that we can find in this historical experience the seeds, the first and very preliminary and contingent hints, of an emergent constitutional patriotism. In 1940, the institutional seats of Belgian constitutional authority and legitimacy were dispersed and weakened. The King remained in the country but his authority and power were considerably lessened through a combination of political maneuvers and personal circumstances. The legislative branch no longer existed and the Pierlot government was operating in exile in London, distant from the quotidian reality of the occupation. The SG governed in a practical sense but as time passed and personnel changes were imposed by the occupying authority, they were perceived more and more as simple yes-men for the Germans. The judicial branch continued to function but in highly compromised circumstances which served to delegitimize the judiciary in the eyes of many Belgians as the occupation went on.

All that remained then, as a potential bulwark against German antisemitic legality, was the Constitution itself. Again as Vivian Curran has so clearly underlined, what really remains in such circumstances is not so much the text of the document, but the ways in which that text and its foundational normativity live in the hearts and minds of its citizens. Naturally, it is without doubt the case that in the historical circumstances studied in this book the idea of a Belgianness underlying the Constitution was, and could only be, rooted in and informed by the extant understandings of the European liberal nation state. Yet, at the same time, it seems equally clear that at some level, perhaps an unconscious one, some nascent or potential broader and deeper understanding of a constitutional order, of a constitutional patriotism as we now understand or seek to deploy the term, was also at work. Those judges and lawyers who sought to subvert Nazi anti-Jewish Decrees could only do so at some level if their actions were informed by a normative context which rejected a narrow "Belgian" understanding of citizenship, of belonging and of equality.

Constitutional order can be, and could only be, defended and invoked as a principled and democratic defense against the institution of legalized hatred, by those whose innermost convictions are and were grounded in an understanding of the key value of social solidarity beyond strictly positivistic constitutional norms of citizenship. The constitution which lives in the minds and hearts of the "citizen" must be an open and welcoming one, one in which the religious, racial or ethnic "Other" is not an enemy, easily discarded at the slightest provocation or opportunity, be it a Nazi invasion, hijacked airplanes or an electoral impasse. The embryonic embodiment of constitutional patriotism to be found in some of the actions of some of the judges and lawyers of Belgium 1940–5 demonstrates the contingency of many of these principles. As long as the invocation of a resistant or alternative normativity was contingent on a narrow understanding of citizenship, some forms of constitutionally informed resistance failed those most in need of protection. The construction of Belgian Jews as "Hebrews" and as "Jews", one group being as a consequence of a narrow taxonomy of citizenship more deserving than the other of constitutional protection, led not to salvation but to the elision of the two categories into the uniquely death-bearing label *Juden*.

As long as citizenship is something which is granted to some, given and lost through the operation of law or of force or of the force of law, it will remain essentially artificial and precarious.[13] If citizenship remains as a core element of constitutional patriotism and public identity, it must be reimagined in a way which will not limit the applicability of norms of human decency when they are most needed. In the case of the Antwerp Bar we have witnessed the fragility of law and citizenship. In the study of the Brussels Bar we learn of its contingent and limited nature. Constitutional patriotism, whatever form it takes, with the coexistence of obligation and service as engaged citizen, embodied in the aspirations of the legal profession as articulated in part at least by those Belgian judges who openly rejected the normative bases of Nazi antisemitism as inimical to Belgian public policy/*ordre public*, has the potential to allow good to triumph. But good can ultimately triumph in times of adversity and crisis, when it is most needed, if it lives in the hearts and minds of the citizens called upon to heed the distress call of the Other. Whether we call this "constitutional patriotism", cosmopolitan justice or some other jurisprudential label which may emerge from current debates about citizenship, belonging and sovereignty, post-9/11, post-globalization, one thing which emerges with some certainty from a study of the role of the Belgian state and legal apparatus in the Shoah is: "It seems that, once introduced into public life, evil easily perpetuates itself, whereas good is always difficult, rare and fragile. And yet possible."[14]

Notes

1 The taxonomies of an anti-Jewish legal order

1 See most recently, Bernard Suchecky, *Résistances juives à l'anéantissement*, Brussels: Luc Pire, 2007. For Belgium, see also Baron Jean Bloch, *Épreuves et combats 1940–1945: Histoires d'hommes et de femmes issus de la collectivité juive de Belgique*, Brussels: Didier Devillez/Institut d'Études du Judaïsme, 2002; Pierre Brodeur, *Des Juifs debout contre le Nazisme*, Brussels: EPO, 1994; Lucien Steinberg, *Le Comité de défense des Juifs en Belgique, 1942–1944*, Brussels: Éditions de l'Université de Bruxelles, 1973; *Hommage aux partisans juifs tombés dans la lutte pour la Libération du pays*, Brussels: Solidarité Juive, 1945.

2 See Marion Schreiber, *Rebelles silencieux: L'Attaque du 20e convoi pour Auschwitz*, Brussels: Racine, 2006.

3 See *Justice Libre*, first publ. Oct. 1941, USHMM, RG. 65.003P, Reel 430, 31390, SVG. While a detailed textual analysis of the legal underground press is another project, even a cursory reading of this publication indicates that the "Jewish question" did not figure prominently in this aspect of "resistance".

4 Stathis N. Kalyvas, "Collaboration in Comparative Perspective", *European Review of History*, 15 (2008), 109–11, 109.

5 The Queen and King intervened in very few cases in favor of Jews and these were limited almost exclusively to "Belgian" Jews. See the files on the royal family held in Paris, CDJC, CDLXIII-57.

6 "Israélites étrangers pour lesquels rien n'a été fait. Aucune suite n'a été donnée. On n'a pas accusé réception". JMDV, A000490.01 et seq. See also files A000464 et seq.

7 See the magisterial study, *L'Étoile et le fusil*, vol. 1, *La Question juive, 1940–1942*, vol. 2, *Les Cent Jours de la déportation des Juifs de Belgique*, vol. 3 (in 2 vols), *La Traque des juifs, 1942–1944*, Brussels: Éditons Vie Ouvrière, 1983, 1984, 1987; *Un pays occupé et ses Juifs: Belgique entre France et Pays-Bas*, Gerpinnes: Éditions Quorum, 1999; *La Persécution des Juifs en Belgique, (1940–1945)*, Brussels: Éditions Complexe, 2004. See also Dan Michman (ed.), *Belgium and the Holocaust: Jews Belgians Germans*, Jerusalem: Yad Vashem, 1998; Rudi van Doorslaer (ed.), *La Belgique docile: Les Autorités belges et la persécution des Juifs en Belgique pendant la Seconde Guerre mondiale*, Brussels: CEGESOMA, 2007.

8 This exemption or exception was sometimes formalized by the Germans themselves. Thus some spouses in some mixed marriages were exempted temporarily from the application of certain provisions relating to forced labor for Jews in 1942, *Verordnung zur Durchführung der Verordnung über die Beschäftigung von Juden in Belgien*, VOBIB, 76, 15 May 1942, § 11.

9 In French, 'l'Association des Juifs en Belgique'; in Flemish, 'Jodenvereniging in België' (JVB); *Verordnung über die Errichtung einer Vereinigung der Juden in Belgien vom 25 November 1941*, VOBIB, 63, 2 Dec. 1941. See generally, Jean-Philippe

Schreiber and Rudi van Doorslaer (eds), *Les Curateurs du Ghetto: L'Association des Juifs en Belgique sous l'Occupation Nazie*, Brussels: Editions Labor, 2004.

10 See Emmanuel Debruyne, "De la politique de tolérance et de ses variations: La Belgique et l'exil des Juifs, (janvier 1933–septembre 1939)", in Rudi van Doorslaer (ed.), *La Belgique docile*, pp. 54 et seq. The leading historical work tracing the changes in Belgian immigration policy remains Frank Caestecker, *Alien Policy in Belgium, 1840–1940: The Creation of Guest Workers, Refugees and Illegal Aliens*, New York and Oxford: Berghan, 2000; cf. Betty Garfinkels, *Belgique, Terre d'Acceuil: Problème du réfugié 1933–1940*, Brussels: Labor, 1974.

11 See Ministry of Justice, Ministry of Foreign Affairs and International Commerce, Ministry of the Interior and Ministry of Labor and Social Security, *Instructions générales du 28 octobre 1936 relatives au Séjour des Étrangers en Belgique*, Herman Bekaert, *L'Expulsion des Étrangers et le Délit de Rupture de Ban*, Louvain: Imprimerie Administrative, 1934; *Le Statut des Étrangers en Belgique, 2 vols*, Brussels: Larcier, 1940.

12 For the background, see Martin Dean, "The Development and Implementation of Nazi Denaturalization and Confiscation Policy up to the Eleventh Decree to the Reich Citizenship Law", *Holocaust and Genocide Studies*, 16 (2002), 217–42.

13 See Correspondence from the Ministry of the Interior, Jan.–March 1942, USHMM, 65.003, Reel 430, SVG.

14 See General Alexander von Falkenhausen, *Mémoires d'Outre-Guerre: Comment j'ai gouverné la Belgique de 1940 à 1944*, Brussels: Arts et Voyages, 1974, for an obviously self-interested account.

15 Correspondence, Jahresbericht Mai 1940–1941, "Judenverordnungen und deren Ausführung", CEGESOMA.

16 "Nous ne pouvons croire que le Pouvoir occupant ait voulu englober dans pareilles mesures ces catégories de personnes auxquelles aucun reproche ne peut être fait sur le plan du plus pur patriotisme."

17 See generally *Rapports sur la Violation du Droit des Gens en Belgique*, vol. 1, Rapports 1 à 12 de la Commission d'enquête, Govt. of Belgium, Paris and Nancy: Berger-Levrault/Librairies-Éditeurs, 1916; *Rapports et Documents d'Enquête*, vol. 4, *Mesures Législatives, Judiciaires etc.*, Brussels: De Wit/Larcier, 1925; Anon., *Les Atrocités allemandes en Belgique*, Paris: Bibliothèque des Ouvrages Documentaires, n.d.; F. Norden, *La Belgique Neutre et l'Allemagne d'après les hommes d'état et les juristes belges*, Brussels: G. Richard, 1915; Fernand Passellecq, *Les déportations belges à la lumière des documents allemands*, Paris and Nancy: Berger-Levrault, 1917; John Horne and Alan Kramer, *German Atrocities 1914: A History of Denial*, New Haven and London: Yale University Press, 2001; Larry Zuckerman, *The Rape of Belgium: The Untold Story of World War 1*, New York and London: New York University Press, 2004. On the legal regime of the occupation see C. L. Louveaux, "La Magistrature dans la tourmente des années 1940–1944", *Revue de Droit Pénal et de Criminologie*, 61 (1981), 619; José Gotovitch, "Note relative à la Magistrature sous l'Occupation", 1972, CEGESOMA, BA L 1/3; Didier Boden, "Le Droit belge sous l'Occupation", in Dominique Gros (ed.), *Le Droit Antisémite de Vichy*, Paris: Seuil, 1996, p. 543. See also, Eugene Hannssens, *Le Pouvoir législatif sous l'occupation allemande en Belgique*, Brussels: Larcier, 1919.

18 See e.g. *Le Bâtonnier Devigne*, Liège: Barreau de Liège, 1947, for an example of the idea that Belgian lawyers embodied, almost by virtue of their profession, the best values of the nation.

19 Many of these protests are collected in Theodor Smolders, *La Jurisprudence belge depuis le 10 mai 1940*, vol. 6, Brussels: Larcier, 1945. For the situation related to forced labor, see generally G. Jacquemyns, *La Société belge sous l'occupation allemande*

1940–1944: Les Travailleurs déportés et leur famille, Brussels: Nicholson & Watson, 1950, and P. Potargent, *Déportation: La Mise au travail de la main-d'œuvre belge dans le pays et à l'étranger durant l'occupation*, Brussels: Edimco, n.d.

20 Ibid. at 12–13. See John H. E. Fried, "Transfer of Civilian Manpower from Occupied Territory", *American Journal of International Law*, 40 (1946), 303–31.

21 See Smolders, *La Jurisprudence belge* and Letter from the Chief Justice (Jamar) and the Attorney-General of the Court of Cassation (Hayoit de Termicourt) to General von Falkenhausen, 31 Dec. 1942, CEGESOMA: Archives Fonteyne, Jean, AA 693/313; Correspondence relating to members of the Bar of Charleroi arrested as hostages, Jan. 1942–Jan. 1943; CEGESOMA, Ministère de la Justice, 1467, VIII-18-19; see also "Memoire of the Belgian Government in Regard to the Deportation and Forced Labor of the Belgian Civil Population Ordered by the German Government", *American Journal of International Law Supp.*, 11(3) (1917), 99–112; Inter-Allied Information Committee, *The Axis System of Hostages*, London: HMSO, 1942; Ellen Hammer, "The Taking of Hostages in Theory and Practice", *American Journal of International Law*, 38 (1944), 20–33. More recently, see Majorie Courtoy, "La Question des Otages en Belgique pendant la Seconde Guerre Mondiale", in Gaël Eismann and Stefan Martens (eds), *Occupation et répression militaire allemandes: La Politique de "maintien de l'ordre" en Europe Occupée*, Paris: Autrement/Institut historique allemand, 2007, p. 104.

22 CEGESOMA, Courrier Ministère de la Justice, AA 1467; Dossier Hayoit, MIC 48; Document concernant la magistrature, AA 1798/1; Walraet, Documents concernant le barreau et la magistrature, AA 1198/10.

23 "La Victoire du Droit", p. 329.

24 Ibid. 1. "Quand les libertés de la patrie étaient déchirées, quand des faiblesses et parfois des lâchetés venaient au secours des usurpateurs du pouvoir, quand des agressions insultaient la justice, quand des juges et des avocats payaient leur résistance par des brimades ou des servitudes, ils songeaient aux fières doctrines qu'eux-mêmes et leurs aînés avaient défendues depuis qu'Edmond Picard, un soir de décembre 1881, avait fondé ce journal pour y server le droit et la vérité."

25 See Foulek Ringelheim, *Edmond Picard: Jurisconsulte de Race*, Brussels: Larcier, 1999.

26 "The Legalization of Racism in a Constitutional State: Democracy's Suicide in Vichy France", *Hastings Law Journal*, 50 (1998), 1–96, p. 95 (footnote omitted).

27 For a detailed and fascinating critique of this opinion and the position of the Hague Convention and Belgian legal norms, see Herman Van Goethem, "La Convention de La Haye, la collaboration administrative en Belgique et la persécution des Juifs à Anvers", *Cahiers d'Histoire du Temps Présent*, 17 (2006), 117–97.

2 The Secretaries-General

1 See Thierry Delplancq, "Une cité occupée et ses Juifs: Quelques aspects heuristiques", *Cahiers de la Mémoire Contemporaine*, 3 (2001), 128–34.

2 For an excellent study of the legal framework and its pernicious consequences, see Herman Van Goethem, "La Convention de La Haye, la collaboration administrative en Belgique et la persécution des Juifs à Anvers", *Cahiers d'Histoire du Temps Présent*, 17 (2006), 117–97.

3 "Problematic National Identity, Outsiders and Persecution: Impact of the Gentile Population's Attitude in Belgium on the Fate of the Jews in 1940–1944", in David Bankier and Israel Gutman (eds), *Nazi Europe and the Final Solution*, Jerusalem: Yad Vashem, 2003, p. 464.

4 Maxime Steinberg, *Un pays occupé et ses juifs: Belgique entre France et Pays-Bas*, Gerpinnes: Quorum, 1998, pp. 25–7.

5 For an introduction to Belgian policy and practice concerning immigrant Jews, Rudi van Doorslaer (ed.), *La Belgique docile: Les Autorités belges et la persécution des Juifs en Belgique pendant la Seconde Guerre mondiale*, Brussels: CEGESOMA, 2007, chs 3 and 4.

6 "Tout étranger, qui se trouve sur le territoire de la Belgique, jouit de la protection accordée aux personnes et aux biens, sauf les exceptions établies par la loi."

7 For a detailed analysis of the jurisprudential history, see Van Goethem, "La Convention de La Haye".

8 *Convention with Respect to the Laws and Customs of War on Land* (Hague, II), 29 July 1899.

"Family honor and rights, individual lives and private property, as well as religious convictions and liberty, must be respected. Private property cannot be confiscated."

9 On these interpretations, see Van Goethem, "La Convention de La Haye", and Juri Michelsen, *The 'Nazification' and 'Denazification' of the Courts in Belgium, Luxembourg, and the Netherlands*, Maastricht: University Press of Maastricht, 2004.

10 See *inter alia*, Jean Stengers, *Léopold III et le gouvernement: Les Deux Politiques belges de 1940*, Brussels: Editions Racine, 1980/2002.

11 See F. E. Oppenheimer, "Governments and Authorities in Exile", *American Journal of International Law*, 36 (1942), 568–93; Henri Fayat, "Legislation in Exile: Belgium", *Journal of Comparative Legislation* (3rd series), 25 (1943), 30–40; François de Kerchove d'Exaerde, "Quelques questions en droit international public relatives à la présence et l'activité du gouvernement belge en exil à Londres (octobre 1940–septembre 1944)", *Revue Belge du Droit International*, 23 (1990), 93–132. On the Pierlot government-in-exile and the Jewish question, see Véronique Laureys, "L'Attitude du gouvernement belge en exil à Londres envers les Juifs et la question juive pendant la Seconde Guerre Mondiale", in Rudi van Doorslaer (ed.), *Les Juifs de Belgique: De l'immigration au genocide, 1925/1945*, Brussels: CREHSGM, 1994, p. 136.

12 See e.g. Maurice Flory, *Le Statut international des gouvernements réfugiés et le cas de la France Libre 1939–1945*, Paris: A. Pedone, 1952.

13 See Jean-Léon Charles and Philippe Dasnoy, *Les Secrétaires-Généraux face à l'Occupant 1940–1944*, Brussels: Arts et Voyages, 1974.

14 See generally, *La Belgique docile*.

15 The prosecuting authorities at the Nuremberg Trials summarized the relationship and governance structure as follows: "This regime of the Secretaries General pleased the Germans, who adopted it." International Military Tribunal, Nuremberg, *The Trial of German Major War Criminals*, 2–13 Feb. 1946, p. 37.

16 See Chapter 1.

17 Loi relative aux délégations de pouvoirs en temps de guerre, *Moniteur Belge*, 11 May 1940, p. 2860. (All Belgian laws are passed in both a French and a Flemish-language version and published in the official Gazette, the *Moniteur Belge* in French and the *Belgisch Staatsblad* in Flemish. For the sake of brevity in these and similar cases, I will limit myself to the French text and citation.)

18 "Lorsque par l'effet des opérations militaires, un magistrat ou un fonctionnaire, un corps de magistrats ou de fonctionnaires … est privé de toute communication avec l'autorité supérieure dont il dépend, ou si autorité a cessé ses fonctions, il exerce dans le cadre de son activité professionnelle et pour les cas d'urgence, toutes les attributions de cette autorité."

19 Proclamation à la population de la Belgique du 10 mai 1940, *Heeresgruppen-Verordnungsblatt für die besetzten Gebiete*, 1, "Que chacun reste à sa place de travail

et vaque à ses affaires, Ainsi chacun rendra service à la patrie, à son peuple, et agira de la sorte également dans son propre intérêt."

20 "Discours de M. Reeder, Militärverwaltungschef, à l'occasion de la première prise de contact avec les Secrétaires généraux le 5 juin 1940." CEGESOMA, Archives Nolet de Brauwere, AA 80-7/1.

21 " … *vous ne nous demanderez rien qui soit incompatible avec notre devoir de fidélité (sic) envers la Patrie*" (emphasis in the original), ibid.

22 See Letter of 6 June 1940 from Pholien and Tschoffen, reproduced in Pierre Leclercq, *L'Equivoque d'une loi*, Brussels: Ferdinand Larcier, 1946, pp. 62 et seq. See also the discussion in the hagiography of Pholien. Francis Delpérée, "Joseph Pholien, juriste: Trois consultations et les mémoires. Le pouvoir exécutif en temps de guerre", in Françoise Carton de Tournai and Gustaaf Janssens (eds), *Joseph Pholien: Un homme d'état pour une Belgique en crises*, Bierges: Editions Mois, 2003, p. 113.

23 The nature and extent of the power to rule by way of these "decrees" or "regulations" would continue to vex not just the relations between the Germans and the Belgian governing authorities, but the relations between and among these actors and the Belgian courts which continued to insist on their ongoing powers to subject the decisions of the Secretaries-General to judicial review. See *inter alia*, *Antoine et Consorts*, Pasicrisie Belge, 1941 (7 April 1941), (Court of Cassation); *Halleux et Consorts*, Pasicrisie Belge, 1942 (30 March 1942); *Procureur du Roi de Nivelles v. C. Mallarme et Jacques*, Pasicrisie Belge, 1943 (27 Jan. 1943); *Verhulst*, Pasicrisie Belge, 1944 (23 Dec. 1943). See also René Hanquet, *Les Pouvoirs des Secrétaires généraux pendant l'occupation*, Brussels: Ad. Goemaere, 1946, and Roger Ockrent, *Les Crises constitutionnelles du pouvoir législatif en Belgique*, Brussels: Université Libre de Bruxelles, Institut de Sociologie Solvay, 1944.

24 "At the order of the Germans this administrative power after a time became a real legislative power." *Trial of German Major War Criminals*.

25 See *Le Protocole Allemand du 12 Juin 1940*, *L'Equivoque d'une loi*, p. 65.

26 See Maxime Steinberg, *L'Étoile et le fusil: La Question juive, 1940–1942*, Brussels: Vie Ouvrière, 1983, esp. pp. 103–19.

27 CEGESOMA, Archives Jean Vossen, Microfilm 74, Mesures Contre Les Juifs, 78.

28 Minutes (*Procès-verbaux*) of the Meeting of the Secretaries-General, 11 Oct. 1940. See also CEGESOMA, Archives Vossen, Microfilm 74, "Question Juive" and "Mesures Contre Les Juifs".

29 Ibid. "Après un bref échange de vues…".

30 "… le Comité des Secrétaires Généraux estime, après un examen approfondi, qu'il ne peut assumer, pour des raisons d'ordre constitutionnel, la responsabilité des mesures envisagées à l'égard des juifs", CEGESOMA, Archives Jean Vossen, Microfilm 74/3.

31 See Chapter 3.

32 For a more detailed critique, see Van Goethem, "La Convention de La Haye".

33 Minutes of the Meeting of the Secretaries-General, 25 Oct. 1940.

34 Ibid. "… M. le Président fait observer que, dans ces conditions, l'administration belge ne peut se soustraire à la mise en pratique de l'ordonnance susdite."

35 Van Goethem, "La Convention de La Haye".

36 "Et dans la mise en œuvre de ces mesures, il aurait fallu que ce soient les Belges qui fassent le sale travail." ("And in implementing these measures, it had to be the Belgians who did the dirty work"). Pierre Stephany, *1940: 366 Jours de l'histoire de Belgique et d'ailleurs*, Brussels: Paul Legrain, 1990, p. 337.

37 Jews, of course, had also been subjected to all the general decrees introduced by the Germans from the time they took over the country. More specifically, however, a few days earlier the occupiers had introduced a law forbidding ritual slaughter of animals, a prohibition which targeted observant Jews without specifically naming them as targets

of the law. See *Verordnung zur Vermeidung von Tierquälerei beim Schlachten von Tieren* ("Decree Avoiding Unnecessary Suffering of Animals during their Slaughter"), VOBIB 18, 25 Oct. 1940. In addition, because the vast majority of Jews present in Belgium at the time were non-citizens, many were subject to regulations governing enemy property. See *Verordnung betreffend das feindliche Vermögen in den besetzten Gebieten der Niederlande, Belgiens, Luxemburgs und Frankreichs*, 23 May 1940 (Decree concerning enemy properties in the occupied territories of the Netherlands, Belgium, Luxemburg and France), VOBIB 2, 17 June 1940.

38 Throughout I use the terms decree and order interchangeably as English-language translations of German legal measures against Jews.

39 *Verordnung über Massnahmen gegen Juden (Judenverordnung) vom 28 Oktober 1940* (Decree of 28 Oct. 1940 concerning measures relating to Jews) (Jewish Decree), VOBIB 20, 5 Nov. 1940.

40 *Verordnung über das Ausscheiden von Juden aus Aemtern und Stellungen, vom 28 Oktober 1940* (Decree of 28 Oct. 1940 concerning the removal of Jews from their positions and employment), VOBIB 20, 5 Nov. 1940.

41 See Richard Weisberg, *Vichy Law and the Holocaust in France*, New York: New York University Press, 1996.

42 Minutes of the Committee of Secretaries-General, 8 Nov. 1940.

43 … les intéressés doivent faire la déclaration à l'Administration communale. S'ils ne font pas cette déclaration, ils sont passibles des peines les plus sévères. En conséquence, les administrations devront, chacune dans la limite de leurs attributions, envisager quelles sont les mesures à prendre. Ibid.

44 Minutes of the Committee of Secretaries-General, 19 Nov. 1940. "Il rappelle que les personnes juives doivent faire elles-mêmes (sic) leur déclaration à l'Administration communale, sous peine de se voir appliquer des sanctions les plus sévères. Il n'y a donc pas lieu pour les administrations de s'occuper de cette inscription."

45 Ibid., 22 Nov. 1940.

46 See e.g. his discussion in "La Tête sur le billot ou la question juive en 1940", in *Un pays occupé et ses juifs*, Gerpinnes: Quorum, 1998, pp. 46–51. The Permanent Council was a purely consultative body but its membership meant that its opinion carried a great deal of prestige and weight. The failure of this body, its institutional paralysis as well as the perceived weaknesses of the Court of Cassation, led to more calls for constitutional reform, including the creation of a Belgian Conseil d'État along French lines i.e. a judicial body which could decide on the constitutional validity of various acts and statutes. See André de Staercke, *De la création d'un conseil d'état en Belgique,* Paris: Presses Universitaires de France, 1939; Jos de Putter, *La Constitution de la Libre Belgique*, Brussels: Les Éditions Libres, 1945; Roger Roch, *Note sur le Conseil d'État*, Commission Belge pour l'Étude des Problèmes d'Après-Guerre, Brussels: Bruylant, 1945; Guy Debeyre, *Le Conseil d'État Belge*, Lille: Douriez-Bataille, 1953.

47 Letter from Secretary of the Council R. Hayoit (de Termicourt) to the Secretary-General of Justice, 21 Nov. 1940, CEGESOMA, Archives Jean Vossen, MIC 74.

48 "… sont les principes fondamentaux de notre droit public placés à la base même de notre organisation administrative et de notre organisation judiciaire." Ibid.

49 " … la *participation* à ces ordonnances excède manifestement le pouvoir légal de MM. les Secrétaires généraux et de tous les fonctionnaires, puisqu'elle constituerait la violation de leur serment d'obéissance à la Constitution…" Ibid.

50 Indeed, this was the position adopted and put into effect by the President (*Bâtonnier*) of the Brussels Bar, Louis Braffort, during the Occupation. Invoking the principles of the Constitution, Braffort refused to hand over a list of names identifying his colleagues as "Jews". When the Germans insisted that he provide them with the entire

list of membership of the Bar, he refused to comply by simply not compiling any list of lawyers for the period. See Chapter 3.

51 Letter of 21 November.

52 Ibid. "Ainsi, à l'estime du Comité permanent, ne sont pas des actes de participation interdite: la soumission des personnes, désignées au § 1 de la 1ère ordonnance, aux interdictions et aux obligations qui leur sont imposées aux §§ 2 et 3, alinéa 3, § 14 de la 1ère ordonnance (§ 1 de la 2 de ordonnance), la soumission au § 9 de la 1ère ordonnance, la tenue du registre des Juifs par les administrations communales ou les commissaires d'arrondissement sur les déclarations spontanément faites par les intéressés (§ 3 de la 1ère ordonnance), l'affichage par les administrations communales requis auprès d'elles par les intéressés, conformément au § 14 de cette ordonnance."

53 Ibid. "Par contre, toute initiative, toutes investigations ou mesures complémentaires, dans le but d'assurer la pleine efficacité de l'une ou de l'autre disposition des ordonnances, est interdite aux fonctionnaires belges. Prendre une telle initiative ou une telle mesure, ce ne serait plus subir l'exécution des ordonnances, ce serait le promouvoir et, par conséquent, participer à la transformation de notre droit public..." At their meetings of 3 and 6 Dec., the Secretaries-General finalized the modalities of passive collaboration.

54 "From Bystander to Actor", *Journal of Human Rights*, 2 (2003), 137–51.

55 Ibid. 138.

56 See David Fraser, *Law After Auschwitz: Towards a Jurisprudence of the Holocaust*, Durham, NC: Carolina Academic Press, 2005.

57 Herman van Goethem has done this brilliantly, "La Convention de La Haye".

58 See Luc Huyse and Steven Dhondt, *La Répression des collaborations 1942–1952*, Brussels: CRISP, 1993; Ganshof van der Meersch, "Réflexions sur la répression des crimes contre la sûreté extérieure de l'état belge", *Revue de Droit Pénal et de Criminologie*, 2 (1946–7), 7–182.

59 See José Gotovitch and Chantal Kesteloot (eds), *Collaboration, répression: Un passé qui résiste*, Brussels: Labor, 2002.

60 For a more detailed discussion of the postwar trials see also, Martin Conway, "Justice in Postwar Belgium: Popular Passions and Political Realities", in István Deák, Jan T. Gross and Tony Judt (eds), *The Politics of Retribution in Europe: World War II and its Aftermath*, Princeton, NJ: Princeton University Press, 2000, p. 133, and Luc Huyse, "The Criminal Justice System as a Political Actor in Regime Transitions: The Case of Belgium, 1944–50", ibid. 157.

61 Minutes, 3 Dec. 1940.

62 "Il est également ordonné que les communes publieront d'urgence un avis rappelant que les Juifs sont tenus de se faire inscrire au registre des Juifs et que les tenanciers d'établissements juifs doivent requérir l'administration communale de procéder à l'affichage prévu par l'ordonnance." Letter from Secretary-General Adam to the Provincial Governors, Local Administrators, Mayors and Councilors, 6 Dec. 1940. USHMM, RG. 65.0001M, Reel 2067, SVG.

63 See generally, "Arrêté royal relative à la mise en disponibilité des agents de l'état", 30 March 1939, *Moniteur Belge*, 2 April 1939 and Cabinet du Premier Ministre, *Statut des agents de l'état: Mise en disponibilité des agents de l'état*, Brussels, 1939.

64 "Ordre de Service", AGR, I 179, # 466, Archives Oscar Plisnier. "Les personnes qui désireraient bénéficier des avantages de la mise en non-activité, doivent en faire la demande avant le 10 décembre."

65 Some Jewish civil servants resisted. Roger Van Praag was summoned by the Secretary-General in charge of his department and was told, that while the Secretary would make no inquiries, he was being put on notice concerning the Jewish Order. Van Praag whose family registered as Jews, fabricated an entire "Christian" family

tree for himself, including forged documents written on old parchment. The Germans approved his "Aryan" status and he went on to play an important role in the resistance. CDJC, "Augenzeugenbericht Roger Van Praag- Zusammenfassung", CDLXI-IP.

66 "… a été mis dans l'impossibilité d'exercer ses fonctions par suite de l'application de l'ordonnance allemande du 28 octobre 1940 (Verordnungsblatt du 5 novembre 1940, No 20)", Ibid., # 260.

67 Ibid., # 466.

68 Note pour Messieurs les Secrétaires-Généraux, ibid.

69 Minutes, 5 Dec. 1941. The Decree concerning the holding of public office in Belgium banned all those who had left the country because of war-related events from state employment. The Military Administration also reserved the right to ban all "undesirable" elements from these positions. *Verordnung über die Ausübung öffentlicher Tätigkeit in Belgien vom 18 Juli 1940*. VOBIB 8, 25 July 1940, §1 and 2 (2).

70 Letter from F. De Fillecyn, Director of Secondary Education (*Enseignement moyen*) to Plisnier, AGR, I 179, Archives Oscar Plisnier, # 256.

71 Ibid., # 260.

72 "Si cette mesure devait aboutir dans certains cas à des conséquences vraiment trop graves pour les intéressés, il conviendrait évidemment d'insister auprès de l'autorité occupante pour que les conditions prévues soient adoucies."

73 There is evidence however that Plisnier continued to provide public funds to the National Committee for the Defence of Jews (Comité National de Défense des Juifs) and to others involved in hiding and protecting Jewish children. See CEGESOMA, Dossier Vossen, Microfilm 74, Letter of 31 March 1945 from the Association d'Aide aux Juifs Victimes de la Guerre to Plisnier.

74 Minutes, 19 June 1942.

75 Minutes, 27 June 1942. The letter was read at the next meeting. Minutes, 3 July 1942.

76 Minutes, 8 Sept. 1942.

77 See generally, Général Alexander von Falkenhausen, *Mémoires d'Outre-Guerre: Comment j'ai gouverné la Belgique de 1940 à 1944*, Brussels: Éditions Arts etVoyages, 1974.

78 CEGESOMA, AA 46, Gaston Schuind, Au Ministère de la Justice Pendant l'Occupation: L'Action de M. Schuind, Secrétaire-Général, pp. 38–9.

79 Maxime Steinberg, *L'Étoile et le fusil: La Traque des Juifs, 1942–1944*, vol. 2, Brussels: Vie Ouvrière, 1986, esp. ch. 7, "La liquidation de la question juive", pp. 217 et seq.

80 See Maxime Steinberg, *L'Étoile et le Fusil*, vol. 2, *1942: Les Cent Jours de la déportation des Juifs de Belgique*, Brussels, Vie Ouvrière, 1984; *Un pays occupé et ses juifs*, pp. 25 et seq. See also Maxime Steinberg, "La Tragédie juive en Belgique occupée: Un ravage de la xénophobie", in Anne Morelli, *Historie des étrangers et de l'immigration en Belgique, de la préhistoire à nos jours*, Brussels: Couleur Livres, 2004, p. 243.

81 *Un pays occupé et ses juifs*, p. 27.

82 An account of Schuind's interventions in favour of Belgian Jews in general and on behalf of certain individual Jews, including the Chief Rabbi, can be found in "Les Persécutions allemandes contre les israëlites [sic] retinrent toute l'attention du Secrétaire Général du Ministère de la Justice", 1945, CEGESOMA, Papiers Schuind, Microfilm 51, pp. 38 et seq.

83 Minutes, 17 Sept. 1943.

84 Minutes, 17 Sept. 1943.

85 Schuind was removed from his position by the Germans notwithstanding a protest from his colleagues.
86 Minutes, 1 Oct. 1943.
87 Minutes, 15 Oct. 1943.
88 Minutes, 17 Dec. 1943.
89 The Association des Juifs en Belgique (AJB) was established in December 1941 by the German military as the official body representing all Jews in the country. A detailed study of this organization is beyond the scope of this book. See Jean-Philippe Schreiber and Rudi van Doorslaer (eds), *Les Curateurs du ghetto: L'Association des Juifs en Belgique sous l'Occupation Nazie*, Brussels: Labor, 2004, for the most recent historiographical developments on the subject.
90 Minutes, 17 Dec.1943.

3 The fragility of law

1   "The Legalization of Racism in a Constitutional State: Democracy's Suicide in Vichy France", *Hastings Law Journal*, 50 (1998), 1–96, 10–11.
2   "Judges are appointed for life. No judge may be deprived of his post or suspended except by a judgment."
3   See below.
4   See below, Chapter 4.
5   See below, Chapter 10.
6   This Belgian legal exceptionalism was noted early in the historiography of the Holocaust in that country. See Joseph Billig, *L'Action Anti-Juive sous l'Occupation Nazie en Belgique*, Paris: CDJC, CCC-58, n.d.
7   *Vichy Law and the Holocaust in France*, New York: New York University Press, 1996, p. 52.
8   *Un antisémitisme ordinaire: Vichy et les avocats juifs*, Paris: Fayard, 1997, p. 108. "Du coté des barreaux français, nulle voix de bâtonnier ou d'ancien bâtonnier ne s'éleva pour dénoncer publiquement des mesures racistes contraires aux principes que le barreau avait toujours revendiqués hautement comme siens."
9   Curran, "Legalization of Racism", 95.
10 See generally, C. L. Louveaux, "La Magistrature dans la tourmente des années 1940–1944", *Revue de Droit Pénal et de Criminologie*, 61 (1981), 619–63; José Gotovitch, "Note relative à la Magistrature sous l'Occupation" (1972), CEGESOMA, BA L 1/3; Didier Boden, "Le Droit belge sous l'Occupation", in Dominique Gros (ed.), *Le Droit Antisémite de Vichy*, Paris: Seuil, 1996, p. 543.
11 Paul Struye (1940–4), Journal de Guerre, Archief/Archives Paul Struye, CEGESOMA, AA 850, now published as *Journal de guerre, 1940–1945*, Brussels: Racine, 2004, especially p. 57.
12 Ibid. 61.
13 Ibid.154.
14 While not in the majority, a significant group of Belgian lawyers clearly fell into a nationalist, corporatist worldview which was either sympathetic to Nazism or downright collaborationist. See e.g. Raymond Ledoux, *La Loi allemande sur les sociétés par actions, comparée à la législation belge*, Brussels: Bruylant, 1941, and Charles Anciaux, *L'État corporatif: Lois et conditions d'un régime corporatif en Belgique*, Brussels: ESPES, 1942.
15 Ibid.
16 Assemblée des Avocats à la Cour de Cassation en date du vendredi 8 novembre 1940, Archives Paul Struye.
17 Ibid.

18 *Journal de Guerre*, p. 155.
19 "Les avocats exerceront librement leur ministère pour la défense de la justice et de la vérité...", *Décret contenant règlement sur l'exercice de la profession d'avocat et la discipline du Barreau*, 14 Dec. 1810, Art. 37.
20 "Les avocats à la Cour de Cassation de Belgique ont été vivement émus à la lecture des ordonnances du 28 octobre 1940 relatives aux mesures contre les juifs. Ces ordonnances ne frappent aucun d'entre eux; elles ne sauraient cependant leur être indifférentes en raison, d'une part, du concours qu'ils pourraient être amenés à apporter pour en assurer l'application, et d'autre part, du caractère inconciliable de ces ordonnances avec la législation belge restée en vigueur et à laquelle ils ont fait le serment d'obéissance." Assemblée des Avocats, Archives Paul Struye.
21 "Faut-il ajouter qu'en raison même de l'activité professionnelle des avocats, il ne parait pas possible d'exiger d'eux une collaboration à des actes dont les conséquences seront de mettre au ban de la société et de réduire finalement à la misère des hommes qui, sans responsabilité dans leurs origines, ont par ailleurs justement revendiqué par la dignité de leur vie et souvent par le dévouement sans défaillance apporté à la chose publique, le droit de conserver la qualité de Belge et de jouir des prérogatives qui s'y attachent." Ibid.
22 "... l'amour de la vérité et de la justice, un zèle éclairé pour les faibles et les opprimés". Ibid.
23 P. Vermeylen, *Règles et usages de l'ordre des avocats en Belgique*, Brussels: Larcier, 1940, pp. 70–1.
24 For the most part I have kept the French names for the courts and legal personnel in Brussels. The Bar at the time was divided according to the jurisdiction before which lawyers predominately practiced. Thus, Louis Braffort was head of the lawyers of Brussels while *Bâtonnier* Veldekens was the President of the lawyers of the Cour de Cassation. In a similar vein I have translated *magistrats* as "judges" rather than as "magistrates". It is important to remember here however, that the Belgian system had and has two types of judges, "sitting" (*assis*) and "standing" (*debout*) judges. The former most closely resemble judges of the common law variety while the latter investigate and prosecute, but are members of the "judiciary".
25 Jahresbericht Mai 1940–1941, Enthält Akten aus den Jahren 1940–1941.
26 I invoke this phrase in homage to Richard Weisberg's interpretation of the ways in which Vichy lawyers accepted the normative framework of French legalized antisemitism and then proceeded to deploy technical skills to argue within that framework without ever questioning or rejecting the law itself – he calls this the "hermeneutic of acceptance". "The Hermeneutic of Acceptance and the Discourse of the Grotesque, with a Classroom Exercise on Vichy Law", *Cardozo Law Review*, 17 (1996), 1875–978.
27 See Sadi Kirschen, *Devant les conseils de guerre allemands*, Brussels: Rossel & Fils, 1919; Thomas Braun, "Le Défenseur", in Stan Dotremont *et al.*, *Le Bâtonnier Louis Braffort: Défenseur et martyr des libertés spirituelles*, Brussels : Larcier, n.d., pp. 49 et seq.; Pierre Henri, "La Défense des belges devant les conseils de guerre allemands pendant la guerre 1940–1945", in *Les Grands Avocats de Belgique*, Brussels: Éditions J. M. Collet, 1984, pp. 271 et seq.
28 Paul Struye, *La Belgique sous L'Occupation Allemande (1940–1944)*, Brussels: Complexe, 2002, p. 53, originally published as *L'Évolution du Sentiment Public en Belgique sous l'Occupation Allemande*, Brussels: Lumière, 1945, p. 28.
29 Maxime Steinberg, *L'Étoile et le fusil: La Question juive 1940–1942*, Brussels: Vie Ouvrière, 1983, p. 114.
30 See Article 100 of the Constitution and the disciplinary rules of the Bar. Vermeylen, *Règles et usages*.

31 Maxime Steinberg, "Le Génocide aux Rendez-Vous du Palais", *Juger*, 6–7 (1994), 13–18. Of course, the question of Nazi law as law was not unique to the Belgian legal system at the time. See David Fraser, "'This is Not Like Any Other Legal Question': A Brief History of Nazi Law Before U.K. and U.S. Courts", *Connecticut Journal of International Law*, 19 (2003), 59–125.

32 P. Graux, "Discours de Me P. Graux", in *Le Bâtonnier Louis Braffort*, p. 95.

33 While Francophones dominated the legal profession at the Bar in the capital, Brussels also had a minority of Flemish-language advocates, see Constant Matheeussen, *Honderd Jaar Vlaams Pleitgenootschap bij de Balie te Brussel 1891–1991*, Tielt: Lannoo, 1992, esp. "De tweede wereldoorlog", pp. 130–5.

34 See generally, Rudi van Doorslaer (ed.), *La Belgique docile: Les Autorités belges et la persécution des Juifs en Belgique pendant la Seconde Guerre mondiale*, Brussels: CEGESOMA, 2007.

35 See generally, Ludo Abicht, *De Joden van Antwerpen*, Antwerp: Hadewijch, 1993; Ephraim Schmidt, *L'Histoire des Juifs à Anvers (Antwerpen)*, Antwerp: Excelsior, n.d.; Lieven Saerens, *Vreemdelingen in een Wereldstad: Een geschiedenis van Antwerpen en zijn joodse bevolking (1880–1944)*, Tielt: Lannoo, 2000. A French-language version was published as *Étrangers dans la cité: Anvers et ses Juifs (1880–1944)*, tr. Serge Govaert, Brussels: Labor, 2005. Subsequent references are first to the Flemish-language original and in parentheses to the French version.

36 See Schmidt, *L'Histoire des Juifs à Anvers*, p. 125.

37 See Saerens, *Vreemdelingen*, pp. 353 et seq. (pp. 416 et seq.).

38 René Victor, *Schets ener Geschiedenis van de Vlaamse Conferentie der Balie van Antwerpen, 1855–1960*, Antwerp: De Vijt, 1960.

39 Saerens, *Vreemdelingen*, pp. 465 et seq. (pp. 543 et seq).

40 Schmidt, *L'Histoire des Juifs à Anvers*, pp. 131–2.

41 Régine Orfinger Karlin, Archief/Archive Orfinger Karlin, CEGESOMA AA 754; see also *Jours de Guerre*, RTBF, # 374, CEGESOMA AA 1450 R. Orfinger (Karlin) and 1ères Ordonnances. Jacqueline Wiener-Henrion, "Régine Karlin-Orfinger", *Cahiers de la Mémoire Contemporaine*, 5 (2003–4), 187–97. Régine Orfinger Karlin merits a mention in Jean-Philippe Schreiber's *Dictionnaire biographique des Juifs de Belgique*, Brussels: De Boeck & Larcier, 2002, but only under her husband's and father's entries, 'Orfinger, Lucien', pp. 266–7, and 'Karlin, Grégoire', p. 191.

42 *Jours de Guerre*.

43 See Jan Verstraete, *De jodenverordeningen en de Antwerpen Balie*, Brussels: Larcier, 2001. See also the chronology and documents reproduced in "L'Exclusion des Juifs de la Magistrature", *Juger*, 6–7 (1994), 36–41.

44 *Jours de Guerre*.

45 Verstraete, *De jodenverordeningen*, p. 70.

46 Victor, *Schets ener Geschiedenis van de Vlaamse Conferentie der Balie van Antwerpen, 1855–1960*, p. 471.

47 Circulars, Auditorat Général, Dossier Collard.

48 See Louveaux, "La Magistrature dans la tourmente", p. 645, and "Le Moindre Mal", *Juger*, 6–7 (1994), 28–30.

49 Article 169 of the Civil Code provided that: "The King's prosecuting attorney of the court of first instance in the arrondissement in which the future spouses propose to celebrate their marriage may dispense, for serious reasons, from the publication and any delay." (Le procureur du roi près d'un tribunal de première instance dans l'arrondissement duquel les impétrants se proposent de célébrer leur mariage peut dispenser, pour des causes graves, de la publication et de délai.) See *Le Pays Réel*, 4 August 1942. In acting this way and using their powers under Article 169, the Crown Attorneys were continuing a practice which had started in the prewar period.

Then, they had used Article 169 to allow couples who would otherwise have fallen foul of the Nuremberg *Rassenschande* prohibitions to marry in Belgium. See Frank Caestecker and David Fraser, "The Extraterritorial Application of the Nuremberg Laws: *Rassenschande* and 'Mixed' Marriages in European Liberal Democracies", *Journal of the History of International Law*, 10 (2008), 35–81.

50 For an example of the difficulties caused by such marriages in postwar divorce or annulment proceedings, see Tribunal Civil de Bruxelles, 9e chamber, 7 April 1945, *Revue Critique de Jurisprudence, Belge*, 1–3 (1947), 31–64.

51 9 Sept. 1942, Note from Plateau to Secretary-Général Schuind, Auditorat général, Procès Schuind, boîte 329, XV, B1. 3.

52 See JMDV, A000299, 3 Aug. 1942, certificate from the Crown Attorney, confirming that Hélène Zylberszac of Anderlecht met the requirements for Belgian citizenship on her 16th birthday.

53 See e.g. the discussion of the Hirsch family's circumstances, Chapter 9 below.

54 AVLg, Bureau du Bourgmestre, 5203.

55 Ibid. "Melle Deitz, sœur germaine de Mr Joseph Deitz, a déjà été rayée du Registre des Juifs par nos soins."

56 Ibid.

57 "Comme j'ai déjà eu l'occasion de vous le dire antérieurement, l'Administration des biens juifs LAISSE AUX AUTORITES BELGES LE SOIN EXCLUSIF DE PROCEDER A LA RADIATION des personnes qui se sont fait inscrire dans les registres des juifs auprès des Administrations communales. J'ai pu obtenir ainsi la radiation dans une Administration d'un faubourg de Bruxelles, d'une personne qui s'était déclarée « à titre de précaution » et qui a pu prouver dans la suite qu'elle n'avait qu'une ascendance juive de 50%. Cette radiation effectuée par l'Administration communale belge a été communiquée aux Autorités allemandes, qui n'ont formulé aucune objection." Ledoux was something of an expert in German law. He was the author of a text extolling the virtues of National Socialist company law.

58 Ibid. Correspondance March 1943. "Un arbre généalogique qui n'est pas appuyé par des actes officiels ne peut suffire de preuve pas plus qu'une attestation de l'association juive."

59 See generally Martin Dean, Constantin Goschler and Phillip Ther (eds), *Robbery and Restitution: The Conflict Over Jewish Property in Europe*, Oxford and New York: Berghan, 2007.

60 See generally, *Hommage à Monsieur le Référendaire Vander Perre*, 25 Oct. 1946, and "Obéissance à la constitution et aux lois du peuple belge", *Jurisprudence Commerciale de Bruxelles*, 35 (1942–4), pp. 221 et seq. See also the discussion in Chapter 10 on Belgian case law.

61 "Obéissance à la constitution", p. 293.

62 Ibid. 224.

63 Ibid. 226.

64 "Il ne se soumettait pas aux lois du peuple belge, il les brandissait comme un drapeau, à la face même de l'ennemi. Et si la loi était son étendard, elle était aussi sa meilleure arme." Ibid.

65 Anne Morelli (ed.), *Les Grands Mythes de l'histoire de Belgique: De Flandre et de Wallonie*, Brussels: Vie Ouvrière, 1995.

66 Edwige Lefebvre, *The Belgian Constitution of 1831: The Citizen Burgher*, Bremen: ZERP, 1997.

67 Martin Conway, *Collaboration in Belgium: Léon Degrelle and the Rexist Movement 1940–1944*, New Haven, CT and London: Yale University Press, 1993, pp. 273–4. On Rex from different perspectives, see Jonathan Littell, *Le Sec et l'humide,* Paris: Gallimard, 2008; Eddy de Bruyne and Marc Rikmenspoel, *For Rex and for Belgium:*

Léon Degrelle and Walloon Political and Military Collaboration 1940–45, Solihull: Helion & Co., 2004.

68 On Gunzburg, see "Le Professeur Nico Gunzburg: Juriste anversois et la culture flamande", in Baron Jean Bloch, *Epreuves et combats 1940–1945: Histoires d'hommes et de femmes issus de la collectivité juive de Belgique*, Brussels: Didier Devillez/Institut d'Études du Judaïsme, 2002, p. 171, and Schreiber, *Dictionnaire biographique*, pp. 146–8.

69 At the time there was no Dutch/Flemish-language official version of the text of the Constitution, which itself guaranteed linguistic equality rights. Ironically, Nico Gunzburg helped draft an unofficial Flemish-language version of the Constitution in the early 1920s.

70 See Chapter 10.

71 *Verordnung zur Vermeidung von Tierquälerei beim Schlachten von Tieren vom 23 Oktober 1940*, VOBIB 18, 25 Oct. 1940.

4 Aryanization, legalized theft and Belgian legality

1 See *Les Biens des victimes des persécutions anti-juives en Belgique: Rapport final de la Commission d'étude sur le sort des biens des membres de la communauté juive de Belgique spoliés ou délaissés pendant la guerre 1940–1945*, Brussels: Services du Premier Ministre, 2001 (Commission Buysse); Rudi van Doorslaer (ed.), *La Belgique docile: Les Autorités belges et la persécution des Juifs en Belgique pendant la Seconde Guerre mondiale*, Brussels: CEGESOMA, 2007; Israël Shirman, "La politique allemande à l'égard des Juifs en Belgique, 1940–1944", Mémoire de licence en Histoire ULB 1970–1971; "La Spoliation Economique des Juifs de Belgique", *Cahiers d'Histoire de la Seconde Guerre Mondiale*, 3 (1974), 65–83; Viviane Teitelbaum-Hirsch, *Comptes d'une mort annoncée: Les Spoliations des Juifs en Belgique*, Brussels: Labor, 1997; Rudi van Doorslaer, "The Expropriation of Property and Restitution in Belgium", in Martin Dean, Constantin Goschler and Philipp Ther (eds), *Robbery and Restitution: The Conflict Over Jewish Property in Europe*, New York: Berghan, 2007, pp. 155 et seq.

2 Cf. Götz Aly's intriguing recent account of the ways in which the looting and redistribution of Jewish property was a key component in the Nazi regime's ability to maintain the support of the majority of Germans. *Hitler's Beneficiaries: How the Nazis Bought the German People*, London: Verso, 2007. On Belgium, see pp. 124 et seq. and pp. 185 et seq.

3 An early example of the legal framework can be found in the First Decree of 20 May 1940, *Verordnung über die ordnungsmässige Geschäftsführung und Verwaltung von Unternehmungen und Betrieben in den besetzten Gebieten der Niederlande, Belgiens, Luxemburgs und Frankreichs (Geschäftsführungs-Verordnung) vom 20 Mai 1940*, VOBIB 2, 17 June 1940. For a detailed description, see the *Report of Police Inspector Guillaume Jans to the Chief Prosecutor* in the context of the immediate post-war investigation of economic collaboration, *"Pro-Justitia"*, 5 April 1945, USHMM, RG. 65.003P, Reel 452, Document 31450, SVG. On economic collaboration generally, and the controversies arsing therefrom, see the competing accounts in e.g. Fernand Baudhuin, *Le Financement des guerres*, Louvain: Institut de Recherches Economiques et Sociales, 1944; *L'Économie Belge sous l'Occupation, 1940–1944*, Brussels: Bruylant, 1945; cf. Robert Billiard, *La Collaboration industrielle et ouvrière avec l'occupant*, Brussels: Author, 1945; *La Contrainte economique sous l'occupation (1940–1944)*, Brussels: Author, 1946; Fernand Demany, *On a volé 64 milliards: L'Histoire de la banque d'Émission*, Brussels: Société Populaire, 1947. On the legal history of economic collaboration, see Dirk Luyten, "Prosecution, Society and

Politics: The Penalization of Economic Collaboration in Belgium After the Second World War", *Crime, History and Societies/Crime, Histoire et Sociétés*, 2 (1998), 111–33.

4 See *Verordnung betreffende das feindliche Vermögen vom 23.5.1940*, VOBIB 2, 17 June 1940. On the interaction between this legal regime regulating enemy property and the later legal category "Jewish" property, see the discussion in Chapter 7.

5 See *Verordnung zur Durchführung und Ergänzung der Feindvermögensverordnung*, VOBIB 5, 6 July 1940.

6 "... nous ignorons si Mr P. Meyer est juif au sens de l'ordonnance du 28 octobre 1940", Déclaration, USHMM, RG 68.001M, Reel 48, Selected Records from the Kingdom of Belgium.

7 Ibid.

8 Ibid.

9 "A notre connaissance, Mr. Borys Rabinovicz est le seul actionnaire qui soit juif". USHMM, Id., Reel 40.

10 Ibid. "Nous ne connaissons pas le nombre de titres possédés actuell par Mr. Rabinovicz."

11 Ibid.

12 "La présente déclaration est remplie en raison du doute sur l'identité racique d'un administrateur de l'entreprise, Mr. Gaston Lehman": ibid.

13 "Les notaires sont les fonctionnaires publics établis pour recevoir tous les actes et contrats auxquels les parties doivent ou veulent faire donner le caractère d'authenticité attaché aux actes de l'autorité publique." Article 1, Loi organique du notariat, 25 ventôse an XI (16 March 1803), as amended. Under the provisions of the Law of 5 March 1935, all Belgian "public servants" (*fonctionnaires*) were obliged to remain at their posts in the case of war or invasion and were subject to severe penalties for any contravention. The Belgian judicial system found itself under severe personnel constraints during the occupation because many judges had indeed fled in May 1940. Those who returned to Belgium were subject to the application of the 1935 statute, which applied to them notwithstanding the guarantees of judicial independence in Belgian law. See the cases of x, Pasicrisie Belge (Cour de Cassation) 24 March 1941, 93; x, Pasicrisie Belge, 5 May 1941, 172. Solicitors (*avoués*) were not considered to be public servants because they acted not for the court or the state but for their client, and therefore were not covered by the law, x, Pasicrisie Belge, 17 June 1941, 231. Notaries, on the other hand, by virtue of the nature of their functions, were considered to be public servants and fell under the provisions of the statute. See *Procureur du Roi c. x, Pasicrisie Belge*, 31 Oct. 1940, 87; x, *Pasicrisie Belge*, 26 May 1941, 210.

14 Albert Rauco and Pierre Cambier, *Traité du Notariat*, Brussels: Larcier, 1948, p. 191.

15 Commission Buysse (see n. 1), pp. 58 et seq.

16 Van Doorslaer (ed.), *La Belgique docile*, pp. 372 et seq.

17 "Ordonnances Relatives aux Juifs", *Recueil Général de l'Enregistrement et du Notariat*, 90 (1941), No. 18144, 11.

18 *Moniteur Belge* (25 Feb. 1941), *Arrêté-Loi relative aux mesures de dépossession effectuées par l'ennemi*, Art. 1, "confiscations, saisies, ventes forcées, ou de toutes autres mesures portant atteinte à la propriété privé". See generally, Jacob Robinson, "Transfer of Property in Enemy Occupied Territory", *American Journal of International Law*, 39 (1945), 216–30.

19 See generally *La Belgique docile*, pp. 375–80.

20 VOBIB 22, 21 December 1943.

21 Op. cit., pp. 58 et seq. The problematic nature of ordinary sales ordered by Belgian courts to satisfy "normal" debts remains more troubling. An intriguing example of the

basic disinterest in the Shoah in Belgian public and legal institutional historiography is found in the official organizational history of the Royal Federation of Notaries of Belgium (Fédération Royale des Notaires de Belgique) which contains not a single word about the heroic actions of the nation's notaries in refusing to certify transactions dealing with Jewish property. Indeed the recounting of the wartime period focuses mainly on the battle to free captured notaries from German POW camps and on the effects of compulsory labor measures on notarial office personnel. *1891–1991: Un siècle au service du notariat*, Brussels: FRNB, 1991, pp. 49–50.

22 Ibid., at pp. 62 et seq.
23 Yad Vashem, O2-396 (Wiener Library-Orfinger File), Auditorat Général Belge, Administration of Jewish Property in Belgium during the War, Rapport sur l'Administration des Biens des Juifs par les allemands pendant la guerre.
24 See e.g. the active involvement of one notary in transferring rental payments on behalf of his Jewish client to the *Verwalter* in JMDV, A00001.01 et seq., Dossier "Goldstein".
25 See e.g. letter of 14 Dec. 1943, concerning the disposition of the furs belonging to the Abraham Klajman company, and associated documents, CEGESOMA, AA 1374, MV 9.
26 Letter of 1 March 1944, and related correspondence, USHMM, RG.65.001M, Reel 1717, Document 24722, SVG, "tous les certificats établissant l'origine aryenne de Madame Kerkhoffs [sic]".
27 *Verordnung über wirtschaftliche Massnahmen gegen Juden (Neufassung) (Dritte Judenverordnung) vom 31 Mai 1941*, VOBIB 44, 10 June 1941.
28 CEGESOMA, AA 120, Copie d'une circulaire envoyée par les Autorités allemandes aux commerçants Juifs, relative à leur inscription au Registre du Commerce, Ministère de la Justice, Crimes de Guerre.
29 Archives de l'État à Liège, UA 1949, 1950, vols 133, 134, 138, Boîtes 1220, 1221TC.

5 Belgian municipalities and the introduction of anti-Jewish Decrees

1 See "Circulaire aux Administrations Communales", re dismissal of civil servants.
2 See *La Loi communale et les lois modificatives: Texte extrait du commentaire pratique*, Frameries, 1900; Alfred Giron, *Essai sur le droit communal de la Belgique*, Brussels: Bruylant, 1868; Louis-Joseph Peeters, *L'Office du Bourgmestre*, Brussels, Larcier, 1887; Robert Wilkin, *Organisation et fonctionnement des autorités communales*, Liège: Invalides, 1938; Union des Villes et Communes Belges, *L'Autonomie Communale en droit belge*, Brussels: Larcier, 1968.
3 Fabrice Maerten, "Secrétaires communaux et résistance en Hainaut Belge: au cœur de la solidarité", in Robert Vandenbussche (ed.), *Les Services publics et la résistance en Zone Interdite et en Belgique (1940–1944)*, Lille: CRHENO/CEGES, 2005, p. 59.
4 Willem C. M. Meyers, "Les Autorités communales belges au début de l'occupation", in *L'Occupation en France et en Belgique*, *Revue du Nord*, no. 2, Hors Série, 2 vols, 1987, vol. 1, p. 195.
5 For example, the 240-page history of local and provincial government of Liège contains one mention of Jews, a simple recording of the introduction of the first anti-Jewish Decrees. Gilbert Mottard, *Des administrations et des hommes dans la tourmente: Liège 1940–1945*, Brussels: Crédit Communal, 1987, p. 54. See Chapter 8.
6 Louis Baillon, *La Résistance administrative: La Lutte secrète des pouvoirs publics contre les Allemands en Belgique, (1940–1944)*, Brussels: Larcier, 1946. See also Bénédicte Rochet, "L'Administration centrale belge: Des fonctionnaires résistants et/ou patriotes?", in Vandenbussche (ed.), *Les Services publics*, p. 13.

7 *Vreemdelingen in een Wereldstad*, Tielt: Lannoo, 2000. See also Nico Wouters, *Oorlogs burgemeesters 40/44: Local bestuur en collaboratie in België*, Antwerp: Lannoo, 2004.

8 "La Convention de La Haye, la collaboration administrative en Belgique et la persécution des Juifs à Anvers", *Cahiers d'Histoire du Temps Présent*, 17 (2006), 117–97.

9 "Des paroles et des actes: L'Administration bruxelloise et le registre des Juifs, 1940–1941", *Cahiers d'Histoire du Temps Présent*, 12 (2003), 141–79; "1940–1942, une cité occupée et ses Juifs: Quelques aspects heuristiques", *Cahiers de la Mémoire Contemporaine*, 3 (2001), 128–34; See also Godelieve Denhaene, "Les Juifs dans certains documents communaux de Schaerbeek pendant la Deuxième Guerre Mondiale", *Cahiers de la Mémoire Contemporaine*, 1 (1999), 133–9.

10 "Une administration face à la législation antisémite: Le Cas d'Ostende, (1940–1942)", *Cahiers de la Mémoire Contemporaine*, 6 (2005), 69–77.

11 See e.g. Sylvain Brachfeld, *Ils ont survécu: Le Sauvetage des Juifs en Belgique occupée*, Brussels: Racine, 2001.

12 In this area, and in all others relating to the Holocaust in Belgium, the most obvious point of reference is Maxime Steinberg's monumental and seminal history of the Shoah, *L'Étoile et le fusil*, Brussels: Vie Ouvrière, 1983, 1984, 1986. See also Steinberg's *Un pays occupé et ses juifs: Belgique entre France et les Pays-Bas*, Gerpinnes: Quorum, 1998, and Dan Michman (ed.), *Belgium and the Holocaust: Jews Belgians Germans*, Jerusalem: Yad Vashem, 1998.

13 See José Gotovitch and Chantal Kesteloot (eds), *Collaboration, répression: Un passé qui résiste*, Brussels: Labor, 2005.

14 "To the annoyance of the Nazis, these measures met with but little response from the Belgian population", *Conditions in Occupied Territories*, New York: United Nations Information Office, 1943. Local mayors came to embody the spirit of Belgian resistance to German occupation, just as they had during the First World War. See Jan-Albert Goris, *A New Code for Belgian Mayors*, New York, NY: Duell, Sloan & Pearce/Belgian Information Center, 1942.

15 In German, *Verordnung*. As noted, I use the English terms "decrees" and "orders" interchangeably throughout to render this and the French *ordonnance*. Both terms give the appropriate sense of binding edicts by the occupying power, having legislative force and effect.

16 "Ces diverses ordonnances n'affectaient qu'un nombre limité de Juifs. En outre, leur exécution se heurtait à l'hostilité ouverte ou à la mauvaise volonté des organismes publics belges chargés d'en assurer l'application". *La Persécution Antisémitique en Belgique*, Liège: Georges Thone, 1947, p. 18. Joseph Billig echoes this account of obfuscation, delay and resistance by local authorities. *L'Action anti-juive sous l'occupation nazie en Belgique*, Paris: CDJC, CCC-58, n.d., pp. 12–13.

17 "Ainsi, nombre d'administrations communales sabotèrent systématiquement l'établissement du registre des Juifs, sous prétexte de surcharge de travail, du manque de matériel ou de main d'œuvre. A cet égard, il est utile de noter que la plupart des Juifs invités à s'inscrire, s'exécutèrent. Quarante-deux mille donnèrent leur nom." Ibid.

18 "A cet égard, on peut noter que la plupart des Juifs s'exécutèrent, quand on les invita à s'inscrire, soit qu'ils fussent animés d'un renouveau de leur fierté d'Israélites, soit que la modération allemande les aveuglât sur les graves conséquences que cet enregistrement pouvait comporter pour eux dans l'avenir." *Rapport du gouvernement belge sur les persécutions des Juifs de Belgique durant l'occupation allemande*, Document 47 (UK 76), IMT, reproduced in Henri Monneray (ed.), *La Persécution des Juifs en France et dans les autres pays de l'ouest*, Paris: CDJC, 1947, p. 202.

19 See Delplancq, "1940–1942, une cité occupée et ses Juifs", p. 128.

20 Rudi van Doorslaer *et al.*, *La Belgique docile: Les Autorités belges et la persécution des Juifs en Belgique pendant la Seconde Guerre mondiale*, Brussels: CEGESOMA, 2007.

21 Ibid., p. 1084. "L'État belge a ainsi adopté une attitude docile en accordant dans des domaines très divers mais cruciaux une collaboration indigne d'une démocratie à une politique désastreuse pour la population juive (belge comme étrangère)."

22 Ibid. pp. 514 et seq.

23 On Liège, see Thierry Rozenblum, "Une cité si ardente: L'Administration communale de Liège et la persécution des Juifs, 1940–1942", *Revue d'Histoire de la Shoah*, 179 (2003), 9–49.

24 See Chapter 8, "Les Autorités belges et les persécutions des Juifs, 1940–1942", pp. 250 et seq.

25 Letter from the Commissaire d'Arrondissement, Philippeville, 5 Oct. 1940, CEGESOMA, AA 92. Arrondissement de Philippeville.

26 "… le culte israélite n'est pas officiellement pratiqué à Verviers". Letter of 1 Aug. 1940, CEGESOMA, AA 51, Administration Communale de Verviers.

27 Ibid. Letter of 1 Oct.

28 Ibid. See also, Jacques Wynants, *Verviers 1940*, Brussels: Crédit Communal, 1980, pp. 215 et seq.

29 CEGESOMA, AA 51, Administration communale de Verviers-Juifs: "nous nous sommes scrupuleusement conformé aux prescriptions".

6 Brussels

1 See "1940–1942, une cité occupée et ses Juifs: Quelques aspects heuristiques", *Cahiers de la Mémoire Contemporaine*, 3 (2001), 128–34, pp. 133–4.

2 Archives de la Ville de Bruxelles (AVB, Cabinet du Bourgmestre, 1940–4), *Inventaire No. 33, Cabinet du Bourgmestre*, p. viii: "La partie du fonds relative à la guerre 1940–1945 offre beaucoup moins d'intérêt. Les documents et surtout la correspondance avec l'autorité occupante ont été trouvés dans un désordre extrême, auquel il n'a été possible de remédier que dans une faible mesure. Il semble d'ailleurs que beaucoup de dossiers aient été détruits ou emportés."

3 AVB, Cabinet du Bourgmestre, 1940–4, File 866 bis (Dossier relative au "registre des juifs"), "Le registre des juifs de Bruxelles a disparu". This does not mean that there is no copy of the Register of Jews for Brussels. Several versions of the Register were created and transferred to various authorities during and after the war. A copy of the Register of Jews for Brussels is available in the holdings of the United States Holocaust Memorial Museum. USHMM, RG. 65. 003 P, Reel 431, SVG and at the Jewish Museum of Belgium (Musée Juif de Belgique) in Brussels. It should also be noted that in the immediate postwar period, Monsieur Warans of the Population Office of the city of Brussels provided, at the request of the Head of the Office of the Registry of Births, Deaths and Marriages of the city, a brief history of anti-Jewish measures and the city administration. Therein Warans notes that on 9 Nov. 1944, the Ministry of the Interior requested that the Register of Jews be handed over to them. This was done, according to Warans, on 30 Nov. 1944. "Note sur les ordonnances concernant les Juifs", 9 Dec. 1944, AVB, Cabinet du Bourgmestre 1940–4, File 866 bis (Dossier relatif au "registre des juifs"). It is however also worth noting here that from the earliest days, city officials decided to maintain two copies of the Register, one of which was to be kept away from public scrutiny and safeguarded in case of loss of the other. See "Instruction Concernant Le Registre des Juifs", AVB, Cabinet du Bourgmestre, 1940–4, File 866 bis.

4 Until the appointment of mayor Coelst, almost all correspondence still extant involving the municipal administration and its officials was in French.

5 There was also "protest" of a more limited kind in relation to the creation or operation of Jewish schools and the use of Belgian police in arresting Jews as discussed later in this chapter. For the Yellow Star Order as giving rise to yet another isolated act of refusal and resistance by officials in Occupied Europe see the story of the Bailiff and Attorney-General of Jersey in David Fraser, *The Jews of the Channel Islands and the Rule of Law 1940–1944: 'Quite Contrary to the Principles of British Justice'*, Brighton and Portland, OR: Sussex Academic Press, 2000, pp. 119–43.

6 "The Legalization of Racism in a Constitutional State: Democracy's Suicide in Vichy France", *Hastings Law Journal*, 50 (1998), 1–96.

7 Created by German Decree, the AJB was put in charge of all details of Jewish life in Belgium and was the sole official point of contact with the occupying power. Debates continue in Belgium, as they do elsewhere, as to whether the actions of that country's *Judenrat* constituted collaboration.

8 See Maxime Steinberg, *Un pays occupé et ses juifs*, Gerpinnes: Quorum, 1998; Pim Griffioen and Ron Zeller, "A Comparative Analysis of the Persecution of the Jews in the Netherlands and Belgium during the Second World War", *The Netherlands Journal of Social Sciences*, 34 (1998), 126–64; Wolfgang Seibel, "The Strength of the Perpetrators: The Holocaust in Western Europe, 1940–1944", *Governance*, 15 (2002), 211–40.

9 Michael Salter, "The Visibility of the Holocaust: Franz Neumann and the Nuremberg Trials", in Robert Fine and Charles Turner (eds), *Social Theory After the Holocaust*, Liverpool: Liverpool University Press, 2000, pp. 197 et seq., p. 213.

10 See Rudi van Doorslaer (ed.), *Les Juifs en Belgique: De l'immigration au génocide*, Brussels: CREHSGM, 1994.

11 Note pour Monsieur le Bourgmestre, 28 May 1940, AVB, Cabinet du Bourgmestre, 1940–4, File 937 (Commission d'assistance publique, 1940–1943).

12 This was not the only time German anti-Jewish legal norms would be applied to Germans in Belgium. The War Damages Order of 14 Aug. 1940, regulating compensation for German citizens seeking to recover war-related losses, required a statement of Aryan background (*Arische Abstammung*) in the claim form and the production of proof of such descent in the case of doubt (*In Zweifelsfällen sind Urkunden beizufügen*). *Verordnung über die Entschädigung deutscher Staatsangehöriger für Kriegssachschäden*, VOBIB 11, 17 Aug. 1940, Question 1 F.

13 "Il est également ordonné que les communes publieront d'urgence un avis rappelant que les Juifs sont tenus de se faire inscrire au registre des Juifs et que les tenanciers d'établissements juifs doivent requérir l'administration communale de procéder à l'affichage prévu par l'ordonnance." Letter from Secretary-General Adam to the Provincial Governors, Local Administrators, Mayors and Councilors, 6 Dec. 1940. USHMM, RG. 65.0001M, Reel 2067, SVG.

14 "Le ff. Secrétaire Général du Ministère de l'Intérieur et de la Santé Publique prescrit que, par ordre de l'Autorité militaire allemande, les communes doivent publier d'urgence le présent avis". USHMM, RG. 65.003P, Reel 430, SVG.

15 "Aux fins de faciliter la tâche qui incombe à leur administration, les communes de l'agglomération bruxelloise ont décidé d'adopter pour le registre le type de fiche ci-jointe. L'autorité militaire allemande décide qu'à moins que des mesures d'exécution aient été déjà prises, le système mis en pratique par les communes de l'agglomération bruxelloise doit être adopté dans tout le pays." Letter from Adam, 6 Dec. 1940.

16 Letter from Pêtre to Van de Meulebroeck, AVB, Secrétariat, Guerre 40–45 (Juifs – Interdictions activités des conseils communaux).

17 For further discussion of the possible interpretations to be given to the mayor's response, see Thierry Delplancq, "Des paroles et des actes: L'Administration bruxelloise et le registre des Juifs, 1940–1941", *Cahiers d'Histoire du Temps Présent*, 12 (2003), 141–79.

18 "Sans doute, certains employés communaux ont rédigé, de concert, une formule
de fiche signalétique sous l'éventualité de la mise en application de l'ordonnance
allemande ... mais les bourgmestres, réunis en conférence, n'ont nullement adopté
ce projet, ni décidé son utilisation dans leur commune. Tout au contraire, constatant
que le paragraphe 16 de l'ordonnance allemande du 28 octobre stipule que 'le chef de
l'administration générale militaire arrêtera les prescriptions nécessaires, afin d'exécuter
et de compléter la présente ordonnance', ils ont décidé d'attendre que les prescriptions
nécessaires afin d'exécuter l'ordonnance du 28 octobre soient édictées pour fixer leur
attitude. Or, ils n'ont eu connaissance de la publication des prescriptions en question
que par votre circulaire précitée. Ils tiennent à souligner qu'ils n'appliqueront des
instructions que contraintes et forcés [sic]." Letter of 13 Dec. 1940, USHMM, RG.
65.003P, Reel 430, SVG.

19 "Des paroles et des actes".

20 JMDV, A004682.01-03.

21 "Communication téléphonique de M. l'Echevin Verhaeghe de Naeyer après la
Conférence des Bourgmestres du 21 novembre 1940", A 004685.01.

22 Letter of 23 Nov. 1940, AVB, Secrétariat, Guerre 40–45 (Juifs).

23 "1- quel service sera chargé de la tenue du registre des Juifs? Sera-ce la Police, les
Cultes ou l'Etat civil? 2- Convient-il d'inviter les Juifs par affiche, à se présenter
pour inscription au Bureau compétent? 3- Ou bien, étant donné que l'ordonnance
dont il s'agit dit dans son article 16 que le Chef de l'administration militaire arrêtera
les prescriptions nécessaires afin d'exécuter et de compléter la présente ordonnance,
y a-t-il lieu de demander des instructions complémentaires à l'Autorité allemande?
4- Le cas échéant, le Service désigné pourra-t-il réunir les délégués des communes
pour leur transmettre les renseignements recueillis afin d'arriver à l'uniformité
d'application." Rapport au Collège, 12 Nov. 1940, AVB, 1940–4, Cabinet du
Bourgmestre, 1940–4, File 866 bis.

24 "Le Collège, en sa séance du 12 novembre, a décidé que le registre des Juifs sera,
comme vous le savez, tenu par l'Etat civil. Il a estimé qu'il ne convenait pas de
demander des instructions complémentaires à l'autorité allemande, mais qu'il y avait
néanmoins lieu d'ouvrir le registre." Note pour Monsieur le Bourgmestre, 21 Nov.
1940, USHMM, RG 65.003P, Reel 430, SVG.

25 Conférence du 16 novembre 1940, relative à l'ordonnance en date du 28 octobre
concernant les mesures contre les juifs, AVB, Cabinet du Bourgmestre, 1940–4, File
866 bis.

26 "Ne pas renvoyer à une date ultérieure les Juifs qui se présenteraient pour se faire
inscrire sur le registre ad hoc. L'Administration n'a pas pour l'instant la mission
d'établir qui doit être considéré comme Juif au sens de l'Ordonnance". Ibid., para. 1.

27 Ibid., paras 3, 4, 5.

28 "Pour tout Juif qui se présente et vient se déclarer, une fiche provisoire sera établie.
Cette fiche sera complétée ultérieurement dans le sens qui nous sera indiqué par
l'ordonnance de l'autorité occupante. Les bureaux de Population ne prendront pas
d'autre initiative". Ibid., para. 5.

29 "Attendre la déclaration des intéressés et la faire signer". Ibid.

30 "Porter au verso du premier volet de la carte d'identité la mention 'A requis son
inscription au registre des Juifs' (texte bilingue)". Ibid., para. 7.

31 "... il résulte que l'inscription faite par les bureaux de la population sur la carte
d'identité ne peut pas faire croire ni permettre de soutenir que l'administration a
désigné quelqu'un comme juif. Il faut qu'apparaisse clairement que c'est l'intéressé
qui est venu se déclarer. Ne pas inscrire simplement 'juif'", 15 Nov. 1940, AVB,
Cabinet du Bourgmestre, 1940–4, File 866 bis.

32 See Delplancq, "Des paroles et des actes", pp. 153 et seq.

33   Conférence du 16 novembre, para. 6.

34   Ibid., para. 8.

35   "En conséquence, comme les déclarations doivent être faites avant le 30 novembre … un fonctionnaire de notre Administration a téléphoné au Ministère de l'Intérieur, afin de savoir si une décision quelconque ou des directives allaient être données. La réponse a été négative. Aujourd'hui, cependant, il semblerait que le dit Département a décidé de s'intéresser à la question, car, Warans, Chef de la Population, a été prié de faire venir le modèle de feuille qui a été établi par vos Services et adopté par les délégués de toutes les communes de l'agglomération, réunis à l'Hôtel de Ville samedi dernier sous la présidence de M. L'Echevin Verhaeghe de Naeyer." Note pour Monsieur le Bourgmestre, 21 Nov. 1940. Councilor Verhaeghe de Naeyer was the presiding officer of the meeting of 16 Nov. at which the eleven decisions concerning the practical implementation of the anti-Jewish Decree were taken. We also know that the Germans themselves had entered into direct contact with various municipal authorities to ensure that the process of registration and signage for Jewish business was proceeding according to plan. When *Stadtkämmer* Kahn, the occupation official in charge of relations with the city of Brussels, made inquiries he was informed in late Nov., before the letter of 6 Dec. and the protest of 13 Dec. that the register was ready. "A la Ville de Bruxelles, il lui a été répondu que le registre d'inscription était prêt". Letter from Governor of Brabant, Houtart, to the Secretary-General for the Interior, 28 Nov. 1940, CEGESOMA, Archives Houtart, MIC 79.

36   "Provisoirement, on pourrait donner acte aux Juifs dire qu'ils se sont présentés, et que, faute d'instructions, ils n'ont pas encore pu être inscrits." Séance de la Conférence des Bourgmestres de l'Agglomération Bruxelloise du 21 Novembre 1940, 66me séance. AVB, Cabinet du Bourgmestre, 1940–4, 866 bis. See also handwritten note replying to Note pour Monsieur l'Echevin Coelst, Registre des Juifs from Director of the Office of the Registry of Births, Deaths and Marriages, 21 Nov. 1940, ibid.

37   I am not suggesting that compliance and resignation were the universal reality. In Jan. 1942, the Office of the Secretary-General of the Interior wrote to local officials informing them that the Germans were unhappy with the level of response in relation to the Register of Jews and that certain municipalities had not yet sent the information to the Security Police. Brussels officials made internal inquiries and informed the Secretary-General that the city of Brussels had complied with the obligations imposed by the Order.

38   "Quant au point de vue juridique, le Service de la Population qui l'a étudié, est à même de répondre actuellement aux questions qui lui seraient posées, mais je pense que vous estimerez comme moi, et d'ailleurs conformément à l'ordonnance, qu'il appartient aux seuls intéressés de décider, si oui ou non, ils doivent requérir leur inscription." Ibid.

39   "En ce qui me concerne, j'ai consenti à ouvrir le registre sur lequel les juifs devaient s'inscrire aux termes de l'ordonnance, parce que j'ai considéré qu'ils avaient la faculté de s'y inscrire ou de ne pas s'y inscrire. Ils conservaient donc la faculté de se soumettre ou de ne pas se soumettre à l'ordonnance. J'avais reçu des demandes de certains juifs qui désiraient s'inscrire pour se mettre en règle. Un seul juif m'a écrit une lettre de protestation." 3 Jan. 1945, CEGESOMA, Archives Houtart, MIC 79.

40   Letter of the Permanent Council of Legislation.

41   AVB, Cabinet du Bourgmestre, 1940–4, File 866 bis.

42   Ibid. "La question posée ci-dessus au Collège offre un intérêt pratique particulier, en ce sens que si aucune inscription ne pouvait être faite à l'heure présente – d'ailleurs contrairement aux stipulations mêmes de l'Ordonnance – le Bureau de la Population ne pourrait pas continuer à mettre sur les cartes d'identité des Juifs qui viennent se déclarer, la mention : 'a requis son inscription au Registre des Juifs' et ne pourrait pas

davantage apposer un J. initiale, à l'inscription des intéressés, dans le Registre de la Population (mention indispensable pour la bonne marche du Service)."

43 Zygmunt Bauman, *Modernity and the Holocaust*, Ithaca, NY and London: Cornell University Press, 1989, p. 106.

44 Letter from Van Glabbeke to Houtart, 27 Nov., AVB, Cabinet du Bourgmestre, 1940–4, File 844 (Correspondance).

45 "… ne pensez-vous pas que l'affiche-avis porterait utilement que la carte d'identité de toutes personnes juives de plus de quinze ans est à présenter?", AVB, Cabinet du Bourgmestre, 1940–4, File 866 bis.

46 Instruction pour l'État Civil, 18 Dec. 1940, AVB, Cabinet du Bourgmestre, 1940–4, File 866 bis.

47 Registre des Juifs, 19 Dec. 1940, AVB, Cabinet du Bourgmestre, 1940–4, File 866 bis.

48 "… indiquer dans la colonne des observations à l'état des mutations un J aux fins de permettre la modification de la fiche". Ibid.

49 USHMM, RG. 65.003 P, Reel 430, SVG.

50 Letter of 20 Dec. 1940, ibid.

51 "Si à Schaerbeek on a pu réduire le format du timbre, c'est vraisemblablement qu'on n'y a pas respecté la formule imposée." Ibid.

52 Letter of 24 Dec. 1940, ibid.

53 For an introduction to the history of the Jews of Schaerbeek, see Godelieve Denhaene, "Les Juifs dans certains documents communaux de Schaerbeek pendant la Deuxième Guerre Mondiale", *Cahiers de la Mémoire Contemporaine*, 1 (1999), 133–9.

54 "Liste des Agents Temporaires Employés à la Confection du Registre des Juifs (Population) et Licenciés le 28 Décembre 1940", AVB, Cabinet du Bourgmestre, 1940–4, File 866 bis.

55 JMDV A004692.01, " la Ville a accompli sa mission. L'administration communale de Bruxelles ne connaît pas de Juifs établis sur son territoire et qui ne se sont pas déclarés". German letter of 31 Jan. to the Provincial Administration, JMDV A004692.02.

56 Letter of 3 April 1941. AVB, Police, Guerre 40–45, File 791.28 (Mesures prises par l'autorité allemande à l'égard de ressortissants des pays en guerre contre l'Allemagne, Sujets Alsaciens-Lorrains).

57 Letter from Joostens, 4 April 1941, ibid.

58 "Liste des établissements soumis à l'obligation de l'affichage", USHMM, RG. 65.003 P, Reel 430, SVG. Correspondance of M. Joostens, Director of Births, Deaths and Marriages, and M. De Tollenaere, Director of the Secretariat, 3 Jan. 1941, ibid. Subsequently the number was amended to 12. See draft letter from the College of Mayors, 8 Jan. 1941.USHMM, ibid.

59 "Ce restaurant est installé au 2d étage, il ne possède ni enseigne, ni écriteau quelconque de nature à le renseigner au public. L'apposition de l'affichette serait de nature à causer un préjudice aux firmes non-juives installées dans le même immeuble et dont les enseignes se trouvent annoncée sur la porte d'entrée." Ibid. The same information was included in a letter intended for the Secretary-General of the Interior summarizing the results of the registration process. See draft letter from the College of Mayors.

60 *Verordnung über das Ausscheiden von Juden aus Aemtern und Stellungen*, § 1 "Direktoren und Schriftleiter in Presse und Radiofunkunternehmen".

61 Letter of 3 Jan. 1941, AVB, Cabinet du Bourgmestre, 1940–4, File 866 bis. For a detailed study of the elimination of Jewish civil servants, see Thierry Delplancq, "L'Exclusion des Juifs de la fonction publique en Belgique 1940–1944: Le Cas des administrations locales bruxelloises", *Revue Belge d'histoire Contemporaine*, 35 (2005), 243–78.

62 I am aware that this is precisely the type of unethical question which Richard Weisberg labels the hermeneutic of acceptance and which he finds repugnant. I do not disagree but since the issues did in fact arise I felt obliged to explain and examine them here.

63 See Joseph Billig, *Le Commissariat Général aux Questions Juives*, 3 vols, Paris: CDJC, 1955, 1957, 1960, especially vol. 2.

64 "Die vorstehenden Bestimmungen wurden in der Judenverordnung des Militär-befehlshabers in Belgien und Nordfrankreich weggelassen, weil sie für die Durchführung der für Belgien im Frage kommenden Judenmassnahmen nicht aktuell sind und weil im Interesse der Erleichterung des Vollsauge durch die belgischen Behörden jede überflüssige Komplizierung des Judenbegriffe vermieden werden sollte." *Jahresbericht-Mai 1940/1941, des Militärbefehlshabers, in Belgien und Nordfrankreich, Judenverordnungen und deren Ausführung*, CEGESOMA.

65 Issues arose as to how to remove, according to legal norms, a stamp JUIF-JOOD, placed in error on the documents of an individual whose father had been "mistakenly" entered in the Jewish Register, see Letter from the Aliens' Office to OFK, Feb. 1942, re K. AVB, Police, Guerre 40–45, File 791.94 (Mesures antisémites) and as to the exact legal definition of Jewishness. See Letter from OFK 672, re M, 22 Sept. 1941, ibid.

66 "Mais depuis la mise en vigueur de l'ordonnance … des particuliers et surtout des notaires, des avocats et des huissiers sollicitent des attestations d'inscription ou de non-inscription au registre des Juifs. Par ailleurs, certaines administrations publiques exigent que toute demande d'admission à un emploi soit accompagnée d'un certificat de non-inscription au registre des Juifs. Cette exigence est apparemment fondée sur l'interprétation de la 2e ordonnance, fournie par votre circulaire du 6 décembre 1940 où il est dit à la page 4: lors des nouvelles nominations, la preuve doit être apportée par document authentique que le candidat n'est pas juif au sens de l'ordonnance." USHMM, RG.65.003 P, Reel 430, SVG.

67 Letter of 16 Jan. 1941 to R. Catteau, ibid.

68 Letter of 16 Jan. 1941 to Dr Vanhoevorst, ibid.

69 Letter of 17 Jan. 1941, ibid.

70 Letter from Secretary of the Council R. Hayoit (de Termicourt) to the Secretary-General of Justice, 21 Nov. 1940, CEGESOMA, Archives Jean Vossen, MIC 74.

71 See David Fraser, "Aryan and Jew in the Nazi *Rechtsstaat*", in Pheng Cheah, David Fraser and Judith Grbich (eds), *Thinking through the Body of the Law*, Sydney and New York: Allen & Unwin and New York University Press, 1996, pp. 63 et seq.

72 "Autoriser la Direction de l'Etat civil à délivrer des déclarations attestant que les intéressés n'ont pas requis leur inscription au registre des JUIFS". Extrait du Registre aux Délibérations du Collège des Bourgmestres et Echevins, 24 Jan. 1941, AVB, Cabinet du Bourgmestre, 1940–4, File 866 bis.

73 The province of Brabant appears to have adopted a somewhat more complex procedure. There anyone seeking to establish their non-Jewish status seems to have offered a written deposition indicating that the definitional provisions of the first anti-Jewish Order (§ 1) did not apply to them. Potentially, this would fall, I believe, more clearly on the side of implicating the administration in a decision-making or at least classificatory process for determining who was or was not a Jew. See Archives Houtart, CEGESOMA, MIC 79, sample document.

74 Letter from R. Vandevelde, Directeur des Affaires Administratives, with attachments, AVB, Secrétariat, Juifs (Personnel Enseignant).

75 "Nombre de personnes juives relevant, directement ou indirectement, de la Ville et des établissements qui lui sont subordonnés, qui ont dû cesser leurs fonctions en exécution de l'ordonnance visant la cessation des fonctions et activités par les juifs." Note from Putyzens, 28 Feb. 1941, AVB, ibid. (Nombre de personnes qui ont dû cesser leurs fonctions).

76 Letter of 5 March 1941, AVB, Secrétariat, Guerre 40–45, Juifs (Nombre de personnes qui ont dû cesser leurs fonctions).
77 "… osciller entre l'exécution passive et une certaine forme de participation déguisée". "Des paroles et des actes", p. 174.
78 Ibid.
79 Ordre de Service, No. 1979, 12 Dec. 1940, AVB, Secrétariat, Guerre 40–45, Juifs; Letter of 9 Jan. 1941 from A. Buez, Ministry of Education to the Head of Public Education, Brussels, ibid., Personnel Enseignant; Letter of 11 Jan. 1941 from Tits, Director of Public Education to City Secretary, ibid. It might be noted here that Tits's letter does contain a typewritten annotation by M. Catteau indicating that certain reasons may exist which would serve to temper the harshness of the Order and of a strict application of Belgian law. "J'ai indiqué à M. Tits certaines raisons d'opportunité [*sic*] qui doivent être prises en considération, et qui tendent à tempérer la rigueur des textes invoqués de part et d'autre."

7 Communicating, informing and deciding

1 Letter from Hauptmann Döring, *Ortskommandantur* to the Mayor, 13 May 1941 and handwritten annotation, AVB, Cabinet du Bourgmestre, 1940–4, File 884 (Documents terminés et transmis à l'autorité allemande).
2 *Verordnung über wirtschaftliche Massnahmen gegen Juden (Dritte Judenverordnung)* (Decree concerning economic measures against the Jews: Third Jewish Order), VOBIB 44, 10 June 1941.
3 See Maxime Steinberg, *Un pays occupé et ses juifs*, pp. 52–4.
4 Letter from the Director of Population Office to M. Putzeys, Secretary of the City of Brussels, 27 June 1941, AVB, Cabinet du Bourgmestre, 1940–4, File 866 bis.
5 Letter of 29 July 1941, USHMM, RG. 65.003 P, Reel 430, SVG.
6 Letter of 5 Aug. from Joostens to Verhaeghe de Naeyer, USHMM, ibid.
7 Letter from Joostens to the College, 12 Aug. 1941, ibid.
8 Letter from the College to Dienstelle des Sicherheitspolizei, 29 Aug. 1941, ibid. Compliance and resignation were not necessarily the universal reality. In Jan. 1942, the Office of the Secretary-General of the Interior wrote to local officials informing them that the Germans were unhappy with the level of response in relation to the Register of Jews and that certain municipalities had not yet sent the information to the Security Police. Brussels officials made internal inquiries and informed the Secretary-General that they had indeed sent the appropriate lists to the German Security officials. See Letter of 22 Jan. 1942 from Croonenberghs; Letter of 26 Jan. from Joostens to Coelst and Letter of 27 Jan. from Coelst to Romsée, USHMM, ibid. Clearly one of the areas of Belgian history which needs to be clarified is the question of compliance and resistance at the level of each municipal government. What seems clear is that Brussels was not a hotbed of resistance.
9 Letter of 23 Sept. 1941, ibid.
10 Letter of 30 Sept, from Joostens to Warans, JMDV, A004698.01.
11 *Verordnung über Aufenthaltsbeschränkungen für Juden vom 29 August 1941* (Order of 29 August 1941 limiting the free circulation of Jews), VOBIB, 5 Sept. 1941.
12 See Bulletin d'informations aux autorités de police et de gendarmerie de l'agglomération bruxelloise, 4 and 11 July 1942, JMDV, A004700.03, 04.
13 Letter from Warans to Joostens, 22 Sept. 1942, JMDV A004704.01,02.
14 Letter of 22 April 1944 to the District Office in Ixelles from the Office of Births, Deaths and Marriages, "Personne décédée avant le 28 octobre 1940 – certificat de non inscription au register des Juifs – Modèle", JMDV A004705.01, accompanied by a Flemish-language model, A004705.02.

15 Letter of 15 Oct. 1941, from Oesterhelt, *Oberfeldkommandantur* to Coelst and reply from Coelst, 24 Oct. 1941, AVB, Cabinet du Bourgmestre, File 845 (Correspondance avec l'autorité allemande).

16 11th Order of 25 Nov. 1941 concerning the Imperial German Nationality Law. This was the local application of the 11th Regulation introduced in Germany itself depriving Jews of their citizenship. For a discussion of the role played by this measure in the German anti-Jewish legal order and in other jurisdictions see David Fraser, "'This is Not Like Any Other Legal Question': A Brief History of Nazi Law Before U.K. and U.S. Courts", *Connecticut Journal of International Law*, 19 (2003), 59–125.

17 Letter of 13 May 1941 from Döring to the Mayor, AVB, Cabinet du Bourgmestre, 1940–4, File 884. The list of names and addresses was due on 15 May and was in fact handed over on 16 May at 11 a.m. There seems to be little evidence of obfuscation and delay here.

18 Perte de Nationalité Allemande par les Juifs Séjournant à l'Etranger, USHMM.

19 "Pour nous couvrir, nous avons exigé la production par les intéressés d'origine allemande: 1- d'un extrait du registre des juifs 2- d'un extrait du ou des registres de population, selon le cas. Sans doute la véritable garantie serait trouvée dans la production d'une pièce émanant de l'autorité allemande elle-même et constatant que l'intéressé a perdu la nationalité allemande par l'application de l'ordonnance de novembre. *Il ne semble pas qu'actuellement tout au moins il soit possible d'obtenir pareille attestation.*" USHMM.

20 "... c'est à l'occasion de mesures d'exécution à prendre par *le Reich* qu'il est prévu que le dossier de l'intéressé doit contenir comme pièce de base une attestation des Services de la Sûreté. Ce texte ne peut nous lier pour la question de délivrance de passeport, de mariage ..." Ibid.

21 See *Verordnung über den Verfall des Vermögens von Juden zu Gunsten des deutschen Reiches vom 22 April 1942* (Order of 22 April 1942 relating to the seizure and confiscation of the property of Jews for the benefit of the German Reich), VOBIB 73, 23 April 1942.

22 Letter from Richter to Mayor Coelst as Chair of the Conference of Mayors, 18 Aug. 1942, AVB, Cabinet du Bourgmestre, 1940–4, File 844. It is worth underlining here that the demand for compliance comes from the office charged with the "administration" of property, more precisely defined as the Aryanization office. The principal effect of the 11th Order was to expropriate expatriate German Jews. Here the city of Brussels provides to the Aryanization officials all of the information necessary to identify those whose property could be taken from them.

23 Séance de la Conférence des Bourgmestres de l'Agglomération Bruxelloise du 20 août 1942, JMDV A004667.01.

24 Letter of 3 March 1942, USHMM, Reel 430 SVG.

25 USHMM, RG.68.001 M, Reel 50, Selected Records from the Kingdom of Belgium.

26 See e.g. "Ressortissants allemands (Sujets Juifs) ayant requis leur inscription au Registre des Juifs", JMDV A004669.01; "Liste des Juifs inscrits aux Registres de la Population de Bruxelles et ayant perdus la nationalité allemande conformément à l'Ordonnance allemande du 25.11.1941", JMDV A004666.01, 12 Sept. 1942.

27 Letter from Piret to Coelst, 9 Sept. 1942, AVB, Cabinet du Bourgmestre, 1940–4, File 866 bis.

28 "Réponses aux Questions Relatives aux Juifs, Posées by M. Le Bourgmestre ff. dans sa Lettre du 9 septembre 1942", ibid.

29 As noted in Chapter 3, the phenomenon of adoption of Jewish children to shelter them from the impact of German policy was a relatively common one and one which vexed the occupying authority.

30 See also the letter from Andrée Erculisse-Souweine to the mayor of the suburb of Ixelles asking him to forward her assertion that she was not a Jew under the terms of the Order to the German authorities at the same time as he sent the list of registered Jews to the Germans in Aug. 1941. USHMM, RG. 68.001 M, Reel 50, Selected Records from the Kingdom of Belgium.

31 *Verordnung über die Kennzeichnung der Juden* (Order establishing a distinctive mark for Jews), VOBIB 79, 1 June 1942.

32 See generally Maxime Steinberg, "Le Pas de l'étoile", in *Un pays occupé et ses juifs*, p. 84.

33 *Verordnung zur Durchführung der Verordnung über die Kennzeichnung der Juden* (Order taken for the application of the Order establishing a distinctive marking for Jews), VOBIB 79, 1 June 1942.

34 Letter to Dr Gentzke, AVB, Cabinet du Bourgmestre, 1940–4, File 846 ("Doubles de lettres reçues et envoyées à l'autorité allemande avec leur traduction (1941–1944)").

35 "Il ne nous appartient pas de discuter avec vous de l'opportunité de la mesure prise contre les Israélites, mais nous avons le devoir de vous faire connaître que vous ne pouvez exiger de nous une collaboration à son exécution. Un grand nombre de Juifs sont belges, et nous ne pouvons nous résoudre à nous associer à une prescription qui porte une atteinte aussi directe à la dignité de tout homme, quel qu'il soit. Cette atteinte est d'autant plus grave qu'elle implique pour ceux qu'elle frappe l'interdiction de porter les insignes de nos ordres nationaux. Nous sommes convaincus que vous reconnaîtrez la légitimité de nos sentiments ..." Ibid.

36 The refusal was also communicated to Joseph Bologne of Liège by a letter from Van Glabbeke, the head of the Mayor's Office the same day. AVB, Cabinet du Bourgmestre, 1940–4, File 866 ("Mesures concernant les juifs"). After keeping a close eye on developments in Brussels, the mayor of Liège also "refused" to implement the Order by invoking the example of the capital and urging the Germans to take over the distribution.

37 Letter from Dr Gentzke to the Mayor of Brussels, 8 June 1942, AVB, Cabinet du Bourgmestre, 1940–4, File 866.

38 AVB, Police, Guerre 40–45, File 791.94, "Mesures antisémites, Ordonnance 27.5.42 établissant une marque distinctive pour les Juifs".

39 JMDV, A004711.01.

40 "... pour que des mesures uniformes soient adoptées pour toute l'agglomération ..."

41 Letter from Gentzke (n. 37), and handwritten annotation, AVB, Cabinet du Bourgmestre, 1940–4, File 866.

42 Rapport 12 June 1942, from Girthy, AVB, Police, Guerre 40–45, File 791.94, "Mesures antisémites, Ordonnance 27.5.42 établissant une marque distinctive pour les Juifs."

43 Letter from Coelst to Dr Callies, *Stadtkommissär* for Brussels, 20 June 1942, AVB, Cabinet du Bourgmestre, 1940–4, File 845.

44 Letter from Grauls and related correspondence, 9 Nov. 1942, AVB, Cabinet du Bourgmestre, 1940–4, File 946 ("Pièces à soumettre à M. le Bourgmestre").

45 Letter of 1 Dec. 1942, from former Councilor Pattou to the Mayor and Council or Brunet, in charge of municipal property, AVB, Cabinet du Bourgmestre, 1940–4, File 948 ("Deux dossiers intitulés Divers 1941–1945 et 1942–1945"), "a laissé, dans l'histoire de la Ville de Bruxelles, un nom célèbre".

46 Letter of 25 July 1944, from Brunet to Grauls, AVB, Cabinet du Bourgmestre, 1940–4, File 948 and positive response from Grauls, 7 Aug. 1944, ibid.

47 *Verordnung über das jüdische Schulwesen*, VOBIB 63, 2 Dec. 1941, §§ 1, 2.

48 Letter of 4 Feb. 1941.

49 "Ecoliers juifs dans les Ecoles moyennes", 25 Feb. 1941, AVB, Cabinet du Bourgmestre, 1940–4, File 884.

50 Letter of 21 April 1942 from Löffler, AVB, Cabinet du Bourgmestre, 1940–4, File 845. The Order on Jewish education had granted sole jurisdiction over Jewish education to the AJB (§ 1). See Schreiber and Van Doorslaer (eds), *Les Curateurs du Ghetto*.

51 Letter of 30 May 1942 to Dr Callies, AVB, Cabinet du Bourgmestre, 1940–4, File 846 ("Correspondance, 1 juillet/30 septembre 1941, juifs").

52 "Nous tenons à vous dire que l'aide apportée jusqu'à ce jour par les administrations communales aux Israélites pour la création d'écoles gardiennes nous a valu de leur part de nombreux témoignages de satisfaction. Un grand nombre d'enfants qui fréquentent ces écoles sont belges, beaucoup d'entre eux sont malheureux. A ce titre ils méritent notre sollicitude. Soyez convaincu que nous continuerons à faire tout ce qui est possible pour atténuer la rigueur des mesures prises contre eux. Mais il importe que vous sachiez que ce que nous avons fait en faveur des écoles gardiennes nous ne pourrons pas le réaliser pour les autres établissements scolaires envisagés." Ibid.

53 All city agencies played a role. The transportation department arranged for trams to adopt appropriate routes to pick up disabled Jewish children so that they could also be brought to a separate Jewish kindergarten. See Letter from Félicie Perelman to the Director of Tramways, 4 May 1942, CDJC, CDLXIII-73.

54 Letter of 4 June 1942, from Dr Callies to the Conference, AVB, Cabinet du Bourgmestre, 1940–4, File 866.

55 Letter from Coelst, 19 June 1942, AVB, Cabinet du Bourgmestre, 1940–4, File 846. "Dans notre lettre du 30 mai, nous disions qu'en raison des mesures pénibles prises à l'égard des juifs dont beaucoup sont nos compatriotes et dont beaucoup sont malheureux ils méritent toute notre sollicitude. Mais, nous n'avons ni le désir ni non plus la possibilité de créer pour eux un enseignement qui leur soit exclusivement réservé.

Les seuls locaux disponibles que nous avons mis immédiatement à la disposition de l'association israélite et ceux qui le deviendront par la suite, ne suffiront point pour héberger les milliers d'élèves primaires auxquels l'accès de nos écoles a été interdit."

56 Letter to Principal Inspector Janssen, 26 June 1942, AVB, Cabinet du Bourgmestre, 1940–4, File 866.

57 Letter of 6 July 1942, to the Conference, AVB, Cabinet du Bourgmestre, 1940–4, File 845.

58 Conference of Mayors, 9 July 1942, AVB, Cabinet du Bourgmestre, 1940–4, File 866, "Les communes sont décidées à aider les Juifs dans toute la mesure de leurs possibilités."

59 Letter from the Department of Public Education to the *Oberfeldkommandantur,* AVB, Cabinet du Bourgmestre, 1940–4, File 846.

60 See Seibel, "Strength of the Perpetrators".

61 Letter from Foucart and Putzeys to the *Oberfeldkommandantur*, AVB, Cabinet du Bourgmestre, 1940–4, File 847 ("juillet/décembre 1942- réquisitions immobilières"). "Les bâtiments scolaires situés Rue du Vautour, 68 ont été réquisitionnés non pour les besoins de l'armée occupante, mais pour l'Organisation TODT, Aucune école, ni aucun grand local n'étant disponible dans ce quartier où les Juifs sont spécialement établis, pour pouvoir satisfaire à votre demande, nous sommes contraints de vous réclamer la mise à notre disposition pour les écoles juives de ce local Rue du Vautour, 68. Nous sommes certains que vous comprendrez cette nécessité et que vous voudrez bien donner des instructions nécessaires pour que cette école soit remise à notre disposition, afin que nous puissions exécuter vos instructions. Cette question, d'après les correspondances que nous avons reçues, devant être résolue rapidement, je me permets de vous demander une solution rapide à la demande de libération du local de la Rue du Vautour."

62 Letter of 2 June 1942 to the Military Administration from the Public Education Department of the City of Brussels, AVB, Cabinet du Bourgmestre, 1940–4, File 846.

63 See Letter of 9 June 1942 from Herinckx, Mayor of Uccle, and reply from Coelst of 10 June 1942, AVB, Cabinet du Bourgmestre, 1940–4, File 945 (Dossier "copies et pieces diverses").

64 Letter of 8 June 1942 from Coelst to the Verwaltungschef, AVB, Cabinet du Bourgmestre, 1940–4, File 945. See also the internal police reports of 5 June 1942 and 3 July 1942. AVB, Police, Guerre 40–45, File 791.822 ("Arrestations illégales").

65 Letter of 3 July 1942, AVB, Cabinet du Bourgmestre, 1940–4, File 845.

66 Letter to Oesterhelt, AVB, Cabinet du Bourgmestre, 1940–4, File 845. The Germans were not pleased and wrote to Houtart, Governor of the Province of Brabant, instructing him to write to Coelst and inform him that his refusal was based in a misunderstanding and incorrect interpretation of the law. Letter from Oesterhelt, 16 July 1942, CEGESOMA, Archives Houtart, MIC 79. Houtart passed the jurisprudential buck to the Secretary-General for the Interior since the German legal position, if correct, would apply to all Belgian police forces. Letter of 22 July 1942, ibid.

67 CEGESOMA, Archives/ Archief Hayoit, MIC 79.

68 Letter of 22 July 1942, ibid.

69 *Verordnung zur Durchführung der Verordnung über die Beschäftigung von Juden in Belgien*, VOBIB 76, 15 May 1942.

70 *Verordnung über die Beschäftigung von Juden in Belgien*, VOBIB 70, 18 March 1942.

71 "Vous penserez sans doute avec moi … que … l'arrestation de sujets juifs aux fins de les contraindre à accepter du travail tombe dans les cas exceptionnels admis par cette ordonnance".

72 Police Report, 4 Sept. 1942, AVB, Cabinet du Bourgmestre, 1940–4, File 945.

73 See *Rapports sur la Violation du Droit des Gens en Belgique*, Paris: Berger-Levrault, 1916.

74 "Logiques administratives et persécutions anti-juives: La Police bruxelloise et les arrestations de 1942", *Cahiers d'Histoire du Temps Présent*, 12 (2003), 181–217. See also "Bulletin d'informations aux autorités de police et du gendarmerie de l'agglomération bruxelloise", AVB, Cabinet du Bourgmestre, 1940–4, File 945, containing the correspondence involving the Police, the Crown Attorney and the Germans in legal debates about the extent of assistance to be rendered by the local police. See also letter of 3 Sept. 1942 from Inspector Tasseel to the Mayor of Brussels detailing other German demands for assistance. Ibid. For an "official" history of the national police, the Gendarmerie, see (Col.) Willy Van Geet, *La Gendarmerie sous l'Occupation*, Brussels: Éditions J. M. Collet, 1992. On the police and the Jews, ibid., pp. 88–9.

75 Letter of 3 July 1942 to Secretary-General Nyns, and reply from Nyns, 9 July 1942, AVB, Cabinet du Bourgmestre, 1940–4, File 947 (Dossier "Questions en suspens").

76 See Maxime Steinberg, *L Étoile et le fusil:1942 Les Cents Jours de la déportation des Juifs de Belgique*, Brussels: Vie Ouvrière, 1984; and *Dossier Bruxelles Auschwitz: La Police SS et l'extermination des Juifs de Belgique*, Brussels: Comité Belge de Soutien à la partie civile dans le procès des officiers SS Ehlers, Asche, Canaris, responsables de la déportation des Juifs de Belgique, 1980.

77 "Bulletin d'information aux autorités de police et de gendarmerie de l'agglomération bruxelloise", 28 Nov. 1940, AVB, Police, Guerre 40–45, File 791.99 ("Renseignements divers demandés par l'autorité allemande").

78 Ibid.

79 Note 16 March 1943, ibid.

80 Rapport 18 March 1943 and attachment, ibid.

81 Ibid., Bulletin d'information, 21 April 1941.
82 Ibid., Bulletin d'information, 28 July 1941.
83 Ibid., Bulletin d'information, 15 Oct. 1941.
84 However, in at least one case, the Belgian police escorted a Mrs L., being hunted by the Gestapo and described as a Polish Jew (*juive polonaise*), to their headquarters on Boulevard Jamar, and reported to their superiors who informed the Germans of her whereabouts. The Gestapo led Mrs L. away from the Brussels police station sometime later. See Rapport, Commissariat de Saint-Gilles to the Police Chief, 12 Sept. 1942, AVB, Police, Guerre 40-45, File 791.94 ("Mesures antisémites").
85 Police of Saint-Josse-Ten-Noode, "Relevé des événements ou incidents importants survenus pendant le mois écoulé et auxquels ont été mêlés des Belges et des Allemands", 1 Nov. 1941, AVB, Police, Guerre 40–45, File 791.329 ("Divers").
86 Rapport, 29 Dec. 1941, AVB, Police, Guerre 40–45, File 791.94 ("Mesures antisémites").
87 Rapport, 21 Jan. 1942, ibid.
88 "Bulletin d'informations aux autorités de police et de gendarmerie de l'agglomération bruxelloise", 22 April 1942, AVB, Police, Guerre 40–45, File 791.99 ("Renseignements divers").
89 Ibid., Letter of 23 April 1942.
90 "Réponse au Bulletin d'Informations du 22/4/42", 23 April 1942, ibid.
91 Rapport, 24 April 1942, ibid.
92 See Commission Buysse, *Les Biens des victimes des persécutions anti-juives en Belgique: Rapport final de la Commission d'étude sur le sort des biens des membres de la communauté juive de Belgique spoliés ou délaissés pendant la guerre 1940–1945*, Brussels: Services du Premier Ministre, 2001.
93 Letter of 14 Aug. to Schneider, AVB, Cabinet du Bourgmestre, 1940–4, File 851 ("1er mai/30 novembre 1943, Immeubles-services"). See also Letter of 24 July re Mr G., ibid.
94 Letter of 28 Aug. 1943, Cabinet du Bourgmestre, 1940–4, File 851.
95 See e.g. Letter of 29 June 1943 from Schneider; letter of 16 July from the Gas and Electricity Board, AVB, Cabinet du Bourgmestre, 1940–4, ibid. Correspondence relating to the Saby Matarasso business, 23 Oct. 1943, AVB, Cabinet du Bourgmestre, 1940–4, File 855 ("Divers 1943–mai 1944").
96 Letter to Schneider, 29 April 1943, concerning Mr K, AVB, Cabinet du Bourgmestre, 1940–4, File 850; Letter to the Office of Jewish Enemy Property (Office de la Propriété Juive), 31 March 1944, re Mrs E., AVB, Cabinet du Bourgmestre, 1940–4, File 855.
97 Letter to Schneider, Matarassso Company, 11 Nov. 1943, ibid.
98 AVB, Cabinet du Bourgmestre, 1940–4, ibid.
99 Letter to Schneider, 1 Aug. 1943, AVB, Cabinet du Bourgmestre, 1940–4, File 851 ("1er mai/30 novembre 1943, Immeubles-services"). The branch in Schaerbeek also entered into contact with the German authorities in order to gain access to unoccupied houses. In order to close the account of their subscribers, they needed to take a final meter reading and seal the meters. The list of fifteen Jewish names of the owners is attached. Administrative efficiency, book-keeping requirements and the closing of accounts above all else seems to have motivated the utility company. Letter, undated, to *Dienststelle* SICHO, AVB, Cabinet du Bourgmestre, 1940–4, File 850.
100 Report, 8 Sept. 1941, AVB, Police, Guerre 40–45, File 791.94 ("Mesures antisémites").
101 AVB, Police, Guerre 40–45, "Entreprises juives – Remise d'ordre de liquidation, Bulletin d'informations", 9 April 1942, File 791.94.
102 See "Legalization of Racism".

8 Liège and its Jews

1 Letter of 17 May to Administrator Schreiber, AVLg, BAP 5 "très précaire".
2 Letter to the mayor, 3 June 1940, AVLg (Police), "environ 20 à 25.000 habitants se sont évacués ou se seront sauvés à la date du 10 mai dernier". See generally Hanna Diamond, *Fleeing Hitler: France 1940*, Oxford and New York: Oxford University Press, 2007.
3 AVLg, Dannes-Camiers, Liquidations.
4 Letter from councilor Jennissen to the Chamber of Commerce, 15 May 1940, ibid.
5 City Council Meeting (Collège *des Echevins*), 24 June 1940, Minutes, AVLg.
6 Letter to Police Commanders, 16 May 1940, AVLg, Dannes-Camiers, Liquidations.
7 Letter of 16 May 1940 from the Receiver-General to Jennissen, ibid., Liquidations 3.
8 Ibid., Liquidations 1, "Déférant au désir que vous avez exprimé, nous vous adressons ci-inclus la liste des maisons israélites et polonaises, liquidées ou en liquidation par l'intervention de la Chambre de Commerce."
9 Letter from the Caisse Communale to Jennissen, 10 July 1940, ibid., draft form, 14 Aug. 1940, Finance Office, AVLg, Liquidations de commerces abandonnés 1940. Généralités.
10 City Council, Meeting of 12 July 1940, Minutes, AVLg.
11 AVLg, Liquidations des commerces abandonnés en 1940. Généralités.
12 See Peter Liberman, *Does Conquest Pay? The Exploitation of Occupied Industrial Societies*, Princeton, NJ: Princeton University Press, 1996; Götz Aly, *Hitler's Benificiaries*, London: Verso, 2007.
13 *Verordnung betreffend das feindliche Vermögen*, 23 May 1940, VOBIB 2, 17 June 1940; *Verordnung zur Durchführung und Ergänzung der Feindvermögensverordnung*, 2 July 1940, VOBIB 5, 6 July 1940; *Durchführungsverordnung zur Feindvermögens-verordnung*, 23 Aug. 1940, VOBIB 13, 30 Aug. 1940; *Dritte Durchführungsverordnung zur Feindvermögensverordnung*, 28 Oct. 1940, VOBIB 19, 1 Nov. 1940.
14 The Belgian Civil Code, Articles 112–14 provided for the appointment of an administrator or trustee to protect the interests of all absent persons.
15 AVLg, Liquidations.
16 Letter of 27 Sept. 1940, ibid.
17 AVLg, Dannes-Camiers, Liquidations de Commerce – Correspondance 1.
18 AVLg, Liquidations, "Comme la Chambre de Commerce seule détient les comptes des intéressés, je vous fais remettre avec la présente un paquet de formulaires qu'il y aura lieu de faire remplir par vos services, étant entendu que la mention finale sera signée par le Receveur communal qui détient les fonds ou par un membre du Collège."
19 AVLg, Dannes-Camiers, Liquidations de Commerce – Correspondance 1.
20 See e.g. the letter of 20 Nov. 1940 from Jennissen to the Population Bureau, asking them to fill in the appropriate forms with an indication of the given names and the nationalities of the persons named in the declaration. The Population Bureau completed its task the very next day. AVLg, Liquidations.
21 AVLg, Liquidations, "Mais voici que se présentent à notre Office des commerçants que nous avons lieu de supposer être des israélites et qui déclarent être revenus au pays avant l'ordonnance du 28 octobre. Je vous serai obligé de me faire savoir le plus tôt possible si je puis remettre les fonds qui leur appartiennent à ces personnes."
22 AVLg, Liquidations.
23 AVLg Dannes-Camiers, Liquidations 3.
24 Ibid., Liquidations – Correspondance 1.
25 Ibid.
26 AVLg, Liquidations, Correspondence échangée avec la Recette Communale.
27 Letter from the councilor in charge of Litigation to the Public Procurement Office, 8 Nov. 1941, AVLg, Dannes-Camiers, Liquidation des Commerces, Correspondance 1.

28 VOBIB 44, 10 June 1941, *Verordnung zur Ergänzung der Judenverordnung vom 31 mai 1941.*

29 "Circulaire envoyée par les Autorités allemandes aux commerçants Juifs, relative à leur inscription au Registre du Commerce", CEGESOMA, AA 120, Ministère de la Justice, Crimes de Guerre.

30 Registre du Commerce, Liège, April–May 1942, AELg. See the discussion in Chapter 4.

31 AVLg, Cabinet du Bourgmestre, Affaires Allemandes, Guerre 40, 3913.

32 Ibid. "J'ai beau expliquer, comme je l'ai pu, que la Ville ne connaît pas les personnes qui appartiennent à la religion juive".

33 Ibid.

34 AVLg, Dannes-Camiers, Liquidations des Commerces – Correspondance 1.

35 AVLg, Liquidations – Commerces 1.

36 Ibid.

37 Ibid.

38 Letter of 7 Feb. 1944.

39 AVLg, Liquidations 2.

40 Ibid.

41 Ibid., "Attendu que les nommés Lindenberg et Hofman doivent encore certaines sommes à la Ville pour taxes".

42 Ibid., "la somme de 1.385 Francs pour taxes dues".

43 Ibid.

44 AVLg, Liquidations-Bloemendael, Chamber of Commerce, 19 May 1940; Councilor for Public Procurement, 19 May 1940; Police Statement, 20 May 1940; Inventory, 20 May 1940; Extract from the Bloemendael Account.

45 Ibid.

46 AVLg, Dannes-Camiers, Liquidations des Commerces – Correspondance, Letter to the Office of Public Procurement, 17 Feb. 1942.

47 USHMM, RG. 68.001 M, Reel 48, Selected Records from the Kingdom of Belgium.

48 AVLg, Liquidations-Dossier C – Liquidation Littman.

49 AVLg, Dannes-Camiers, Liquidations des Commerces – Correspondance 1, 24 Nov. 1940.

50 Lettre du Commandant Militaire à la Caisse Communale, 18 Nov. 1941. (Transmis du Bureau du Bourgmestre au Service de Finances et à l'Echevin du Ravitaillement "pour disposition".) AVLg, Cabinet du Bourgmestre Guerre 40, Affaires Allemandes, 3545, and AVLg, Liquidations-Dossier C – Liquidation Littman, Juda.

51 AVLg, Dossier C – Liquidation Littman Juda.

52 AVLg, Liquidations des Commerces – Correspondance 1.

53 Ibid., "le juif polonais".

54 Ibid.

55 AVLg, Liquidations-Dossier 154 – Liquidation Licklatzki (*sic*).

56 Ibid., Letter of 18 Nov. 1940. "Mais ce dernier n'étant pas rentré, les sommes que nous détenons en son nom sont considérées comme biens ennemis et peut-être comme propriété juive. Nous ne pouvons donc nous en désaisir (sic) et nous devons les déclarer à l'office de Déclaration de la Propriété ennemie."

57 AVLg, Dannes-Camiers, Liquidations des Commerces – Correspondance 1 – Déclarations des Biens Ennemis.

58 Letter of 23 Nov. 1940 from Compagnie Dufrane & Minon to the Receiver; Letter of 26 Nov. from the Receiver to Jennissen; Letter of 30 Nov. from Jennissen to the company. AVLg, Liquidations – Liquidation Micklatzki – Dossier 154.

59 Letter of 5 Dec. 1940 from Jennissen to the councilor in charge of Legal Affairs; Tribunal de première instance, 25 Nov. ibid. Letter from SICO to Jennissen, 12 Dec. 1940.

60 Letter to the mayor, transmitted to the Finance Department for settlement, 16 and 18 Dec. 1940, ibid.

61 Ibid.

62 Ibid.

63 Ibid.

64 USHMM, RG 68.001M, Reel 48, Selected Records from the Kingdom of Belgium. "L'entreprise a été liquidée en juin 1940 par les soins de la Chambre de Commerce de Liège, sur réquisition de la Ville de Liège."

65 AVLg, Liquidations – Dossier 154 – Liquidation Micklatzki.

66 "S'il y a nécessité de pourvoir à l'administration de tout ou partie des biens laissés par une personne présumée absente, et qui n'a point de procureur fondé, il y sera statué par le tribunal de première instance, sur la demande des parties intéressées" (Art. 112). (If there is a necessity to provide for the administration of all or part of the assets left by a person presumed missing and who has no authorized agent, it will be so determined by the court of first instance on the application of interested parties.)

67 Ibid., Letter of 25 Jan. 1941.

68 Ibid., Letter of 22 Feb.

69 Ibid.

70 Ibid., "dans une situation très précaire".

71 Letter of 7 March 1941, ibid. "le montant net restant après avoir couvert toutes les dettes".

72 Letter to Jules Glineur, 12 March 1941. "Il s'ensuit que seul le Code civil belge contient les prescriptions à suivre dans cette liquidation."

73 Ibid.

74 Letter from the Receiver to Jennissen, 4 April 1941, ibid.

75 Letter of 10 June 1941, ibid.

76 AVLg, Cabinet du Bourgmestre – Guerre 1940 – Affaires Allemandes – 7648.

77 Letter of 3 July 1944, AVLg, Liquidations-Dossier 154 – Liquidation Micklatzki.

78 Ibid.

79 Brogna survived the latter stages of German persecution in hiding at a Liège hospital, l'hôpital Bavière, but died shortly after the return of the rest of the family from France in 1945. See Charlotte Goldberszt, "Varsovie-Liège 1940–1942: Sur une correspondance", Revue d'Histoire de la Shoah, 187 (2007), 289–304.

80 AVLg, Liquidations-Dossier 170 – Affaire Goldberst (sic).

81 Ibid., and AVLg, Liquidations.

82 AVLg, Dannes-Camiers, Liquidations des Commerces – Correspondance 1.

83 AVLg, Liquidations-Dossier 170 – Affaire Goldberst.

84 Letter of 18 Oct. 1940, ibid.

85 Letter of 2 Nov. 1940, ibid. "Je me permets de vous signaler que M. le Receveur des Contributions insiste pour obtenir le payement des impôts, ce que je ne peux faire sans entrer en possession de l'argent déposé à la Ville."

86 Ibid. "A cette occasion, je me permets de vous signaler la récente ordonnance de l'autorité allemande au sujet des Juifs."

87 USHMM, RG.69.001M, Reel 48, Selected Records from the Kingdom of Belgium.

88 JMVD, Dossier Goldberszt, A009206.1. Letter of 8 Nov. 1940. "Je crois aussi qu'il est de votre intérêt, vu les récentes mesures prises par l'autorité, de terminer le plus tôt possible, cette affaire."

89 JMDV, Dossier Goldberszt, A009282.

90 Ibid, A009293 and A 009284, Letter of 7 Jan. from Maître Elie Burthoul to Me Mottart and reply of 8 Jan. Article 112-14 of the Civil Code provided for the judicial appointment of an administrator in the case of recognized absence only.

91 AVLg, Liquidations – Affaire Goldberst – Dossier 170. Letter of 8 Jan. 1941 to l'Echevin du Ravitaillement.
92 Ibid. A009211.4. Letter of 9 Jan. from Glineur to Mme Horenblas, JMDV, A009285. Letter from Glineur to Me Mottart, 11 Jan., JMDV, A009286; Déclaration Formulaire A, signed by Mme Horenblas, 28 Feb. 1941.
93 JMDV, A009287.
94 Letter from l'Echevin du Ravitaillement, 13 Jan. 1941, AVLg, Liquidations –Affaire Goldberst – Dossier 170. Letter of 11 Feb. from Echevin du Ravitaillement to Receveur Communal, ibid. Letter from Glineur to Echevin du Ravitaillement, 13 Feb. 1941. Ibid.
95 JMDV, A009288, Letter from greffier Glineur to Me Mottart, 15 Jan. 1941.
96 JMDV, 009290, Letter of 16 Jan. 1941.
97 JMDV, A009291, A009292, A009293, A009294.
98 JMDV, A 009289. Letter of 15 Jan. 1941.
99 JMDV A009295, Letter to Me Delfosse, avoué, 13 Feb.. These costs and fees totaled 194.50 BEF. Letter from avoué Delfosse to Mottart, 25 Feb., JMDV, A009296.
100 AVLg, Liquidations – Affaire Goldberst – Dossier 170, Letter from the Military Command to Glineur, 22 Feb. 1941.
101 Ibid., Letter from Jennissen to Glineur, 14 Feb. 1941.
102 JMDV, A009297, Letter from Avoué Delfosse to Me Mottart, 6 March 1941.
103 AVLg, Liquidations – Affaire Goldberst – Dossier 170, Letter of 18 March 1941 to Jennissen.
104 Ibid.
105 JMDV, Dossier Goldberszt, A009299.
106 JMDV, A009220, Letter of 13 June 1941.
107 JMDV, A009301; A009302; A009303; A009303.V.
108 A009305, Letters of 13 May 1941, to Mme Horenblas and to the City Receiver.
109 AVLg, Liquidations – Affaire Goldberst – Dossier 170, Letter of 16 May 1941.
110 JMDV, A009308.
111 JMDV, A009309 and A009310, Letter from Mottart, 5 June 1941; Reply from Mme Horenblas, 7 June 1941.
112 JMDV, A009311 and A009311.V, Letter of 1 July 1941: "s'élèveront à la somme de 800 francs à laquelle s'ajouteront quelques déboursés".
113 JMDV, A009312, Letter to Me Mottart, 4 July 1941.
114 JMDV, A009313, Letter to Me Mottart, 24 July 1941.
115 JMDV, A009258.1, Letter to the Receiver, 2 Aug. 1941, with annotations.
116 JMDV, A009528.2, Letter from the Receiver, 9 Oct. 1941.
117 JMDV, A009316; A009317; A009320.
118 JMDV, A009245; A009251; A009252.
119 AVLg, Liquidations – Liquidation Lindenberg – Dossier OPM.
120 Ibid., "apatride d'origine polonaise".
121 AVLg, Liquidations – Liquidation Lindenberg – Dossier OPM, Oppositions déposées, Me Firmin Debatty, Huissier, 2 July, 1 Oct., 15 Dec. 1940, Correspondance 8, 14, 31 May 1941, 17, 19, 22, and 23 July 1941.
122 Arrêté, 4 Nov. 1940, Collège des Bourgmestres et Echevins, ibid.
123 Letter from Novita to the City, 8 Jan. 1941, ibid.
124 Ibid.
125 See additional correspondence on 9 and 22 Aug.
126 Ibid., Letter of 23 July 1941.
127 Ibid., Letters of 25 July and 1 Aug. "Il faut inviter cet officier ministériel (l'huissier Debatty) à suivre les règles de la procédure édictées par les articles 557 et suivants du Code de procédure."
128 Ibid. See also his letter of 15 Oct. 1941.

129   Ibid., Letter of 5 Sept. 1941.
130   Ibid., Letter of 8 Sept. 1941: "est conforme à l'attitude que nous avons décidée il y a
        déjà de nombreux mois, et je ne vois aucune raison de la modifier. Nous ne pouvons pas
        nous libérer valablement en mains d'un tiers, sans l'accomplissement de ces formalités,
        à défaut de l'accord de notre créancier."
131   Letter from the councilor in charge of Legal Services to the Public Procurement, 11
        March 1942. Order of the Council, 16 March 1942. "A la rigueur des principes, nous
        pourrions nous opposer au payement et exiger une procédure régulière. Toutefois, vu la
        modicité de la somme, il y a intérêt, même pour la personne en cause, à ce que la prime
        soit liquidée. La théorie de la gestion d'affaires ... pourrait justifier le décaissement."
132   Ibid., Letter of 13 Oct. 1942. "Il s'agit ici du bien d'un juif polonais".
133   AVLg, Dannes-Camiers, Liquidations des Commerces 2.
134   AVLg, Liquidations – Liquidation Lindenberg – Dossier OPM.
135   Ibid.
136   Ibid., Letter of 11 July 1944. "Pourriez-vous me faire savoir quelles raisons ont provoqué
        la différence entre le paiement fait à Monsieur Debatty et l'autorisation allemande?
        Comment pourrions-nous justifier le versement de 1.350 Francs fait selon les indications
        de Monsieur Boelen de votre Service (il s'agit des taxes)."
137   AVLg, Liquidations des Commerces-1, Letter of 19 July 1944.
138   AVLg, Liquidations – Liquidation Lindenberg – Dossier OPM.
139   Ibid.
140   AVLg, Liquidations, Dossier 23, Bloemendael.
141   Ibid., Letter to the Council from the Receiver, 7 Jan. 1947.
142   AVLg, Liquidations – Liquidation Lindenberg – Dossier OPM. "M. Lindenberg, Joseph,
        sujet juif, toujours absent".
143   AVLg, Liquidations – Affaire Cingler – Dossier 85. "Attendu que Mr CYNGLER n'a
        pas voulu entrer en possession de l'entièreté de cette somme et qu'un solde de Frs.
        2.194,20 reste provisoirement consigné en mains de Mr le Receveur communal; qu'il y
        a licu de régulariser la situation. Sur la proposition de MM. Les Echevins des Finances
        et du Ravitaillement: Autorise Mr le Receveur communal à porter en recettes sur l'article
        No— du budget de 1946, la somme de DEUX MILLE CENT NONANTE QUATRE
        FRANCS 20 CENTIMES (Frs 2.194,20)."
144   AVLg, Liquidations – Liquidations Lindenberg – Dossier OPM.
145   Ibid., Note of 3 Sept. 1947.
146   Correspondance septembre–octobre 1947, AVLg, Correspondance 3.
147   AVLg, Liquidations 2: "Mr Lindenberg a quitté le pays, pour les Etats-Unis, alors qu'il
        est encore redevable de plusieurs taxes, suivant détail: ... Il faut un mandat pour "apurer"
        le compte de M. Lindenberg".

9   Hirsch & Co.: a case study

1   *Verordnung betreffende das feindliche Vermögen in den besetzten Gebieten der
      Niederlande, Belgiens, Luxemburgs und Frankreichs (Feindvermögensverordnung) vom
      23.5.1940*, VOBIB 20, 17 June 1940.
2   *Verordnung sur Durchführung und Ergänzung der Feindvermögensverordnung*, 2 July
      1940, VOBIB 20, 6 July 1940.
3   Articles of Incorporation of the Brüsseler Treuhandgesellschaft, contracted before
      Notary Brunet, 12 Oct. 1940, Article 3, Service des Victimes de la Guerre: "toutes
      opérations civiles et commerciales relatives à la gestion, l'administration, la liquidation
      et le contrôle des biens appartenant à des particuliers ou à des sociétés ainsi que toutes
      autres activités financières ou industrielles se rapportant directement ou indirectement à
      cet objet."

4 On the operation of the German spoliation apparatus in Belgium, see Commission Buysse, *Les Biens des victimes des persécutions anti-juives en Belgique: Rapport final de la Commission d'étude sur le sort des biens des membres de la communauté juive de Belgique spoliés ou délaissés pendant la guerre 1940–1945*, Brussels: Services du Premier Ministre, 2001, pp. 40 et seq.

5 See Jean-Philippe Schreiber, *L'Immigration Juive en Belgique du Moyen Age à la Première Guerre Mondiale*, Brussels: Éditions de l'Université de Bruxelles, 1996, pp. 96 et seq.

6 See Véronique Pouillard, *Hirsch & Cie: Bruxelles, 1869–1962*, Brussels: Éditions de l'Université de Bruxelles, 2000, pp. 9 et seq.

7 Ibid., pp. 14 et seq. See also the entry for "Hirsch, Lévi dit Léo", in Jean-Philippe Schreiber, *Dictionnaire biographique des Juifs de Belgique*, Brussels: De Boeck & Larcier, 2002.

8 See their entries in Schreiber, *Dictionnaire biographique*.

9 Ibid., and Pouillard, *Hirsch & Cie*, pp. 67–8.

10 A leading Brussels lawyer, Botson was among those local members of the Bar, fluent in German, who undertook the representation of Belgians before German military tribunals during the occupation. He participated in resistance activities during the war and was subsequently elected head of the Bar (*Bâtonnier*) in 1945. See the entry "Henry L. Botson", in Pierre Henri, *Grands Avocats de Belgique*, Brussels: Éditions J. M. Collet, 1984.

11 AGR, Maison Hirsch I 288, # 100, Procurations, 8 June 1940.

12 Ibid., Procuration, 10 Sept. 1940.

13 Pouillard, *Hirsch & Cie*.

14 "Situation Racique de la Maison Hirsch & Cie", AGR, Hirsch & Cie, I 288, # 89.

15 See the entry "Hirsch, Arthur", in Jean-Philippe Schreiber, *Dictionnaire biographique*.

16 "Messieurs Hirsch ont donc 50% de sang aryen et ne professent nullement la religion israélite." AGR, I 288, # 89.

17 Ibid., # 107, Administration allemande.

18 Letter of 11 July 1941. AGR, I 288, # 108, Administration allemande: "et que la qualité de Juive de son épouse n'est pas établie à suffisance".

19 Ibid., *Verordnung zur Ergänzung der Judenverordnung vom 31 mai 1941*, VOBIB 44, 10 June 1941, §§ 7 and 11.

20 Note of 23 July 1941, AGR, I 288, # 108, Administration allemande.

21 "N.B. – Il ne peut jamais être fait état de ce document vis-à-vis de tiers. Si le besoin s'en révèle, il faut faire état de la confirmation que j'ai adressée le 11 juillet au Dr. Wilhelm Pée, administrateur-commissaire désigné par le Commandant Militaire pour la Sté Hirsch & Cie." AGR, I 288, # 108, Administration Allemande.

22 Pouillard, *Hirsch & Cie*, p. 75.

23 Correspondence, 14, 21 and 23 July, AGR, I 288, # 105.

24 "Note sur l'Entretien que J.-P. H. et Me Botson ont eu le 4.4.41 avec MM. Lehembre et Huart de la Banque de Bruxelles", AGR, I 288, Projet de Vente, # 104.

25 Ibid., Letter of 13 May 1941.

26 Ibid., Letter of 21 July 1941.

27 Ibid., # 243, Letter of 3 Oct. 1941.

28 Ibid., Letters of 3 Oct.

29 Ibid., # 242.

30 With Pée's agreement, it would be divided equally among the brothers and the Jewish two-thirds Aryanized by depositing the monies in a blocked account. Ibid., Letter of 25 Oct. 1941.

31 Ibid.

32 Ibid.

33 Ibid., # 243.
34 Letter of 25 Feb. 1942, # 342.
35 Ibid.
36 Ibid.
37 Ibid., # 242. A request was made by Jean-Paul to keep two of the books, *Aus seinem Leben*, by Philippe Freundenberg, his grandmother's brother and *Les Lois ouvrières en Grande-Bretagne*, the only copy of the work by his father Arthur, for personal family reasons. It was rejected by the *Einsatzstab* because they were "typically Jewish books" (*deux livres typiquement Juifs*). Letter from Pée to Jean-Paul, 2 March 1942; Reply from Hirsch to Pée, 3 March 1942. Lettre from Pée to Hirsch, 7 April 1942; Letter from *Einsatzstab* to Pée, 7 April (*... weil es sich gerade dabei spezifisch jüdische Bücher handelt*).
38 See Chapter 10.
39 Letter of 9 March 1942, # 342.
40 Ibid., Letter from Thoumsin-Saintenoy, 25 March 1942.
41 Ibid.
42 Ibid., # 242.
43 AGR, Maison Hirsch & Cie, I 288, # 105, Administration allemande.
44 Letter of 20 May 1942, ibid.
45 Letter of 22 May 1942, ibid.
46 Correspondence 8 June, 10 June 1942, ibid., # 242.
47 Expert's letter to Thoumsin-Saintenoy, 11 June 1942, # 342.
48 Letter to Jean-Paul Hirsch, 18 June 1942, ibid.
49 "Cahn est un individu dangereux. Il ne répond même plus à son avocat. Ne pas faire de nouvelles affaires avec lui."
50 Letter of 15 July 1942, # 242.
51 Letter of 23 July 1942.
52 Letter of 11 Sept. 1942, "Relations entre la direction et le Verwalter", # 110.
53 Letter to Müller, 15 Sept. 1942; Letter from Müller, 6 Oct. 1942, ## 333, 340.
54 Letter of 10 Oct. 1942, # 342.
55 Letter to Paul Sandelin, 15 Oct. 1942, ibid.
56 Ibid., # 244.
57 Ibid., Letter of 15 Feb. 1943.
58 See the detailed discussion later in this chapter.
59 Letter of 12 Oct. 1944 to the Crown Attorney, ibid. # 342.
60 Letter of 14 Nov. 1944 from Gerrebos and Mestdagh to Ghislain, ibid.
61 Letter of 20 Feb. 1945, # 342.
62 Ibid.
63 AGR, I 288, Hirsch & Cie, # 96.

10 Belgian lawyers, Belgian judges, Jewish cases

1 See Richard Weisberg, *Vichy Law and the Holocaust in France*, New York: New York University Press, 1996; Dominique Gros (ed.), *Juger sous Vichy*, Paris: Seuil, 1994; Dominique Gros (ed.), *Le Droit Antisémite de Vichy*, Paris: Seuil, 1995; Robert Badinter, *Un antisémitisme ordinaire*, Paris: Fayard, 1997; Philippe Fabre, *Le Conseil d'État et Vichy: Le Contentieux de l'antisémitisme*, Paris: Publications de la Sorbonne, 2001.
2 The Conseil de Prud'hommes was a body with tribunal-like powers established in 1926 to settle disputes in the workplace, between and among employers and employees. Conciliation was the main aim of the system but the tribunal was given the power to issue binding judgments where conciliation failed. See P. Wauwermans and L. Th. Léger, *Les Conseils de Prud'hommes*, Dison: Imprimerie Disonaise, n.d.

3 "Louage d'Ouvrage", no. 505, in Th. Smolders, *La Jurisprudence belge depuis le 10 mai 1940*, vol. 2, Brussels: Ferdinand Larcier, 1941 (hereafter, *La Jurisprudence belge*), 146 (Prud'h. Brux.), 29 Oct. 1940.

4 AEA, Conseil des Prud'hommes de Bruxelles, Versement 2000, boîte 161, PV No. 2504, Rép. No. 1354.

5 The court record contains this letter "Brüssel, den 9 Oktober 1940 / Bescheinigung / Der Jude Friedrich Rothmann war bei der Firma Ready beschäftigt. Da Die Deutsche Wehrmacht nicht duldet, dass Juden in einem ausschließlich für die Deutsche Wehrmacht schaffenden Betriebe tätig sind, wurde der Jude auf unsere Anweisunghin fristlos entlassen. / Schulter / Kriegsverwaltungsrat".

6 *Jurisprudence Commerciale de Bruxelles* (hereafter *JCB*), 35 (1942–4), 300. (Tribunal de Commerce de Bruxelles), 24 Jan. 1941; (Cour d'Appel de Bruxelles), 2 June 1944. "La dissolution des sociétés à terme ne peut être demandée par l'un des associés avant le terme convenu, qu'autant qu'il y en a de justes motifs, comme lorsqu'un des associés manque à ses engagements, ou qu'une infirmité habituelle le rend inhabile aux affaires de la société, ou autres cas semblables, dont la légitimité et la gravité sont laissées à l'arbitrage des juges." (The dissolution of limited-term partnerships may be sought by one of the partners before the agreed time upon showing just reasons, such as when another partner fails to meet his obligations, or a long-term infirmity renders him incapable of participating in the business of the partnership, or other similar cases, the legitimacy and gravity of which are to be determined by the judges.)

7 Ibid. 302.

8 Ibid. 309. "les gens de ce pays se montrent ordinairement plus compréhensifs, plus indulgents, plus tolérants".

9 *Journal des Tribunaux* (hereafter *J des T*) (1944–5), 224 (Comm. Gand), 26 Feb. 1942). The case was also reported in *Revue de l'Administration et du Droit Administratif de la Belgique*, 87 (1945), 12.

10 "Attendu qu'il ne souffre aucun doute que cette loi en exécution de laquelle toutes les mesures énoncées ci-dessus ont été prises contre les frères Windmuller, constitue une loi politique qui a comme telle un caractère essentiellement territorial et en peut conséquemment avoir aucun effet en dehors des frontières du pays où elle a été promulguée ..." Ibid.

11 "Que le législateur allemand est sans qualité pour organiser l'expropriation ou la saisie de cette créance et pour faire faire respecter par les tribunaux belges les susdites mesures pour la seule raison que la créance dont s'agit [*sic*] doit être recouvrée contre des débiteurs belges." Ibid.

12 Article 11 provides that: "No one may be deprived of his property except for reasons of public purpose, in the instances and in the manner prescribed by law and with a just and reasonable indemnity" ("Nul ne peut être privé de sa propriété que pour cause d'utilité publique, dans les cas and de la manière établie par la loi, et moyennant une juste et préalable indemnité"). Article 545 of the Civil Code repeats Article 11 of the Constitution and Article 544 sets out that "Ownership is the right to enjoy and dispose of things in an absolute manner, provided that one does not engage in a use prohibited by law or by regulation." ("La propriété est le droit de jouir et de disposer des choses de la manière la plus absolue, pourvu qu'on n'en fasse pas un usage prohibé par les lois ou par les règlements.")

13 "... est une des bases fondamentales des institutions nationales belges que l'on ne peut faire fléchir en considération d'une loi étrangère sans troubler profondément l'ordre établi sur le territoire." Ibid.

14 "... pas plus que l'ordonnance du 28 octobre 1940". Ibid.

15 It is perhaps worth noting that the entire profession did not wrap itself in positivist glory in this case since the German *Verwalter* was of course represented by a Belgian lawyer

who was apparently happy to plead before the court that Belgian law permitted the expropriation of German Jews and that Belgian courts should assist in the process.

16 See *inter alia*, José Gotovitch and Chantal Kesteloot, *Collaboration, répression: Un passé qui résiste*, Brussels: Labor, 2002.

17 *JCB* (1942), 244, 25 March 1942.

18 "Copie d'une circulaire envoyée par les Autorités allemandes aux commerçants Juifs, relative à leur inscription au Registre du Commerce", CEGESOMA, AA 120, Ministère de la Justice, Crimes de Guerre.

19 *Rosiers* (see n. 17), p. 246. On the fate of Article 46 of the Hague Convention, see Herman van Goethem's seminal article, "La Convention de la Haye, la collaboration administrative en Belgique et la persécution des Juifs à Anvers (1940–1942)", *Cahiers d'Histoire du Temps Présent*, 17 (2006), 117–97.

20 *JCB*, 276, 26 Nov. 1942.

21 Ibid., 13 May 1943, "à la requête de la Société anonyme ... représentée par son Kommissarischer Verwalter , M... et pour autant que de besoin par son conseil d'administration, composé de MM... ", p. 277.

22 "... soient investies, pour agir au nom de la société, d'un pouvoir dont les Tribunaux belges, organes de la souveraineté belge dans le domaine dévolu au pouvoir judiciare, devraient reconnaitre la validité, c'est-à-dire la conformité à la législation nationale belge." Ibid.

23 *JCB*, 278, 13 Sept. 1943.

24 *JCB*, 277–8. "Le Kommissarischer Verwalter n'est ni l'organe, ni un mandataire de la société dans la gestion de laquelle il intervient. C'est un tiers imposé par l'autorité occupante à la tête de l'entreprise. Il est le délégué, l'instrument de cette autorité, qui l'a chargé de réaliser une mainmise sur l'entreprise. Il est responsable de ses actes envers elle seule. Il ne représente point le propriétaire de l'entreprise."

25 "La Convention de la Haye"; *Pasicrisie belge* (1916), vol. 1, pp. 383 and 413 et seq. (Cour de Cassation), 20 May 1916.

26 *The 'Nazification' and 'Denazification' of the Courts in Belgium, Luxembourg and the Netherlands*, Maastricht: University of Maastricht Press, 2004.

27 *JCB* 35 (1942–4), 294, 26 April 1944. See also *JCB*, 36 (1946), 162, 29 Nov. 1944.

28 *La Jurisprudence belge*, vol. 5 (1943), p. 167 (Civ. Bruges), 3 Dec. 1942.

29 For a contemporary description see Magdalene Schoch, "Divorce Law and Practice Under National Socialism in Germany", *Iowa Law Review*, 28 (1942–3), 225–55. Another useful discussion, with references to relevant German cases, can be found in Oscar Janowsky and Melvin Fagen, *International Aspects of German Racial Policies*, New York: Oxford University Press, 1937, pp. 196–9. See also Ingo Müller, *Hitler's Justice*, Cambridge, MA, and London: Harvard University Press, 1991, 90–119.

30 "Les époux pourront réciproquement demander le divorce pour excès, sévices ou injures graves de l'un envers l'autre."

31 Rapport au Conseil des Ministres, and Avis Officiels, 10 Jan. 1941, *Pasinomie*, Arrêté-loi du 10 Janvier 1941.

32 *Blondin v. Johnen et Gohy*, 28 Dec. 1944, *La Jurisprudence belge*, vol. 6 (1945), p. 146; *J des T*, 187, 18 Feb. 1945.

33 Ibid. "Attendu qu'il suffit de lire le texte de diverses ordonnances allemandes pour se rendre compte que toutes ces dispositions contre les sujets juifs ont le caractère d'une véritable spoliation des biens; que l'autorité allemande a procédé à des déportations, des incarcérations et des confiscations de biens, ce sans aucun fondement juridique et contrairement aux dispositions du droit international public; que toute la législation allemande contre les Juifs devait aboutir à la confiscation de leurs biens et à l'extermination de leur race; que ces lois iniques sont contraires au droit naturel et au droit international public... "

34 *J des T* (1944–5), 304 (J. P. Bruxelles, 2e cant.), 14 Feb. 1945.
35 *Journal des Juges de la Paix / Tijdschrift van de Vrederechters* (1945), 289.
36 Ibid. 290.
37 Ibid., "que l'appartement devra être remis à la disposition de M. Levy, dès qu'il en exprimera le désir".
38 *Moniteur Belge* (12 March 1945).
39 Ibid., articles 30, 31 and 32.
40 Op. cit., 291.
41 *Journal des Juges de la Paix / Tijdschrift van de Vrederechters* (1946), 248, 5 Oct. 1945.
42 *J des T* (1944–5), 292 (J. P. Ixelles, 2e cant.), 26 March 1945.
43 Code Civil, Art. 1239, "Le payement doit être fait au créancier ou à quelqu'un ayant pouvoir de lui, ou qui soit autorisé par justice ou par la loi à recevoir pour lui" ("Payment must be made to the creditor or to someone authorized by him, or by the court, to receive it on his behalf").
44 *J des T* (1945–6), 562.
45 *Benanom and Laskar v. Roeben and Sadee*, ibid. 563 (J. P. Bruxelles, 3e cant.), 16 Oct. 1945.
46 *Jenckiel Zaleman v. Culot and Jeanneret*, ibid. (J. P. Bruxelles, 2e cant.), 17 Oct. 1945, "La prudence la plus élémentaire… " See also *Ressner v. Longero and Meulenbergh*, ibid. (J. P. Bruxelles, 1er cant.), 26 July 1945.
47 Ibid. (J. P. Bruxelles, 3e cant.), 16 Oct. 1945.
48 Ibid., *Kilimin v. Librarie Le Condunant* (J. P. Bruxelles, 3e cant.), 19 Sept. 1945.
49 Ibid. (J. P. Ixelles, 1er cant.), 4 Oct. 1945.
50 *JCB*, 39, 35 (1946), 12 Dec. 1945.
51 *Weisburger and Maier v. Me G. Louveaux, administrateur provisoire ad hoc de la société Té Dé*, ibid. 40. This did not prevent a number of *Verwalteren* from holding such meetings in order to sell of the shares held by Jews. Nor did it prevent non-Jewish Belgians from purchasing such shares. See e.g. CEGESOMA, AA 829, S. Reich, Comptoir des Jouets, Correspondence Feb. and March 1943.
52 *A. Jacob v. La Baloise*, *JCB* 39, 138 (1946), 17 May 1946; *J des T* (1946), 371. It is perhaps worth noting that insurance companies did not hesitate to seek and to obtain the payment of annual premiums from the *Verwalter*. See e.g. Correspondence from the Compagnie des Propriétaires Réunis to Ernst Müller, *Verwalter*, Nov. 1943. USHMM, RG. 65.001M, Reel 1575, SVG. See also discussion in Chapter 7 on the imbroglio involving the payment of insurance premiums from funds held in trust for the Jewish owners of abandoned businesses by the city of Liège.
53 "Any act whatsoever of a person which causes damage to another obliges the person by whose fault it occurred to make reparation" ("Tout fait quelconque de l'homme, qui cause à autrui un dommage, oblige celui par la faute duquel il est arrivé à le réparer").
54 *Stella v. J.M.*, *JCB*, 243 (6 Nov. 1946). See also *JCB,* 41, 216 (1948), 18 Aug. 1947, *Stella v. N.P.*
55 *Roszinski v. Joulet*, *J des T* (1946), 565 (Juge de la Paix d'Anderlecht), 28 June 1945.
56 *Patrowsky v. Tabarznick et al.*, ibid. (Juge de la Paix d'Anderlecht), 11 Oct. 1945.
57 *Dickarz v. Vanden Brande and Ghilneux*, ibid. (Juge de la Paix, 2e cant. Brussels), 16 July 1945.
58 *Erste Verordnung über die Neuordnung des Filmwesens in Belgien vom 6 August 1940*, VOBIB 9, 7 Aug. 1940.
59 *Verordnung über den Betrieb von Theatern und Unterhaltungsstätten vom 23 September 1940*, VOBIB 15, 28 Sept. 1940.
60 Other cinema operations declared their "Jewish" ownership interests pursuant to the First Order. See e.g. Declaration of Jewish Undertaking, Les Grands Théâtres SA,

10 Dec. 1940, and Les Grands Palais d'Attractions Pathé Frères SA, 10 Dec. 1940, USHMM RG.68.001M, Reel 40, Selected Documents from the Kingdom of Belgium. Each declared in identical terms that as publicly held companies they were unable to determine the identity of their shareholders but they thought that the majority of shares was not in the hands of Jews: "nous pensons que la majorité n'est pas entre les mains des juifs". For each company, the two Jewish members of the board had already resigned.

61 *La Jurisprudence belge*, vol. 1 (1941), p. 79.

62 *Moniteur Belge* (22 March 1940), Arrêté-loi.

63 "If during the period of a lease the thing rented is wholly destroyed by a fortuitous event, the lease is terminated as a matter of law; if it is destroyed only in part, the lessee may, according to the circumstances, demand either a reduction of the price or the termination of the lease itself. Neither case gives rise to indemnification." ("Si, pendant la durée du bail, la chose louée est détruite en totalité par cas fortuit, le bail est résilié de plein droit; si elle n'est détruite qu'en partie, le preneur peut, suivant les circonstances, demander ou une diminution du prix, ou la résiliation même du bail. Dans l'un et l'autre cas, il n'y a lieu à aucun dédommagement.")

64 *Becker v. De Becker and Metro Goldwyn Meyer (sic)*, *La Jurisprudence Belge*, vol. 1 (1941), p. 158 (Comm. Brux.), 23 Jan. 1941.

65 *S.A. Metro Goldwyn-Mayer. S.A. Immobilière de la Porte de Namur*, *La Jurisprudence Belge*, vol. 4 (1943), 135 (Civ. Brux.), 17 Dec. 1941.

66 "The lessor is obligated, by the nature of the contract and without the need for any specific stipulation: 1) To deliver to the lessee the thing leased; 2) To maintain such thing in such a condition to serve the purpose for which it was leased; 3) To provide peaceful enjoyment to the lessee for the duration of the lease." ("Le bailleur est obligé, par la nature du contrat, et sans qu'il soit besoin d'aucune stipulation particulière, 1- De délivrer au preneur la chose louée 2- D'entretenir cette chose en état de servir à l'usage pour lequel elle a été louée 3- D'en faire jouir paisiblement le preneur pendant la durée du bail".)

67 "A rental contract terminates by the loss of the thing rented and by the default respectively of the lessor and the lessee to fulfil their undertakings." ("Le contrat de louage se résout par la perte de la chose louée, et par le défaut respectif du bailleur et du preneur, de remplir leurs engagements.")

68 "… puisque l'interdiction peut n'être que temporaire et qu'il pourrait dépendre du pouvoir occupant", p. 137.

69 Ibid.

70 "He (the lessee) is responsible for deteriorations or losses which occur during his enjoyment, unless he proves that they occurred without his fault." ("Il répond des degradations ou des pertes qui arrivent pendant sa jouissance, à moins qu'il ne prouve qu'elles ont eu lieu sans sa faute.")

71 Ibid. 138.

72 *Metro Goldwyn Mayer v. Propriétaires du Forum*, *Jurisprudence de Liège* (1940–8), 53 (Justice de Paix de Liège), 2 Sept. 1946, "suite à des nouvelles informations d'où il ressort que la firme – Metro Goldwyn Mayer – est une exploitation juive".

73 Extraits d'un jugement du Tribunal civil de Liège (9e chambre), 18 Nov. 1941, *Revue Critique de Jurisprudence Belge*, 1–3 (1947), 273.

74 *S.A. Métro-Goldwyn Mayer v. Beckers et al.*, *Revue Critique de Jurisprudence Belge*, 1–3 (1947), 268, 27 June 1946.

75 *Metro Goldwyn Mayer v. Propriétaires du Forum*, *Jurisprudence de Liège* (1940–8), 53 (Justice de Paix de Liège), 2 Sept. 1946.

76 "*Res judicata* applies only to that which was the subject-matter of the decision. It is necessary that the claim be the same; that the action have the same object; that the action be between the same parties and constituted by them and against them in the

same capacity." ("L'autorité de la chose jugée n'a lieu qu'à l'égard de ce qui a fait l'objet du jugement. Il faut que la chose demandée soit la même; que la demande soit demandée sur la même cause; que la demande soit entre les mêmes parties, et formée par elles et contre elles en la même qualité.")

77 The applicability of the 12 March 1945 Order in such cases was also confirmed by the Justice of the Peace (2e cant.), Brussels, in *Jenkiel Zaleman v. Culot and Jeanneret,* 17 Oct. 1945, *J des T* (1946), 565, 17 Oct. 1945.

78 *Metro Goldwyn Mayer v. Propriétaires du Forum, Jurisprudence de Liège* (1940–8), 53, 55.

79 Ibid. "… qu'il est certain que la demanderesse a tenté vainement de trouver des solutions conciliant ses intérêts et ceux des bailleurs; qu'il est évident que toutes ses démarches étaient vouées à l'avance à un échec certain, les Allemands désirant mettre la main sur cet établissement pour y installer la 'Bruciné' et en tout cas en exclure définitivement … une entreprise juive".

11 Constitutional patriotism and the fragility of law

1 Maroun Labaki and Pascal Martin, Interview with Daniel Cohn-Bendit, "Forcer les Flamands à se decider!", *Le Soir,* 28 Nov. 2007.

2 Elaine Sciolino, "Calls for Breakup Grow Even Louder in Belgium", *New York Times,* 21 Sept. 2007; Jon Henley, "Bye Bye Belgium?", *Guardian,* 13 Nov. 2007.

3 Guy Verhofstadt, *Rapport au Roi Albert II sur la réforme des instituions dans le cadre de ma mission d'information et de formation,* Brussels: Office of the Prime Minister, 2008.

4 "Voici l'accord de gouvernement", *Le Soir,* 18 March 2008; "Leterme 1 peut commencer", *La Libre Belgique,* 18 March 2008; David Coppi, "Leterme devant le Parlement ce jeudi", *Le Soir,* 20 March 2008; "Accord de confiance pour le gouvernememt", *La Libre Belgique,* 22 March 2008.

5 Tony Judt, "Is there a Belgium?", *New York Review of Books,* 2 Dec. 1999, p. 49; "The Stateless State: Why Belgium Matters", *Reappraisals,* London: William Heinemann, 2008, pp. 233–49.

6 See e.g. Karl-Heinz Ladeur, "'We, the European People…' – Relâche?", *European Law Journal,* 14 (2008), 147–67.

7 On the philosophical nature of the crisis, see Jacques Derrida, "Le Souverain Bien: Ou l'Europe en mal de souveraineté", *Cités,* 30 (2007), 103–40.

8 *The German Occupation of Belgium 1940–1944,* New York: Peter Lang, 1993, p. 108. See also Wolfgang Seibel, "The Strength of the Perpetrators: The Holocaust in Western Europe, 1940–1944", *Governance,* 15 (2002), 211–40.

9 "'La Belgique docile': Des qualités et de l'ambigüité d'un monument historiographique", *Points critiques,* 281(2) (2007), 5–8.

10 See Jan-Werner Müller, *Constitutional Patriotism,* Princeton, NJ and Oxford: Princeton University Press, 2007.

11 See Christian Joerges and Navraj Singh Ghaleigh, *Darker Legacies of Law in Europe: The Shadow of National Socialism and Fascism over Europe and its Legal Traditions,* Oxford: Hart, 2003.

12 Jürgen Habermas, "The European Nation State: Its Achievements and its Limitations. On the Past and Future of Sovereignty and Citizenship", *Ratio Juris,* 9 (1996), 125–37, 133. See also "Citizenship and National Identity", in *Between Facts and Norms: Contributions to a Discourse Theory of Law and Democracy,* Cambridge, MA: MIT Press, 1998, pp. 491 et seq.

13 Jacques Derrida, *Le Monolinguisme de l'autre* (Paris: Galilée, 1996), pp. 32–7.

14 Tzvetan Todorov, *The Fragility of Goodness: Why Bulgaria's Jews Survived the Holocaust,* tr. Arthur Denner, Princeton, NJ: Princeton University Press, 2001, p. 40.

Bibliography

Abicht, Ludo, *De Joden van Antwerpen*, Antwerp: Hadewijch, 1993.

Aly, Götz, *Hitler's Beneficiaries: How the Nazis Bought the German People*, London: Verso, 2007.

Anciaux, Charles, *L'État corporatif: Lois et conditions d'un régime corporatif en Belgique*, Brussels: ESPES, 1942.

Anon., *Rapports sur la Violation du Droit des Gens en Belgique*, vol. 1, Rapports 1 à 12 de la Commission d'enquête, Govt. of Belgium, Paris and Nancy: Berger-Levrault/ Librairies-Éditeurs, 1916.

—— "Memoire of the Belgian Government in Regard to the Deportation and Forced Labor of the Belgian Civil Population Ordered by the German Government", *American Journal of International Law, Supp.*, 11(3) (1917), 99–112.

—— *Rapports et Documents d'Enquête*, vol. 4, *Mesures Législatives, Judicaires etc.*, Brussels: De Wit/Larcier, 1925.

—— "Obéissance à la constitution et aux lois du peuple belge", *Jurisprudence Commerciale de Bruxelles*, 35 (1942–4), 221 et seq.

—— *Conditions in Occupied Territories*, New York: United Nations Information Office, 1943.

—— *Hommage aux partisans juifs tombés dans la lutte pour la Libération du pays*, Brussels: Solidarité Juive, 1945.

—— *Hommage à Monsieur le Référendaire Vander Perre*, 25 Octobre 1946.

—— *Le Bâtonnier Devigne*, Liège: Barreau de Liège, 1947.

—— *L'Occupation en France et en Belgique*, Revue du Nord, no. 2, Hors Série, 2 vols, 1987.

—— "Leterme 1 peut commencer", *La Libre Belgique*, 18 March 2008.

—— "Voici l'accord de gouvernement", *Le Soir*, 18 March 2008.

—— "L'Exclusion des Juifs de la Magistrature", *Juger*, 6–7 (1994), 36–41.

—— "Accord de confiance pour le gouvernememt", *La Libre Belgique*, 22 March 2008.

—— *Les Atrocités allemandes en Belgique*, Paris: Bibliothèque des Ouvrages Documentaires, n.d.

Badinter, Robert, *Un antisémitisme ordinaire: Vichy et les avocats juifs*, Paris: Fayard, 1997.

Baillon, Louis, *La Résistance administrative: La Lutte secrète des pouvoirs publics contre les Allemands en Belgique (1940–1944)*, Brussels: Larcier, 1946.

Baudhuin, Fernand, *Le Financement des guerres*, Louvain: Institut de Recherches Economiques et Sociales, 1944.

—— *L'Économie Belge sous l'Occupation, 1940–1944*, Brussels: Bruylant, 1945.

Bauman, Zygmunt, *Modernity and the Holocaust*, Ithaca, NY, and London: Cornell University Press, 1989.

—— "From Bystander to Actor", *Journal of Human Rights*, 2 (2003), 137–51.

Bekaert, Herman, *L'Expulsion des étrangers et le délit de rupture de ban*, Louvain: Imprimerie Administrative, 1934.

—— *Le Statut des Étrangers en Belgique*, 2 vols, Brussels: Larcier, 1940.

Bankier, David and Gutman, Israel (eds), *Nazi Europe and the Final Solution*, Jerusalem: Yad Vashem, 2003.

Billiard, Robert, *La Collaboration industrielle et ouvrière avec l'occupant*, Brussels, 1945.

—— *La Contrainte économique sous l'Occupation (1940–1944)*, Brussels, 1946.

Billig, Joseph, *L'Action Anti-Juive sous l'Occupation Nazie en Belgique*, Paris: CDJC, CCC-58, n.d.

Bloch, Baron Jean, *Épreuves et combats 1940–1945: Histoires d'hommes et de femmes issus de la collectivité juive de Belgique*, Brussels: Didier Devillez/Institut d'Études du Judaïsme, 2002.

Boden, Didier, "Le Droit belge sous l'Occupation", in D. Gros (ed.), *Le Droit Antisémite de Vichy*, Paris: Seuil, 1996, p. 543.

Brachfeld, Sylvain, *Ils ont survécu: Le Sauvetage des Juifs en Belgique occupée*, Brussels: Racine, 2001.

Braun, Thomas, "Le Défenseur", in Stan Dotremont *et al.*, *Le Bâtonnier Louis Braffort: Défenseur et Martyr des Libertés Spirituelles*, Brussels: Larcier, n.d., p. 49.

Brodeur, Pierre, *Des Juifs debout contre le Nazisme*, Brussels: EPO, 1994.

Caestecker, Frank, *Alien Policy in Belgium, 1840–1940: The Creation of Guest Workers, Refugees and Illegal Aliens*, New York and Oxford: Berghan, 2000.

Caestecker, Frank and Fraser, David, "The Extraterritorial Application of the Nuremberg Laws: Rassenschande and "Mixed" Marriages in European Liberal Democracies", *Journal of the History of International Law*, 10 (2008), 35–81.

Carton de Tournai, Françoise and Janssens, Gustaaf (eds), *Joseph Pholien: Un homme d'état pour une Belgique en crises*, Bierges: Éditions Mois, 2003.

Charles, Jean-Léon, and Dasnoy, Philippe, *Les Secrétaires-Généraux face à l'Occupant 1940–1944*, Brussels: Arts et Voyages, 1974.

Commission Buysse, *Les Biens des victimes des persécutions anti-juives en Belgique: Rapport Final de la Commission d'étude sur le sort des biens des membres de la communauté juive de Belgique spoliés ou délaissés pendant la guerre 1940–1945*, Brussels: Services du Premier Ministre, 2001.

Conway, Martin, *Collaboration in Belgium: Léon Degrelle and the Rexist Movement 1940–1944*, New Haven, CT and London: Yale University Press, 1993.

—— "Justice in Postwar Belgium: Popular Passions and Political Realities", in István Deák, Jan T. Gross and Tony Judt (eds), *The Politics of Retribution in Europe: World War II and its Aftermath*, Princeton, NJ: Princeton University Press, 2000, p. 133.

Coppi, David, "Leterme devant le Parlement ce jeudi", *Le Soir*, 20 March 2008.

Crabb, John H., *The Constitution of Belgium and the Belgian Civil Code*, Buffalo, NY: Fred B. Rothman & Co., 1982.

Curran, Vivian G., "The Legalization of Racism in a Constitutional State: Democracy's Suicide in Vichy France", *Hastings Law Journal*, 50 (1998), 1–96.

Dean, Martin, "The Development and Implementation of Nazi Denaturalization and Confiscation Policy up to the Eleventh Decree to the Reich Citizenship Law", *Holocaust and Genocide Studies*, 16 (2002), 217–42.

Debeyre, Guy, *Le Conseil d'État Belge*, Lille: Douriez-Bataille, 1953.

de Kerchove d'Exaerde, François, "Quelques questions en droit international public relatives à la présence et l'activité du gouvernement belge en exil à Londres (octobre 1940–septembre 1944)", *Revue Belge du Droit International*, 23 (1990), 93–132.

Delpérée, Francis, "Joseph Pholien, juriste: Trois consultations et les mémoires. Le pouvoir exécutif en temps de guerre", in Françoise Carton de Tournai and Gustaaf Janssens (eds), *Joseph Pholien: Un homme d'état pour une Belgique en crises*, p. 113.

Delplancq, Thierry, "1940–1942, une cité occupée et ses Juifs: Quelques aspects heuristiques", *Cahiers de la Mémoire Contemporaine*, 3 (2001), 128–34.

—— "Des paroles et des actes: L'Administration bruxelloise et le registre des Juifs, 1940–1941", *Cahiers d'Histoire du Temps Présent*, 12 (2003), 141–79.

—— "L'Exclusion des Juifs de la fonction publique en Belgique 1940–1944: Le Cas des administrations locales bruxelloises", *Revue Belge d'Histoire Contemporaine*, 35 (2005), 243–78.

—— "Une administration face à la législation antisémite: Le Cas d'Ostende (1940–1942)", *Cahiers de la Mémoire Contemporaine*, 6 (2005), 69–77.

Demany, Fernand, *On a volé 64 milliards: L'Histoire de la banque d'Émission*, Brussels: Société Populaire, 1947.

Denhaene, Godelieve, "Les Juifs dans certains documents communaux de Schaerbeek pendant la Deuxième Guerre Mondiale", *Cahiers de la Mémoire Contemporaine*, 1 (1999), 133–9.

de Putter, Jos, *La Constitution de la Libre Belgique*, Brussels: Les Éditions Libres, 1945.

Derrida, Jacques, *Le Monolinguisme de l'autre*, Paris: Galilée, 1996.

—— "Le Souverain bien: Ou l'Europe en mal de souveraineté", *Cités*, 30 (2007), 103–40.

de Staercke, André, *De la création d'un conseil d'état en Belgique*, Paris: Presses Universitaires de France, 1939.

Diamond, Hanna, *Fleeing Hitler: France 1940*, Oxford and New York: Oxford University Press, 2007.

Dotremont, Stan, *et al.*, *Le bâtonnier Louis Braffort: Défenseur et martyr des libertés spirituelles*, Brussels: Larcier, n.d.

Fabre, Philippe, *Le Conseil d'État et Vichy: Le Contentieux de l'antisémitisme*, Paris: Publications de la Sorbonne, 2001.

Fayat, Henri, "Legislation in Exile: Belgium", *Journal of Comparative Legislation* (3rd series), 25 (1943), 30–40.

Fine, Robert and Turner, Charles (eds), *Social Theory After the Holocaust*, Liverpool: Liverpool University Press, 2000.

Flory, Maurice, *Le Statut international des gouvernements réfugiés et le cas de la France Libre 1939–1945*, Paris: A. Pedone, 1952.

Fraser, David, "Aryan and Jew in the Nazi *Rechtsstaat*", in Pheng Cheah, David Fraser and Judith Grbich (eds), *Thinking through the Body of the Law*, Sydney and New York: Allen & Unwin and New York University Press, 1996, p. 63.

—— *The Jews of the Channel Islands and the Rule of Law 1940–1944: 'Quite Contrary to the Principles of British Justice'*, Brighton and Portland, OR: Sussex Academic Press, 2000.

—— "The Fragility of Law: Anti-Jewish Decrees, Constitutional Patriotism and Collaboration in Belgium 1940–1944", *Law and Critique*, 14 (2003), 253–75.

—— "' This Is Not Like Any Other Legal Question': A Brief History of Nazi Law Before U.K. and U.S. Courts", *Connecticut Journal of International Law*, 19 (2003), 59–125.

—— "A Passive Collaboration: Bureaucracy, Legality and the Jews of Brussels, 1940–1944", *Brooklyn Journal of International Law*, 30 (2005), 365–420.

—— *Law After Auschwitz: Towards a Jurisprudence of the Holocaust*, Durham, NC: Carolina Academic Press, 2005.

Fried, John H. E., "Transfer of Civilian Manpower from Occupied Territory", *American Journal of International Law*, 40 (1946), pp. 303–31.

Garfinkels, Betty, *Belgique, terre d'acceuil: Problème du réfugié 1933–1940*, Brussels: Labor, 1974.

Gerard-Libois, J. and Gotovitch, José, *L'An 40: La Belgique occupée*, Brussels: CRISP 1971.

Giron, Alfred, *Essai sur le droit communal de la Belgique*, Brussels: Bruylant, 1868.

Goldberszt, Charlotte, "Varsovie-Liège 1940–1942: Sur une correspondance", *Revue d'Histoire de la Shoah*, 187 (2007), 289–304.

Goris, Jan-Albert, *A New Code for Belgian Mayors*, New York: Duell, Sloan & Pearce/ Belgian Information Center, 1942.

—— (ed.), *Belgium Under Occupation*, New York: Moretus Press/Belgian Government Information Center, 1947.

Gotovitch, José, "Note relative à la Magistrature sous l'Occupation" (1972), CEGESOMA, BA L 1/3.

Gotovitch, José and Kesteloot, Chantal, *Collaboration, répression: Un passé qui résiste*, Brussels: Labor, 2002.

Graux, P., "Discours de Me P. Graux", in Dotremont *et al.*, *Le Bâtonnier Louis Braffort: Défenseur et martyr des libertés spirituelles*, p. 95.

Griffioen, J. W. (Pim) and Zeller, Ron, "A Comparative Analysis of the Persecution of the Jews in the Netherlands and Belgium during the Second World War", *The Netherlands Journal of Social Sciences*, 34 (1998), 126–64.

Gros, Dominique (ed.), *Juger sous Vichy*, Paris: Seuil, 1994.

—— (ed.), *Le Droit antisémite de Vichy*, Paris: Seuil, 1995.

Habermas, Jürgen, "Citizenship and National Identity (1990)", in *Beyond Facts and Norms: Contributions to a Discourse Theory of Law and Democracy*, Cambridge, MA: MIT Press, 1996, pp. 491 et seq.

—— "The European Nation State: Its Achievements and its Limitations. On the Past and Future of Sovereignty and Citizenship", *Ratio Juris*, 9 (1996), 125–37.

Hammer, Ellen, "The Taking of Hostages in Theory and Practice", *American Journal of International Law*, 38 (1944), 20–33.

Hanquet, René, *Les Pouvoirs des Secrétaires généraux pendant l'occupation*, Brussels: Ad. Goemaere, 1946.

Henley, Jon, "Bye Bye Belgium?", *Guardian*, 13 Nov. 2007.

Henri, Pierre, "La Défense des belges devant les conseils de guerre allemands pendant la guerre 1940–1945", in *Les Grands Avocats de Belgique*, Brussels: Éditions J. M. Collet, 1984, p. 271.

Horne, John and Kramer, Alan, *German Atrocities 1914: A History of Denial*, New Haven, CT, and London: Yale University Press, 2001.

Huyse, Luc, "The Criminal Justice System as a Political Actor in Regime Transitions: The Case of Belgium, 1944–50", in István Deák *et al.* (eds), *The Politics of Retribution in Europe: World War II and its Aftermath*, p. 157.

Huyse, Luc and Dhondt, Steven, *La Répression des Collaborations 1942–1952*, Brussels: CRISP, 1993.

Inter-Allied Information Committee, *The Axis System of Hostages*, London: HMSO, 1942.

Janowsky, Oscar, and Fagen, Melvin, *International Aspects of German Racial Policies*, New York: Oxford University Press, 1937.

Joerges, Christian, "The Darker Side of a Pluralist Heritage: Anti-Liberal Tradition in European Social Theory and Legal Thought", *Law and Critique*, 14 (2003), 225–8.

—— and Ghaleigh, Navraj Singh (eds), *Darker Legacies of Law in Europe: The Shadow of National Socialism and Fascism over Europe and its Legal Traditions*, Oxford: Hart, 2003.

Judt, Tony, "Is there a Belgium?", *New York Review of Books*, 2 Dec. 1999, pp. 49–53.

—— "The Stateless State: Why Belgium Matters", *Reappraisals*, London: William Heinemann, 2008, pp. 233–49.

Kalyvas, Stathis N., "Collaboration in Comparative Perspective", *European Review of History*, 15 (2008), 109–11.

Karlin, Régine Orfinger, Archief/Archive Orfinger Karlin, CEGESOMA AA 754 (n.d.).

—— *Jours de Guerre*, RTBF, # 374, CEGESOMA AA 1450, R. Orfinger (Karlin) and 1ères Ordonnances.

Kirschen, Sadi, *Devant les conseils de guerre allemands*, Brussels: Rossel & Fils, 1919.

Labaki, Maroun and Martin, Pascal, Interview with Daniel Cohn-Bendit, "Forcer les Flamands à se decider!", *Le Soir*, 28 Nov. 2007.

Ladeur, Karl-Heinz, "'We, the European People…': Relâche?", *European Law Journal*, 14 (2008), 147–67.

Laureys, Véronique, "L'Attitude du gouvernement belge en exil à Londres envers les Juifs et la question juive pendant la Seconde Guerre Mondiale", in Rudi van Doorslaer (ed.), *Les Juifs de Belgique: De l'immigration au genocide, 1925/1945*, p. 136.

Leclercq, Pierre, *L'Equivoque d'une loi*, Brussels: Ferdinand Larcier, 1946.

Ledoux, Raymond, *La Loi allemande sur les sociétés par actions, comparée à la législation belge*, Brussels: Bruylant, 1941.

Lefebvre, Edwige, *The Belgian Constitution of 1831: The Citizen Burgher*, Bremen: ZERP, 1997.

Liberman, Peter, *Does Conquest Pay? The Exploitation of Occupied Industrial Societies*, Princeton, NJ: Princeton University Press, 1996.

Littell, Jonathan, *Le Sec et l'humide*, Paris: Gallimard, 2008.

Louveaux, C. L., "La Magistrature dans la tourmente des années 1940–1944", *Revue de Droit Pénal et de Criminologie*, 61 (1981), 619–63.

—— "Le Moindre Mal", *Juger*, 6–7 (1994), 28–30.

Luyten, Dirk, "Rozenblum, Thierry, "Une cité si ardente: L'Administration communale de Liège et la persécution des Juifs, 1940–1942", *Revue d'Histoire de la Shoah*, 179 (2003), 9–49.

Saerens, Lieven, *Vreemdelingen in een Wereldstad: Een geschiedenis van Antwerpen en zijn joodse bevolking (1880–1944)*, Tielt: Lannoo, 2000.

—— *Étrangers dans la cité: Anvers et ses Juifs (1880–1944)*, tr. Serge Govaert, Brussels: Labor, 2005.

Salter, Michael, "The Visibility of the Holocaust: Franz Neumann and the Nuremberg Trials", in Robert Fine and Charles Turner (eds), *Social Theory After the Holocaust*, p. 197.

Schmidt, Ephraim, *L'Histoire des Juifs à Anvers (Antwerpen)*, Antwerp: Excelsior, n.d.

Schoch, Magadelene, "Divorce Law and Practice Under National Socialism in Germany", *Iowa Law Review*, 28 (1942–3), 225–55.

Schreiber, Jean-Philippe, *L'Immigration juive en Belgique du Moyen Age à la Première Guerre Mondiale*, Brussels: Éditions de l'Université de Bruxelles, 1996.

—— *Dictionnaire biographique des Juifs de Belgique*, Brussels: De Boeck & Larcier, 2002.

—— "La Belgique et les Juifs sous l'occupation nazie: L'Histoire au-delà des mythes", *Les Cahiers de Mémoire Contemporaine*, 4 (2002), 59–97.

—— "'La Belgique docile': Des qualités et de l'ambigüité d'un monument historiographique", *Points critiques*, 281(2) (2007), 5–8.

Schreiber, Jean-Philippe and Van Doorslaer, Rudi (eds), *Les Curateurs du ghetto: L'Association des Juifs en Belgique sous l'Occupation Nazie*, Brussels: Labor, 2004.

Schreiber, Marion, *Rebelles silencieux: L'Attaque du 20e convoi pour Auschwitz*, Brussels: Racine, 2006.

Sciolino, Elaine, "Calls for Breakup Grow Even Louder in Belgium", *New York Times*, 21 Sept. 2007.

Seibel, Wolfgang, "The Strength of the Perpetrators: The Holocaust in Western Europe, 1940–1944", *Governance*, 15 (2002), 211–40.

Servais, Jean, and Mechelynck, E., *Code Civil précédé de la Constitution Belge*, Brussels: Émile Bruylant, 1924.

Shirman, Israël, "La Politique allemande à l'égard des Juifs en Belgique, 1940–1944", Mémoire de licence en Histoire, ULB 1970–71.

—— "La Spoliation Economique des Juifs de Belgique", *Cahiers d'Histoire de la Seconde Guerre Mondiale*, 3 (1974), 65–83.

Smolders, Theodor, *La Jurisprudence belge depuis le 10 mai 1940*, vols 1–6, Brussels: Ferdinand Larcier, 1940–5.

Steinberg, Lucien, *Le Comité de défense des Juifs en Belgique, 1942–1944*, Brussels: Éditions de l'Université de Bruxelles, 1973.

Steinberg, Maxime, *Dossier Bruxelles Auschwitz: La Police SS et l'extermination des Juifs de Belgique*, Brussels: Comité Belge de Soutien à la partie civile dans le procès des officiers SS Ehlers, Asche, Canaris, responsables de la déportation des Juifs de Belgique, 1980.

—— *L'Étoile et le fusil: La Question juive, 1940–1942*, Brussels: Vie Ouvrière, 1983.

—— *L'Étoile et le fusil: 1942: Les 100 Jours de la déportation des Juifs de Belgique*, Brussels: Vie Ouvrière, 1984.

—— *L'Étoile et le fusil: La Traque des juifs, 1942–1944*, 2 vols, Brussels: Vie Ouvrière, 1986.

—— "Le Génocide aux Rendez-Vous du Palais", *Juger*, 6–7 (1994), 13–18.

—— *Un pays occupé et ses juifs: Belgique entre France et les Pays-Bas*, Gerpinnes: Quorum, 1998.

—— *La Persécution des Juifs en Belgique, 1940–1945*, Brussels: Complexe, 2004.

—— "La Tragédie juive en Belgique occupée: Un ravage de la xénophobie", in Anne Morelli (ed.), *Historie des étrangers et de l'immigration en Belgique, de la préhistoire à nos jours*, Brussels: Couleur Livres, 2004, p. 243.

Stengers, Jean, *Léopold III et le gouvernement: Les Deux Politiques belges de 1940*, Brussels: Éditions Racine, 1980/2002.

Stephany, Pierre, *1940: 366 Jours de l'histoire de Belgique et d'ailleurs*, Brussels: Paul Legrain, 1990.

Stolleis, Michael, *Law Under the Swastika*, Chicago, IL: University of Chicago Press, 1998.

Struye, Paul, Journal de Guerre (1940–4), Archief/Archives Paul Struye, CEGESOMA, AA 850.

—— *L'Évolution du sentiment public en Belgique sous l'occupation allemande*, Brussels: Lumière, 1945.

—— *La Belgique sous l'occupation allemande (1940–1944)*, Brussels: Complexe, 2002.

—— *Journal de guerre, 1940–1945*, Brussels: Racine, 2004.

Suchecky, Bernard *Résistances juives à l'anéantissement*, Brussels: Luc Pire, 2007.

Teitelbaum-Hirsch, Viviane, *Comptes d'une mort annoncée: Les Spoliations des Juifs en Belgique*, Brussels: Labor, 1997.

Todorov, Tzvetan *The Fragility of Goodness: Why Bulgaria's Jews Survived the Holocaust*, tr. Arthur Denner, Princeton, NJ: Princeton University Press, 2001.

Union des Villes et Communes Belges, *L'Autonomie communale en droit belge*, Brussels: Larcier, 1968.

Vandenbussche, Robert (ed.), *Les Services publics et la résistance en Zone Interdite et en Belgique (1940–1944)*, Lille: CRHENO/CEGES, 2005.

Van der Meersch, W. J. Ganshof, "Réflexions sur la répression des crimes contre la sûreté extérieure de l'état belge", *Revue de Droit Pénal et de Criminologie*, 2 (1946–7), 7–182.

Van Doorslaer, Rudi, *Les Juifs de Belgique: De l'immigration au genocide, 1925/1945*, Brussels: CREHSGM, 1994.

—— (ed.), *La Belgique docile: Les Autorités belges et la persécution des Juifs en Belgique pendant la Seconde Guerre mondiale*, Brussels: CEGESOMA, 2007.

—— "The Expropriation of Property and Restitution in Belgium", in Martin Dean, Constantin Goschler and Philipp Ther (eds), *Robbery and Restitution: The Conflict Over Jewish Property in Europe*, New York, NY: Berghan, 2007, p. 155.

Van Goethem, Herman, "La Convention de La Haye, la collaboration administrative en Belgique et la persécution des Juifs à Anvers", *Cahiers d'Histoire du Temps Présent*, 17 (2006), 117–97.

Verhofstadt, Guy, *Rapport au Roi Albert II sur la réforme des institutions dans le cadre de ma mission d'information et de formation*, Brussels, 2008.

Vermeylen, P., *Règles et usages de l'ordre des avocats en Belgique*, Brussels: Larcier, 1940.

Verstraete, Jan, *De jodenverordeningen en de Antwerpen Balie*, Brussels: Larcier, 2001.

Victor, René, *Schets ener Geschiedenis van de Vlaamse Conferentie der Balie van Antwerpen, 1855–1960*, Antwerp: De Vijt, 1960.

Von Falkenhausen, Alexander, *Mémoires d'Outre-Guerre: Comment j'ai gouverné la Belgique de 1940 à 1944*, Brussels: Éditions Arts et Voyages, 1974.

War Crimes Commission, Kingdom of Belgium, *Rapport du gouvernement belge sur les persécutions des Juifs de Belgique durant l'occupation allemande*, Document 47 (UK 76), 1946, IMT.

—— *La Persécution Antisémitique en Belgique*, Liège: Georges Thone, 1947.

Warmbrunn, Werner, *The German Occupation of Belgium 1940–1944*, New York, NY: Peter Lang, 1993.

Wauwermans, P. and Léger, L. Th., *Les Conseils de Prud'hommes*, Dison: Imprimerie Disonaise, n.d.

Wynants, Jacques, *Verviers 1940*, Brussels: Crédit Communal, 1980.

Weisberg, Richard, "The Hermeneutic of Acceptance and the Discourse of the Grotesque, with a Classroom Exercise on Vichy Law", *Cardozo Law Review*, 17 (1996), 1875–1978.

—— *Vichy Law and the Holocaust in France*, New York: New York University Press, 1996.

Wiener-Henrion, Jacqueline. "Régine Karlin-Orfinger", *Cahiers de la Mémoire Contemporaine*, 5 (2003–4), 187–97.

Wilkin, Robert, *Organisation et fonctionnement des autorités communales*, Liège: Invalides, 1938.

Zuckerman, Larry, *The Rape of Belgium: The Untold Story of World War 1*, New York and London: New York University Press, 2004.

Index

Adam, M. (Ministry of Interior Inspector-General) 25, 26, 32, 33, 36, 75, 88–9, 96
adoption of Jewish children 42, 56, 127
AJB (Association des Juifs en Belgique) 5, 39, 85, 129, 131, 132, 133–4, 135, 138
Aliens' Office 6, 96, 99, 102, 103, 109, 125, 142
Aliens Police (*Police des Étrangers*) 86, 151
aliens/foreigners 1, 5–6, 14
Allied governments, report praising Belgian population (1943) 77
Alsace-Lorraine 108–9
amusement facilities *see* theaters and amusement facilities
Anderlecht 202
anti-Jewish Decrees: Belgian administrative structures operating side by side with 34, 169, 176, 181, 187, 199, 201, 227; Belgian "passive collaboration" in 13, 23, 26, 27, 211; cases of Belgian courts' refusal to comply with 207, 208–9; in daily legal practices of bureaucrats 125; Decree prohibiting ritual animal slaughter 62; discussions between German authority and SG about 19–22, 25–6, 201; distinctions applied to Jews 5–6; Eleventh Decree stripping Jews of citizenship (November 1941) 6, 123, 124, 125–6; First Order offering legal definition of "Jew" (October 1940) 6–7, 22, 24, 52, 64, 75, 89, 90–101, 102, 105, 112, 154–5, 174, 207; on forced labor for Jews (May 1942) 139; on Jewish Education (December 1941) 133–8; legal and

governmental "resistance" to 3, 10, 60; legal professionals' attitudes in post-Liberation cases 213; letter from legal officials protesting about 48–52, 211–12, 225; police participation in implementing 142; relating to economic measures against the Jews 70–3, 153, 154, 158, 173–4, 180, 194, 195, 196, 199, 208–9; relating to reorganization of film industry 218, 219–20; Second Decree removing Jews from public employment 22, 23, 33, 35, 44, 52, 63–4, 111, 203; viewed in historical frame as German measures 11, 23, 28, 41, 42, 78–9
antisemitism: Belgian confusion about Nazi racial taxonomies 189, 212–13; Belgian government as first victim of 28; cases of Belgian courts' refusal to engage with 206–7, 208, 210, 211, 227–8, 230; Edmond Picard's writings 9; embedded in bureaucratic administrations 174, 227; first reported case before anti-Jewish Decrees 202–3; legal profession in Antwerp 53–6, 60–1, 61–2; legalization of 41, 42, 84, 87, 114, 126, 139; local officials' participation in effecting 15, 21, 87, 107, 116, 144, 227; role in rise of Flemish nationalism 52–3, *see also* Nazi racial ideology
Antwerp: Bar's response to Decree against Jewish legal professionals 52, 53–6, 60–1, 227, 230; as center of Flemish nationalism 52–3; Jews forced to move from 121; as one of few cities Jews were permitted to move to 122; police compliance with forced labor for Jews